THE BRITISH NAT[illegible]AL PARTY

This book examines the recent development of the far-right in Britain, with a particular focus on the British National Party (BNP), the most electorally successful far-right party in British history. It brings fresh perspectives to our understanding of the BNP in order to make a significant contribution to scholarly debate on the nature of far-right extremism, both nationally and internationally.

The book is significantly different from other literature in the field, primarily because of its focus on three important yet underdeveloped themes, which are reflected in the structure of the book itself. These are:

- the ideological and cultural politics of the contemporary BNP;
- responses to the BNP;
- the BNP's place within the contemporary domestic and international far-right milieu.

Written by an outstanding line-up of renowned experts in this field, this is essential reading for all those with an interest in British politics, fascism, political parties, race relations and extremism.

Nigel Copsey is Professor of Modern History at Teesside University, UK. Major publications include *Anti-Fascism in Britain* (2000) and *Contemporary British Fascism* (2004; 2008). He is also co-editor of *British Fascism, the Labour Movement and the State* (2005) and *Varieties of Anti-Fascism* (2010).

Graham Macklin was Leverhulme Trust Early Career Fellow at Teesside University, UK (2007–9). Major publications include *Very Deeply Dyed in Black: Sir Oswald Mosley and the Resurrection of British Fascism after 1945* (2007).

THE BRITISH NATIONAL PARTY

Contemporary perspectives

Edited by Nigel Copsey and Graham Macklin

University of Nottingham
Hallward Library

LONDON AND NEW YORK

1006285021

First published 2011
by Routledge
2 Park Square, Milton Park, Abingdon, Oxon, OX14 4RN

Simultaneously published in the USA and Canada
by Routledge
270 Madison Avenue, New York, NY 10016

Routledge is an imprint of the Taylor & Francis Group

© 2011 Nigel Copsey and Graham Macklin for selection and editorial matter; individual chapters, the contributors

Typeset in Bembo and Stone Sans by
Florence Production Ltd, Stoodleigh, Devon
Printed and bound in Great Britain by
CPI Antony Rowe, Chippenham, Wiltshire

All rights reserved. No part of this book may be reprinted or reproduced or utilised in any form or by any electronic, mechanical, or other means, now known or hereafter invented, including photocopying and recording, or in any information storage or retrieval system, without permission in writing from the publishers.

British Library Cataloguing in Publication Data
A catalogue record for this book is available from the British Library

Library of Congress Cataloging in Publication Data
The British National Party: contemporary perspectives/edited by
Nigel Copsey and Graham Macklin.
p. cm.
Includes bibliographical references and index.
1. British National Party (1982–). I. Copsey, Nigel, 1967–.
II. Macklin, Graham.
JN1129.B75B75 2011
324.241′093 – dc22 2010035634

ISBN 13: 978–0–415–48383–4 (hbk)
ISBN 13: 978–0–415–48384–1 (pbk)
ISBN 13: 978–0–203–83019–2 (ebk)

CONTENTS

ILLUSTRATIONS

Figures

Tables

CONTRIBUTORS

Karin Bottom is Research Fellow at the Institute of Local Government Studies (INLOGOV) at the University of Birmingham. Since obtaining her PhD, she has researched and published on small parties in British local government. Currently, she is researching the BNP's use of populism in local government and small-party lifecycles in multilevel contexts.

Nigel Copsey is Professor of Modern History at Teesside University. He is the author of *Anti-Fascism in Britain* (2000) and *Contemporary British Fascism: The British National Party and the Quest for Legitimacy* (2004; 2008). He is also co-editor of *British Fascism, the Labour Movement and the State* (2005) and *Varieties of Anti-Fascism: Britain in the Inter-War Period* (2010). His current research project is an international history of anti-fascism.

Colin Copus is Professor of Local Politics and Director of the Local Governance Research Unit in the Department of Public Policy, De Montfort University. He is the author of *Leading the Localities: Executive Mayors in English Local Governance* (2006) and *Party Politics and Local Government* (2004) and numerous journal articles. He has recently concluded two major research projects: the first, a Leverhulme-funded project exploring the role and impact of small political parties, independent politics and political associations in local government; the second, a Nuffield-funded comparative project examining the roles, responsibilities and activities of councillors across Europe.

Roger Griffin is Professor of Modern History at Oxford Brookes University. He is the author of over eighty works relating to generic fascism, including *The Nature of Fascism* (1991), *Modernism and Fascism: The Sense of a Beginning under Mussolini and Hitler* (2007) and the collection of essays *A Fascist Century* (2008). He has also edited anthologies of primary and secondary sources relating to fascism, including

Fascism (1995), *International Fascism. Theories, Causes and the New Consensus* (1998), and (with Matthew Feldman) the five volumes of *Critical Concepts in Political Science: Fascism* (2003).

Graham Macklin was Leverhulme Trust Early Career Fellow at Teesside University (2007–9). He is the author of *Very Deeply Dyed in Black: Sir Oswald Mosley and the Resurrection of British Fascism after 1945* (2007) as well as numerous articles on the history of British fascism and extreme right-wing politics. His current research revolves around the rise of white racial nationalism in Britain. He is currently an Honorary Research Fellow at the Parkes Institute for Jewish/Non-Jewish Relations at Southampton University.

Anthony M. Messina is John R. Reitemeyer Professor of Politics at Trinity College in Hartford, Connecticut. He has written widely on the politics of ethnicity and immigration in Western Europe. His recent books include *The Logics and Politics of Post-World War II Migration to Western Europe* (2007) and the co-edited *The Migration Reader* (2006) and *The Year of the Euro* (2006). He is currently co-editing a book on nationalist, ethno-nationalist and religious challenges to the emergence of a European identity.

James Rhodes is Simon Research Fellow in the Department of Sociology at the University of Manchester. His previous research has focused on the localized breakthrough of the BNP and has been published in *Patterns of Prejudice, British Politics, Sage Race Relations Abstracts* and *Ethnicities*. His current research project is a comparative study of de-industrialization and the shifting dynamics of 'race' and class in the US and the UK.

John E. Richardson is Senior Lecturer in the School of Arts and Culture, Newcastle University. He is on the editorial boards of *Discourse and Society, Social Semiotics* and the *Journal of Language and Politics*, and is Special Issues Editor for *Critical Discourse Studies*. His research interests include structured social inequalities, British fascism, racism in journalism, critical discourse studies and argumentation. His recent books include *Language and Journalism* (2009) and *Analysing Journalism: an approach from critical discourse analysis* (2007), and he is currently writing a book contextualizing and analysing the multimedia discourses of the British National Party (Bloomsbury Academic, 2012).

Fabian Virchow is Professor of Social Theory and Theories of Political Action at the University of Applied Sciences, Düsseldorf. He has published widely on the German extreme right, Holocaust denial and the armed forces. He is the author of *Gengen den Zivilismus* (2006) and has edited several collections of essays, including, with Tanja Thomas, *Banal Militarism* (2006) and, with Rikke Schubart, Debra White-Stanley and Tanja Thomas, *War Isn't Hell It's Entertainment: Essays on Visual Media and the Representation of Conflict* (2009).

Steven Woodbridge is Lecturer in Politics in the School of Social Science, Kingston University, Surrey. His PhD was based on a study of British fascist ideology during the interwar period, and he specializes in the history of the extreme right in Britain. He has published on British fascist and neo-fascist ideas during the twentieth century. His most recent publication is a study of the attitude of early British fascists towards Mosley and the New Party.

INTRODUCTION

Contemporary perspectives on the British National Party

Nigel Copsey

In June 2009, the British National Party (BNP) won its first ever seats in the European Parliament. 'The most demonised and lied about party in British politics has made a massive breakthrough tonight', a jubilant Nick Griffin, chairman of the party, declared in his victory speech in Manchester. That the BNP was now representing Britain in the European Parliament sent a shock wave across Britain's political establishment. Harriet Harman, Labour Party deputy leader, described it as 'terrible'. Referring to the BNP as 'completely beyond the pale', Conservative Party leader David Cameron was equally 'sickened'. Nick Clegg of the Liberal Democrats rounded on the BNP as a 'party of thugs and fascists'. The BNP had first threatened to break through to the European Parliament in 2004. Five years later, after obtaining 6.2 per cent of the vote (some 943,598 votes in total, 1.3 per cent more than in 2004), the BNP secured the election of two MEPs. Representing North West England and Yorkshire and the Humber, respectively, on 14 July 2009 Griffin and Andrew Brons took up their seats (numbers 780 and 781) in the Strasbourg Chamber. It was a 'sad day for Britain', Glenis Willmott, leader of the European Parliamentary Labour Party lamented, 'Two UK fascists are taking their seats in this parliament for the first time.' Certainly, the election of the BNP to the European Parliament marked a historic moment in British politics, as never before had a British far-right party broken through in a national election.

In view of its previous inability to offer any kind of credible electoral challenge to the mainstream, the British extreme right has long been dismissed as a lamentable political failure. This is the central motif that runs through standard narratives of British right-wing extremism, even if more nuanced interpretations based on the interwar period have drawn attention to its relative 'success' as a (sub)cultural phenomenon (Spurr, 2003; Gottlieb and Linehan, 2004). The accepted wisdom is that a variety of institutional, political and cultural factors have always prevented Britain's right-wing extremists from establishing themselves in the national political arena. As if inscribed on tablets of stone, it has become de rigueur for successive generations of observers to list these factors – the first-past-the-post electoral system, mainstream ownership of the immigration issue, deeply-rooted civic values – as the reasons why British society remained impervious to right-wing extremism (see, for example, Ignazi, 2003: 184–6). At this point, stock notions of British 'exceptionalism' are all too readily (and often rather simplistically) invoked.

Admittedly, until recently, Britain appeared immune to the contagion of right-wing extremism that has, since the 1980s, afflicted continental Europe. But, even when this apparent immunity still obtained, indeed well before the BNP had emerged from political obscurity, cautionary words were being said about the underlying potential for extreme-right mobilization on Britain's shores. The issue, as we saw it, was that a significant minority of British voters remained infused with deep-seated anti-immigrant populism (and authoritarian attitudes) but were deprived of a respectable (or even quasi-respectable) right-wing populist party to represent them (see Griffin, 2001). For that reason, writing at the turn of the twenty-first century, Roger Eatwell (2000: 190) had the prescience to reflect that, were the far-right to modernize – to distance itself from its historic identity – 'the potential for a British Le Pen-type party has never been greater'. For several of us, then, the emergence of the BNP did not come entirely out of the blue.

With *some* of this potential for extreme-right mobilization now being realized, it finally gives the lie to comforting notions of British 'exceptionalism'. Of course, it would be wrong to overstate the BNP's electoral potency. When waxing lyrical about how the 'perfect storm' will somehow propel it into Downing Street, the BNP resides in the Never-Never Land of British politics. As the results of the 2010 general election bear out, there is scarcely any chance that the BNP will secure the election of even one of its candidates to Westminster, let alone form a government. Moreover, the potential introduction of an alternative vote (AV) electoral system will make it even harder for the BNP to capture a parliamentary seat, simply because it will require the BNP to poll at least 50 per cent of the vote in any constituency. The AV system also does away with the possibility of winning a seat on a minority vote share (25–33 per cent) in either a four-way or three-way contest. That the BNP might have gained its first ever Member of Parliament on the basis of a one-quarter or one-third vote share was a possibility that did occasion some concern in the run up to the 2010 general election. Nick Griffin had confidently calculated that, were there to be a split vote among the 'old parties' in Barking, it might result in the BNP winning the seat on a 27 per cent vote. This was always an unlikely prospect, but after Griffin had announced his intention to contest the Barking constituency, one online betting site did offer odds of 7/2 on the BNP winning a seat in the 2010 general election (a probability of just over 22 per cent). As it turned out, however, Griffin performed well below expectations and could only muster a 14.6 per cent share, below the percentage polled by the BNP candidate in the same constituency in 2005. Needless to say, the BNP will not seek advantage from any public clamour for electoral reform by campaigning for AV – its preference is for a 'pure' system of proportional representation (Griffin believes that such a system would have awarded the BNP twelve MPs in May 2010).

Looking forward into a new era of British politics, Griffin's post-election musings have seen him forecast that, with massive cuts in public spending,

> the Bank of England prediction that whoever won this election will end up being 'out of power for a generation' is now going to apply to two of the three old parties. That's bad news for Britain, but good news for us.
>
> (BNP e-newsletter, 11 May 2010)

Perhaps, but the major beneficiary is more likely to be the Labour Party opposition, especially if, in its traditional heartlands, Labour can speak to people's concerns over immigration (an issue that dominated early encounters in the Labour Party leadership contest). The caveat to this is that the promise of even tougher controls on immigration might do little to address extant hostility towards established ethnic minorities, particularly Muslims. Recent studies have identified a positive relationship between the proportion of Bangladeshi and Pakistani residents and higher levels of support for the BNP, particularly in white enclaves in ethnically diverse urban districts (Bowyer, 2008; Goodwin et al., 2010).

Rather than imagining representatives of the BNP sitting in the House of Commons, a more realistic scenario is for the BNP to further implant itself at local level, particularly in a non-general election year when turnout is lower. Studies have demonstrated that, when fewer people turn out to vote, the proportion of people voting for the BNP tends to increase. This is said to be the consequence of two trends. The first is simply because non-BNP voters are failing to turn out; the second is that low voter turnout is symptomatic of disengagement with mainstream politics, an attitudinal characteristic that can drive people to vote for the BNP as a radical alternative to the Westminster parties (see Chappell et al., 2010). While further local-level implantation lies within the BNP's reach, the possibility that it might take control of a local authority now looks increasingly distant. For a moment, the local authority of Barking and Dagenham, where the BNP was the official opposition, seemed vulnerable. But, in the May 2010 local elections, the BNP lost every single one of its twelve councillors in Barking and Dagenham; nationally, it lost all but two of the twenty-eight council seats that it was defending. Does all this now mean that the threat at the polls that the BNP represents is a hollow one? In the wake of the 2009 European elections, when revealing that, across a number of localities, the Conservative Party had collaborated with the Labour Party in taking on the BNP, Conservative Party chairman Eric Pickles had warned that the BNP:

> are going to be a very serious force in British politics and the mainstream political parties have got to get their act together and start confronting them. We have got to start working in those areas where they have got contact, harder than we have ever worked before. That's the way you are going to

> defeat the BNP – you have got to take the BNP on. They have filled that vacuum which Labour retreated from so long ago.[1]

One can, of course, accuse Pickles of scaremongering and dismiss the BNP as an entirely insignificant and totally irrelevant political force. After all, in the 2009 European elections, a second-order election, its share of the vote was only the sixth largest, and, while it received the fifth largest share of the national vote in the 2010 general election, its share was a measly 1.9 per cent. Even so, we must still strike a note of caution. What we are being confronted with is a right-extremist party that has experienced growth over the longer term. The average number of votes cast for BNP candidates in the 2010 general election was roughly fifty more than in 2005, from nearly three times the number of candidates, and, in some constituencies (Barnsley Central, Rotherham), its vote actually increased sharply. Geographically, its strongest regions were Yorkshire and Humber and the West Midlands, where it averaged 4.7 per cent of the vote per candidate. It is also worth bearing in mind that, in the 2010 local elections, the BNP still managed to garner more than 20 per of the vote in no fewer than twenty-five council wards (see *Searchlight*, no. 420, June 2010). Moreover, when based on opinion poll findings that a significant minority of Britons (between one-fifth and one-third) feel threatened by multiculturalism (John et al., 2006: 22), it would appear that the BNP has yet to realize its (admittedly hypothetical) full growth potential. There are, as Robert Ford puts it, 'many British voters who share the concerns of the extreme right but do not currently vote for it' (Ford, 2010: 164).

One study of latent support for the BNP by Peter John and Helen Margetts (2009) identified a significant subset of the electorate – up to 18 per cent in one poll – that would consider voting for the BNP. In theory, as the BNP ratchets up its electoral intervention – and in the wake of the 2010 general election Griffin has announced his intention to 'overhaul' the BNP's 'elections fighting machine' (BNP e-newsletter, 4 June 2010) – so this latent support could conceivably translate into actual support, provided that underlying drivers, such as popular anxiety over immigration, remain salient (unsurprisingly, BNP voters are most likely to identify immigration as the most important issue facing Britain today). According to John and Margetts, the BNP has already 'moved to the mainstream of the British political system, losing some of its negative image among the voters' (2009: 511). This was their conclusion even before Nick Griffin's controversial appearance on the BBC's flagship *Question Time* programme in October 2009. This broadcast, the first time ever that the BNP had been invited to share a national TV platform with mainstream panellists, represented an important milestone in the party's quest for legitimacy. Despite the fact that a nervous Griffin performed badly and came across as a 'smirking extremist', in the first opinion poll taken after his appearance, more than one-fifth of the British public (22 per cent) said they would 'seriously consider' voting for the BNP in a future local, general or European election. Of course, we should avoid reading too much into such headline figures. The number of people who said they would 'definitely vote' for the BNP remained stubbornly low at just 4 per cent (*Daily Telegraph*, 24 October 2009), and BNP voting intention has fallen back to the 1.5–3 per cent range since (see for example, YouGov/*Sunday Times* poll, 10–11 June 2010).

The rise of the BNP

If, from 2001, the rise of the BNP has become more obvious, the early shoots of its electoral growth had already sprouted at the end of the 1990s (Copsey 2008: 116). However, it was the BNP's performance in the 2001 general election – in Oldham and Burnley it captured more than 10 per cent of the vote – that first claimed our wider attention. In the Oldham West and Royton constituency, the BNP's Nick Griffin won 16.4 per cent of the vote, the highest vote for a far-right party since the National Front's Martin Webster had polled 16.2 per cent in a 1973 parliamentary by-election in West Bromwich. On election night, the image of Griffin on the platform at the Oldham West declaration, a gag in his mouth and wearing a t-shirt that read 'GAGGED FOR TELLING THE TRUTH', was relayed into millions of households. And even if, at the 2005 general election, the BNP's vote in the Oldham West and Royton constituency fell by 6.9 per cent – Griffin stood in Keighley – the 2005 general election still confirmed an expansion in BNP support. In over thirty constituencies, the party obtained more than 5 per cent of the vote. The number of deposits that the BNP saved was up sevenfold on 2001, and in three seats it polled more than 10 per cent of the vote, garnering as much as 16.9 per cent in the Barking constituency. The BNP candidate in Barking, Richard Barnbrook, came within twenty-eight votes of second place. Five years later, Nick Griffin polled more votes in Barking (6,620) than Barnbrook did in 2005 (4,916), though his overall share of the vote dropped to 14.6 per cent, a decline of 1.7 per cent. The BNP also saved deposits in more seats (seventy-two, as opposed to thirty-four in 2005) and saw its average vote per candidate increase from 1,620 (in 2005) to 1,668 (in 2010).[2]

Yet, it has been in local elections that the rise in the BNP vote has been especially marked (Wilks-Heeg, 2009). The local elections in 2002 saw three BNP candidates elected councillors in Burnley. In terms of winning representation to public office, this constituted the first major electoral breakthrough for the BNP since 1993, when Derek Beackon won a by-election in the Millwall ward of Tower Hamlets. Further confirmation of the BNP's upward trajectory came with the results of the 2003 local elections, when the BNP captured some thirteen council seats. This figure increased to twenty-one in June 2004; by 2006, the BNP's tally of local councillors stood at fifty-four. Following the local elections in 2008, the BNP held some fifty-five councillors across twenty-two local authorities. A seat in the Greater London Assembly elections was also won in May 2008, followed in June 2009 by the addition of three county-council seats. Although Eric Pickles is right – it has been in Labour's traditional heartlands where it has performed best – the BNP has nonetheless established a broader electoral presence. In June 2009, it polled over 10 per cent of the vote in no fewer than fifty-two local authority areas.

Particularly high polls were recorded in Thurrock (17.5 per cent), Barnsley (16.7 per cent) and Rotherham (15.4 per cent). And although the number of its councillors dropped back to twenty-eight following the May 2010 local elections, the BNP still averaged over 10 per cent of the vote in 147 wards across twelve local authority areas. In four local authority areas it captured over 15 per cent of the vote: Barking and Dagenham (18.2 per cent), Pendle (16.9 per cent), Stoke-on-Trent (16.5 per cent) and Burnley (15.8 per cent).

Academic responses to the BNP

Despite this obvious rise in electoral support, academic research is only now beginning to catch up. During the 1980s and 1990s, the BNP was the subject of little academic scrutiny. This is hardly surprisingly: its electoral forays were eminently forgettable. Though originally formed in 1982, academic studies of the BNP did not materialize until over a decade later, following its Millwall local council by-election victory. This victory, which the BNP mistakenly considered the harbinger of a national electoral breakthrough, occasioned several case studies, first by Husbands (1994), then by Copsey (1996) and later revisited in comparative context by Eatwell (1998a). What emerged from this early literature was the significance of legitimacy as a key dynamic in determining extreme-right electoral breakthrough. The issue of legitimacy was especially problematic for the BNP, a party heavily tainted by its historical association with neo-Nazism. Without legitimacy, as Eatwell (1998b: 153) had understood, 'The BNP has no hope of becoming a serious national force: it is too delegitimized by association with fascism and violence. But a more respectable form of new party is another matter.'

In 1999, as if right on cue, in stepped Nick Griffin, who succeeded closet neo-Nazi John Tyndall as BNP chairman. Griffin joined forces with the BNP 'modernizers' and, in their quest for political legitimacy, worked to 'rebrand' the BNP, to distance it from its fascist past. Griffin aspired to give the party a far more respectable identity and in so doing make it electable. Although in no sense was this strategy of 'normalizing' the BNP singularly responsible for its electoral rise, it must be considered a factor (even for the third of BNP voters who, in one recent poll, believed that there is a difference in intelligence between the average black Briton and the average white Briton). For increasing numbers of BNP voters (and members), the party has been able to transcend its old neo-Nazi image. On the other hand, it still remains widely reviled as a *racist* political party. Refuting allegations of 'fascism' is one thing, but unless it can more effectively refute allegations of racism, it stands little chance of winning over a broader (non-racist) immigration-sceptic electorate.

It was the run of BNP local election victories from 2002 onwards that rekindled academic interest in the BNP, as commentators sought to understand the reasons for its local electoral emergence. Preliminary work on the party's success between 1999 and 2003 was first undertaken by historian David Renton (2003). Renton identified tabloid hostility towards asylum seekers and political disaffection with the 'crowded centre' of mainstream politics as factors facilitating the rise of the BNP. Nonetheless, he remained sanguine, believing that the party's lack of members would count against wider electoral success. This optimism found an echo in his review of the BNP's performance at the June 2004 European, local and London mayoral elections (Renton, 2005). Following the BNP's failure to break through in 2004, Renton concluded that there was now a 'strong possibility that a line might finally be held, and the BNP prevented from further growth' (2005: 45).

Such optimism proved misplaced. Elsewhere, political scientist Roger Eatwell (2004: 77) felt that, 'the BNP's prospects have never been better'. This reading was based on two observations. The first concerned ownership of the immigration issue by the Conservatives, which he felt was 'weakening', and, second, the popular saliency of the immigration issue, which he felt was likely to continue. Meanwhile, informed by a longer-term historical perspective, Tom Linehan (2005: 161) called our attention, not to short-term factors, but to the decline of class-based politics and the structural reconfiguration of the British labour movement as 'more fundamental to the advance of the far-right'. Well before data became available to corroborate Linehan's thesis, he was astute enough to theorize that the BNP's support base was populated by a high proportion of working-class voters who felt abandoned by New Labour's neo-liberal project.

The first book-length study of the BNP did not appear until 2004, with Nigel Copsey's detailed account of the party's historical development (see Copsey, 2004). This emphasized that the factors underpinning support for the BNP were not dissimilar to those that had contributed to the growth of the extreme right on the continent, that is to say 'the socio-political construction of the immigration/asylum "problem", popular racism, systemic factors such as political alienation and protest, and most significant of all – since right-wing extremists would remain ghettoised without it – the construction of legitimacy' (2004: 167). Written before the 2004 European elections, the claim that the BNP stood on the cusp of a national breakthrough was perhaps a little premature. Yet this scenario, as the European elections of 2009 were to play out, was hardly far-fetched. Later, in a revised and expanded second edition, Copsey warned of the potential for the BNP to win representation in the Greater London Assembly in 2008, as well as the European Parliament in 2009 (2008: 173). In both cases, his grounds for pessimism were vindicated. Drawn principally from the white working-class, pessimistic and estranged from Westminster's political elite, economically insecure and overwhelmingly opposed to immigration and asylum, the BNP vote was never going to disappear overnight.

First in 2004, and then reiterated in the second edition, Copsey called on academia to bring fresh perspectives to bear on this most recent incarnation of Britain's fascist tradition. And, in recent years, a flurry of new studies on the BNP has appeared written by historians, sociologists, political scientists and even psychologists. These have included examinations of the BNP's local implantation in both Burnley (Copsey, 2005; Rhodes, 2006; 2009a) and in Dagenham (Goodwin, 2008); the decline of local party competition as a factor in the emergence of the BNP (Wilks-Heeg, 2009); 'white enclaves' and patterns of BNP support in urban neighbourhoods (Bowyer, 2008); the importance of legitimacy to BNP breakthrough (Goodwin, 2007; Rhodes, 2009b); support, and latent support, for the BNP (Cruddas et al., 2005; John et al., 2006; John and Margetts, 2009); individual and contextual predictors of BNP support (Ford and Goodwin, 2010); activism in the BNP (Goodwin, 2010); the BNP's ideological modernization (Copsey, 2007); similarities between BNP populism and the radical-left populism of Respect (Clark et al., 2008); BNP representations of Muslims after the July 2005 bombings (Wood and Finlay, 2008); religion and the BNP (Woodbridge, 2010); and BNP foreign policy (Griffin, 2007). Adopting a more holistic approach to extremism, the BNP, alongside Islamist extremism, is extensively discussed in a recent edited volume on twenty-first-century extremism in Britain (Eatwell and Goodwin, 2010). A forthcoming book-length study of BNP activists by Matthew Goodwin (2011) is also eagerly anticipated.

What has emerged from the literature so far is that academics are generally unconvinced by the extent to which the BNP has genuinely 'modernized'; they also tend to agree that there exists considerable *potential* support for the extreme right; that immigration is a core concern for BNP voters, but it often acts as a surrogate for other local issues; that the BNP vote is largely rooted in a politically abandoned and economically insecure (male) white working class; that the party's quest for legitimacy is a fool's quest, because the BNP is still widely perceived as a racist (if not fascist) political party; and that it will remain frustrated by the anti-racist norms of British society, which arguably constitute the biggest obstacle to its transition from a 'big small party' to a 'small big party'. Nick Griffin, having digested academic scholarship on the subject, recognizes that one of the BNP's key limitations is that it needs a far stronger 'reputational shield'. In other words, despite all his efforts to nurture 'modernization', Griffin bemoans the fact that the BNP still struggles to defend itself against external perceptions that it is a racist political party (see *Identity*, no. 99, February 2009). Perhaps finally sensing that, without a more credible and respectable leader, the BNP will never attract a much broader coalition of voters, over the weekend of 22–23 May 2010 Griffin announced his intention to stand down from the leadership of the party in 2013, a development that cannot come soon enough for some party activists who, at the time of writing, are mounting a leadership challenge.

There are, however, still significant gaps in our current knowledge, which this volume attempts to fill. In our view, these gaps are best approached through three important, yet underdeveloped, themes. These themes are, first, the ideological and cultural politics of the BNP; second, responses to the BNP; and third, international perspectives. These overarching themes divide Part I, Part II and Part III of this volume, respectively.

Part I: Ideological and cultural politics

So far, most studies of the BNP's 'modernization' have centred upon the lessons learned from its continental counterparts, particularly the French National Front.

Turning the focus back on Britain, in the first chapter of this volume Graham Macklin locates the 'modernization' of the BNP within its largely ignored domestic context. This chapter considers the BNP's relationship, not with its immediate predecessor, the National Front, but with its underexplored 1960s historical namesake. In so doing, Macklin examines how the leadership of today's BNP has deliberately rewritten the internal history of British fascism in order to further legitimize and revise current strategy. Macklin pays particular attention to the figure of John Bean, eulogized by Nick Griffin for having blazed the trail for 'modern' British nationalism in the 1960s. But what Macklin uncovers is no more than historical subterfuge, a duplicitous attempt by Griffin and fellow BNP 'modernizers' to disguise the extremist provenance of their party. To parody the lyrics of the 1960s British rock band the Kinks, the BNP remain 'dedicated followers of fascism'.

This theme of duplicity is then carried over into the second chapter. In this chapter, John Richardson dissects the discursive representation of race and racial difference in texts produced and/or circulated by the BNP. As Richardson points out, his chapter is based on two presuppositions: first, that contemporary fascist discourse is inherently duplicitous, claiming one thing while being committed to something else. Second, when examining this dishonesty, it is vital to differentiate between the *exoteric*, the surface arguments in fascist discourse, and the *esoteric*, the underlying ideological commitments. Richardson's analysis owes much to the pioneering work of both Michael Billig and Stan Taylor on the 1970s National Front. Billig was one of the first to distinguish between the exoteric and esoteric in British fascism, arising from the 'conflict between ideological purity and the desire for a mass basis' (Billig, 1978: 124). According to Richardson, on the surface members of the BNP appear to be 'racial populists', a category that falls, he feels, within the acceptable limits of democratic British politics. But, at its ideological core, the BNP's political ideology remains heavily indebted to the historical traditions of British racial fascism.

From a more sociological perspective, James Rhodes then delineates the contours of the BNP's relationship to multiculturalism. In the final chapter of Part I, Rhodes shows that, as mainstream critiques of multiculturalism have gathered pace, so the BNP, through its own critique of multiculturalism, has been able to inhabit more and more mainstream territory. Rhodes discusses how – at the same time as opposing multiculturalism – the BNP also borrows from its rhetoric. By claiming to defend the interests of 'beleaguered' and 'abandoned' white communities, the BNP promotes a white 'minority consciousness'. According to this construct, whites are said to be under threat by expanding black and minority ethnic communities, particularly Muslims, and are dispossessed by a political establishment with no interest in the 'indigenous' people. Through adopting such language, Rhodes draws our attention to the ways in which the BNP is able to capitalize on a broader 'white backlash' against multiculturalism. However, not unlike Richardson, Rhodes concludes that the party's more esoteric ideology reveals that the BNP is not just another (subcultural) group expressing its hostility to multiculturalism, but a 'counter-cultural' group that retains a highly racially exclusionary concept of nation.

Part II: Responses to the BNP

The second part of this volume is primarily concerned with *responses* to the BNP, in the media, from extreme-right competitor groups, from anti-fascists and from within the council chamber. Nigel Copsey and Graham Macklin open Part II with their chapter exploring the relationship between the media and the contemporary far-right in Britain. Needless to say, the media can exert important effects, setting agendas that have been favourable to the BNP, as well as boosting the party's visibility and legitimacy. It is no coincidence that the rise of the BNP has occurred during a period when press coverage of asylum and immigration issues has grown significantly; nor is it any coincidence that, when coverage of immigration peaks, so too does coverage of the BNP (John et al., 2006: 22). What Copsey and Macklin contend is that, although the media's rejection of the BNP is an effect of British society's anti-fascist and growing anti-racist norms, this rejection operates in conjunction with populist acceptance/legitimization of many of the BNP's thematic concerns. Denunciation of the BNP, in the context of repeated expressions of media negativity towards refugees, asylum seekers and other migrant groups, offers a convenient way for the media to demonstrate 'traditional' British values of tolerance, decency and fair play. Meanwhile, for the BNP – still immersed in the depths of conspiracy theory – the media are equivalent to a 'lying, treacherous cancer which has a star role in the slow genocide inflicting our British race and nation' (*Identity*, no. 101, 2009).

Steven Woodbridge then unpicks the variegated response to the rise of the BNP from extreme-right groups (or more accurately *groupuscules*) outside the BNP. Woodbridge surveys the responses of three variants of the non-BNP extreme right: first, the Mosleyites, second, the National Front and, third, Tyndallite 'racial nationalists'. For Woodbridge, the defining characteristic of the extreme-right critique of the BNP from outside the party has been its ambivalence. For sure, Woodbridge argues, the BNP has been berated for its position on Europe, for its populism and for its outward betrayal of the racial nationalist cause, but there have also been instances of 'empathy, furtive regard and even open admiration'. The response to the BNP from rival groups has therefore been far more complex and nuanced than we would have expected, especially considering Nick Griffin's propensity to sneer 'Nazi cranks' at other extreme-right pretenders.

We then move to the opposite side of the political spectrum and examine the shifting dynamic of the anti-fascist movement and its response to the BNP. Since the 1970s, the strategy of militant anti-fascist opponents was largely predicated on the belief that Britain's fascists were intent on denying the left credibility by creating a climate of physical intimidation on the streets. 'It was necessary', as the former National Front Activities Organizer, Martin Webster, had once remarked, 'to kick our way into the headlines.' In the mid 1990s, however, as Nigel Copsey reveals, the BNP set off in a new direction. It abandoned the National Front-style 'march and grow' tactic of its past in favour of community politics and local electioneering. In this context, militant anti-fascism was rendered increasingly untenable. Copsey's chapter, which surveys the period from the mid 1980s to the present day, maps anti-fascism's awkward transition from direct action to community action and reflects on the ways in which anti-fascists have been forced, albeit with varying degrees of success, to recalibrate their campaign strategies.

If parts of this chapter make for uncomfortable reading, then the final chapter of this section is sure to touch a raw nerve with those anti-fascists who lampoon the BNP for its 'do-nothing councillors'.[3] This chapter, by Karin Bottom and Colin Copus, explores the impact of the arrival of BNP councillors into local government, paying particular attention to how they organize within councils and carry out the activities and responsibilities of being a councillor. What is more, it also discusses how other parties have responded to the institutional presence of the BNP. Revealingly, in the first such analysis of its kind, Bottom and Copus contend that BNP councillors are actually quite unremarkable. There is, they argue, little that evidences them as 'exceptional'. What is exceptional, they maintain, are both the (racial) nature of their preferred constituencies and the negative reaction that their institutional presence triggers from councillors of other political parties. Much of the BNP 'bad councillor' narrative, if not always fictionalized, appears to be at least 'over-dramatized'.

Part III: International perspectives

One political trend that has affected Western Europe since the 1980s has been the electoral advance of anti-immigrant parties and movements. In various forms, these actors have appeared throughout Western Europe, afflicting every major, and several minor, immigrant-receiving states to a greater or lesser extent. For that reason, the anti-immigrant BNP should not be studied in isolation from its counterparts elsewhere. How politically relevant are these actors? To what degree have their presence and activities influenced mainstream political discourse and the contents of state immigration policy? While we now know much about their respective impact in countries such as Austria, France and Germany (see Williams, 2006), we still know next to nothing about their relative impact in Britain.

Not surprisingly, while it labours under the delusion that it will one day enter the corridors of power, the BNP is wont to emphasize how it exerts an influence on British politics far in excess of its relatively modest base of elected representatives. It has, for instance, claimed direct influence over government policy on several occasions: in April 2002, just weeks before the local council elections, when Home Secretary David Blunkett published a series of measures targeting illegal immigration; the decision, in 2004, to allow the influx of white labour from Eastern Europe as opposed to 'racially different' Third World migrants; the announcement after the 2005 general election that the government would move to a tighter points-based immigration system; and in 2006, with Labour MP Margaret Hodge's remarks regarding housing for native-born Britons in her Barking constituency (see *Identity*, no. 84, November 2007).

In the first chapter of Part III, Anthony Messina attempts to fill this particular gap in our understanding. He examines, in an international comparative context, the BNP's possible influence on public attitudes towards settled immigrants and immigration, major party political discourse and the formulation of national public policy. His conclusions provide little to gladden the hearts of BNP members. Messina contends that, unlike extreme-right parties elsewhere, the BNP has *not* significantly influenced public opinion, major party political discourse or national policy. The main problem for the BNP, according to Messina, lies both in its illiberal origins and the prevailing opportunity structure, in which the Conservative Party has effectively monopolized ownership of the immigration issue.

Our penultimate chapter sees Roger Griffin offering a panoramic view of the BNP's place within the international topography of contemporary fascism. For Roger Griffin, the BNP occupies a distinctly unimpressive place. There is, as he sees it, a mediocre façade to the 'modernized' BNP comprised of neo-populist architectural features copied from elsewhere with minimum intellectual adaptation. Once this façade is stripped away, a deeply unflattering picture of BNP leader Nick Griffin emerges. As Roger Griffin views him, regardless of several chameleon-like changes in ideological identity, the umbilical cord to neo-Nazism remains uncut. Roger Griffin is equally contemptuous of the BNP's prospects. Once again placing the BNP in its international context, he suggests that Nick Griffin should have copied, not the *Front National* but the former *Allianza Nazionale* – a party that genuinely de-fascistized. The problem, of course, is that Nick Griffin is no Gianfranco Fini.

The final chapter represents an Anglo-German attempt by Graham Macklin and Fabian Virchow to test Roger Eatwell's thesis regarding the necessary prerequisites for an extreme right-wing breakthrough (see Eatwell 1998a). To do so, the two authors compare and contrast the BNP and *Nationaldemokratische Partei Deutschlands* (NPD, the German National Democratic Party) in their respective strongholds of Stoke-on-Trent in the West Midlands and the states of Saxony and Mecklenberg–Western Pomorania in the former East Germany. As the authors point out, not only are the BNP and NPD two ideologically aligned parties, they are also organizationally linked. Furthermore, both parties have similarly experienced local electoral breakthroughs, and yet little attempt has been made to study their local implantation in any comparative context. This chapter investigates the similarities and differences between the campaigning methods employed by these two parties in order to establish both the potential and the limitations of right-extremist attempts to construct local legitimacy.

This brings us to our conclusion, where Graham Macklin focuses on avenues for future research. Our mission statement, in publishing this volume, was to fill important lacunae and open up areas for further debate and research. But, as Graham Macklin explains, whether we have been successful in broadening these parameters can only be judged by the nature of the research that this volume engenders. We see the research agenda on the BNP as a work in progress. It remains unfinished. At the end of 2009, the BNP boasted its highest ever membership of 13,000 and a turnover approaching £1.5 million (BNP e-newsletter, 22 December 2009). As we entered the second decade of the twenty-first century, for a buoyant Nick Griffin, the BNP stood 'like a political megalith, proud, strong and unshakeable' (BNP e-newsletter, 31 December 2009). Thankfully, such remarks reveal more about Nick Griffin's delusions of grandeur than, as this volume confirms, his fascist party's true political ballast.

Notes

1 See http://news.bbc.co.uk/1/hi/uk_politics/8103626.stm (accessed 15 December 2009).
2 See www.manchesteruaf.org/2010-elections/202-graph-bnp-vote-in-general-elections.html (accessed 16 June 2010).
3 See, for example, http://lancasteruaf.blogspot.com/ (accessed 15 December 2009).

References

Billig, M. (1978) *Fascists: a social psychological view of the National Front*, London: Harcourt Brace Jovanovich.

Bowyer, B. (2008) 'Local context and extreme right support in England: the British National Party in the 2002 and 2002 local elections', *Electoral Studies*, 27 (4): 611–20.

Chappell, L., Clifton, J., Gottfried, G. and Lawton, K. (2010) *Exploring the roots of BNP support*, London: Institute for Public Policy Research.

Clark, A., Bottom, K. and Copus, C. (2008) 'More similar than they'd like to admit? Ideology, policy and populism in the trajectories of the British National Party and Respect', *British Politics*, 3, 511–34.

Copsey, N. (1996) 'Contemporary fascism in the local arena: the British National Party and "rights for whites"', in Cronin, M. (ed.) *The failure of British fascism: the far right and the fight for political recognition*, Basingstoke: Macmillan.

Copsey, N. (2004) *Contemporary British fascism: the British National Party and the quest for legitimacy*, Basingstoke: Palgrave-Macmillan.

Copsey, N. (2005) 'Meeting the challenge of contemporary British fascism? The Labour Party's response to the National Front and the British National Party', in Copsey, N. and Renton, D. (eds) *British fascism, the Labour movement and the state*, Basingstoke: Palgrave-Macmillan.

Copsey, N. (2007) 'Changing course or changing clothes? Reflections on the ideological evolution of the British National Party, 1999-2006', *Patterns of Prejudice*, 4 (1): 61–82.

Copsey, N. (2008) *Contemporary British fascism: the British National Party and the quest for legitimacy*, 2nd edn, Basingstoke: Palgrave-Macmillan.

Cruddas, J., John, P., Margetts, H., Rowland, D. and Weir, S. (2005) *The far right in London: a challenge for local democracy?* York: Joseph Rowntree Trust.

Eatwell, R. (1998a) 'The dynamics of extreme right electoral breakthrough', *Patterns of Prejudice*, 32 (3): 3–31.

Eatwell, R. (1998b) 'Britain: the BNP and the problem of legitimacy', in Betz, H.-G. and Immerfall, S. (eds) *The new politics of the right: neo-populist parties and movements in established democracies*, Basingstoke: Macmillan.

Eatwell, R. (2000) 'The extreme right and British exceptionalism: the primacy of politics', in Hainsworth, P. (ed) *The politics of the extreme right: from the margins to the mainstream*, London: Pinter.

Eatwell, R. (2004) 'The extreme right in Britain: the long road to "modernization"', in Eatwell, R. and Mudde, C. (eds) *Western democracies and the new extreme right challenge*, London: Routledge.

Eatwell, R. and Goodwin, M. J. (eds) (2010) *The new extremism in 21st century Britain*, London: Routledge.

Ford, R. (2010) 'Who might vote for the BNP?', in Eatwell, R. and Goodwin, M. J. (eds) *The new extremism in 21st century Britain*, London: Routledge.

Ford, R. and Goodwin, M. J. (2010) 'Angry white men: individual and contextual predictors of support for the British National Party', *Political Studies*, 58 (1): 1–25.

Goodwin, M. J. (2007) 'The extreme right in Britain: still an "ugly duckling" but for how long?', *The Political Quarterly*, 78 (2): 241–50.

Goodwin, M. J. (2008) 'Backlash in the "hood": determinants of support for the British National Party (BNP) at local level', *Journal of Contemporary European Studies*, 16 (3): 347–61.

Goodwin, M. J. (2010) 'Activism in contemporary extreme right parties: the case of the British National Party (BNP)', *Journal of Elections, Public Opinion and Parties*, 20 (1): 31–54.

Goodwin, M. J. (2011) *The new British fascism: the rise of the British National Party*, London: Routledge.

Goodwin, M. J., Ford, R., Duffy, R. and Robey, R., (2010) 'Who votes extreme right in twenty-first century Britain?', in Eatwell, R. and Goodwin, M. J. (eds) *The new extremism in 21st century Britain*, London: Routledge.

Gottlieb, J. and Linehan, T. (eds) (2004) *The culture of fascism: visions of the far right in Britain*, London: I.B. Tauris.

Griffin, R. (2001) 'No racism, thanks, we're British. How "right-wing populism" manifests itself in contemporary Britain', in Eisman, W. (ed.) *Rechtspopulismus in Europa. Analysen und Handlungsperspektiven*, Graz: Czernin-Verlag, 90-111. Reprinted in Feldman, M. (ed.) (2008) *A fascist century: essays by Roger Griffin*, Basingstoke: Palgrave-Macmillan.

Griffin, R. (2007) 'Non angeli, sed angeli: the neo-populist foreign policy of the "new" BNP', in Liang, C. S. *Europe for the Europeans: the foreign and security policy of the populist radical right*, Aldershot: Ashgate.

Husbands, C. T. (1994) 'Following the "continental model"?: implications of the recent electoral performance of the British National Party', *New Community*, 11 (2): 65–79.

Ignazi, P. (2003) *Extreme right parties in Western Europe*, Oxford: Oxford University Press.

John, P. and Margetts, H. (2009) 'The latent support for the extreme right in British politics', *West European Politics*, 32 (3): 496–513.

John. P., Margetts, H., Rowland, D. and Weir, S. (2006) *The BNP: the roots of its appeal*, Colchester: Democratic Audit.

Linehan, T. (2005) 'Whatever happened to the Labour movement? Proletarians and the far right in contemporary Britain', in Copsey. N and Renton, D. (eds) *British fascism, the Labour movement and the state*, Basingstoke: Palgrave-Macmillan.

Renton, D. (2003) 'Examining the success of the British National Party, 1999-2003', *Race & Class*, 45 (2): 75–85.

Renton, D. (2005) '"A day to make history"? The 2004 elections and the British National Party', *Patterns of Prejudice*, 39 (1): 25–45.

Rhodes, J. (2006) 'The "local" politics of the British National Party', *SAGE Race Relations Abstracts*, 31 (5): 5–20.

Rhodes, J. (2009a) 'The political breakthrough of the BNP: the case of Burnley', *British Politics*, 4 (1), 22–46.

Rhodes, J. (2009b) 'The banal National Party: the routine nature of legitimacy', *Patterns of Prejudice*, 43 (2): 142–60.

Spurr, M. A. (2003) ' "Living the Blackshirt life": culture, community and the British Union of Fascists, 1932–1940', *Contemporary European History*, 12 (3): 305–22.

Wilks-Heeg, S. (2009) 'The canary in a coalmine? Explaining the emergence of the British National Party in English local politics', *Parliamentary Affairs*, 62 (3): 377–98.

Williams, M. H. (2006) *The impact of radical right-wing parties in West European democracies*, New York: Palgrave-Macmillan.

Wood, C. and Finlay, W. M. L. (2008) 'British National Party representations of Muslims in the month after the London bombings: homogeneity, threat, and the conspiracy tradition', *British Journal of Social Psychology*, 47: 707–26.

Woodbridge, S. (2010) 'Christian credentials? The role of religion in British National Party ideology', *Journal for the Study of Radicalism*, 4 (1): 25–54.

PART I

Ideological and cultural politics

1

MODERNIZING THE PAST FOR THE FUTURE[1]

Graham Macklin

> It is possible, however, that the true future of British racialist politics lies with the British National Party, which is the only organisation formally to have broken away from the Fascist traditions of the 1930s . . . In the past three or four years it has advanced at a quicker rate than any other racialist organisation. It is smaller than the Mosley movement . . . but it is so closely tailored to current racial tension that it possesses a definite potential.
>
> Colin Cross (*New Society*, 3 June 1965)

> The phrase Modern Nationalism . . . is a genuinely very recent synthesis. While it is true that there have been several brief and short-lived spring flowerings of this ideology – starting with John Bean's early efforts in the 1960s – it has not formed a coherent and firmly based position until our time.
>
> Nick Griffin (*Identity*, no. 66, May 2006)

Introduction

Much academic research into the 'modernization' of the contemporary British National Party (BNP), led since 1999 by Nick Griffin, has highlighted, quite rightly, the important influence of the 'continental model' provided by Jean-Marie Le Pen's *Front National* (FN) (Copsey, 2008). Indeed, the existence of this 'continental model' indicates that the 'modernization' of the BNP did not take place in isolation. Across Western Europe, extreme-right parties have sought to modernize themselves, shed their 'fascist baggage' and, in so doing, acquire political legitimacy and thus electoral support: a process that, in Italy for instance, culminated in a marked radical departure from the past, but that in Germany and Britain has proved little more than cosmetic. That the BNP looked to the FN to provide 'the winning formula' (Kitschelt, 1995) or 'master frame' (see Rydgren, 2004) is hardly surprising. The differences between the two parties could not have been more marked. The electoral success of the FN, following its breakthrough in Dreux in 1983, stood in stark contrast to that of the BNP, which, having been founded the previous year, spent the next two decades in the electoral doldrums, operating more as a street gang than a legitimate political party. The current electoral success (recently somewhat tarnished following its performance in the 2010 local and general elections) enjoyed by the BNP has led to renewed comparisons with the rise of the FN.[2]

Less often commentated upon was not so much the influence of the British National Front in the 1970s upon Le Pen but, prior to this, his relationship with the British National Party (BNP) in the 1960s, led by John Bean. Le Pen was a subscriber to *Combat*, the BNP journal edited by Bean, whom he visited in London in 1961 or 1962. 'I recall clearly that we met under the clock outside The Cock public house where Fleet Street joins the Strand. I was holding a copy of *Combat* so he could identify me,' recounted Bean:

> One thing I am pretty certain we talked about was opposition to a centralised Federal Europe – as opposed to Tyndall's isolationism . . . His English, though far from perfect was better than my French. Two colleagues of that era whom I am still in touch with recall standing with him at one of our meetings in Trafalgar Square, and both still recalled the long raincoat that he wore and his enthusiastic clapping.
>
> (John Bean, letter to the author, 22 February 2001)

The above incident illustrates, as indeed do the two opening quotes, that there is an important dimension missing from the scholarly study of the contemporary BNP. First and foremost, there is the historical domestic context in which its 'modernization' has taken place, which has also had an impact beyond national borders. Understanding this internal historical continuum is crucial if we are to understand, not just the revisionist nature of the BNP 'modernization' project itself, but also the way in which the party has sought to revise and recalibrate its own history in order to shape its own political future. Indeed it reveals the lengths to which leading party strategists and ideologues have gone in order to obfuscate the racial-fascist ideological roots of the party and its founding cadres. The purpose of this exercise is to anchor their 'new' political project in a supposedly more 'moderate', far-right historical tradition, free of the taint of such extremism that, despite the election of Nick Griffin and Andrew Brons to the European Parliament in June 2009, continues to bedevil its quest for legitimacy.

Many shades of black, and grey . . .

Nowhere is the attempt to revise the internal history of British fascism more apparent than in John Bean's autobiography, *Many shades of black: inside Britain's far right* (1999), which, on the face of it, is a remarkably candid account of half a century of far-right activism. Born in 1927 into a middle-class family in Carshalton, Surrey, his father a bookkeeper for the family confectionery business in Bermondsey, Bean was brought up by his step-mother following the death of his father, his mother having already died when he was a child. Too young to see active service in the Second World War, Bean served in the Royal Navy from 1945 to 1948, which took him to Trinidad three times. He subsequently took up employment as an industrial chemist with a firm of paint manufacturers, who dispatched him to India in 1950, ostensibly for three years but as it transpired only for six months. Nevertheless, of these combined experiences Bean later noted that they:

> Signposted the political path I was to follow . . . I had become aware of the racial differences that had created the varied cultures of mankind. This made me a racialist, but certainly not a 'race hater'. Twenty years of radical right activity were to make me realize that there can be, unfortunately, a rather narrow dividing line.
>
> (Bean, 1999: 35–57)

Having returned to England, Bean's 'quest for the political truth' (Bean, 1999: 43) began in earnest, first as a member of Oswald Mosley's Union Movement (UM). In his autobiography, Bean recounts his involvement with the British far-right, from his early involvement with the UM's 'Keep Brixton White' campaign, through to his becoming northern organizer for the League of Empire Loyalists (LEL), which he left in 1958 to found his own group, the National Labour Party (NLP), together with a young John Tyndall, the future founder of the present BNP. The NLP sought to appeal to working-class Labour Party supporters through a mixture of racial nationalism and 'a kind of popular socialism, shorn of left-wing ideology' (Tyndall, 1988: 182).

During its brief existence, the NLP distinguished itself as a violent, racist groupuscule. On 27 February 1960, it merged with the White Defence League (WDL), led by Colin Jordan (1923–2009), to create the British National Party (BNP), a *völkisch* racial-nationalist organization dedicated to 'the preservation of Northern European civilisation and the heritage of Britain', which echoed the influence of pan-Nordic umbrella groups such as the Northern League, dedicated to propagating 'scientific' racism, to which the NLP and the WDL were both affiliated (*Combat*, no. 1, 1958). Given Bean's later claim to moderation, point two of the original BNP policy is instructive:

> To fight to free Britain from Jewish dominance and the coloured influx and to restrict permanent residence to Northern European foil; to terminate all non-European immigration, inclusive of Jews; and wherever possible to transfer humanely all racial aliens to their own lands.
>
> (Special Branch report, 22 February 1960)

The BNP split in 1962 over Jordan and Tyndall's Nazi-inspired histrionics (Thurlow, 1998: 234). Tyndall and Jordan subsequently founded the National

Socialist Movement (NSM) on 20 April 1962, Hitler's birthday. Bean meanwhile retained the BNP name and the bulk of the membership, at the expense of a party headquarters, which remained in Jordan's hands. This incarnation of the BNP – the third organization to bear the name, the current being the fifth – existed until February 1967, when it recombined with the LEL and the Racial Preservation Society (RPS) to create the National Front (NF).

Without doubt, Bean was an important figure in the history of the British far-right. Some commentators on the far-right aver that, had Bean not retired from politics shortly after the foundation of the NF in 1967, and had that organization stuck to the strategy he pioneered, then the British far-right could have been spared three decades of political failure. Suffice to say that Bean has been reconceptualized, by the contemporary far-right and by Nick Griffin personally, as the harbinger of the 'modern' British 'nationalism' and, some might say, the best leader British fascism never had. Bean's ideological and strategic innovations were not just recognized by Colin Cross in his 1965 *New Society* article. The anti-fascist magazine *Searchlight* paid Bean a backhanded compliment when it wrote that *Combat*, the magazine Bean edited, which regularly railed against 'The Black Invasion', was 'one of the best publications ever turned out by the far-right. Bean . . . wrote with wit and hate. He was also one of the best street speakers the British far-right had after Mosley' (*Searchlight*, no. 226, April 1994).

Bean's re-emergence as a significant figure for the British far-right has not been accidental. The first observation to make is that, in championing the account of British fascism set forth by Bean in *Many shades of black*, the leadership of the current BNP has quite deliberately sought to manufacture a useable version of its historical past to validate its current strategic goals and, in doing so, serve the political future. BNP ideologues have highlighted Bean's alleged attempt to purge his version of the BNP of anti-Semitism and his determination to prioritize electioneering and community politics, both goals of the current BNP. This serves a particular political purpose. In promoting the version of history propounded in *Many shades of black,* the contemporary BNP has sought to invent for itself a 'moderate' and, it has to be said, non-existent historical continuity that shifts the centre of gravity towards Bean rather than founding BNP chairman John Tyndall (1934–2005). This feeds into the party's agenda of insulating itself against charges of racist political extremism, of which Tyndall was the personification. This failure to make a clean break with the past, opting instead to emphasize another part of the fascist historical tradition, indicates perhaps a less than whole hearted commitment to modernizing that party. Indeed, were the contemporary BNP genuinely committed to achieving democratic legitimacy, it would surely make more sense to break with the past entirely, instead of engaging in such quixotic efforts to edit history. Perhaps the easiest way to account for the desire of Griffin et al. to maintain a direct link with their political predecessors is that the core principles of 'race and nation' enunciated by groups such as the 1960s BNP are also the *idées fixes* of the contemporary BNP. To turn its back on the historical tradition from which it emerged, the contemporary BNP would have to reject the essential 'truth' of its own ideology and thus its whole reason for being.

Bean has been complicit in this historical subterfuge. This is not surprising. Despite his advancing years, Bean plays an important role within the contemporary BNP as the editor of its journal *Identity*. Bean quietly inherited the editorial chair from Griffin in April 2003 and has edited the journal ever since.[3] 'When you said you'd do it, with your past record, I was delighted', enthused Griffin in an hour-long interview with Bean, which was subsequently circulated to party cadres and the public as a DVD entitled *John Bean – a true Nationalist*. The BNP website was equally delighted, lauding Bean as a 'veteran nationalist who has given over a half a century to the movement' and, in doing so, 'has made a massive contribution to nationalism and has always been part of the progressive movement drivng [sic] nationalism forward to electoral success'.[4]

Tyndall, in contrast, barely warrants a mention on the BNP website and, since his death in 2005, has rarely been mentioned in party publications either. His apparent airbrushing from the history of the party he founded in 1982 can be deduced from the choice of words used on the BNP website to describe Bean, who, incidentally, only joined the BNP after Griffin became chairman in 1999, having been largely politically quiescent since the early 1980s, aside from the occasional contribution to *Spearhead*. 'Progressive' and 'successful' are the key words to fasten upon. Tyndall was neither of these things, and, during his tenure as chairman, neither was the BNP. Bean, on the other hand, represents, to a certain extent, the image that Griffin wishes to project of the BNP: modern and electable.

In order to understand the importance of this latter point, it is necessary to view Bean's elevation to the position of 'elder statesman' within the context of the 'modernization' process itself. *Many shades of black* was privately published in 1999 during the increasingly acrimonious leadership contest between John Tyndall and Nick Griffin, who defeated the founder of the party to become BNP chairman in September 1999. *Many shades of black*, the pointed personal observations on the failure of British fascism by a veteran activist back from the political grave, had an obvious appeal to the 'modernizing' faction within the party. They consciously used the book and the observations contained therein to validate their own pointed criticisms of both Tyndall and his leadership.

Effusive reviews appeared in *Patriot*, mouthpiece of the 'modernizing' BNP faction, serving to heighten the historical potency of their attacks on the shortcomings of their soon to be deposed chairman. Bean's autobiography was seen to buttress the case for 'modernization' made contemporaneously by Griffin and his cohorts. The book was subsequently reviewed in the inaugural issue of *Identity*, the new BNP journal, which praised it for giving 'an unusually objective assessment of past errors and the future potential of our cause'. The review lingered upon Bean's closing comment that: 'The BNP has shown that it is growing up; becoming more mature, with a subsequent increase in growth. Much of this has been due to the influence and new generation of racial nationalists' (*Identity*, no. 1, January/February 2000).

Such testimony served to further undermine Tyndall. It was ironic that Bean's autobiography should have a role to play in the struggle for the soul of racial nationalism in 1999, given that he himself had been engaged in an almost identical battle with Tyndall and Jordan to 'modernize' British fascism during the early 1960s, a battle that Tyndall ultimately won – and the 'modern nationalism' alluded to by Griffin in the introduction lost – when Tyndall became chairman of the National Front in 1972.

Aside from its immediate value as a tool to blacken Tyndall's political reputation during and after the leadership contest, *Many shades of black* had held another attraction for the 'modernizers'. Detailed analysis of the book reveals the familiar autobiographical traits of sanitization and self-exculpation, in which Bean expunged his racist and anti-Semitic record, as well as, perhaps inevitably, his shortcomings as a political leader, which, for party 'modernizers' keen to reinvent the history of both their party and indeed the tradition from which it emerged, held an obvious appeal.

For the 'modernizers', *Many shades of black* offered a greater opportunity, the possibility of inventing, quite literally, the paradox of a 'non-extremist' extremist historical tradition, with Bean rather than Tyndall at the centre. It was to Bean that the 'modern' BNP owed a historical intellectual debt, the 'modernizers' now argued, not Tyndall. Bean had opted to develop community campaigning techniques and an electoral machine that was to bear fruit for the BNP during the 1964 general election, whereas Tyndall plumped for paramilitarism, jackboots and jail, contributing in no small measure to the negative image the public had of the British far-right. Therefore, in rejecting Tyndall and embracing Bean, the contemporary BNP attempts, not only to obfuscate the extremist origins of the party and indeed many of its own leading officers, but also to root its current strategic thinking in the past and, in doing so, to project it forwards as the future.

This deliberate distortion of the political record is commonplace for committed party apparatchiks, who are wont to dismiss anything prior to 1999 as an irrelevance to the 'modern' party. *Many shades of black* contributed to this internal narrative within the BNP at the very moment that, outwardly at least, the party was making attempts to move away from its virulently racist and anti-Semitic antecedents. This attempt to rewrite history was also overtaken by a more breathless attempt to erase it altogether. This can be gainsaid from the front page of *Patriot*, a mouthpiece for the 'modernizers' that portrayed the election of Nick Griffin in 1999 as a veritable year zero, under the banner headline 'New Millennium . . . New Leader!' (*Patriot*, no. 5, 1999), which rendered the years of party history prior to this singular event 'non-decades', to be derided or, better yet, simply ignored.

Whitewashing anti-Semitism

In *Many shades of black,* Bean portrays himself as presiding over the first attempt to purge British fascism of its addiction to both Nazism and biological anti-Semitism. In this respect, this early attempt to 'modernize' British fascism can be seen to parallel the 'modernization' of the BNP led by Nick Griffin after 1999. In both cases the figure of John Tyndall, an unreconstructed National Socialist, loomed large. Bean expelled both Tyndall and Jordan from the BNP in 1962 largely on account of their National Socialism. The parallels are rendered more explicit by the role that Bean has played in Griffin's attack on the 'Judeo-obsessives' – a shorthand for the Tyndallites and other hard-liners who refuse to recognize the efficacy of Griffin's 'modernization' programme – within the contemporary BNP. Following Tyndall's death in 2005, Griffin continued to face a residual challenge from some of his remaining supporters. In March 2006, Griffin launched a major offensive against the 'insane and politically disastrous obsession' that many BNP members had with 'the Jews'. These ideologically intransigent members succeeded in mounting a leadership challenge against Griffin in 2007, which he won with a comfortable 91 per cent majority of the vote. Bean's open support for Griffin, of whom he stated, 'In my 50 years I have not met anybody with a superior all-round political ability to that of Nick Griffin', administered a historical *coup de grace* to the pretensions of Griffin's admittedly already doomed rivals.[5]

However, the assertion made both in *Many shades of black* and by the contemporary BNP, that Bean purged the party of anti-Semitism, simply cannot be taken at face value. His party was in the vanguard of support for Nazi war criminal Adolf Eichmann, whose trial in Israel began on 11 April 1961 and ended with his execution on 1 June 1962, galvanizing Britain's anti-Semites and fascists to action. Bean and Jordan drove across central London carrying posters proclaiming 'Eichmann trial – Jews caused World War II' and 'Punish atrocities by Jews'. They stopped outside the Princes Theatre, High Holborn, where a Jewish meeting to commemorate the Warsaw ghetto was taking place. All eight occupants, including Jordan and Bean, were arrested and fined for insulting behaviour (*The Times*, 18 April 1961 and 2 May 1961).

In his autobiography, Bean blamed the entire incident on Jordan, claiming the episode gave him nightmares for years afterwards (Bean, 1999: 150–2). Colin Jordan issued a scathing refutation of Bean's version of events. The article, entitled 'John Bean recants', ridiculed his autobiography as 'a chronicle of clammy repentance and renunciation' through which Bean, 'whitens the hairs of his image in his old age by dint of blackening mine'. Jordan noted that Bean had raised no objection whatsoever to the constitution of the BNP, which explicitly recognized the 'Jewish problem', pointing out that Bean regularly pontificated on the subject in *Combat* ('The voice of race and nation'). Bean had claimed that he did not realize that the Warsaw ghetto exhibition was the intended target of their anti-Semitic activism. Jordan stated that this was a 'downright and deliberate lie':

> He advances in this dishonesty to pretend that on the afternoon during that campaign when, by prior planning, we circled with a placarded Land-Rover a central London theatre where Jews were meeting in exploitation of Eichmann's kidnapping he did not know in driving the vehicle the nature of the target, the object of the exercise. It so happened that it was Bean's silly backchat to a police superintendent, when that officer initially was only requiring Bean to drive out of the area, that caused all of the men inside the

> cabin and packing the open back to be arrested and then fined. Such falsification is the measure of the man seeking to set me up as a scapegoat.
> (*Gothic Ripples*, no. 40, April 2000)

The book was not only dishonest, argued Jordan, but it also trimmed at core principles. Jordan, a vociferous critic of the BNP, noted sardonically that the party under Griffin, which had been seeking to improve its image by banishing overt anti-Semitic discourse, had thus, 'responded favourably to this kindred spirit'.

It is hard not to agree with this observation. One of the principal claims made in *Many shades of black* was that Tyndall's anti-Semitism had repelled potential NF supporters and was thus responsible for its failure. On a personal note, Bean stated that the 'sly digs' at Jews to be found in *Spearhead*, the journal edited by Tyndall from 1964 to 2005, and other BNP publications was one of the reasons he did not join the BNP until after 1999, when *Spearhead* ceased to be the semi-official mouthpiece of the organization (Bean, 1999: 228–9). He neglected to mention, however, that during the late 1990s *Spearhead* was not edited by Tyndall but by Nick Griffin, under the pseudonym 'Tom North'. Indeed, in his praise for the new generation of nationalists emerging within the BNP, Bean neglects to make any mention at all of Griffin's own anti-Semitic record or his conviction for inciting racial hatred in 1998 as a result of articles he had published in his own anti-Semitic journal, *The Rune*, which have had an equally detrimental effect on public perceptions of the BNP.

Although Bean may not have been 'Judeo-obsessive' in the sense that Tyndall was, there can be no doubt that Bean 'accepted' anti-Semitism 'without demur' and, as Jordan argued, was now seeking to pass the historical buck in order to gain 'respectability' at his expense (*Gothic Ripples*, no. 40, April 2000). With regards to the Eichmann trial, the relevant issue of *Combat*, the journal edited by Bean, reveals that Bean contemporaneously applauded the very action he condemned in his autobiography. Furthermore, to coincide with the trial, Bean and Jordan produced a special 'Jewish atrocity' supplement to *Combat,* claiming the trial was 'a Jewish propaganda stunt' designed 'to smear and discredit . . . any and every form of criticism and opposition to their world power'. It also accused Jews of faking concentration camp photographs and included an article entitled 'the great lie of the six million', which denied the existence of Nazi gas chambers (*The Eichmann Trial – 'Combat' Supplement*). Other issues of *Combat* acquitted Eichmann as a 'fabricated monster' and branded the Holocaust 'palpable balderdash' (*Combat*, no. 11, March–April 1961, and *Combat*, no. 12, May–July 1961). This cannot be blamed on Jordan's influence. Prior to his involvement with him, Bean had penned numerous anti-Semitic articles railing against 'the growing power of Jewry', while, in the same issue, Tyndall demanded the 'elimination' of the Jewish 'cankerous microbe'. *Combat* also carried adverts for *The protocols of the elders of Zion* and printed a letter, without editorial comment, which stated 'the whole story of 6 million dead Jews is pure fiction' (*Combat*, no. 3, April–June 1959, and *Combat*, no. 5, January–March 1960). Bean also authored an article entitled 'Who are the Jews?', which argued that Jewish 'influence' represented a profound spiritual threat to national identity that:

> threatens to kill any further development of the bearers of the highest culture of mankind: the European, and particularly the Nordic section . . . all Europe must be freed from the malaise of Jewishness by the humane departure of these non-European peoples to their own national state of Israel.
> (*Combat*, no. 14, November-December 1961).

Bean's whitewashing of his own anti-Semitic record and his subsequent adoption of an anti-anti-Semitic stance were both pragmatic and personal. While Bean still appeared to believe in the traditional shibboleths of 'Jewish influence' in the media and finance, not to mention Jewish internationalism, he recognized that the obsession of many racial nationalists with Jewish 'plots' had led the movement 'up a blind alley' when the real danger, he argued, came from multiculturalism and global financial institutions, 'gentile as well as Jewish' (*Heritage and Destiny*, no. 6, January/February 2001). As Bean himself concedes, his views have 'hardened' rather than moderated in the past fifty years. 'International finance' and 'globalization' represent 'the same enemy, the same threat to the British way of life, to the European way of life, to the life of the West' (BNPtv, DVD).

Ultimately what differentiated Bean's anti-Semitism from that of Tyndall (and indeed Jordan) was his eventual recognition that such pronouncements damaged the BNP's political credibility and legitimacy. Even for appearances' sake, Tyndall was unable able to accept that 'Islam' represented a greater threat than 'Zionism' (*Spearhead*, no. 427, September 2004). Bean, on the other hand, who had more 'Strasserite' radical anti-capitalist leanings (something he has in common with Griffin), has come to view the real enemy as being a combination of 'globalization' and 'Islamification'. Echoing the anti-Semitic arguments used by Sir Oswald Mosley against the Jews in the 1930s, Bean argued on the BNP website, *pace* Griffin, that 'nationalists' should not shrink from the 'strategically useful, and morally legitimate' task of fighting 'bad' Jews, but that party activists needed to employ an '*ethnorealpolitik*' and recognize that the Jews were not necessarily a 'permanent' enemy, and within the ideological framework of the BNP campaign against 'Islam' represented potential allies. 'The master key to a sensible attitude towards the Jews is this', argued Bean, '*treat them like any other foreign people*' [my emphasis]. Arguing against party hard-liners, Bean stated that the idea that the Jews were responsible for 'all' our problems was ridiculous, not least because it ignored gentile involvement in globalization and 'the drive for world government'. Bean was at pains to explain, however, that 'our reformed Jewish policy has mainly been adopted for our own benefit', as overtly anti-Semitic pronouncements threatened the BNP 'modernization' drive.[6]

There is one final caveat to add with regards to the anti-anti-Semitic stance that Bean propagates, in both *Many shades of black* and his subsequent writings for the BNP. This was the fact that Bean, as he admits, deliberately toned down his past anti-Semitism 'to get the book published'. It was an endeavour in which he was singularly unsuccessful. Before self-publishing his autobiography, Bean approached twenty-seven publishing houses, intimating that at least one rejection was due to the director having a Jewish sounding name, while the remainder, he claimed, rejected the book because of 'left-wing' bias (*Heritage and Destiny*, no. 6, January/February 2001, and *Spearhead*, no. 375, May 2000). As he also conceded to Tyndall, 'If I have appeared to go too far in minimizing Jewish political and cultural influences it is because I do not wish to be seen as an "anti-Semite"' (*Spearhead*, no. 370, December 1999).

Southall and the BNP

The second major issue raised by *Many shades of black* that found favour with the 'modernizing' faction of the BNP was its focus on electioneering and the consequent legitimacy that this bestowed upon the racial-nationalist cause. This, so BNP 'modernizers' believed, offered a historical validation of the strategy they themselves had recently begun rigorously to pursue, which would begin to pay dividends in 2002 and 2003. During the early 1960s, Bean's BNP had increasingly focused its attention upon Southall in the borough of Ealing in west London. This was perceived to be fertile ground for a far-right anti-immigration campaign. Southall had a large Indian Punjabi community drawn from the subcontinent. In 1951, Southall's population stood at 55,896, of which 330 were immigrants. A decade later, the population had declined to 52,983, of which 2,540 were immigrants. By 1964, the year the BNP seriously set its sights upon the constituency, the immigrant population had increased to 6,500 (Woolcott, 1965: 31–54).

The BNP campaign in Southall took place against a backdrop of pre-existing local anti-immigrant campaigning. Local concerns, particularly with regards to housing and education, articulated through a racial prism were expressed by the Southall Residents Association (SRA), founded in September 1963 and chaired by Arthur E. Cooney. The SRA had evolved from the Palgrave Residents Association (PRA), a hastily convened group that had successfully petitioned the Labour council to purchase a property in Palgrave Avenue in order to keep it in 'white hands', thereby denying prospective Indian buyers (Walker, 1977: 51), although another account pinpoints its birth in (white) parental dissatisfaction at the number of immigrant children at a local primary school, which then exceeded 50 per cent (Woolcott, 1965: 35). The SRA advanced a similar agenda, coming to an agreement with a local estate agent that property bought through the association should only be sold to white buyers (Frederking, 2007: 103).

The driving force behind the PRA, leading local Conservative activist Margaret Penn, promptly joined the SRA as its secretary, seeking to steer the group towards becoming a fully-fledged community pressure group. She resigned in February 1964, however, as did three other leading members, alarmed that 'a new policy is emerging within the association, directed towards colour discrimination'. This was a reference to Cooney's obdurate refusal to work with the local Indian community. Although he asserted the SRA was political, Cooney denied the possibility or indeed desirability of racial integration. 'I think the British National Party has got something on immigration', he stated. The previous April, he and SRA treasurer Doris Hart had signed the nomination papers for two BNP candidates, Jack McConville, who polled 479 votes (27.3 per cent) in Hamborough ward, pushing the Conservatives into third place, and Ron Cuddon, who polled 257 votes (13.5 per cent) in Glebe ward. The clearly defined racist tendency within the SRA caused further resignations during the course of 1964, while another member, H. W. Johnson, resigned in order to stand as a BNP candidate in the Ealing borough council elections. Cooney later became treasurer of the Racial Preservation Society (RPS), which became a component of the National Front in 1967 (Walker, 1977: 52, 60; Woolcott, 1965: 36; *Combat*, no. 22, May/June 1963).

Although there were several strident voices calling for immigration restrictions during the 1960s, the proposal by the SRA for racially segregated education in January 1964 was out of step with contemporary political opinion. However, the strength of feeling against immigration in Southall was such that local Labour MP George Pargiter was moved to call for 'a complete ban on immigration to Southall' that same month, a position that did not reflect mainstream Labour Party opinion. The Conservatives held similarly robust attitudes, calling for a fifteen-year qualification period before immigrant families could get on the council-housing list. 'The issue of immigration created political chaos in Southall', noted one commentator (Walker, 1977: 52). Into the breach stepped the BNP.

The 'doorstep' campaign, which handed the BNP such 'immediate and spectacular' results in Southall in 1963, was 'primarily' due to the efforts of Ron Cuddon, the West Middlesex BNP organizer who sat on its governing body, the National Council. Bean credits Cuddon as 'one of the first to see the futility of the "coat trailing" meetings which ended in violence'. This tactic of meetings and marches, designed to provoke an outcry and thus gain publicity but that frequently served only to attract violent opposition, was the dominant model of activism for most far-right groups at the time. Cuddon's principal innovation was to build a 'local' team of activists, men and women, the majority of whom were from outside the milieu of extremist politics and 'who worked methodically talking to people on their doorsteps who shared the same disquiet at what was going on, and the same feeling of being let down by the orthodox parties' (Bean, 1999: 170). The use of female members in door-to-door canvassing was 'particularly effective in offsetting the "fascist" image being pushed by the mainstream parties' (Ulster Nation, 2002: 12). The Southall BNP branch also concentrated upon getting its message across through sustained literature sales of *Combat*, which were higher in Southall than anywhere else in the country (BNP members bulletin, 26 June 1964).

It was against this flurry of community-orientated politicking that Bean announced that he was to stand in Southall in the 1964 general election. Ironically, Bean had originally intended to contest Deptford, although he changed his mind following the arrest of a Deptford BNP activist for planning a bank robbery, the adverse local publicity persuading Bean to accept an offer from Cuddon to stand in Southall instead. In hindsight, the BNP campaign appears less deliberately focused than it was in reality. Bean lacked both funds and members to campaign properly elsewhere. Furthermore, this newfound concentration on the ballot box caused the BNP to begin haemorrhaging younger members who flocked towards the excitement provided by more militant organizations, such as John Tyndall's Greater Britain Movement (GBM), which had emerged during the course of 1964 from a split in Colin Jordan's NSM. The lack of confrontation also deprived the BNP campaign of publicity. However, had the remainder of the party been of the same 'quality' as the Southall branch, Bean believes that the BNP 'could have become a mass movement' (Bean, 1999: 170–72).

Key to its success in the run up to the general election was the 'considerable, though not unanimous support' that the BNP had derived from the SRA (Bean, 1999: 172). On 27 April, the SRA staged a hustings in the local British Legion Hall, inviting all three prospective parliamentary candidates, George Pargiter, the sitting Labour MP, Barbara Maddin, the Conservative candidate, and Bean. That said, SRA support for the BNP was already beginning to dissipate, as the group's pretensions to become a national organization began to manifest itself. Furthermore Maddin, the Conservative candidate, assiduously courted the SRA, campaigning heavily against immigration in an effort richly rewarded when both Cooney and his secretary, Grace Woods, voted for her and not the BNP (Foot, 1965: 216).

At the general election in October 1964, Bean polled 3,410 votes (9.1 per cent), the highest vote of any far-right candidate at that time. He had hoped to top 5,000 votes, however, but amid a national swing to the Conservatives and the anti-immigration stance adopted by the local Conservatives, which siphoned off some of the racist vote, Bean was satisfied with the result. His analysis of the vote indicated that approximately half of his vote – 4.75 per cent – came from disillusioned Labour supporters rather than Conservatives. In Deptford, where the BNP had stood twice previously but did not stand in 1964, its activists campaigned for an anti-immigrant independent candidate, Colin Atkins, who subsequently polled 2,386 votes (8.4 per cent), which the BNP claimed to have cultivated (*Combat*, no. 29, January 1965).

Bean's achievement at the ballot box was overshadowed, however, by the victory in Smethwick of Conservative candidate Peter Griffiths, who had defeated the Labour Foreign Secretary Patrick Gordon Walker on an anti-immigration ticket. Griffiths' campaign descended into gutter racism, however, when supporters began issuing material supporting him bearing the slogan 'if you want a nigger neighbour, vote Labour', which Griffiths failed to condemn. The Birmingham organizer of Mosley's UM had invented the slogan, Bean later recalled, and 'we heard that BNP members were also using the slogan and although I did not approve of it, I must confess to turning a blind eye'. Although the BNP did not have a candidate in Smethwick in 1964, some of its Birmingham members had canvassed on Griffiths' behalf. 'We had begun to appreciate the usefulness of tactical voting', Bean later observed. 'In some respects Griffiths' victory was a victory for us' (Bean, 1999: 172).

The reason for the success of the BNP in Southall in 1964 had less to do with the number of immigrants in the constituency – it was often far higher in other constituencies with no visible far-right support, such as Brixton in the south London borough of Lambeth – and more to do with its success in latching on to a 'self-generated and self-sustaining' campaign, further politicizing its prejudices while embedding itself deeper into the local community, a precursor to the 'community campaigning' model employed by today's BNP.

The 1964 general election success proved a chimera, however. Bean was unable to replicate its success. In March 1966, 'in spite of months of assiduous canvassing and organization in the previous eighteen months', their percentage of the vote in Southall declined from 3,410 votes (9.1 per cent) to 2,768 votes (7.4 per cent). The anti-immigrant vote in Deptford similarly dipped from the 2,386 votes (8.4 per cent) achieved by the anti-immigrant independent to 1,906 (7 per cent). An ill-prepared intervention in Smethwick meanwhile gained only 508 votes (1.5 per cent) (Walker, 1977: 57). Amid a broader national swing towards Labour, there were a number of reasons for the decline. The BNP had spread itself too thin and did not canvass as hard as it had in Southall in 1964, and, perhaps more saliently, it lacked the support of the SRA, which, having begun to dissociate itself from the BNP in 1964, continued to do so afterwards and diminished the local appeal of the BNP in the process. Other reasons included a combination of 'white flight' from the borough by many BNP supporters and the 'tougher' stance by mainstream political parties on immigration, which ate into the BNP appeal in the intervening two years. For Bean, ultimately the Southall campaign was a failure. 'They wouldn't listen', he lamented to Griffin, 'and now it's an Asian enclave' (BNPtv, DVD).

Bean might have failed to hold back the demographic tide, but the principal strategic lesson of the Southall campaign for a younger generation of activists struggling to extricate themselves from under the 'dead hand' of fascism was 'the discovery by Bean that racial populism and the issue of coloured immigration could turn an obscure fanatical sect into a potential mass movement' (Thurlow, 1998: 241). Vehement opposition to immigration has since become the cornerstone of far-right campaigning in Britain and indeed Europe, though to suggest that this was in any way owing to the model provided by Bean would be unduly to exaggerate his importance (Prowe, 1994: 289–313).

Furthermore, although the contemporary BNP has made much of its predecessor's pioneering community-led electioneering, it is important not to overstate the case. Serious community-orientated campaigning proved brief and ultimately transient. From 1965, the BNP reverted to 'poster parades' and marches in favour of causes such as white supremacist rule in Rhodesia, which had then begun to galvanize the far-right following its Unilateral Declaration of Independence (UDI) in November. Bean was arrested and fined following one such meeting (*Identity*, no. 86, January 2008). Ironically, considering the argument for community-led electioneering made both in Bean's autobiography and by the contemporary BNP, it was this reversion to marching that, Bean recorded, 'marked the beginning of a twelve month period when *support* for the BNP rose considerably, although actual membership increased only slightly' (Bean, 1999: 179).

Praise for the supposed electoral path pursued by Bean was at the centre of a review of *Many shades of black*, penned by Tony Lecomber, that appeared in the penultimate edition of his own journal, *Patriot*. Lecomber, one of the leading 'modernizers' within the contemporary BNP and a key ally of Nick Griffin, lauded Bean and Cuddon for their perceptive concentration on local organization building and sustained electoral work in Southall from 1963. 'Reading these passages', noted Lecomber, 'I was immediately struck by the similarities to then and now' making a pointed comparison between Cuddon in Southall in 1963 and BNP elections officer Eddy Butler in Tower Hamlets in 1993 (*Patriot*, no. 7, 2000).

It is interesting to note that the same edition of *Patriot* carried an article on strategy and tactics from Butler, then the BNP elections officer, who at that point in time had masterminded the party's sole electoral breakthrough in 1993. Butler argued that *Many shades of black* was 'well worth studying', particularly with regards to local community campaigning in targeted wards, which was pioneered by the original BNP but, adopted only sporadically, was completely undermined by 'a low boredom threshold' among far-right activists, who denied themselves 'any sustained success' as a result (*Patriot*, no. 7, 2000). While the parallel drawn between Cuddon and Butler is interesting, the roots of Butler's 1993 success have more immediate origins, attributable to the politicization of race by the local Liberal Democrat group, which paved the way for the 'legitimacy' enjoyed by the BNP and its 'rights for whites' campaign, rather than its being the result of any genuine historical continuity (Copsey, 1996: 118–41).

The main thrust of Lecomber's review, however, had an avowedly partisan political point to make. 'The sad fact is that it has taken us more than 35 years to reach the same point as the original BNP', he observed. 'Why is this? Bean's book doesn't provide the answer, at least not directly. But it is there for those with eyes to see and the brains to understand.' For Lecomber, *Many shades of black* reaffirmed his belief that the failure of British fascism could be laid squarely at Tyndall's door. 'Thinking on all of this, one wonders what might have been had Bean and not Tyndall been the dominant personality in the 1970s', noted Lecomber ruefully. Lecomber buttressed his argument by reiterating the statement made by A. K. Chesterton, the first chairman of the NF, at its 1967 AGM, in which he warned of the 'incalculable' harm that would be done to the nascent organization by:

> The man who thinks this is a war that can be won by mouthing slogans against dirty Jews and filthy n★★★ers is a maniac whose place should not be in the National Front but in a mental hospital . . . A nation once noble and great cannot be rescued from the mire by jackasses who play straight into the enemies hands by giving the public that image of us that the enemy most dearly wants to be given.

Setting aside the fact that it was Chesterton who arranged for Tyndall's inclusion in the NF, Lecomber's inclusion of this quote in his review clearly implies that Tyndall was one of those 'jackasses' who had caused 'incalculable' harm to the cause of British 'nationalism' (*Patriot*, no. 7, 2000). This was certainly a case of the pot calling the kettle black, given Lecomber's apparent record of racist political violence, which led ultimately to his dismissal from the upper echelons of the BNP leadership in 2006.

Despite a personal affection for Tyndall, Bean concurred, stating that Tyndall was both the 'greatest asset' and the 'greatest liability' for the BNP. Tyndall's pugnacious leadership and longevity were neutralized by photographs of him wearing Nazi-style uniform in the 1960s, which was a public-relations disaster for racial nationalism, he argued (Bean, 1999: 238).

For the 'modernizing' faction, *Many shades of black* underlined the fact that Tyndall was a liability whose insistence on the tactics of 'march and grow' while chairman of the NF had led that organization into a cul-de-sac in the 1970s, and had led the BNP to a similar denouement thirty years later. Tyndall, it was claimed, was 'slow to learn' the lessons of the original BNP, which pointed towards organizational building, sustained electoral work and the avoidance of confrontation for confrontation's sake (*Patriot*, no. 7, 2000).

Despite these stinging criticisms, which were used to particular effect by the BNP 'modernizers' in the standoff with Tyndall in 1999, it should be noted that *Many shades of black* represents an exercise in the application of hindsight. Bean's reminiscences ignored the central fact that he too had been instrumental in facilitating Tyndall's entry into the NF and so cannot have been overly appalled by either his politics or the strategy he pursued. During the course of 1966, the disparate strands of the far-right embarked upon a series of discussions, which, in February 1967, would lead to the establishment of the NF. Bean was a key player in the merger talks, as was Tyndall, who had been calling for 'unity' since July 1966. However, when Ron Cuddon, the man credited with the BNP's electoral success, learned that Bean and another BNP National Council member had met with Tyndall, he resigned from the BNP, announcing that 'a neo-Nazi plot was afoot' (Walker, 1977: 63, 74). Bean claimed that Cuddon had resigned despite being 'assured' that Tyndall would not be a part of the merger and that the anti-Semitism and pro-Nazism of his organization, the GBM, 'would most certainly not be part of National Front policy'. Bean reassured *Combat* readers that, despite Cuddon's departure, 'the majority of Southall ex-BNP members support the National Front' (*Combat*, no. 40, 1967). Bean's autobiography reveals, however, that Cuddon's resignation was more damaging than he let on at the time, precipitating the departure of 'half of the Southall branch', as well as a number of other activists (Bean, 1999: 189).

Cuddon's departure was a warning sign that was ignored. Despite outward utterances, Chesterton and Bean, who resigned as BNP national organizer in September 1966 lest his own past extremism jeopardize negotiations, both appear determined to admit Tyndall, observing that tactically he had to be excluded from the 'formation stages' of the merger. As a sign of his good faith, Tyndall disbanded the GBM in June 1967, its membership quietly joining the nascent NF, while *Spearhead* offered the new organization its 'wholehearted support'. Bean later credited Tyndall with playing a 'significant' role in the formation of the NF (Bean, 1999: 183–4).

The contemporary BNP has sought to characterize the 1960s version as its precursor in an attempt to disconnect itself from its immediate political antecedent, the NF, an organization it now derides as 'neo-fascist'. However, this contemporary chicanery founders on Bean's pivotal role in the formation of the NF. He was one of the organization's three founders, not just founding members, and noted that the populist racial ideology espoused by the BNP and the NF, some minor points aside, was 'basically the same' (*Combat*, no. 40, 1967).

Bean did attempt to influence the nascent NF to learn the lessons of Southall, which, quoting from the Institute of Race Relations newsletter, meant that, as everyone knew he was 'anti-immigrant', Bean could 'concentrate on trying to make his party respectable', developing a full raft of policies so that, when he spoke of immigration, which consumed less than half his platform, he was able to appear 'reasonable and undramatic'. Race 'is still the basis of politics' he reassured his readers, but clearly he believed that the NF needed to follow the strategic model defined by the BNP three years previously (*Combat*, no. 40, 1967). However, although Tyndall initially remained outside the NF, he and Bean were soon co-operating with each other to a significant degree, which certainly suggests a certain ideological symmetry. The duo exchanged articles for each other's respective publications, in spite of the objections of Bean's closest collaborator, Andrew Fountaine (1918–97), the vice-chairman of the NF and former BNP activist, who disliked Tyndall personally and politically. Bean evidently disregarded Fountaine's objections. *Combat* and *Spearhead* began sharing offices, and, when *Combat* folded in the autumn of 1968, Bean handed its subscription list to Tyndall, which certainly implies that he approved of the magazine's content (Bean, 1999: 205).

Ultimately, Bean assigned the NF's failure to a combination of six factors: the Conservatives' tough stance on immigration in 1979, white flight, internal feuding, marches that were surrounded by an aura of violence, left-wing 'smear' leaflets and anti-Semitism. It is to be noted that three of the reasons were in essence presentational, a principal concern of BNP 'modernization'. Bean claimed to have been appalled by the tone of party publications, which, he asserted, had a baleful effect on would-be members who were concerned over immigration but, confronted with 'open racial abuse' in *National Front News* and Holocaust denial in *Spearhead*, 'decided that it was true after-all. The National Front were anti-Semitic, and they could see why they were being called Nazis' (Bean, 1999: 228–9). Tyndall's protracted review of *Many shades of black* in *Spearhead* only served to reinforce the point. Tyndall, who claimed past political associations were 'completely irrelevant' to a party's image, likewise proved unable to accept that public perceptions of violence or the discussion of 'background issues', such as alleged Jewish power, really had damaged NF support (*Spearhead*, no. 369, November 1999).

On the website of the contemporary BNP, Bean recently wrote that, 'Seeing it [the NF] become more extreme under the leadership of John Tyndall, I resigned.'[7] This is misleading. Bean, despite his apparent objections to NF anti-Semitism, remained an NF member, albeit an inactive one, until the end of 1978, when he allowed his membership to lapse (something slightly different to resigning) shortly before the implosion of the organization in the wake of its disastrous showing in the 1979 general election. Tyndall had been the dominant figure throughout this period, chairing the organization twice. Thereafter, largely out of personal loyalty to Fountaine, Bean backed the National Front Constitutional Movement (NFCM), though he continued contributing occasional articles to *Spearhead*. The NFCM represented another missed opportunity for the British far-right. The organization's chief ideological innovation was to recognize that compulsory repatriation was not a vote winner, a proposal greeted with 'horror and disbelief' by one leading NF member, Andrew Brons, who today is a BNP MEP for Yorkshire and Humberside region (*New Nation*, no. 1, 1980).

Conclusion

Many shades of black represents an important window through which one can observe the battle for political legitimacy being waged both publicly and privately by the BNP. The book swiftly became a cipher for the party's own modernization efforts. Used as a discursive weapon against the historical record of political opponents, the BNP 'modernizing' faction was, unsurprisingly, uninterested in the veracity of the account presented by Bean, no doubt aware that a dose of historical reality would have undermined its usefulness as a tool to buttress their claims that the party had distanced itself from its overtly extremist roots. Ironically, although the BNP has sought to expunge the debt the party owes to party founder John Tyndall, in its attempt to anchor its new political project in the history of the 1960s BNP led by John Bean, it has rooted itself in a historical tradition every bit as racist and anti-Semitic as the one it seeks to distance itself from.

This being the case, it rather begs the question as to why the BNP has pursued the exercise so doggedly. Why try to rehabilitate history? Why not start from scratch? That the 'modern' BNP has sought to revise its history to make it more electable and to use this to marginalize Tyndall is perhaps largely unsurprising. As noted at the opening of this chapter, however, the BNP appears unable to transcend its roots to become a genuine 'post-fascist' party, precisely because its ideologues and activists, socialized within earlier extremist groups stretching back, in some cases, to the early 1950s, would have to reject the essential 'truth' of the BNP's racial-nationalist ideology and, with it, a racial *Weltanschauung* that they genuinely believe in and that, ultimately, they thus have no personal or political desire to repudiate. This is perhaps one of the principal reasons why, although the contemporary BNP has succeeded in becoming the most successful electoral manifestation of the extreme right, it has so conspicuously failed to erect a convincing 'reputational shield' (Ivarsflaten, 2006) to deflect accusations of racism and extremism.

Seen from the outside, this seemingly inexplicable commitment to preserving ideological continuity has ensured that the contemporary BNP has been no more successful than its historical namesake in expunging either racism or anti-Semitism from its ranks, despite a much-vaunted 'modernization'. For instance, despite claiming to have 'no time for anti-Semites' (*The Independent on Sunday*, 4 January 2009), party chairman Nick Griffin continues to frame arguments within the parameters of recognizably anti-Semitic discourse. Furthermore, recent polling data also suggest that 33 per cent of BNP voters agreed, completely or in part, with the proposition that there exists a major international Jewish/communist conspiracy to undermine the traditional Christian values of Britain and other Western countries.[8]

In the conclusion to *Many shades of black,* John Bean paid homage to the 'influence and new generation of racial nationalists' who, by implication, had learned the lessons of the 1960s BNP. In the original proofs for the book, Bean had singled out Griffin by name, but removed reference to him in deference to a request from Tyndall (BNPtv, DVD). Even here, Bean is not entirely candid. As late as 2001, two years after Griffin seized control of the BNP from Tyndall, Bean was to write that 'in my mind the British National Party would be better served with John Tyndall as chairman' (*Heritage and Destiny*, no. 6, January/February 2001). This did not imply, however, that in supporting Tyndall he depreciated Griffin's efforts. 'He is rather like me at his age!' observed Bean, in a rather telling comment (*Heritage and Destiny*, no. 7, March/April 2001). Although *Many shades of black* represents a concerted attempt to revise the history of the British far-right in order to make it serviceable for future ideological exigency, the historical record indicates strongly that it was not just John Tyndall who was 'slow to learn'.

Notes

1 I would like to thank the Leverhulme Trust for funding this research.
2 See www.guardian.co.uk/commentisfree/2009/oct/22/bnp-nick-griffin-le-pen (accessed 8 November 2009).
3 Paul Golding, BNP director of publicity, edited *Identity* until his expulsion. Nick Griffin edited *Identity* from May 2002 for the next ten issues until April 2003, when Bean became editor; see *Identity*, no. 19, April 2002; *Identity*, no. 20, May 2002; and *Identity*, no. 31, April 2003.
4 See www.identitymagazine.org.uk/editorial.html (accessed 8 November 2009).
5 See www.bnp.org.uk/2007/12/why-i-support-nick-griffin/ (accessed 8 November 2009).
6 See www.bnp.org.uk/articles/judeo_obsession.htm (accessed 26 June 2006).
7 See www.bnp.org.uk/2007/12/why-i-support-nick-griffin/ (accessed 8 November 2009).
8 See www.channel4.com/news/media/2009/06/day08/yougovpoll_080609.pdf (accessed 8 November 2009).

References

Bean, J. (1999) *Many shades of black: inside Britain's far right*, London: New Millennium.

Copsey, N. (1996) 'Contemporary fascism in the local arena: the British National Party and "rights for whites",' in Cronin, M. (ed.) *The failure of British fascism: the far right and the fight for political recognition*, Basingstoke: Macmillan.

Copsey, N. (2008) *Contemporary British fascism: the British National Party and the quest for legitimacy*, 2nd edn, Basingstoke: Palgrave-Macmillan.

Foot, P. (1965) *Immigration and race in British politics*, Harmondsworth: Penguin.

Frederking, L. C. (2007) *Economic and political integration in immigrant neighbourhoods*, Selinsgrove: Susquehanna University Press.

Ivarsflaten, E. (2006) 'Reputational shields: why anti-immigrant parties fail'. Paper presented to the annual conference of the American Political Science Association, Philadelphia, 30 August–3 September.

Kitschelt, H. (1995) *The radical right in Western Europe*, Ann Arbor: University of Michigan Press.

Prowe, D. (1994) 'Classic fascism and the new radical right in Western Europe: comparisons and contrasts,' *Contemporary European History*, 3 (3): 289–313.

Rydgren, J. (2004) *The populist challenge: political protest and ethno-nationalist mobilization in France*, New York: Bergahn.

Thurlow, R. (1998) *Fascism in Britain: from Oswald Mosley's Blackshirts to the National Front*, London: IB Tauris.

Tyndall, J. (1988) *The eleventh hour: a call for British rebirth*, London: Albion.

Ulster Nation (2002) *Freedom struggle: half a century in British nationalist politics – an interview with John Bean*, Belfast: Glenwood Publications/Ulster Nation.

Walker, M. (1977) *The National Front*, London: Fontana/Collins.

Woolcott, D. (1965) 'Southall', in Deakin, N. (ed.) *Colour and the British electorate 1964: six case studies*, London: Pall Mall Press.

2

RACE AND RACIAL DIFFERENCE

The surface and depth of BNP ideology[1]

John E. Richardson

Introduction

This chapter examines the discursive representation of race and racial difference in texts produced and/or circulated by the British National Party (BNP). The chapter draws on critical discourse analysis and assumes that language is a social practice that, like all practices, is dialectically related to the contexts of its use. In other words, 'speaking and writing always represent, produce and reproduce attitudes, beliefs, opinions and ideologies' (Heer and Wodak, 2008: 10). In so doing, language use contributes to the production and *re*production of social realities. As Reisigl and Wodak (2001: 1) argue, racism and discrimination manifest themselves discursively, in that 'racist opinions and beliefs are produced and reproduced by means of discourse [. . .] through discourse, discriminatory exclusionary practices are prepared, promulgated and legitimized'. Hence, the strategic use of many linguistic strategies to construct in- and out-groups is fundamental to political (and discriminatory) discourses in all kinds of settings. Ruth Wodak's discourse–historical approach to discourse analysis (see Reisigl and Wodak 2001; 2009; Richardson and Wodak, 2009a; 2009b; Wodak, 2009) is particularly useful in analysing the discourse of fascist parties, owing to the way it aims to integrate and triangulate knowledge about historical sources and the background of the social and political fields within which discursive events are embedded.

The chapter is based on two contentions, hopefully substantiated by my discussion: first, that the discourse of fascist parties seeking mass electoral support is inherently duplicitous, claiming one thing while the party is committed to something else. Second, in examining this dishonesty, it is essential to distinguish between the surface arguments in fascist discourse and the underlying ideological commitments. As Mannheim (1960: 120) pointed out, in the case of fascist ideology, 'more than in most others, it is essential to separate the propaganda from the real attitude in order to gain an understanding of its essential character'. Consequently, the chapter will argue that an understanding of fascist political ideology requires comparative analysis of texts produced at different times and for different audiences (insider and outsider; potential voter and party initiates). On the surface, BNP members appear to be racial populists, a categorization that places them within the acceptable limits of (right-wing, nationalist, authoritarian) democratic British politics. However, as Nick Griffin has himself noted, the BNP has its ideological roots 'in the sub-Mosleyite whackiness of Arnold Leese's Imperial Fascist League' (Griffin, 2003, cited in Copsey, 2007: 70). As I will show below, the ideological core of the BNP, as revealed in the political beliefs and commitments of party leaders and activists, still draws strength from Leese's anti-Semitic racial fascism and remains committed to the racial purification of the national space.

Patterns of stability and change

A consistent dilemma for fascists since 1945 has been the extent to which they should be open and honest in their propaganda about what they actually stand for. Understandably, the Nazi industrialization of mass murder during the Second World War meant that there was little electoral cachet in labelling your party, or movement, 'fascist', which led to two perpetually recurring strategies: dissociating yourself from, or rehabilitating, Nazism (Sykes, 2005: 95). The latter strategy led, inexorably, to an extra-parliamentary, pseudo-revolutionary path and, in Britain, was advocated most consistently by Colin Jordan, having taken the reins from his mentor Arnold Leese (see Gorman (1977) and Morell (1980) for discussions of this legacy). The former strategy led to a duplicitous path, initially exemplified by Mosley and the Union Movement, wherein pre-war fascist euphemistic commonplaces, such as 'national unity', 'common culture' and 'strong government', were rebranded and relaunched as 'a synthesis of the best elements of fascism and of the old democracy' (Mosley, n.d.: 17; also see Macklin, 2007). Thus, in Union Movement discourse, fascism became 'European Socialism', the free-to-be-exploited Empire became 'Europe–Africa', single-party rule became 'definite, conscious and economic leadership' (Skidelsky, 1981: 495–6) and 'Fascist Man' became the 'creative individual' (Mosley, n.d.: 12).

Since this post-war rebranding, fascist parties intent on building a mass movement have always maintained two faces, a private one and a public one, drawing, respectively, on an 'esoteric' appeal to 'intellectual' insiders and a grossly simplified 'exoteric' appeal to both the mass membership and the electorate (Taylor, 1979: 127, adapting the work of Almond, 1954). In this respect, British fascism is not unique, of course; most political parties adopt different argumentative, and even ideological, appeals when addressing different sections of the electorate, and maintain front-of-stage and back-stage personas (Wodak, 2009). Equally, parties in power may use ideologically obfuscatory language (Fairclough, 2000) or may equivocate, particularly in discourse on sensitive or 'taboo' subjects such as race (Dummett, 1973; Foot, 1965; Miles and Phizacklea, 1984). However, the post-war political landscape has meant that the esoteric ideological arguments of British fascists are 'much more complex and far-reaching than the "exoteric" appeal than is the case with other British parties' (Taylor, 1979: 129).

The construction and exploitation of public concern over immigration in the 1970s brought a change of fortune for Britain's fascist fringe. Similarly, since 2001, and particularly since the July bombings in 2005:

> the BNP has gone all out to tap a rich vein of anti-Muslim sentiment [. . .] Party members are now rebuked for discussing the Holocaust and told to focus on terrorism, the evils of Islam, and scare stories of Britain becoming an Islamic state.
>
> (Oborne, 2008)

This, too, is part of an explicitly Janus-faced policy. In an article published in the magazine *Patriot* soon after his first trial for incitement to racial hatred, Griffin outlined to BNP activists his plans for the 'modernization' of the party:

> As long as our own cadres understand the full implications of our struggle, then there is no need for us to do anything to give the public cause for concern [. . .] we must at all times present them with an image of moderate reasonableness [. . .] Of course, we must teach the truth to the hardcore, for, like you, I do not intend this movement to lose its way. But when it comes to influencing the public, forget about racial differences, genetics, Zionism, historical revisionism and so on – all ordinary people want to know is what we can do for them that the other parties can't or won't.
>
> (*Patriot*, no. 4, 1999)

The importance of this extract – acknowledging that the BNP adopts a 'moderate' public face to hide an ideological core – cannot be over-emphasized, given the way that Griffin explicitly makes a distinction between exoteric and esoteric appeals: that it is possible to appeal to 'ordinary people' at the same time as teaching 'the truth to the hardcore'. Further, perhaps because the magazine *Patriot* could have been read by journalists, politicians or academics seeking to attack the BNP, the article indexes this strategy of exoteric/esoteric appeals in a more fundamental way. Writing for party members on the subject of strategically moderating the BNP's 'careless extremism', Griffin partially conceals 'the truth' to which he and his party remain wedded: 'racial differences' is a code for racial hierarchies; 'genetics' is a code for scientific racism, and specifically theories of genetic racial superiority/inferiority; 'Zionism' is a code word for Jews, the 'Jewish Question' and the myth of a Jewish world conspiracy in particular (Billig, 1978); and 'historical revisionism' refers to Holocaust denial. In their place, Griffin argues that the party needs to concentrate its propaganda on 'idealistic, unobjectionable, motherhood and apple pie concepts' (ibid.): freedom, democracy, security and identity (see Copsey, 2007; 2008). Employing this campaign tactic, coupled with factors such as, inter alia, the financial crisis, high unemployment and general dissatisfaction with the mainstream parties, the BNP is currently achieving a level of electoral success that is unparalleled in the history of British fascism (see John et al., 2006).

Despite their variance, both the exoteric and esoteric racial ideologies of British fascism are united by a cluster of common presuppositions: the existence of distinct races; that all human civilization and development spring from the 'spirit' inherent, unchangeably, in these races; that different races have different capacities for 'civilization' and, partly as a result, are in conflict with each other; that these races form a hierarchy in which some are 'naturally' more valuable and beneficial than others; and, consequently, that these higher races need protecting from the threats posed by the lower and competing races. This chain of presuppositions formed the central commitments to Aryan superiority and racial purity in *Mein Kampf*, and the racial ideology of British fascism draws deeply on this racist heritage. Thus, in 1976, *Spearhead*, John Tyndall's fascist magazine and then-mouthpiece of the National Front, asserted: 'the achievements of the civilisation are the achievements of the race. Race has been, thus far, the cradle of civilisations and nations' (*Spearhead*, no. 99, November 1976). Thirty years later, in an internal document, the BNP argued: 'People are a product of their genes, and a country is the product of its people' (BNP, *Hostile media questions for BNP candidates and officials*, 2005). As we will see, in exoteric rhetoric, the ideological commitment to protecting the white race is reformulated as a love of an in-group identity, culture and country. But this is a tactical rather than ideological difference, as the esoteric discourse of the BNP still displays a notable preoccupation with the four euphemistically named subjects that Griffin listed in his 1999 *Patriot* article: 'racial differences, genetics, Zionism, historical revisionism'.

The surface of BNP racial ideology

The party has a highly developed propaganda network, producing a newspaper, a magazine, four regularly updated websites, a range of official and unofficial blogs, a monthly video news service DVD, a wide variety of leaflets on national and local issues and, most recently, a record label and Internet radio station. The volume of this material is staggering, meaning that a close examination of all texts in which race and racial difference are invoked is beyond the reach of this chapter. This first section provides a summary of leaflets, as the prototypical genre produced for the mass membership and electorate. The leaflets selected are representative examples of local and national campaign materials, distributed in a number of British electoral constituencies; all their contents were authorized by the party's director of publicity. In the later sections, these leaflets are contextualized – and contrasted – with texts intended for insider audiences.

The principal argumentation strategy of the BNP's exoteric media is a patriotic appeal to Britain and Britishness and, on the surface at least, claims similar political ground to the mainstream political parties. Indeed, from 2007 onwards, the Labour Party and the BNP shared 'British jobs for British workers' as a campaign slogan (see Richardson and Wodak, 2009b) (see Figure 2.1).

FIGURE 2.1 Photomontage of recent BNP leaflets[2]

In publicly disseminated campaign materials, the BNP uses red, white and blue and the Union Flag as its major symbolic resources, emphasizing its support for 'Britain' and British cultural identity. It supports the NHS and is in favour of more police on the streets, the protection of greenbelts and a range of populist, political commonplaces that many democratically minded Britons would be hard-pressed to object to (see Richardson, 2008; Richardson and Wodak, 2009a; 2009b). If the claims in Figure 2.1 were taken on face value, the BNP would appear to reside within the democratic limits of British politics, albeit British politics of the right-wing, nationalist and authoritarian variety. What marks the BNP out, however, is the rationale for its politics: as I detail elsewhere (Richardson, 2008), the presence of minority ethnic communities underwrites all of its exoteric policies, though this presence is usually alluded to, euphemized or discussed via a strategy of 'calculated ambivalence' (Engel and Wodak, 2009), in which the BNP does not explicitly name the 'ethnic Other'. The reason why the resources of the NHS are stretched? Too many 'non-British' people. The reason for the high crime rate and need for more police? Too many 'non-British' people. The reason why the greenbelt is under threat? Too many 'non-British people'. Unemployment? And so on – using scapegoating that is typical of far-right parties across the EU (Betz and Meret, 2009; Mudde, 2007; Pelinka and Wodak, 2002). The BNP is, therefore, not so much a single-*issue* party as a *single-explanation* party; its exoteric policies appear linked because they are all, implicitly or explicitly, linked to a single cause: the presence of too many undesirable 'non-British' (that is, immigrant) people in Britain.[3]

A key ideological argument of the BNP since the violent disturbances in the north of England and the attacks on America in 2001 has been what the party calls the *Islamification* of Britain. However, since the Racial and Religious Hatred Act (2007) came into force, and two high-profile, failed prosecutions of the party leadership, there has been a noticeable 'visual turn' in the leaflets of the BNP (see Richardson and Wodak, 2009a). Take, for example, the very wordy leaflet distributed in Burnley (2003), for the unsuccessful candidate Jim Cowell, shown in Figure 2.2.

Here, in a rather standard racist argument for 'keeping them out', Cowell rails against 'MULTI-CULTURALISM' and 'MULTI-RACIALISM' (capitalized throughout) and warns that 'in a few years your vote will count for nothing as ethnic minorities are invited to settle in Burnley'. Compare this with a leaflet distributed in the Midlands town of Stoke in 2008, shown in Figure 2.3.[4]

In Figure 2.3, the upper montage combines images of a Church tower, a group of white women, standing with a child and a dog outside a terraced house, and the distinctive bottle kilns of the potteries; the lower montage combines an image of Muslim women wearing the *niqab* and the silhouettes of domed roofs topped with crescent moons.[5] The viewer's attention is directed by the use of the arrows on the left, pointing, in the lower montage, to a woman putting up two fingers – ironically, a rather English gesture of defiance or abuse – aimed at the photographer and, hence, transferred to the viewer. The repeated use of 'this' is a particularly effective rhetorical device and is the principal element that allows a cross-fertilization between the visual and verbal components of the leaflet. On their own, the linguistic aspects of these leaflets are equivocal in what exactly they are arguing for:

> From this: Hanley 70 years ago
> To this: Is this what you want for our city centre?
> The choice is yours!

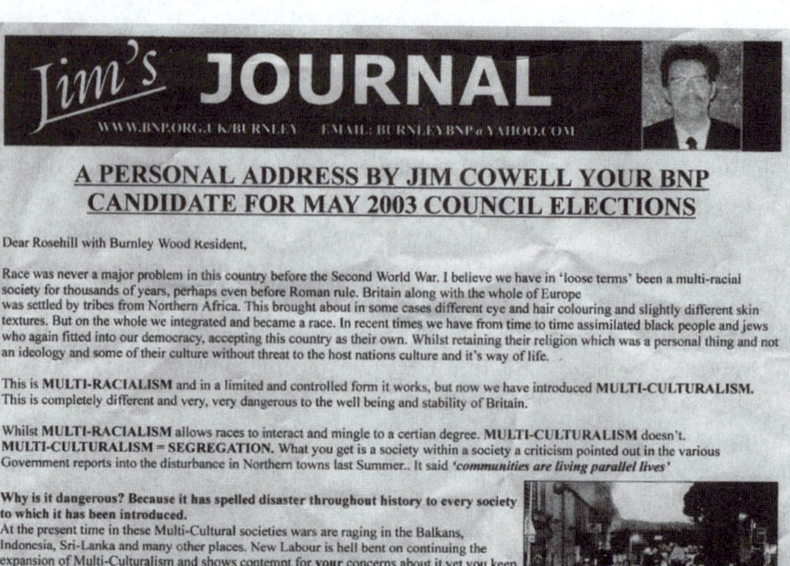

Jim's JOURNAL

WWW.BNP.ORG.UK/BURNLEY EMAIL: BURNLEYBNP@YAHOO.COM

A PERSONAL ADDRESS BY JIM COWELL YOUR BNP CANDIDATE FOR MAY 2003 COUNCIL ELECTIONS

Dear Rosehill with Burnley Wood Resident,

Race was never a major problem in this country before the Second World War. I believe we have in 'loose terms' been a multi-racial society for thousands of years, perhaps even before Roman rule. Britain along with the whole of Europe was settled by tribes from Northern Africa. This brought about in some cases different eye and hair colouring and slightly different skin textures. But on the whole we integrated and became a race. In recent times we have from time to time assimilated black people and jews who again fitted into our democracy, accepting this country as their own. Whilst retaining their religion which was a personal thing and not an ideology and some of their culture without threat to the host nations culture and it's way of life.

This is **MULTI-RACIALISM** and in a limited and controlled form it works, but now we have introduced **MULTI-CULTURALISM.** This is completely different and very, very dangerous to the well being and stability of Britain.

Whilst **MULTI-RACIALISM** allows races to interact and mingle to a certian degree. **MULTI-CULTURALISM** doesn't. **MULTI-CULTURALISM = SEGREGATION.** What you get is a society within a society a criticism pointed out in the various Government reports into the disturbance in Northern towns last Summer.. It said ***'communities are living parallel lives'***

Why is it dangerous? Because it has spelled disaster throughout history to every society to which it has been introduced.

At the present time in these Multi-Cultural societies wars are raging in the Balkans, Indonesia, Sri-Lanka and many other places. New Labour is hell bent on continuing the expansion of Multi-Culturalism and shows contempt for your concerns about it yet you keep them in power! This is not the old traditional Labour party. The founders would be turning in their graves. Our country is awash with revenue from North Sea Oil yet our pensioners are being evicted from Nursing homes and your children are unlikely to receive an old age pension. Existing private pensions have now been raided and we are told any pension above £50 is to be taxed at 50%!

Above: When Multi-Culturalism goes wrong

FIGURE 2.2 Cowell, Burnley 2003 (extract)

In the absence of explicit elaboration, the two images fill in the referential blanks created through the repeated use of the indexical but ambiguous 'this'. The choice to depict Muslim women in *niqab* and the use of silhouettes of mosques and crescent moons in the photomontage make it difficult to construct any interpretation of the lower image other than one that emphasizes their Muslimness. And this foregrounding of the women's Muslimness acts to emphasize the white, Christian, non-Muslimness of the women and children in the upper image. Hence, from this contrast, we can construe that the women of Hanley have changed, or are in the process of changing:

> 'From this [white, Christian] to this [Muslim]'

The presupposedly undesirable nature of this change rests on the figure of contrast that the leaflet sets up between the *women qua women* of Hanley's past and women presented as more typical of Hanley's present. The white women of the past are friendly and domesticated, reflecting a patriarchal view in which women 'remain primarily responsible for the family and the home' (Amesburger and Halbmayr, 2002, cited in Mudde, 2007: 93); in contrast, the Muslim women are unwelcoming and abusive. However, the leaflet also raises the possibility of change *back* – of resistance to this change and the negative effects that the party imply have arisen from it. The method by which this change is to be brought about is not defined,

FIGURE 2.3 Hanley, Stoke 2008

and is all the more threatening for that. Instead, the reader is simply offered a choice – between *this* [white, Christian] and *this* [Muslim]. Discursive enactments such as these are based on the BNP's 'white fantasy' (Hage, 1998: 85) that they have the right and the ability to regulate the ethnic parameters of British society, to tolerate or proscribe, to include or exclude, both physically and verbally.

In this way, the images perform a double function: they, first, convey in a vivid and evocative way a putative change in the 'face of the country', presenting 'facts' that you can see with your own eyes. These particular images entail an 'Islamification' of Hanley, through evoking the religious difference signified by clothing and places of worship, despite the fact that the women in the photo and silhouetted mosque aren't *in* Hanley. The implicit indexing of religion removes the need for the linguistic element of the leaflet to use any racial or religious terms, thereby fulfilling their second function: they inject a degree of deniability to the argumentation – that is, the BNP could, conceivably (though rather implausibly), claim 'they weren't being racist', even while arguing for the ethnic purification of Stoke city centre. This is propaganda that almost denies it is presenting a propagandistic argument.

Under the surface

In contrast to the image presented in BNP leaflets and election broadcasts, there is ample evidence of enduring racism in the party just beyond such mass-distributed texts. The BNP's website is, more than likely, the first place that people would consult if, having received a leaflet, they wanted to find out more about the party and what it stands for. The website functions as both a news service and a social network, building a community of BNP activists, voters and supporters through, among other ways, forums and groups that members can opt to join.[6] One of the largest of these social network groups is called 'Our foundation the BNP', with 806 members at the time of writing. The welcome screen of this social group spells out its racist *raison d'être* in forthright, rather ungrammatical, terms:

> stand tall, stand together and be proud to be a member of this great party, spread the word the BNP is comming to take back every town and city thats what the english people want there country not over run with ethnics. making protest about how some other country should be freed why dont they go back and free it themselfs.
>
> we can not take anymore, and we dont want any fooking more. we are not interested in there religion or beleives dont they get the hint
>
> [. . .]Time for a BNP march to show the country we are not scared!!! and we will claim our country back from the people that want to islamify us.[7]

On reading this statement, there is little chance of anyone misunderstanding the 'foundations' of these BNP members' political beliefs: Britain contains too many 'ethnics'; their influence is not welcome; and the BNP is working to 'take back every town' in the name of English people. Given that discussion boards frequently contain racist diatribes such as this, it is tempting to conclude that this is simply typical of online discourse. However, we should remember that, 'Our foundation the BNP' is, like all the social network groups accessible via the BNP homepage, moderated by senior party officials. If the party leadership viewed this racism as problematic, it would remove it from the site. The only ambiguity arises at the end of the above quote: who are the people that want 'to islamify us'? Are they Muslim or some third party? I will return to this question of agency later in the chapter.

All news reports, and most other texts, published on the website are comment-enabled. Each BNP news report is written by (usually unnamed) party officials in such a way to provoke outrage among its readers – outrage that the commentators duly express in their comments. For example, one article forcefully criticized the 'Mumbai-born "artist" Anish Kapoor' for an article, published in the National Trust magazine, in which he suggested that Britain needs to open up to 'the best in modern art, design and architecture'. In response, the BNP argued: 'Pseudo-artists like Mr Kapoor – who is not an indigenous British person – are responsible for the cultural deconstruction of thousands of years of British history, tradition and culture.' The vituperative sentiment was echoed in over 100 comments from registered members, in arguments that emphasized Kapoor's impertinence for being Indian (by birth) and expressing an opinion, sneered at 'Indian slums' and 'mud huts', and widely agreed that Kapoor's article, despite being intended to improve the artistic and cultural life of Britain, meant that he was no longer welcome in this country.[8]

News articles on 'race science' occasionally surface on the BNP homepage. For example, the BNP gleefully reported that the UK Border Agency is running a pilot research project testing the DNA of asylum applicants, to help distinguish between deserving Somalis and undeserving Kenyans, as this news (apparently) 'has confirmed the existence of race'.[9] The basic scientific facts that genetic variation is not the same as 'race', and that a 'historic link' between DNA and geography is not the same as nationality, were passed over in favour of supporting a scheme designed to limit the number of (black) refugees entering the UK. However, it is the end of this article that is most revealing. Here, the report suggests some recommended reading: *Race, evolution and behaviour: a life history perspective,* by Professor J. Philippe Rushton. The recommendation claims:

> Using evidence from psychology, anthropology, sociology and other scientific disciplines, this book shows that: There are at least three biological races (subspecies) of man [. . .] There are recognizable profiles for the three major racial groups on: Brain size; Intelligence; Personality and temperament; Sexual behaviour, and Rates of fertility, maturation and longevity.

The report then directs the reader to the BNP's own *Excalibur* merchandizing wing, where the book is available for purchase. Why is such a book noteworthy?

Philippe Rushton is an ex-doctoral student of Hans Eysenck, the famous purveyor of racial science, and the book draws heavily on the research of Eysenck and others closely associated with the eugenics journal *Mankind Quarterly* (*MQ*).[10] Echoing these racial scientists, Rushton's work claims to show that black people are 'on the whole, smaller brained, slower to mature, less sexually restrained and more aggressive' than white people (Mehler, 1989: 17). It should go without saying that Rushton's work is repudiated by the overwhelming majority of psychologists working in the area of intelligence and difference. However, in 1987, Richard Lynn, an associate editor of *MQ*, invited Rushton to write an article on the social consequences of his theories of biological determinism. Rushton duly obliged, arguing that the white majority (in this case, in the US) was 'unlikely to maintain their position' as the dominant group 'given the differential birth rate' between the white and non-white populations (Rushton, 1987: 392, cited in Mehler, 1989: 20). Rushton's solution, that immigration should be discouraged, and genetically superior people (white, of course) should be encouraged to have large families in order to save Western civilization, is no doubt what appeals to the BNP.

The party's obsession with genetics and racial difference is also indexed in an internal document (BNP, *Hostile media questions for BNP candidates and officials*, 2005). Indeed, of the fifteen hostile questions that the document provides model answers for, only two didn't relate to these subjects.[11] In their answers, they use a standard definitional stop to categorize a racist as 'someone who hates people of other races'; in contrast, they love the 'indigenous British', which shouldn't be viewed as racism. However, the knots in which they tie themselves while attempting to describe the 'indigenous British population' reveal both their continued belief in biological races and their continued commitment to discrimination on biological grounds – which can only be conceived of as racism. Thus, they argue:

> To be truly British one has to have a British genotype [. . .] Blacks and Asians born here are legally British [. . .] but they are not genetically British.
>
> We believe that Britain's proud history of glorious achievements demonstrates this British genotype is valuable and deserves to be preserved.
>
> While an individual mixed marriage – or mixed race child – in Britain won't, in itself, make a great deal of difference, if this is encouraged as it is at present then inevitably the traditional British genotype will be endangered.

A favourite expression of the racial fascist Leese was that 'race is the basis of politics' (Billig, 1978: 152), and it is in the extracts above that Leese's commitment to the politics of 'racial purity' is most clearly rearticulated. Simply replacing the word 'race' with the more scientific sounding 'genotype' doesn't obviate the racist implications of their arguments. The final extract above not only argues against 'race mixing', it also introduces the idea that mixed marriages are being 'encouraged', despite the endangerment that this brings to the 'British genotype'. Who would be encouraging such a thing? Are these the same people as those who want to 'Islamify' us? Again, the party is tight-lipped; I revisit this later in the chapter.

Elsewhere in this internal document, the BNP maintains that its belief that Europeans are 'some 15% above [more intelligent than] people of African origin' doesn't make it racist. Its advice for candidates and officials continues: 'if the interviewer says that "if we believe blacks are less intelligent then we are saying they are inferior", we can point out that blacks have other abilities where they are superior, such as certain sports'. The party seems blissfully unaware that this racist stereotype of black physicality has a long, historic pedigree. On the basis of the 'intellectual inferiority' of 'people of African origin', the BNP propose a stratified system of rights, wherein non-British races would have limited influence on the country: 'We have no objection to a limited number of people of different races or cultures, but they shouldn't be so many that they actually change the area they live in'. Later, they argue that Britain is 'being colonised by foreign populations' and, in response, a system of enforced and voluntary (that is, paid) repatriation is needed – a policy that 'while "colour blind" in theory, in practice [. . .] will impinge mainly on non-whites'. They remain committed, therefore, to the racial 'cleansing' of Britain, leaving only 'British' – that is, white – people remaining.

Other internal documents also reveal the party's continued dedication to biological racism. The BNP's *Language and concepts discipline manual* (2005), for example, aims to instruct party members and activists in how to 'stick to the party's true message and convey it to the voting public in a clear and consistent way' (p. 1). The following rules are important, given the contents of the BNP leaflets briefly discussed in the earlier section:

> Rule #15. BNP activists and writers should never refer to 'black Britons' or 'Asian Britons' etc, for the simple reason that such persons do not exist. These people are 'black residents' of the UK etc, and are no more British than an Englishman living in Hong Kong is Chinese. Collectively, foreign residents of other races should be referred to as 'racial foreigners', a non-pejorative term that makes clear the distinction needing to be drawn. [. . .]
>
> Rule #17. Britain does not have 'immigrants,' a term proper for use in settler societies like Canada, Argentina, and the USA. It has 'guest workers,' 'foreign workers,' or 'descendants of foreign workers'. They are, depending on who they are, 'racial foreigners,' 'religious foreigners' or 'persons of foreign religion,' or 'ethnic foreigners'. The last term is meant to apply to persons racially similar to Britons, but ethnically dissimilar, like Dutchmen.
>
> (BNP, *Language and concepts discipline manual*, 2005)

Thus, despite its protestation and self-construction as a 'modern democratic party', the BNP retains key racist commitments: non-white (and, seemingly, non-Christian) Britons 'do not exist'. The only British people are white, and so when the nominals 'British' or 'Briton' are used, this should axiomatically be taken to exclude these variously defined 'racial foreigners', 'religious foreigners', 'persons of foreign religion' or 'ethnic foreigners'. With the benefit of this contextualization and elucidation, the repeated use of 'British' in Figure 2.1, and throughout their propaganda, hardly needs further analysis: they support '[white] jobs for [white] workers'; they are concerned about '[white] wages' and 'would invest in [white] jobs'; and they make sure '[white] families are housed first'.

Thus, in contrast to their frequent denials, the BNP is a racist party: it remains wedded to a belief in racial inequality and a racial explanation of social and historic progress; it also remains committed to a white Britain, with black communities 'repatriated' or otherwise removed from any public influence. However, the racist ideology of the BNP runs still deeper.

The depths of BNP racial ideology

To reveal the fascist core of the BNP, analysis needs to rely a little less on traditional exoteric texts, such as party manifestos, leaflets and election broadcasts, and adopt a wider, more contextually informed view, focused on the political movement 'as a whole, on their history, cultures and heritage, on forms of party socialization and membership, and ideology and internal discourse' (Mammone, 2009: 176). With some regularity, organizations such as *Searchlight* expose the continued commitment of BNP members to fascist, and on occasion National Socialist (Nazi), ideology and political aims. At the time of writing, the latest additions to this cast are four BNP activists photographed at the Nazi music and politics festival, *Fest der Völker*, in East Germany, on 12 September 2009 (*Searchlight*, no. 412, October 2009). Nina Brown, a BNP parish councillor in Brinsley (Nottingham), and her husband Dave Brown, also a Brinsley parish councillor and the BNP candidate for the Broxtowe District Council, were photographed in front of 'a banner depicting two steel-helmeted soldiers of the German army and bearing the clapped-out fascist slogan Europe Awake'. Nina Brown spoke to the festival crowd, sharing the stage with leading European fascists in attendance, including Sweden's Dan Erikkson, a representative of the violent anti-Semitic Info14 network.[12]

These are by no means aberrant cases. A YouGov poll on the political views of the British adult population conducted on the eve of the 2009 European elections asked respondents if they agreed or disagreed with the following statement: 'There is a major international conspiracy led by Jews and Communists to undermine traditional Christian values in Britain and other western countries.' It found that 33 per cent of respondents who intended to vote BNP considered the statement completely or partially true.[13] On the eve of the 2010 general election, *Searchlight* (no. 419, May 2010: 12–13) published brief biographies of nineteen BNP election candidates, showing their commitment to political extremism. Included in this list were:

- Shelly Rose (Parliamentary candidate for Luton North), part of a social group of BNP activists in the East Midlands and an anti-Semite who wrote on her Facebook page, 'I would rather put myself out and pay a bit more at a smaller local shop, than line the pockets of the kikes that run Tesco'.

- Robin Evans (Parliamentary candidate for Blackburn), who resigned from the BNP in 2003 and joined the openly fascist British National Socialist Party, before returning to the BNP.
- Ken Booth (Parliamentary candidate for Newcastle Upon Tyne central), a former North East National Front organizer who, in 2007, compared the Nazi death camp at Auschwitz to Disneyland and refused to believe the 'official figures' of those who died in the Holocaust.
- Richard Hamilton (Parliamentary candidate for Milton Keynes North), who took part in the 'mock trial and execution' of a gollywog at the 2009 'Red, white and blue' festival. A *News of the World* report suggested that, before the trial, 'Hamilton's ghettoblaster blared out songs supporting Hitler and attacking "niggers"'. The BNP claimed his membership had been 'suspended' as a result of the affair, though evidently for less than a year.
- Chris Beverley (Parliamentary candidate for Morley and Outwood), a leading figure in Yorkshire BNP and a key link with the German neo-Nazi National Democratic Party (NPD). Beverley recently refused to condemn Hitler in a radio broadcast.
- Barry Bennett (Parliamentary candidate for Gosport) who was, until recently, a regular user of the Stormfront website, where he wrote: 'I believe in National Socialism, WW2 style, it was best, no other power had anything like it. The ideology was fantastic. The culture, nothing like it. If it was here now, I'd defect to Germany.'
- Marlene Guest (Parliamentary candidate for Rotherham), the Rotherham BNP organizer, who appeared in Sky TV documentary *BNP Wives* and claimed that the number of deaths in the Holocaust had been exaggerated and that the Jews were putting Germany on a guilt-trip. Asked if any good had come out of the Holocaust, she replied: 'Well, apparently, didn't they get a lot of dentistry and plastic surgery', apparently in reference to Nazi 'medical experiments'.

Significant portions of the BNP leadership also remain wedded to such anti-Semitic conspiracy theories and to Holocaust denial. When Ernst Zundel, the author of *The Hitler we loved and why*, was released from a German prison in Germany on 1 March 2010, after serving five years for Holocaust Denial, Richard Edmonds – a party veteran and member of the executive 'Advisory Council' – was among the small gathering of supporters that greeted him.[14] On an official party blog in September 2009, Lee Barnes, the legal officer of the BNP, argued that the Holocaust was a defensive action against 'Jewish Bolsheviks'. Accordingly:

> The Holocaust was the price ordinary Jews of Europe paid for the actions of the Bolshevik Jews in Russia after the Russian Revolution [. . .] It was the actions of Bolshevik filth like Rosa Luxemberg in Germany during the Spartacist Uprising that allowed Hitler to equate Jews and Bolshevism – and thereby prepare the way for the Holocaust.[15]

Towards the bottom of the post, Barnes provides a source of the information that 'supports' his argument: an article published by the notorious 'historical revisionist' – that is, Holocaust denial – organization, the Institute for Historical Review.[16] Famously, Nick Griffin was successfully prosecuted for incitement to racial hatred in 1998, for Holocaust denial material published in his magazine *The Rune*. In the police interview during the investigation of this crime, which Griffin himself released as part of a fighting fund campaign, he argued:

> *Griffin:* I cannot see how any Jew should be upset, erm, if they find out that such large numbers of their people weren't horribly killed. It's good news! I can't see it's insulting to anybody [. . .]
>
> *Police questioner:* By promoting the fact that they believe, as history bears out, that the Holocaust occurred –
>
> *Griffin:* History does not bear that out.
>
> *Police questioner:* Well, the recognized history, for the majority of people then, the –
>
> *Griffin:* The orthodox history accepts it in the same way that people once thought that, erm, that the sun goes round the earth, yes.

Griffin has never distanced himself from, or retracted, these statements. Indeed concealed camera footage filmed in 2004, by journalist Dominic Carman (Griffin's unofficial biographer), shows he still believes 'The Jews' have 'simply bought the West, in terms of press and so on, for their own political ends'. He went on to suggest that, 'If Hitler hadn't been so daft, they'd have exterminated the German Jews.'[17] The continuing anti-Semitism of the BNP is such that, just before the 2010 general election, Alby Walker, the Stoke BNP council group leader and local branch organizer, left the party and announced on a regional BBC programme that 'there's a vein of Holocaust denying within the BNP that I cannot identify myself with. They've still got senior members of the BNP who will be candidates in the general election that have Nazi, Nazi-esque sympathies.'[18]

For those who can recognize the codes and euphemisms, BNP literature is replete with references to vague or unidentified people who are working against the interests of Britons (that is, white Britons). There are two instances of this in extracts cited above: people encouraging mixed relationships, and 'the people that want to islamify us'. These people are a crucial link in the BNP's ideological chain, an explanation for why, in the words of Philippe Rushton (1987), whites have adopted ideologies that 'discourage nationalist and religious beliefs' (cited in Mehler, 1989: 20). The explanation is 'the Jews'. For British fascists, 'it has long been axiomatic that multiculturalism is a Jewish conspiracy' (Copsey, 2007: 74). It is the Jew ('*Der Jude*', in Nazi argumentation), the arch-internationalist architect of both communism and capitalism, who is the real enemy of the nationalist; it is the Jew who is responsible for mass immigration, in a bid to weaken the white race; it is the Jew who has pulled the wool over the eyes of white people, through control of the mass media (see Billig (1978) for extensive discussion; Nugent and King, 1979).

At points in the history of British fascism, this *Judenhass* has been open and unambiguous. In *Spearhead* magazine, John Tyndall argued: 'if Britain were to become Jew-clean she would have no nigger neighbours to worry about [. . .] It is the Jews who are our misfortune: T-h-e J-e-w-s. Do you hear me? THE JEWS' (*Spearhead*, no. 4, February 1965). Later, Nick Griffin's pamphlet *Who are the MIND-BENDERS?* (1997, reprinted 1999) detailed the 'Jewish conspiracy' to brainwash the British (white) people in their own country (see Chapter 4 by Copsey and Macklin in this volume). However, given the overwhelming distaste for political anti-Semitism, and its association with Nazism and the Holocaust, references in modern fascist literature to this conspiracy are almost always coded, even in esoteric arguments. The All-Party Parliamentary Inquiry into Antisemitism (2006: 25) examined 'numerous examples' of BNP sourced materials using coded language to cover up anti-Semitic belief and argument, including references to international groups (at the heart of conspiracies for global government) and the term 'Zionists' as a euphemism for 'Jews'. For example, the report cites 'an article in the BNP *Voice of Freedom* speaking of soldiers risking their lives in Iraq because "Tony Blair swapped British blood for donations from a clique of filthy-rich Zionist business-men".'[19] Similarly, in 'its 2005 general election manifesto, the BNP included a promise not to go to war for "neo-con adventures on behalf of the Zionist government of Israel".'[20] There are frequent references to men in 'international finance', unnamed-but-financially-powerful string-pullers, 'big business', money power, the backers of international political or economic institutions (e.g. the EU, the IMF, the UN) and, increasingly, globalists. To find out more about the significance and the role of these 'internationalists', inquisitive readers have to dig a little deeper, to texts recommended by the party.

A large number of texts circulate among the members of political parties, texts that are not produced by the party but are congruous with the party's ideology and, hence, resonate with its members. Advertised on the BNP's main website is another site, described as 'Britain's leading independent nationalist blog, *British Nationalist*'. At the time of writing (9 October 2009), the homepage displayed an article headlined 'Euro Fascism: The joint creation of the Banksters and the left', which advanced the favourite fascist canard of a conspiracy between capitalism and communism:

> in some of the nations of the former British empire, specifically the UK and Canada, leftists together with the forces of international capitalism have joined together to encroach most dangerously on human freedom [. . .] This is what happens when people with mediocre intelligence and moral sensibility embrace a chimerical vision of human perfectibility and are manipulated by more cunning and vicious masters.
>
> The useful fools, the so called leftist intelligentsia, whose blogs you see and whose articles you read in the *Guardian* repeat endlessly the nonsense

> that these [race relations] laws all are to protect the rights of the minorities in 'our multicultural society', not having the wit to see that rapacious international CAPITALISM HAS CREATED THESE MINORITIES, REFUGEES FROM THEIR OWN LANDS WHO ARE DELIBERATELY IMPORTED TO EUROPE TO DILUTE AND DESTROY THE POWER OF THE LOCAL INDIGENOUS PEOPLES.[21]

The code words used in this extract index a long-established fascist tradition of presenting anti-Semitic conspiracy theories while disavowing the accusation of anti-Semitism. Central here are manipulation 'by more cunning and vicious masters' and the notion of a *deliberate* plan to use immigration to 'dilute and destroy the [. . .] indigenous peoples'. While, at face value, this conspiracy, between leftists/Marxists/communists and capital, seems completely ridiculous, in fact it 'enables a reconciliation of contradictions' (Billig, 1978: 162) in fascist ideology:

> If both communism and capitalism are seen as common enemies in the same evil conspiracy then working-class support can be solicited with an anti-capitalist rhetoric and middle-class support can be solicited with an anti-communist rhetoric. The language of revolution can be used simultaneously with the language of tradition.
>
> (ibid.)

Book clubs and distribution lists have a long history within British fascist parties and are the principal means for the transmission of this conspiracy theory. Following the Second World War, the first political activities of Mosley and his followers amounted to setting up and infiltrating books clubs in order to disseminate and discuss fascist propaganda (Rose, 1948). From the 1960s to the 1980s, the National Front (NF), the National Party and the British Movement (BM) operated book clubs 'for the study of literature dealing with the Jewish Question and other racial problems', which were 'protected from the Race Relations Act as well as from the suspicions of uninquisitive members' (Billig, 1978: 133).

The current BNP book list, for sale via the Excalibur website, continues to contain a range of 'racial eugenics' books and the white supremacist tome *March of the Titans – a history of the white race*, written by Arthur Kemp, the party's foreign affairs spokesman. The sections of Kemp's book that cover interwar Germany and the Second World War bear all the classic hallmarks of modern-day Holocaust denial, in which Nazi barbarity is minimized, openly denied or, where this is impossible, only partially acknowledged, followed by an ameliorating '*but* . . .' Thus, he claims: the Nazi Nuremburg 'Blood Protection Law [. . .] was done to promote the further dissolution of *Jewish* genes'; that it was a 'Jewish assassin Ernst vom Rath in Paris, [who] triggered the "Crystal Night" [*Kristallnacht*] *retaliation attacks* on Jewish targets in Germany'; and that 'anti-Jewish feeling' and the '*internment* of large numbers of Jews inside Germany' were justified as 'On 24 March 1933 [. . .] the leaders of the world's Jews had declared war on Germany' [my emphasis throughout].

Kemp's concluding thoughts on the death camps are also revealing: 'All things said, to have been a Jew in Nazi Germany could not have been a pleasant experience: but [. . .] certainly far fewer died than what is most often claimed.'[22] As Griffin argued, the BNP 'must teach the truth to the hardcore' if it doesn't want 'this movement to lose its way'; book lists, such as Excalibur's, are evidence that this teaching is still going on.

The anti-Semitic conspiracy theory is also indexed in other ways. As Copsey points out:

> The January 2005 issue of *Identity* featured an article entitled 'The Hidden Hand' that argued that, as the work of the likes of the British conspiracy theorist A. K. Chesterton had shown, the Bilderberg Group was taking all the major decisions affecting the world and that its final goal was one of world dictatorship.
>
> (Copsey, 2007: 77)

Fascist disciples would not have missed the significance of an article on global conspiracy, with such a headline, that also referred to the work of A. K. Chesterton. Chesterton was a key figure in the development of British fascism, being a leading member of the British Union of Fascists in the 1930s and more anti-Semitic than Oswald Mosley. As late as 1996, the catalogue for the BNP Book Service still sold the conspiracy text *The new unhappy lords*, by A. K. Chesterton. This book asks the question 'Are these master manipulators and master-conspirators Jewish?', and takes over 200 pages to answer:

> [. . .] almost certainly 'yes'. Whether or not One World is the secret final objective of Zionism, World Jewry is the most powerful single force on earth and it follows that all major policies which have been ruthlessly pursued through the last several decades must have had the stamp of Jewish approval.
>
> (Chesterton, 1965: 204)

The Hidden Hand was an alternative title for the viciously anti-Semitic magazine *Jewry Über Alles*, published in the 1920s by The Britons. Referring to Chesterton's work and invoking *The Hidden Hand* – in this 2005 article in the BNP's leading magazine – demonstrate an unbroken link back through the 'populist' fascism of the 1970s, the British National Socialism in the 1960s, as far as the British Union of Fascists and National Socialists in the 1930s. The inter-textual reference is a favourite method of the modern-day fascist, in which they hide their devotion to anti-Semitic conspiracy theories in clear view.

Occasionally, the esoteric conspiracy theory crashes into public view, through being explicitly used in exoteric campaign literature. On 7 and 8 June 1999, the leaflet shown in Figure 2.4 was hand-delivered to homes in the Avenues area of Hull, as part of the BNP's European election campaign.

OUR POLITICIANS ARE TRAITOR CRIMINALS

DID ANY POLITICIAN ever seek or obtain a mandate from the British people to repeal the law of TREASON - aiding and abetting a foreign invasion - a hanging offence? Did our 'democratic government' ever ask the British people if they wanted our country to be run by multinational capitalists and spoiled by millions of immigrants from the Third World, to make us into a mongrel race of docile low-paid wage slaves? THEY DID NOT.

'No man in his senses would expect to improve or modify a breed in any particular manner, or keep an old breed true and distinct, unless he separated his animals.'

Charles Darwin, *The Variation of Animals and Plants Under Domestication*

Jews are in England unlawfully, since the Edict of Expulsion of 1290 has never been repealed. Now these illegal immigrants completely control our news and TV, and never miss an opportunity to portray the MULTI-CULTURAL MESS as a normal state of affairs. It was Jews who wrote the Race Relations Act, now called the Public Order Act, a law used exclusively against British men who defy THE NEW TYRANNY in which people are afraid to say what they think. If the BLEEDING HEARTS can call for an economic boycott of South Africa, allowing the natives, squatting beside the refuse of a prosperous civilisation created by European settlers, to turn that country into the murder capital of the world, where Whites are being raped and murdered every day, we recommend the same.

VOTE BNP IN THE EURO ELECTION ON JUNE 10

PUBLISHED BY HULL BNP, PO BOX 531, HULL HU5 4YT

FIGURE 2.4 Hull anti-Semitic leaflet, June 1999

The leaflet was apparently designed by Simon Sheppard and then authorized by Dave Hannam, the organizer for the newly constituted Hull branch. In the days that followed, John Tyndall and Richard Mulhall (the regional agent for Yorkshire and The Humber) received injunctions against them by the National Executive of the Labour Party, proscribing further distribution of the leaflet, and both Simon Sheppard and Dave Hannam were arrested and charged with printing or distributing racially inflammatory material.[23] The text draws on several argumentative topoi in the vilification of Jews: the law and right, justice, democracy (with an inversion of a free-speech argument in the form of the 'new tyranny') and abuse. It also manages to address both the primary and secondary aspects of the anti-Semitic conspiracy – namely, immigration and 'racial mongrelisation' are a Jewish plot; and Their control of the media hides this from Us – within the space of a single page. Accordingly, Jews are not only in the UK 'unlawfully' but are guilty of treason owing to their 'aiding and abetting a foreign invasion' (only citizens could be guilty of treason, but the leaflet is silent on this inconsistency). This 'invasion' is intended to 'make us into a mongrel race', depress our wages and reduce quality of life. And, in the height of perversion, their complete 'control of our news and TV' enables 'Jews' to 'portray the MULTI-CULTURAL MESS as a normal state of affairs'. Rarely has the party put its name to such openly anti-Semitic and racist material, or distributed a leaflet that draws so explicitly on the racial fascism of Arnold Leese.

Sheppard was subject to disciplinary proceedings, and his membership of the party was terminated. This corrective response could no doubt be cited by the BNP as evidence that they are no longer the Holocaust-denying party of old and take explicit anti-Semitism of party members seriously. However, it wasn't the leaflet's racism and anti-Semitism that bothered the party leadership – at least, not directly. The initial communication from Griffin to Sheppard noted that the 'hysterical tone [of the leaflet] could only put off ordinary people and can only do us harm [. . .] If you are responsible for it, forget any future co-operation on publishing projects'.[24] At no point did Griffin argue that the leaflet was prejudiced or fallacious, merely that it was unhelpful to the party's election ambitions, which can hardly be regarded as excoriating Sheppard's anti-Semitism.

The party's punishment of Dave Hannam, as the organizer of the Hull branch, was far less severe. Indeed, it was non-existent. Hannam served his three-month sentence and rejoined the party, going on 'to become the BNP's regional treasurer and a close confidant of party leader Nick Griffin'.[25] In 2005 he co-wrote the song 'Corporal Fox' with Griffin, which was used in the 2005 BNP party election broadcast, before heading the BNP's nationalist record label, Great White Records, from its launch at the end of 2005 until summer 2009. At the time of writing, he is the BNP national treasurer, in which capacity he is present at Advisory Council Meetings, the highest committee of party leadership.[26] The only possible conclusion is that a conviction for distributing anti-Semitic material is not viewed as blocking advancement in the BNP; in fact, for some, it can lead to promotion and the trust of the party leader.

Conclusion

The BNP presents itself as a party that has made a complete break with the past fascist activities of its leadership and members. On its websites, its members, activists and supporters all make repeated, strident claims that the BNP is not a racist party, and certainly not fascist. Indeed, these claims are often reversed, arguing that the mainstream media and 'Old Parties' are racist, because of the ways they apparently ignore the beliefs and wishes of the white majority, and are fascist because of their support for anti-hate speech legislation. To accept these arguments at face value would be the height of foolishness. In fact, the BNP should be viewed as a continuation of previous parties of the British fascist fringe – certainly the National Front and National Party, but also incorporating the ideological commitments of racial fascism and British National Socialism from the 1960s.

These continuations in racial ideology are traceable in both content and strategy, but only through close intertextual examination – not only of the campaign materials (leaflets, brochures, manifestos etc.) that they produce and distribute across the UK; not only of the articles they write and the social networks they host on their websites; but also of the texts they recommend and circulate through book clubs and by other means.

Notes

1 The author would like to thank Michael Billig, Cristina Marinho, Ruth Wodak and anonymous reviewers for their helpful comments on earlier drafts of this article.

2 This montage is comprised of sections of leaflets, collected between 2007 and 2009 in Barrow, Bradford, Loughborough, Oxford and Quorn, and a national leaflet on wildcat strikes, available at bnp.org.uk

3 See Richardson (2008) and Richardson and Wodak (2009b) for an extended discussion of this argument.

4 An almost identical rhetorical structure was used on the front page of the four-page leaflet that the party produced during the London mayoral and GLA elections in 2008 (see Richardson and Wodak, 2009a). The structure also appears indebted to a leaflet distributed by the Danish People's Party in 2002, headlined 'Denmark today'. Criminal charges were brought against leading members of the party's youth organization for distributing the leaflet (see Betz and Meret, 2009).

5 Incidentally, neither of these aspects of the montage have anything to do with Hanley or the wider city of Stoke-on-Trent: the image was taken in the Sparkhill area of Birmingham (UK) on 31 January 2007, and the conspicuous lack of a mosque on this scale in Stoke has required the BNP art department to mock up these silhouettes.

6 See also BNP News (2009) 'The importance of social networking', 13 October 2009; available at http://bnp.org.uk/2009/10/the-importance-of-social-networking/ (accessed 14 October 2009).

7 Taken from http://bnp.org.uk/groups/the-bnp (accessed 9 October 2009).

8 BNP News (2009) 'Britain lacks "cultural confidence" Indian "artist" tells National Trust', 5 October 2009; available at: http://bnp.org.uk/2009/10/britain-lacks-%E2%80%9Ccultural-confidence%E2%80%9D-indian-%E2%80%9Cartist%E2%80%9D-tells-national-trust/ (accessed 9 October 2009).

9 BNP News (2009) 'Race doesn't exist? The UK Border Agency says it does', 2 October 2009; available at: http://bnp.org.uk/2009/10/race-doesn%E2%80%99t-exist-the-uk-border-agency-says-it-does/ (accessed 9 October 2009).

10 Eysenck, the author of *The inequality of man*, was interviewed for the first issue of the National Party's publication *Beacon* (1977). In this interview, Eysenck explained why he believed that blacks were genetically less intelligent than whites.

11 Question 2 is 'What is your attitude to homosexuals?' (they answer that homosexuality 'is by definition an aberration'); their answer to Question 12 denies that the BNP 'is a fascist and undemocratic party'.

12

> info-14 supports all sound patriotic activities, both parliamentary and extra-parliamentary. The struggle for freedom must be fought on a broad front, both in polling stations as well as in the streets. All roads are worth exploring in order to take power back from the hands of the people traitors and give it back to the Swedes
>
> (www.info14.com, accessed 7 October 2009)

The number 14 in their name indexes the '14 words' coined by David Lane and used by white supremacists: 'We must secure the existence of our people and a future for white children'.

13 YouGov (2009) 'European elections', Fieldwork dates 29 May–4 June 2009, available at: www.channel4.com/news/media/2009/06/day08/yougovpoll_080609.pdf (accessed 2 August 2010).

14 See: www.zundelsite.org/news_english/0089.html and http://thecst.org.uk/blog/?p=1257 (accessed 1 August 2010).

15 Taken from http://leejohnbarnes.blogspot.com/2009/09/ww2-time-to-tell-truth.html (accessed 1 August 2010).

16 Weber, M. 'The Jewish role in the Bolshevik Revolution and Russia's early Soviet regime', Institute for Historical Review, available at: www.ihr.org/jhr/v14/v14n1p-4_Weber.html (accessed 1 August 2010).

17 See www.youtube.com/watch?v=9LR8-uXEHAM (accessed 12 May 2010).

18 Williams, D. (2010) 'Dissident derails Stoke BNP election campaign', *Searchlight Online*, available at: www.searchlightmagazine.com/index.php?link=template&story=320 (accessed 11 May 2010).

19 'Blair's evil war', *Voice of Freedom*, August 2004, cited in the *Report of the All-Party Parliamentary Inquiry into Antisemitism* (2006: 25).

20 BNP general election manifesto (2005), cited in the *Report of the All-Party Parliamentary Inquiry into Antisemitism* (2006: 25).

21 http://british-nationalist.org.uk/2009/09/euro-fascism-the-joint-creation-of-the-banksters-and-the-left/ (accessed 9 October 2009).

22 Kemp, A. 'The Final Solution', in *March of the Titans*; available at www.white-history.com/hwr64iv.htm (accessed 1 August 2010).

23 On 14 June 2000, they were convicted at Hull Crown Court, with Sheppard receiving a sentence of nine months imprisonment; Hannam was sentenced to three months imprisonment after pleading guilty.

24 These extracts are taken from Sheppard's racist and anti-Semitic website: www.heretical.com/British/bhullbnp.html, for which he was found guilty of sixteen counts of inciting racial hatred in 2009. See: www.cps.gov.uk/news/press_releases/101_09/ (accessed 29 September 2009).

25 See 'Holocaust deniers skip bail to claim asylum', *Searchlight Magazine*, available at: www.searchlightmagazine.com/index.php?link=template&story=237 (accessed 29 September 2009).

26 Minutes of the Advisory Council Meeting, Sunday 26 April 2009, available at: http://bnp.org.uk/resources/ac-meetings/april-2009/ (accessed 28 January 2010).

References

All-Party Parliamentary Group against Antisemitism (2006) *Report of the All-Party Parliamentary Inquiry into Antisemitism*, London: The Stationary Office LTD.

Amesburger, H. and Halbmayr, B. (eds) (2002) *Rechtsextreme Parteien: eine mögliche Heimat für Frauen?*, Opladen: Leske & Bundrich.

Betz, H.-G. and Meret, S. (2009) 'Revisiting Lepanto: the political mobilisation against Islam in contemporary Western Europe', *Patterns of Prejudice*, 43 (3-4): 313–34.

Billig, M. (1978) *Fascists: A social psychological view of the National Front*, London: Harcourt Brace Jovanovitch.

Chesterton, A. K. (1965) *The new unhappy lords*, London: Candour Publishing Co.

Copsey, N. (2007) 'Changing course or changing clothes? Reflections on the ideological evolution of the British National Party 1999-2006', *Patterns of Prejudice*, 41 (1): 61–82.

Copsey, N. (2008) *Contemporary British fascism: the British National Party and the quest for legitimacy*, 2nd edn, Basingstoke: Palgrave-Macmillan.

Dummett, A. (1973) *A portrait of English racism*, Harmondsworth: Penguin.

Engel, J. and Wodak, R. (2009) 'Kalkulierte Ambivalenz: Störungen und das Gedankenjahr: Die Causen Siegfried Kampl und John Gudenus', in de Cillia, R. & Wodak, R (eds) *Gedenken im Gedankenjahr*, Innsbruck: Studienverlag.

Fairclough, N. (2000) *New Labour, new language*, London: Routledge.

Foot, P. (1965) *Immigration and race in British politics*, Harmondsworth: Penguin.

Gorman, R. M. (1977) 'Racial antisemitism in England: the legacy of Arnold Leese', *Wiener Library Bulletin*, 43/44: 65–70.

Hage, G. (1998) *White Nation: fantasies of white supremacy in a multicultural society*, Annandale: Pluto Press.

Heer, H. and Wodak, R. (2008) 'Collective memory, national narratives and the politics of the past', in Heer, H., Manoschek, W., Pollak, A. and Wodak, R (eds) *The discursive construction of history: remembering the Wehrmacht's war of annihilation*, Basingstoke: Palgrave-Macmillan.

John, P., Margetts, H., Rowland, D. and Weir, P. (2006). *The BNP: the roots of its appeal*, London: Joseph Rowntree Charitable Trust.

Macklin, G. (2007) *Very deeply dyed in black: Sir Oswald Mosley and the resurrection of British fascism after 1945*, London: IB Tauris.

Mammone, A. (2009) '*The eternal return?* Faux populism and contemporarization of neo-fascism across Britain, France and Italy', *Journal of Contemporary European Studies*, 17 (2): 171–92.

Mannheim, K. (1960) *Ideology and Utopia*, London: Routledge & Kegan Paul.

Mehler, B. (1989) 'Foundation for fascism: the New Eugenics Movement in the United States', *Patterns of Prejudice*, 23 (4): 17–25.

Miles, R. and Phizacklea, A. (1984) *White man's country: racism in British politics*, London: Pluto Press.

Morell, J. (1980) 'Arnold Leese and the Imperial Fascist League: the impact of racial fascism', in Lunn, K. and Thurlow, R. C. (eds) *British fascism: essays on the radical right in inter-war Britain*, London: Croom Helm.

Mosley, O. (1951) *European socialism*, London: Euphorian Books.

Mudde, C. (2007) *Populist radical right parties in Europe*, Cambridge: Cambridge University Press.

Nugent, N. and King, R. (1979) 'Ethnic minorities, scapegoating and the extreme right', in Miles, R. and Phizacklea, A. (eds) (1979) *Racism and political action*, London: Routledge and Kegan Paul.

Oborne, P. (2008) 'Fear of Islam: Britain's new disease', *The Independent*, 4 July 2008.

Pelinka, A. and Wodak, R. (eds) (2002) *Dreck am Stecken*, Vienna: Czernin Verlag.

Reisigl, M. and Wodak, R. (2001) *Discourse and discrimination. Rhetorics of racism and antisemitism*, London: Routledge.

Reisigl, M. and Wodak, R. (2009) 'The discourse–historical approach', in Wodak. R. and Meyer. M. (eds) *Methods of critical discourse analysis*, London: Sage.

Richardson, J. E. (2008) '"Our England": discourses of "race" and class in party election leaflets', *Social Semiotics*, 18 (3), 321–36.

Richardson, J. E. and Wodak, R. (2009a) 'The impact of visual racism: visual arguments in political leaflets of Austrian and British far-right parties', *Controversia: an international journal of debate and democratic renewal*, 6 (2): 45–77.

Richardson, J. E. and Wodak, R. (2009b) 'Recontextualising fascist ideologies of the past: right-wing discourses on employment and nativism in Austria and the United Kingdom', *Critical Discourse Studies*, 6 (4): 251–67.

Rose, L. (1948) *Fascism in Britain* [pamphlet].

Skidelsky, R. (1981) *Oswald Mosely*, London: MacMillan.

Sykes, A. (2005) *The radical right in Britain*, Basingstoke: Palgrave-Macmillan.

Taylor, S. (1979) 'The National Front: anatomy of a political movement', in Miles, R. and Phizacklea, A. (eds) (1979) *Racism and political action*, London: Routledge & Kegan Paul, 125–46.

Wodak, R. (2009) *The discourse of politics in action*, Basingtoke: Palgrave-Macmillan.

3

MULTICULTURALISM AND THE SUBCULTURAL POLITICS OF THE BRITISH NATIONAL PARTY

James Rhodes

Introduction

The emergence of the British National Party (BNP) since 2000 has coincided with a decisive shift away from multiculturalism as the principal approach to 'race relations' in Britain. The 2001 summer riots in Oldham, Bradford and Burnley, coupled with the 9/11 and 7/7 attacks, have seen a move by politicians, the media, and sections of the public away from viewing ethnic diversity as something to celebrate; instead, it is now cast as a source of anxiety and fear (McGhee, 2008). Indeed, opposition to multiculturalism has been a central tenet of BNP ideology under the leadership of Nick Griffin (Copsey, 2007). Here, the vision of the party has cohered around the perceived liberal folly of multiculturalism, viewing it as a political strategy that serves to marginalize the 'indigenous' population at the expense of 'immigrants' and minority ethnic groups. However, at the same time, the party has also borrowed the rhetoric and symbols of multiculturalism as a means through which the rights of the majority white population can be pursued. In this sense, the BNP situates its own opposition to multiculturalism within an increasingly favourable political context. Because of this, the actions and ideology of the party can, to some extent, be characterized less as counter-cultural, than as subcultural. The following chapter examines the basis of the BNP's critique of multiculturalism, locating it within a broader context where New Labour has returned to a policy of 'integration', which more closely resembles assimilation rather than the safeguarding of ethnic and cultural plurality (Back et al., 2002; Kundnani, 2007). The way in which the BNP borrows from the logic of multiculturalism, as it has been conceived in Britain, will also be considered. The BNP's claims to champion a marginalized white ethnicity will be examined in relation to what has been identified as an emergent 'white backlash' (Hewitt, 2005), where claims to defend 'rights for whites' appear to carry greater political currency. The chapter will conclude by asserting that, although the BNP attempts to portray itself as a subcultural movement within the field of the politics of multiculturalism, it remains opposed to the norms and values of the dominant culture.

Opposing multiculturalism

Nick Griffin's ascent to party leader in 1999 saw the BNP introduce an agenda of 'modernization' (Copsey, 2004; 2007; Eatwell, 2004). This not only meant a renewed focus on community-based politics and the development of the party machine, it also marked the emergence of a new ideological framework forged around the themes of security, freedom, identity, and democracy (Copsey, 2004; 2007). This vision involves the party asserting its commitment to: defend national interests through the right to self-determination and economic protectionism; represent the will of 'ordinary' people; protect the nation's borders by ending immigration; and defend the rights of the indigenous white population (ibid.). Uniting these themes is the BNP's hostility towards globalization and multiculturalism. As Douglas Holmes observed while conducting interviews with BNP activists in the East End of London during the 1990s, the abstract nature of the rise of globalization and the spread of global capitalism means that its most visible manifestation – immigrants, particularly non-white immigrants – come to be viewed as the 'symptoms and agents' of social change (Holmes, 2000: 114). As a result of this, multiculturalism is identified as a political project that champions the rights of 'outsiders' at the expense of the 'native' white population. Modood observes how multiculturalism in Britain has been racialized as it is intrinsically linked to immigration: 'specifically, the immigration from outside Europe, of non-white people into predominantly white countries' (2007: 2). It is this association between multiculturalism, globalization, and non-white immigration that the BNP has sought to both emphasize and critique. Holmes found that, in the account of a BNP activist he interviewed,

> The path to multiculturalism annihilates the social contract that sustained memorialized Britain. Few he insists, are willing to describe its ruinous progression . . . the proliferation of crime, the murder of police officers, the turning of young people to drug addiction are the consequence of a pluralist society that subverts the traditional social order.
>
> (Holmes, 2000: 125)

It is argued by the BNP that multiculturalism marks the abandonment of the white working classes by the political elites, especially New Labour. The party's 2005 election manifesto declared that:

> The present regime is engaged in a profound cultural war against the British people, motivated by the desire to create a new ethnic power base to replace the working class which they have abandoned in pursuit of their enthusiasm for globalisation.
>
> (BNP, 2005)

It is stated that the pursuit of cultural pluralism has served to destabilize the traditional basis of the white community, particularly among the white working classes. The party suggests that the 'decline' of such 'authentic' communities, both materially and culturally, can be explained through the presence of non-white populations, who are aided and abetted in their destructive tendencies through the political ideology of multiculturalism, which promotes the interests of non-whites at the expense of the established white British population. Multiculturalism is seen as encouraging, 'social atomization and alienation with all that implies for social breakdown, decay and personal unhappiness' (Heydon, 2007: 24). It is argued that the forces of immigration and multiculturalism have led to both local and national decline. In an interview on Radio 4's *The Report* in April 2009, Nick Griffin suggested that non-white immigration and multiculturalism amounted to a form of 'bloodless genocide'.[1] Such a perception results from the view that multiculturalism, 'is evil because it dispossesses the native British of their inheritance fostering a deep sense of grievance which will fester for untold generations'. This process, 'crushes their natural preference to live amongst their own people in their own way, and stamps on their ability to make their culture flourish and to express it' (Heydon, 2007: 24). The BNP argues that multiculturalism has led to the increased regulation of public space, where national traditions are chastised as outmoded and offensive to minority ethnic groups. It is argued that this leads to the curtailment of civil liberties and freedom of speech, as well as the repression of white cultural expression.

It is the figure of the Muslim that the BNP draws upon most heavily in opposing multiculturalism. For the party, Muslims represent threats to national and individual security, to the hegemony of white cultural values and traditions, as well as to the numerical predominance of the 'indigenous' population. Martin Wingfield (2008) suggests that districts across the country have become 'Balkanized' as a result of the presence of an expanding Muslim population; 'the new "majority community", these very colonists, are now re-engineering local society to replicate Muslim societies that they ostensibly left behind in Pakistan, or wherever, when they came to Britain'. As well as being more likely to stand candidates and receive more votes in more homogeneously white wards located in districts with larger Pakistani and Bangladeshi Muslim populations (John et al., 2006; Bowyer, 2008), symbolically, representations of Muslims are used by the BNP to portray the negative effects that multiculturalism has exerted on romanticized notions of a stable, harmonious white community. An example of this came in the party's campaign for the 2008 London mayoral elections, in which Richard Barnbrook was elected to the London Assembly. The campaign flyer, entitled *The Londoner,* juxtaposed the image of a street party with an exclusively white constituency with the image of a number of Muslim women wearing the full veil (see also Goodwin, 2008). Beneath the image, the party bemoans the loss of London's historic character. The city is portrayed as being, 'at ease with itself, friendly, happy and secure', and if voters want London to return to this then they are implored to vote BNP. The opposition of the BNP to multiculturalism and its political growth has coincided with the emergence of a rightward shift in relation to 'race relations' and multicultural policies. In this sense, rather than going against the grain, the party's hostility towards multiculturalism can be located within a much broader and more mainstream set of oppositional views, which emerged in the wake of the 2001 riots in Oldham, Burnley, and Bradford.

From multiculturalism to 'integration'

For the BNP, the 2001 riots provided evidence of the inherent danger of mixing 'incompatible' cultures. It interpreted the disturbances as confirming its own critiques of multiculturalism. Nick Griffin identified Oldham as the location where the 'Multiracial "dream" died' (2001: 4):

> In white working-class estates on the edges of Muslim areas all over the country the liberal fantasy of multi-racial harmony is dead and gone forever . . . The only question is how long its putrid corpse will bring hatred, violence and death to innocent people of all colours before we are in a position to give it a decent burial.
>
> (*Identity*, no. 9, May 2001)

It was not just the BNP that saw the riots as resulting from the excesses of multiculturalism. Increasingly, the government and many liberal politicians and commentators came to share a sense that somehow multiculturalism was to blame for the disturbances. With the coming to power of New Labour in 1997, it was hoped that there would be a move away from traditional, racialized conceptions of national identity. The party espoused a commitment to celebrate diversity and to tackle the issues of racial inequality and violence, evident in the passage of the 2000 Race Relations (Amendment) Act. However, the governmental response to the 2001 riots and the 9/11 and 7/7 attacks has marked a dramatic shift away from this apparent initial commitment to create a more pluralistic vision for the nation (Back et al., 2002; Kundnani, 2007; McGhee, 2008; Pilkington, 2008).

The primary cause identified for the disturbances was a lack of 'community cohesion' (Cantle, 2001). It was argued that the tendency of South Asians to self-segregate served to create a context of resentment and mistrust in which different 'communities', defined in terms of ethnicity, were leading distinct, separate lives (ibid.). Although racism, the impacts of structural inequality, and the active role of the BNP in the disturbances were all cited as factors, these were often de-emphasized in favour of a narrative that located blame for the riots as residing within the 'cultures' and dispositions of particular individuals and groups, which the report defined in terms of ethnicity (Back et al., 2002; Kundnani, 2007; McGhee, 2008; Pilkington, 2008; Rhodes, 2009). For instance, the Cantle Report stated that, 'It is easy to focus on systems, processes and institutions and to forget that community cohesion fundamentally depends on people and their values' (Cantle, 2001: 18). A key outcome of the official response to the riots was the introduction of citizenship tests, advocated by then Home Secretary David Blunkett in December 2001. This presented South Asian Muslims as a distinct group, whose weak sense of citizenship and failure to accept British values had led to problems of conflict and community tensions. It was clear that this response was shaped, not just by the events in Burnley, Bradford, and Oldham, but also by the subsequent terrorist attacks in New York. In February 2002, David Blunkett set out his new vision for 'managing' diversity and immigration: '*We* have norms of respectability . . . and those who come into *our* home – for that is what it is – should accept those norms just as we would have to do if we went elsewhere' (cited in Younge, 2002; italics added).

The response of New Labour in 2001 was highly significant, as it marked a shift away from its promise to establish a more pluralistic sense of national identity and seriously to address issues of racial inequality and institutional racism (McGhee, 2008; Pilkington, 2008). McGhee states that this 'retreat from multiculturalism' has been ambiguous and contradictory as, 'multiculturalism is attacked but the ideals of multiculturalism including respect for diversity remain prominent in Government discourses' (2008: 6). One example of this ambiguity is evident in the calls for a 'new Britishness' that have emerged post-2001 and the 7/7 London bombings. As McGhee states, this new Britishness calls for a more ethnically inclusive sense of national identity, based upon 'civic' rather than 'ethnic' values (2008: 130). For instance, at a speech given to the Commonwealth Club in February 2007, Gordon Brown declared that, 'we are a country united not so much by race or ethnicity but by shared values that have shaped shared institutions'. He advocated a recovery of Britain's historically 'strong sense of duty. The Britain of local pride, civic duty, civic society and the public realm.' However, again, such a vision places the emphasis on others to adapt to a 'British way of life' forged upon '2,000 years of successive waves of invasion, immigration, assimilation'.[2] For McGhee, despite the claims for a nation forged upon ethnic pluralism and a respect for difference, this form of nationalism is less about a two-way process between, for example, 'host' and 'newcomer' in an attempt to develop 'shared values'; instead, this form of 'civic assimilationism' represents a reassertion of 'our' traditional British values, amid calls for these values to be universally respected as a matter of 'duty' (2008: 128–33). This also ignores the extent to which some South Asian Muslims perceive national identity and values to be heavily racialized, as it is sometimes felt that, 'integration had been defined from a purely white British perspective' (Bagguley and Hussain, 2008: 121).

A result of this shift has been that New Labour has dramatically reduced the distance between itself and the British new right, whose various groups and ideologues have been vocal opponents of multiculturalism since the 1980s (Ansell, 1997). Indeed, the BNP and the British new right chart similar ideological territory in relation to their opposition to multicultural policies, reflected in, and produced through, the historic associations between the new right and the far-right in the UK (ibid.). New Labour's actions served to return debates over citizenship and national identity to the 'assimilationism' of the 1960s and the rise of Powellism

(Back et al., 2002). This reasserted a racialized conception of belonging, as, 'despite New Labour's gestures towards cultural diversity and inclusion its body politic beats to the rhythm of a white heart' (ibid.: section 5.7). It is certainly the case that the BNP's opposition to multiculturalism has become much less controversial in the wake of the 2001 riots, 9/11, and 7/7. Kundnani argues that, although hostility towards cultural diversity has long been central to the political right, since these events, 'cultural diversity has been attacked equally vigorously by liberals and by those on the centre left' (2007: 122). Indeed, the riots of 2001 simultaneously marked the proliferation of multicultural critiques from those of all political persuasions and the increasing legitimacy of the BNP. Following the riots, the party received unprecedented media attention. During the summer months, Nick Griffin appeared on BBC's *Newsnight*, the *Today* programme, Channel 4 *News*, *Tonight with Trevor McDonald*, and GMTV as, 'areas of the media that had hitherto been closed to right-wing extremists now opened up' (Copsey, 2004: 134).

As in the case of the BNP, opposition to multiculturalism has come to focus in particular around anxieties regarding Britain's Muslim population. The aftermath of the 2001 riots, 9/11, and the onset of the 'War on Terror' saw Muslims, both here and abroad, become a target of fear, suspicion, and hostility, portrayed as a potentially threatening and disloyal group. This negative perception of the Muslim community increased in the wake of the 7/7 London bombings and the discovery that those involved in the attacks were British-born Muslims. For the BNP, the events once again confirmed the inherent danger of Britain's policy of multiculturalism, ethnic plurality, and the clash between Islamic and British values (Griffin, 2005: 4). The 7/7 bombings also marked an intensification in political, media, and public suspicion of the broader Muslim community. New Labour, in particular, moved further away from multiculturalism towards a strategy of 'integration'. Kundnani (2007) suggests that this new strategy for community relations in the UK is more adequately reflected by the term 'integrationism'. He argues that this reveals how the logic and rhetoric of assimilationism are now subsumed within the apparently more 'progressive' and benign discourse of 'integration'. However, such a strategy operates on the basic premise that Muslims are a problematic group, a distinct set of 'others' that need to be managed and reshaped in order to foster a more cohesive society.

For Kundnani, the hostility towards Muslims and the perceived incompatibility of this group with dominant British values increasingly unite politicians on both the political left and right: 'whereas the right is pessimistic about the possibilities of absorbing this alien population into modern Britain, the left integrationists feel that Muslims can be assimilated through suitably aggressive policies' (2007: 126). During 2006, New Labour deployed an increasingly aggressive strategy that made greater demands on the Muslim community to integrate. In October 2006, Jack Straw declared the wearing of the veil by Muslim women to be 'a visible statement of separation and difference', preventing greater integration and community cohesion (cited in Morris, 2006: 6). Similarly, in December 2006, Tony Blair re-emphasized, within a speech concerned particularly with the rise of Muslim extremism, the 'duty' that 'immigrants' had to conform to British values: 'The right to be in a multicultural society was always implicitly balanced by a duty to integrate, to be part of Britain, to be British and Asian, British and black, British and white.'[3] In August 2006, the Communities Secretary, Ruth Kelly, suggested that, 'we have moved from a period of uniform consensus on the value of multiculturalism, to one where we can encourage that debate by questioning whether it is encouraging separateness'. She suggested that the failure to impose a core set of shared values had led to the fragmentation of British society.[4] This reflected an increasing sense of unease regarding multiculturalism and the belief that its divisive tendencies had contributed to increased cultural polarization. The BNP certainly saw this shift away from multiculturalism as evidence of its own growing influence on the political mainstream:

> The old clichés about diversity being 'a strength' have been shelved in favour of an abject admission of multiculturalism's failure. Although Kelly and Blair's speeches do not quite say everything the BNP would have wished, who can deny the unseen hand the BNP had in writing them?
>
> (Liddell, 2007: 16)

Post-2001 and 7/7, there has also been a significant intensification of mainstream media opposition to multiculturalism. This was revealed in particular during the BBC's *White Season*, which was screened in March 2008. The timing of the documentary series coincided with the fortieth anniversary of Enoch Powell's 'Rivers of blood speech', in which he predicted the inevitable conflict that would result from non-white immigration and the advent of a multiracial society. The centrepiece of the BBC series was a film that revisited Powell's speech, purporting to examine both its impact and legacy. It appeared to operate on the premise that, in the wake of the 2001 riots and the 7/7 bombings, multiculturalism had failed, and Powell's dystopian image of racial conflict had to a large extent come to fruition. In fact, Simon Darby (2008), the deputy leader of the BNP, credited Nick Griffin as stating that, 'If we had given BNP TV the remit to do a Powell documentary it wouldn't have differed too much from this.' Indeed, Griffin saw the BBC *White Season* as, 'dramatic evidence of a paradigm shift in the position of the left-liberal elite' (2008: 4). He added that,

> Powell was suddenly presented as a true prophet; still controversial, but broadly proven right. The Beeb didn't actually apologise but, as near damn it, put it on record that Enoch had been right all along . . . their broadcast marked the end of an era for uncritical support for multi-culturalism, and [the] beginning of something very different.
>
> (ibid.: 4–5)

For Griffin, this shift can be explained by growing opposition to immigration. He argued that the BBC documentary was simply 'the breach that has doomed the dam', as the tide of opposition to multiculturalism has created a context in which the BNP's ideas possess more legitimacy (ibid.: 7). It is clear that the BNP has sought to locate itself within a broader oppositional culture towards the politics of multiculturalism: a culture in which the BNP's public projections appear far less dissonant than they did prior to the summer of 2001. However, simultaneously, the BNP also draws upon the symbols and rhetoric of multiculturalism to advance its claims of 'rights for whites'. Here, the BNP attempts to project itself as a subcultural movement, imitating the ideas and dispositions of the dominant culture more effectively than the political mainstream.

Multiculturalism, ethnic difference, and whiteness

Multiculturalism has not only been increasingly opposed as a result of the perceived threat posed by Muslim extremism. It has also been criticized for encouraging the separation of communities along ethnic lines. In April 2004, Trevor Phillips, the head of the then Commission for Racial Equality (CRE), advocated the abandonment of multicultural policies owing to their divisiveness.[5] This has long been a key criticism of multiculturalism in the UK, and something that the BNP has been keen to capitalize upon. The party has been aided by the tendency of multiculturalism to present ethnicity as the primary indicator of 'difference' and to fix and essentialize notions of ethnicity and culture (Modood, 2007). Indeed, 'the positing of minority or immigrant cultures, which need to be respected, defended, publicly supported and so on, appeals to the view that cultures are discrete, frozen in time, impervious to external differences, homogeneous and without internal dissent' (ibid.: 89). With Nick Griffin's rise to leadership in 1999, the party, at least superficially, abandoned the idea of inherent biological racial hierarchy in favour of a discourse centred on notions of cultural difference and incommensurability. As Copsey states, 'such a view allows its proponents to support the "right to difference", casting aside accusations of Nazi-style racism while still opposing multiracial society' (2007: 71). What the BNP has sought to do is simultaneously to oppose multiculturalism while also seeking to locate itself within its field, by claiming to defend the interests of what it casts as a beleaguered white community. The party also asserts the right of 'different' cultures to celebrate their own traditions and values. It is argued, then, that, 'The BNP [are] not racists but legitimate defenders of ethnic and cultural identity' (ibid.: 74). A principal way in which the party has sought to demonstrate this is through its claims to advocate an ethno- rather than racial form of nationalism (ibid.: 78). The BNP highlights its opposition to white immigration from European countries as evidence of this. Nick Griffin stated in 2006 that, 'unlike racial nationalist purists, we would be opposed to the arrival at Dover of several million German or Swedish immigrants' (2006: 6).

The BNP has also concerned itself with borrowing the set of discursive and representative repertoires and techniques utilized by other multicultural groups in Britain. As Modood states, multiculturalism in Britain has offered a political framework within which groups have sought to mobilize collective identities, often in response to negative ascriptions and marginal status positions. Within such discourses, 'There is a sense of groupness in play, a mode of being, but also subordination or marginality, a mode of oppression, and the two interact in creating an unequal "us–them" relationship' (2007: 37). In this sense, 'an oppressed group challenges not just its oppression but the prevailing wisdom about its mode of oppression. It claims to know something, to name an experience because the "difference" is addressed from the inside by the victims' (ibid.: 42). So the BNP claims that whites, particularly working-class whites, have been abandoned by a government more interested in the pursuit of multiculturalism, which favours the redistribution of rights and privileges to 'outsiders'. It is argued that whites have become the predominant marginalized group in British society. This is evident in the BNP's claim to represent 'rights for whites', a slogan that has been central to party campaigning since the start of the 1990s. Back and Keith argue that this term obscures the racialized structure of inequality, as well as drawing upon apparently universal claims to 'equality' and 'fairness'. However, 'such appeals are far from universal. Rather, they are bound into a context in which the debate about racism and racial inequality is frozen in the present, so that histories of racism and disadvantage are rendered inadmissible' (1999: 149). What the BNP has sought to encourage and capitalize upon is a 'minority consciousness' (Baumann, 1996) among whites, in which this group is deemed to be under threat from an expanding minority ethnic population and a government no longer interested in the plight of 'native' peoples. Indeed, the encouragement of this 'minority consciousness' is recognized as being central to BNP strategy:

> Minorities, properly encouraged and organised, are always fiercer upholders of their identity than majorities. This is particularly true of oppressed minorities, and there is no bigger more oppressed minority in Britain than the 'invisible ghosts' of the old population stubbornly holding on in the places where they are now foreigners in their own streets.
>
> (Griffin, 2007: 5)

For Baumann, the 'cultivation' of this white 'minority consciousness' emerges most frequently and forcefully within the contest for material resources and public services, forged around notions of white exclusion and preferential treatment towards minority ethnic groups through a form of 'positive discrimination' (ibid.: 138). Indeed, in the areas in which the BNP has experienced significant electoral success, the party has been able both to capitalize upon and to foster notions of 'unfairness' to whites. In Burnley, the success of the BNP during the 2002 and 2003 elections, in particular, was forged around the idea that the South Asian community was receiving a disproportionate share of council resources (Copsey, 2004; John et al., 2006; Goodwin, 2008; Rhodes, 2010). This sense of marginalization is evident in quotes from Carol Hughes, who was elected as a BNP councillor in Burnley in 2002. She described her motivation for joining the party: 'I saw what was happening in Burnley: white people being discriminated against, white people being blamed for "racism", white people having their culture attacked.' Hughes identifies her 'main hope for the future' as being:

> to deal with the racism issue. And by that I mean to put a stop to anti-white racism that white people in Burnley and all over the country are continuously subjected to. I am working for fairness and an end to discrimination against white people like me.[6]

In Burnley, BNP voters regularly employed the notion of equality as a means of justifying their support for the party, as demonstrated in the following quote from a party supporter: 'I think if everybody were treated equally I wouldn't have a problem but they're ["Asians"] not treated equally, they're treated better' (Rhodes, 2010: 87).

This sense of unfairness and the resulting BNP demands for 'equality' have been integral to successful local election campaigns in other areas. In Barking and Dagenham in 2006, the BNP had twelve local councillors elected. Here, the party pedalled the idea that 'immigrants' and asylum seekers were being favoured in the allocation of housing, ahead of the established white population (John et al., 2006; Goodwin, 2008; Rhodes, 2010). More recently, the BNP has made similar claims regarding the poor response of police and the criminal justice system to racially motivated attacks on whites, particularly in light of the manslaughter of BNP activist Keith Brown in July 2007 in Stoke-on-Trent, during a domestic dispute with a Muslim neighbour. In an article that appeared on the BNP website in 2008, the party argued that racist attacks on whites constituted a 'race war' that was being ignored by politicians, the liberal establishment, and the media: 'There are no public inquiries into the white victims of racism and no monuments are built to mark their tragedies. The blood on the pavements of white victims of racism is quickly hosed away and they are simply forgotten.'[7]

During the 1990s, Roger Hewitt (2005) identified what he saw as the development of a new and dominant theme within white racism – 'unfairness' to whites. He located the roots of this 'white backlash' within the developing hostility to multiculturalism and anti-racist policies that had emerged in the early 1980s, encouraged in particular by Thatcher and the new right's critique of such political initiatives. Although Hewitt recognizes how notions of 'unfairness' to whites mobilize around claims for a more equitable redistribution of material resources and equality before the law, he also demonstrates how it reflects a strong sense of white cultural marginalization and disenfranchisement. He found that the focus of multicultural and anti-racist policies on the culture of ethnic groups led to a perception among some that there was a failure to recognize and celebrate white English culture (Hewitt, 2005; also Baumann, 1996; Nayak, 1999). Hewitt's research among youths in Greenwich found that, 'white children – especially young people from working-class homes – experienced themselves as having an invisible culture, of being even cultureless' (2005: 126).

Claims to the marginalization of the white English gathered apace towards the end of the 1990s in the context of devolution, the rise of the European Union, and moral panics over asylum seekers and immigrants. The publication of the Macpherson and the Parekh Reports were also significant here. Macpherson's attack on the existence of institutional racism within the police, produced in response to the murder of Stephen Lawrence, was seen by the right-wing press as an attack on Englishness and national values (Kundnani, 2000; Hewitt, 2005). As Kundnani states, the response to charges of the existence of institutional racism suggested that, 'if racism is the result of institutions ignoring the specificity of particular racial groups, then surely, the right argued, the most discriminated group of all are the English, for they can claim no special privileges' (2000: 12). The Parekh Report's calls to move beyond a conservative, racialized conception of English identity were received in a similarly negative fashion by the political right (Hewitt, 2005). The BNP saw the Parekh Report as marking the advancement of race relations legislation, which 'treats our dispossession and deculturalisation as something that only needs formalising' (Hamilton, 2005: 9). Kundnani (2000) suggests that this period marked the intensification of a new English nationalism that articulates a sense of marginality, both material and cultural. In this context, the shift of the BNP during 2006 towards a more overt English nationalism, manifest in calls for the creation of an English parliament, is evident of its attempts to co-opt such sentiments. This has also provided a means through which the party can attempt to position itself within more mainstream discourses relating to the defence of culture, nation, and sovereignty, much as Scottish and Welsh nationalism has done (Hannam, 2007).

Responding to the 'white backlash'

For Hewitt (2005), support for the BNP is just one manifestation of the emergent 'white backlash' he identifies. Although he locates this opposition to multicultural policies as existing particularly among the white working classes, he acknowledges that it is a phenomenon that transcends neat class distinctions. Indeed, although support for the BNP is primarily located within the white working classes (Bowyer, 2008; Goodwin, 2008), restricting the extent of the 'white backlash' to these groups, or indeed to the level of BNP support itself, ignores the much broader scope of this form of political sentiment. Despite the cross-sectional nature of these views, the BBC *White Season* focused solely on the 'white working class'. The BBC's commissioning editor, Richard Klein, suggested that the aim of the series was to address the feelings of 'abandonment' and 'neglect' felt by the white working class, many of whom, 'see themselves as an oppressed ethnic minority too, and lower down the ladder than other groups on the hierarchy of victimhood' (cited in Ware, 2008: 2.5). This notion of the marginalized nature of the white working class was also put forward by Dench et al.'s (2006) study of *The new East End*. Drawing on incredibly simplistic and uncritical conceptions of the 'white working class', the book argued that the 'indigenous' population felt increasingly threatened and displaced as a result of the presence of minority ethnic groups, primarily Bangladeshis. White resentment results, it is argued, owing to the way in which welfare and resource allocation is made on the basis of need, serving to undermine traditional communities. The BNP has been keen to reproduce the findings of this study within party literature, as a means of legitimating its own views and locating itself as the only true voice of sentiments that are widely acknowledged but rarely acted upon:

> This is an important book because leftwingers have finally realised the bitterness of the working class which can be persuaded to shift its allegiance elsewhere. The working class has always been cheated by all parties but it still exists and is not in forgiving mood.
>
> (Mayhew, 2007: 13)

This increased media and academic focus on the white working class is reflected within the Labour Party. This is driven both by fears of losing the support of its traditional base and by the rise of the BNP itself. The local electoral successes of the party since 2001 made it an increasing source of anxiety for the Labour government, partly owing to the fact that it is in traditional Labour strongholds such as Barking and Dagenham, Burnley, and Stoke-on-Trent that the party has fared best (John et al., 2006; Bowyer, 2008; Goodwin, 2008). Indeed, the retreat from multiculturalism has, in part, been driven by fears over the way in which it is perceived to have fostered white antagonism and resentment, particularly among the working class, playing into the hands of the BNP (Back et al., 2002; McGhee, 2008). In December 2001, in the wake of the riots, the CRE warned the government that working-class whites felt left out within a political culture that was perceived to grant preferential treatment to minority ethnic groups. More recently, in 2006, the Labour MP for Barking, Margaret Hodge, suggested that white working-class voters were turning from Labour to the BNP as a result of the failings of the party to address the concerns of its traditional supporters. Hodge suggested that the concerns of her white working-class constituents resulted from a failure to control immigration, with little mention of shared experiences of unemployment, deprivation, and the effects of de-industrialization:

> They can't get a home for their children, they see black and ethnic minority communities moving in and they are angry . . . Nowhere else has changed so fast. When I arrived in 1994, it was a predominantly white, working class area. Now, go through the middle of Barking and you could be in Camden or Brixton. That is the key thing that has created the environment the BNP has sought to exploit.
>
> (cited in Kite, 2006: 1)

The interpretation and framing of the debates around immigration and the 'plight' of the 'white working class' are extremely problematic and serve to consolidate rather than challenge those discourses used by the BNP. Indeed, Hodge was widely criticized when, just weeks after her comments, the BNP had twelve local councillors elected in Barking and Dagenham. The 'white working class' is presented as a fixed 'community' that has been fundamentally altered, not through social, political, and economic processes associated with de-industrialization, neo-liberalism, and economic restructuring, but through immigration, principally non-white immigration. Ware contends that these debates mean that increasingly, 'in the critique of multiculturalism, white working-class resentment is viewed as a rational, understandable response to the pressures caused by successive waves of immigration since the founding of the welfare state' (2008: 1.1). She suggests that vocalizing this sense of white resentment, rather than diluting its potency, actually legitimates it by accepting the framing of these issues that groups such as the BNP seek to forward. This reflects the government's willingness to address immigration rather than systemic inequality, as Hodge's comments demonstrate. Again, the BNP argues that it is the only political movement through which these concerns can be adequately addressed. In response to Hodge's speech, the BNP stated that:

> She seems so much out of her depth, like she was overwhelmed by the seriousness of the situation yet at the same time unable to say just how serious it was . . . Mrs Hodge got caught in a trap. It's one that establishment politicians are frequently finding themselves in, and it's a result of them serving two constituencies – that of the ethnic minorities and that of the white majority. The problem in Barking and Dagenham is that government-sponsored mass third world immigration is in the process of destroying the white community, materially, spiritually, and morally . . . But of course Mrs Hodge couldn't articulate her constituents' problems so precisely.
>
> (Priestley, 2006)

The danger is that presenting the difficulties experienced by white communities as the preserve of whites alone plays into the BNP's critique of multiculturalism and its attempts to borrow the logic of multiculturalist discourse through the creation of a white 'minority consciousness'.

The counter-cultural politics of the BNP

It has been asserted, then, that the BNP has simultaneously opposed multi-culturalism while also borrowing its rhetoric, through its assertion of a marginalized white English/British identity and its adherence to notions of cultural difference and incommensurability. The BNP's critique has emerged at a period in which there has been a marked shift away from multiculturalism, towards a strategy of integration, which mirrors the assimilationism of previous decades (Back et al., 2002). This opposition has been heightened as a consequence of the 2001 riots, the 9/11 and 7/7 attacks, as well as the War on Terror. At the same time, the BNP's claim to represent a besieged white 'native' population has also occurred within a broader 'white backlash' against multiculturalism (Hewitt, 2005), which, it is argued, serves to disenfranchize the white – particularly the white English – population.

Within this context, the BNP seeks to legitimize itself by claiming simply to be a party able to vocalize and to champion these concerns, unlike the mainstream political parties who, while increasingly aware of the existence of such resentments, are bound by political correctness and the etiquette of the liberal political establishment. In this sense, as argued above, the party presents itself as simply a subcultural movement, imitating the values and norms of the dominant political culture, and claiming to employ the rhetoric, concerns, and demands for recognition made by minority ethnic groups. However, it is necessary to distinguish between the image the BNP overtly presents of itself as the guardian of English/British ethnic and cultural identity who, like other groups, simply wants to protect the right of the indigenous population, and the more esoteric ideology of the party. In reality, the BNP remains a counter-cultural movement, totally opposed to the norms and values of the dominant culture and reliant on a racially exclusive, anti-democratic political ideology. Nigel Copsey's work (2004; 2007) has been particularly important in demonstrating the distance that exists between the public face that the BNP projects to the public and the private face that is largely concealed from scrutiny.

For Copsey (2007), while the BNP has attempted to cast itself as a more 'respectable' political actor, through an apparent commitment to democracy and strategies of national populism, its ideological core remains more sinister. He notes that the party retains a commitment to totalitarian principles such as control of the media, as well as policies focused on putting an end to immigration, deporting all illegal immigrants, voluntary repatriation, the advocacy of policies based on national preference, as well as a continuing belief in the scientific basis of 'race' and notions of genetic superiority/inferiority (ibid.: 74–5). It is also the case that, while the BNP seeks to locate itself as one of many critics of multiculturalism, its own viewpoint goes beyond those of the broad political mainstream. Although New Labour has moved away from overt support for multiculturalism and fails to recognize the racialized basis of its integrative project (McGhee, 2008), it does not preclude minority ethnic groups from belonging to the nation, even if this inclusion is conditional on deference to white cultural norms and the marginalization of particular forms of ethnic identity. It also combines this with an ambiguous and limited commitment to address continuing racial inequalities (McGhee, 2008; Pilkington, 2008). In contrast to this, an extract leaked from the party's 'Language and concepts discipline manual' stated that, 'BNP activists and writers should never refer to "black Britons" or "Asian Britons" etc., for the simple reason that such persons do not exist'.[8]

Similarly, while the government strategy of 'integration' seeks as its aim more harmonious relations and greater levels of interaction, the BNP favours, 'a policy of cultural and biological separation, whereby people "can enjoy each other's cultures but they must stick to their own"' (Copsey, 2007: 75). For the BNP, the idea of integration is a 'fallacy', as it is seen as transcending scientific laws that govern which groups can successfully interact: 'It is the real world in which we must live, a world in which race is a determinate characteristic, telling us more about the nature of any individual than any other features by which we must judge him' (Baxter, 2005: 26). The BNP still sees repatriation beyond the borders of the nation as being the best solution to the 'problem' of 'diversity':

> The only sure-fire way to end the hatred, instability, murder and horror visited on us by multi-racialism and multi-culturalism is to return, as quickly and as far as is humanely, practically, and politically possible, to the more homogenous Britain for which the heroes of the first two World Wars fought and died.
>
> (Griffin, 2005: 4)

Here, then, the more esoteric ideology of the BNP reveals the extent to which, despite attempts to place itself as just another group within the field of multiculturalism seeking to defend the interests of its own ethnically defined constituency, the party remains beyond the pale. Similarly, its opposition to multiculturalism is not only based on increasing fears of ethnic and cultural difference, in much the same way as the critiques that exist within the political mainstream. Rather, the BNP relies on notions of scientific racism, a highly racially exclusionary concept of nation, and a belief in the spatial separation of different ethnic groups. To conclude, while the party has attempted to locate itself as simply another political actor within the mainstream political opposition to multiculturalism, the BNP remains a counter-cultural rather than a subcultural movement, opposed to the dominant values of British society.

Acknowledgements

This research was possible as a result of the ESRC Postdoctoral Fellowship scheme (Award number: PTA-026–27–1819). Thanks are also due to Graham Macklin and Nigel Copsey for their comments and advice.

Notes

1 'BNP leader defends policy on race', BBC website, 23 April 2009. Available online at: http://news.bbc.co.uk/go/pr/fr/-/1/hi/uk_politics/8011878.stm (accessed 24 April 2009).

2 'Full text of Gordon Brown's speech', 27 February. Available online at: www.guardian.co.uk/politics/2007/feb/27/immigrationpolicy.race (accessed 14 June 2010).

3 'Conform to our society, says PM', BBC website, 8 December 2006. Available online at: http://news.bbc.co.uk/go/pr/fr/-/1/hi/uk_politics/6219626.stm (accessed 12 December 2006).

4 'In full: Ruth Kelly speech', BBC website, 24 August 2006. Available online at: http://news.bbc.co.uk/go/pr/fr/-/1/hi/uk_politics/5281572.stm (accessed 17 October 2006).

5 'Race chief wants integration push', BBC website, 3 April 2004. Available online at: http://news.bbc.co.uk/go/pr/fr/-/1/hi/uk/3596047.stm (accessed 16 December 2004).
6 'Interview with Burnley BNP councillor Carol Hughes', *Identity*, August 2002: 14–15.
7 'The race war against the indigenous Britons continues', 2 August 2008. Available online at: www.bnp.org.uk/racismcutsbothways/?p+167&print=1 (accessed 5 September 2008).
8 'BNP leader defends policy on race', BBC website, 23 April 2009. Available online at: http://news.bbc.co.uk/go/pr/fr/-/1/hi/uk_politics/8011878.stm (accessed 24 April 2009).

References

Ansell, A. E. (1997) *New right, new racism: race and reaction in the United States and Britain*, New York: New York University Press.

Back, L. and Keith, M. (1999) 'Rights and wrongs: youth, community and narratives of racial violence', in Cohen, P. (ed.) *New ethnicities, old racisms?* London: Zed Books.

Back, L., Keith, M., Khan, A., Shukra, K. and Solomos, J. (2002) 'New Labour's white heart: politics, multiculturalism and the return of assimilationism', *Sociological Research Online*, 7(2).

Bagguley, P. and Hussain, Y. (2008) *Riotous citizens: ethnic conflict in multicultural Britain*, Aldershot: Ashgate.

Baumann, G. (1996) *Contesting culture: discourses of identity in multi-ethnic London*, Cambridge: Cambridge University Press.

Baxter, D. (2005) 'Fallacies of integration', *Identity*, November: 24–6.

BNP (2005) *Rebuilding British democracy. British National Party general election 2005 manifesto*, Welshpool, Powys.

Bowyer, B. (2008) 'Local context and extreme right support in England: the British National Party in the 2002 and 2003 local elections', *Electoral Studies*, 27: 611–20.

Cantle, T. (2001) *Community cohesion: a report of the Independent Review Team*, London: Home Office.

Copsey, N. (2004) *Contemporary British fascism: the British National Party and the quest for legitimacy*, Basingstoke: Palgrave-Macmillan.

Copsey, N. (2007) 'Changing course or changing clothes? Reflections on the ideological evolution of the British National Party 1999–2006', *Patterns of Prejudice*, 41 (1): 61–82.

Darby, S. (2008) 'Batten down the hatches', 9 March. Available online at: http://simondarby.blogspot.com/2008/03/batten-down-hatches.html (accessed 14 March 2008).

Dench, G., Gavron, K. and Young, M. (2006) *The new East End: kinship, race and conflict*, London: Profile Books.

Eatwell, R. (2004) 'The extreme right in Britain: the long road to "modernization"', in Eatwell, R. and Mudde, C. (eds) *Western democracies and the new extreme right challenge*, London: Routledge, 62–79.

Goodwin, M. (2008) 'Backlash in the 'hood: determinants of support for the British National Party (BNP) at the local level', *Journal of Contemporary European Studies*, 16 (3): 347–61.

Griffin, N. (2001) 'The night before the storm: how the multiracial "dream" died in Oldham', *Identity*, May: 4–5.

Griffin, N. (2005) 'The death of the multicultural fantasy', *Identity*, September 2005: 4–7.

Griffin, N. (2006) 'Modern nationalism: the new force in politics', *Identity*, May: 4–8.

Griffin, N. (2007) 'The big picture behind our electoral targets', *Identity*, October: 4–7.

Griffin, N. (2008) 'The Last Days of "Normal"', *Identity*, April: 4–7.

Hamilton, D. (2005) 'Decline into tyranny', *Identity*, December: 8–9.

Hannam, D. (2007) 'The rise of English nationalism', *Identity*, October: 14–16.

Hewitt, R. (2005) *White backlash and the politics of multiculturalism*, Cambridge: Cambridge University Press.

Heydon, T. (2007) 'A question of trust', *Identity*, November: 24–7.

Holmes, D. R. (2000) *Integral Europe: fast-capitalism, multiculturalism, neofascism*, Princeton, NJ: Princeton University Press.

John, P., Margetts, H., Rowland, D. and Weir, S. (2006) *The BNP: the roots of its appeal*, Essex: Democratic Audit.

Kite, M. (2006) 'White voters are deserting us for BNP, says minister', *Sunday Telegraph*, 16 April: 1, 10.

Kundnani, A. (2000) 'Stumbling on: race, class and England', *Race and Class*, 41 (4): 1–18.

Kundnani, A. (2007) *The age of intolerance: racism in 21st century Britain*, London: Pluto.

Liddell, C. (2007) 'How Labour changes its colours due to the BNP's popularity', *Identity*, November: 14–16.

Mayhew, D. (2007) 'The new East End', *Identity*, April: 12–13.

McGhee, D. (2008) *The end of multiculturalism? Terrorism, integration and human rights*, Maidenhead: Open University Press.

Modood, T. (2007) *Multiculturalism*, Cambridge: Polity.

Morris, N. (2006) 'Straw says he feels uncomfortable talking to women who wear veils', *The Independent*, 6 October: 4.

Nayak, A. (1999) 'White English ethnicities': racism, anti-racism and student perspectives', *Race, Ethnicity and Education*, 2 (2): 177–202.

Pilkington, A. (2008) 'From institutional racism to community cohesion: the changing nature of racial discourse in Britain', *Sociological Research Online*, 13 (3).

Priestley, J. (2006) 'What Mrs Hodge said', 19 April. Available online at: www.bnp.org.uk/columnists/joepr2.php?joeId=17 (accessed 19 October 2006).

Rhodes, J. (2009) 'Revisiting the 2001 riots: New Labour and the rise of "colourblind racism"', *Sociological Research Online*, 14 (5).

Rhodes, J. (2010) 'White backlash, 'unfairness' and justifications of British National Party (BNP) support', *Ethnicities*, 10 (1): 77–99.

Ware, V. (2008) 'Towards a sociology of resentment: a debate on class and whiteness', *Sociological Research Online*, 13 (5).

Wingfield, M. (2008) 'What does the future hold for the British ethnic minority?', 3 September. Available online at: www.bnp.org.uk/2008/09/what-does-the-future-hold-for-the-british-ethnic-minority/ (accessed 5 September 2008).

Younge, G. (2002) 'Britain is again white', *The Guardian*, 18 February 2002.

PART II

Responses to the BNP

4

'THE MEDIA = LIES, LIES, LIES!'

The BNP and the media in contemporary Britain

Nigel Copsey and Graham Macklin

> We in the BNP know only too well that the mass media, and the deceitful low-life journalists that infest it, are liars. They lie all the time, every day, every hour, and in every new story . . . It is no underestimation to say that the mass media is Public Enemy No. 1 . . . We must not relent until the British people have realised the true extent of the media's diabolical role in the wholesale cultural genocide of our people. THE MEDIA = LIES, LIES, LIES!
>
> (Paul Golding, *Identity*, no. 99, February 2009).

Introduction

Although there are a number of important studies into the relationship between the media and race (see for example, Ferguson, 1998; Gabriel, 1998), studies of the relationship between the far-right and the mainstream media in contemporary Britain are notably absent. To date, this relationship has attracted barely any scholarly attention. But does this matter? What, if anything, is so important about this relationship? It is our contention that the potential significance of the media might be best viewed through Roger Eatwell's model regarding the dynamics of far-right electoral breakthrough (see Eatwell, 1998: 3–32). For this breakthrough to occur, argues Eatwell, there needs to be a conjunction of three factors: an individual sense of personal *efficacy*; a view that an insurgent far-right party possesses a level of *legitimacy*; and a declining sense of *trust* in the sociopolitical system. Such an analysis rejects the tendency to see the British National Party (BNP) vote as simply an impulsive protest vote. Moreover, the media can play an important role in mediating this transition from pariah to paragon, acting as a gate-keeper to the second factor, the much sought after *legitimacy* the BNP craves.

The British media do not play a passive role in this process. The far-right in Britain is not, nor has it ever been, in a position to manage its own image. Barry

Troyna has shown, in his research into the National Front (NF) in the 1970s, that in essence parties such as the BNP challenge the conservative consensus of mainstream media values, which cuts across right/left and quality/tabloid distinctions. British media outlets are committed to the overarching principles of liberal democracy, which explains the 'passionate hostility' with which they react to those who have placed themselves beyond these values (Troyna, 1980: 25–30; 1987: 275–91). There is a tension, of course, between how the media report on the far-right and how they report 'race' and immigration, their 'common-sense' reporting of which shapes attitudes and prejudices and contributes to the rise of the very political phenomenon that it condemns as illegitimate. This chapter will explore this tension.

In a recent study of the media and the far-right in Western Europe (which regrettably does not include the British case), Antonis Ellinas (2010: 204–5) contends that the media can facilitate the emergence of right-extremist parties in three main ways. First of all, they can drop 'barriers of entry into the electoral market by giving new parties the means to disseminate their message across a wider audience than their organizational or financial resources would allow'. Second, the media can bestow on newcomers respectability and legitimacy. Third, they can 'provide momentum to minor parties by giving the impression of a mass following that signals their political viability. Such signals can reduce the possibility that their potential voters will strategically desert them in fear of wasting their votes'. For Ellinas (2010: 7), media effects are most pronounced at earlier stages in a party's development – the pre-electoral breakthrough stage – and can (potentially) 'lift marginal parties from obscurity and push them into the political mainstream' (see also Mudde, 2007: 253). So, far from holding the far-right in check, have the media actually fuelled its rise in contemporary Britain?

The roots of the media's strategy for reporting British fascism first developed during the 1930s. In late 1933, Sir Oswald Mosley, leader of the British Union of Fascists (BUF), had gained the backing of media mogul Lord Rothermere, owner of a number of national newspapers, who placed his newspapers, including the *Daily Mail* – it famously led with the headline 'Hurrah for the Blackshirts' – at Mosley's disposal. This newfound respectability led to a 'sharp boost' in new members for the BUF. Rothermere's support continued for six months until 7 June 1934, when Mosley held a meeting in London's Olympia that ended in considerable violence. Thereafter, Rothermere recoiled from openly supporting fascism. Mosley blamed pressure from Rothermere's Jewish advertisers, a charge he failed to substantiate (see Mosley, 1968: 346–7).

It was the last time Mosley, or indeed any British fascist organization, was able to count on the backing of a 'respectable' news organ. Rothermere's decision to withdraw open support for the BUF was of pivotal importance: without it, the membership went into sharp decline, its activities indelibly associated with violence and thus beyond the pale in terms of permissible media discourse. Hitler's 'Night of the long knives', which took place on 30 June, further bolstered this impression (see Thurlow, 1998: 69–74). Thereafter, Mosley, who had previously been invited to debate fascism with opponents on the British Broadcasting Corporation (BBC) on several occasions, found himself out in the cold, as the BBC opted for a strategy denying him the oxygen of publicity. His own attempts to crack the monopoly of the state broadcaster, circumventing it entirely through the development of alternative media outlets such as a foreign-based radio station, met with failure (Barnes and Barnes, 1990: 11–16). Only in 1966, when the European Court of Human Rights ruled that the BBC was acting unlawfully by denying Mosley a right to reply, was an aged Mosley allowed to return to the airwaves. In November 1967, Mosley finally appeared on ITV's *Frost Programme*. The following year, after an absence of thirty-four years, he appeared on the BBC's *Panorama* – 8.5 million people watched his performance (Dorrill, 2006: 637–8).

Reporting the BNP: the broadcast media

Since his election as BNP chairman in 1999, Nick Griffin has attempted, with a modicum of success, to 'modernize' the party, giving it a more 'media-friendly' face in order to win legitimization (Eatwell, 2004: 62–81). Far from being the subject of a 'media blackout' as it frequently claims, the BNP has been granted access to the airwaves in a way that would have been inconceivable had party founder John Tyndall still been at the helm. On 26 June 2001, in the wake of serious disorder in the northern mill town of Burnley, Griffin was invited on to the BBC's flagship news programme *Newsnight,* followed in quick succession by appearances on the BBC Radio 4 *Today* programme, ITV's *Tonight with Trevor McDonald* and on BBC News 24's *HardTalk*. The idea of 'no platform' for fascists, which had been a dominant strategy for dealing with fascists since the 1930s, was beginning to break down (see Copsey, 2008: 133–4).

In tandem with this erosion of the 'no-platform' doctrine, unthinkable only a few years previously, there were a number of high-profile investigative documentaries scrutinizing the BNP's 'modernization'. These have included 'Under the skin', screened on 25 November 2001 as part of the BBC's flagship investigative showcase *Panorama*, which exposed the enduring racism and criminality that survived at the very highest echelons of the BNP, despite its much vaunted makeover.[1] This was followed on 15 July 2004 by a second BBC documentary, *The secret agent,* which reaffirmed this view as an undercover reporter filmed several BNP members confessing to criminal acts or making what were deemed to be racially inflammatory remarks.[2] The screening of the documentary led to the arrest of fifteen BNP members, including Griffin, who was later tried twice, though acquitted on both occasions, on charges relating to the incitement of racial hatred in 2006.

The BBC is not the only broadcaster to subject the BNP's veneer of respectability to scrutiny through the medium of documentary filmmaking. On 7 November 2003, Channel Four screened a devastating exposure of Mark Collett entitled 'Young, Nazi and proud', which revealed his racism, anti-Semitism and overt admiration of Nazi Germany and Hitler.[3] Collett, then the leader of the Young

BNP, the party youth wing, and later the BNP director of publicity, was to be arrested and tried with Griffin in 2006 as a result of *The secret agent* documentary.

Not all broadcast coverage of the BNP has cast the party in such a negative light, however. In 2001, BBC Radio 4's *Today* programme, which interviewed Griffin in the aftermath of the race riots in Oldham, was fiercely criticized for giving the BNP publicity and credibility it did not warrant. *Today* editor Rod Liddle refused to apologize for the broadcast, stating that it would be 'undemocratic' not to give the BNP a platform, suggesting also that it was far more illuminating to tackle the BNP's hypocrisy, including claims in its election material that it wanted to 'heal' Oldham's problems, rather than resorting to censorship.[4] Liddle subsequently resigned from the BBC in 2003 and currently writes regularly for the right-wing periodical *The Spectator,* through which he has since criticized the BBC for its 'biased' coverage of the BNP (*The Sunday Times*, 30 January 2005). Following Griffin's arrest, resulting from *The secret agent*, Liddle penned an article for *The Sunday Times* entitled, 'Alas, I must defend the BNP', though his real target was the supposed inconsistency and hypocrisy of the Crown Prosecution Service rather than a spirited defence of the BNP per se, arising from his belief that Griffin's 2006 prosecution was political rather than criminal in inspiration (*The Sunday Times*, 5 February 2006, and *The Spectator*, 1 January 2005). In *The Spectator* and in the Channel Four documentary *Immigration is a time bomb*, Liddle has authored a number of polemics attacking the benefits of 'multiculturalism' as opposed to cultural integration, highlighting the supposed incompatibility of fundamentalist Islam with liberal democracy, a stance upon which the BNP constantly campaigns. This is not to suggest that Liddle is, as some BNP members seem to imagine, 'pro-BNP'. Such a perception from within the far-right glosses over Liddle's authorship of several strident and extremely derogatory articles attacking the 'utterly ghastly' BNP, its leadership, members and voters, who are derided as racist and plebeian (*The Spectator*, 23 September 2004).

On the whole, the impression conveyed by the mainstream broadcast media vis-à-vis the BNP is overwhelmingly negative, with instances of more lenient treatment being the result of the idiosyncrasies and peccadilloes of individual editors and producers, rather than the result of deliberate policy.

Reporting the BNP: print journalism

Far more complex and vexatious is the relationship between the BNP and the mainstream media as expressed through print journalism. In 1993, hostility to the BNP was summed up by the *Daily Mirror* headline 'Sieg Heil . . . and now he's a British Councillor', which followed the election of Derek Beackon, the party's first councillor in East London (*Daily Mirror*, 18 September 1993). Almost without exception, the mainstream press reports the BNP in a manner that the BNP would regard as being uniformly hostile. Even newspapers that continually agitate against immigration, migrant workers, asylum seekers and other 'irregulars', such as the *Daily Express*, *Daily Mail* and *The Sun*, have remained staunchly opposed to the

BNP. Prior to the May 2003 elections, the *Daily Mail* branded the BNP 'poisonous bigots', while the *Daily Express* ran a stridently anti-BNP campaign in the week preceding the 2003 local elections, with one columnist going so far as to state that, 'any reader who actually voted BNP should consider themselves ineligible to buy this newspaper' (*Daily Express*, 29 April 2003). In 2004, *The Sun*, Britain's most popular tabloid, ran the front-page headline 'BNP: Bloody Nasty People', followed by a leading article that stated unequivocally that the BNP were 'a collection of evil, hate-filled moronic thugs . . . wicked men . . . criminals who should be locked up' (*The Sun*, 15 July 2004). There are, of course, the occasional anomalies. The *Evening Standard* and the *Daily Mail* have both printed vacuous 'lifestyle' features on Griffin, without any serious examination of his politics. That said, both newspapers have also featured stinging investigations into the BNP.

However, it is also clear that the relationship between print journalism and the far-right is complex and, in some cases, seemingly symbiotic, given the tone in which some sections of the tabloid media have embraced large portions of the BNP platform. Nowhere is this more evident than in relation to asylum and immigration and the perceived threat of 'Islam', discussion of which has become inseparable from the debate on terrorism and national security. But causality is never straightforward. Newspapers may just as well be catering to the prejudices of their readers as influencing them. For its part, the BNP appears to believe that the casuality is in fact straightforward, and thus the sensationalist manner in which many mainstream media outlets report the issues of race, immigration and asylum has contributed to the legitimization and normalization of the BNP platform. This is typified by the statement of deputy BNP chairman Simon Darby, prior to his election as a councillor in Dudley in 2003, that:

> We've had quite a bit of luck in that the newspapers have become obsessed with the asylum issue . . . I have not been able to believe the *Daily Express*. Issue after issue, day after day, asylum this, asylum that. So we now have the luxury of banging on people's doors with the mainstream issue of the day.

Asked if he really attributed the advances of the BNP to *The Sun*, *Daily Mail* and *Daily Express*, Darby retorted, 'Oh yeah, totally. It has legitimised us. We are mainstream now' (*The Guardian*, 30 April 2003). BNP leader Nick Griffin concurred: 'One could today be forgiven for thinking that the editors of five of Britain's national daily papers – the *Daily Star*, *The Times*, *Daily Mail*, *Daily Express* and *Daily Telegraph* – had all suddenly become BNP converts.'[5]

If the BNP is to be believed, then the tenor of tabloid reporting on Islam has helped the party hone its political platform based upon similar themes. As Griffin told a meeting in Burnley, rather than 'bang on' about the Jews, which would render the party obviously extremist and unelectable, the BNP has coldly and calculatedly chosen to campaign against 'Islam', because the continually hostile coverage of Islam by the mainstream media makes it an issue the general public can identify with, as opposed to arcane, anti-Semitic conspiracy theories adhered to only by the party hardcore. The BNP view assumes that anti-Islamic sentiment is, to an extent, manufactured by the mainstream media and that, if they can align themselves with the major trends emanating from it, then they will be the political beneficiaries (Tameside Election BNP DVD 2006).

'From pariahs to panellists': Nick Griffin on *Question Time*

On 22 October 2009, Nick Griffin, the BNP chairman, succeeded, as a result of his election as an MEP in the June European elections, in fulfilling an enduring political ambition: to appear on *Question Time*, the flagship current affairs programme broadcast by the BBC. The announcement by the BBC was met with anguished outrage from the political establishment and the media. The agreement of the Conservative Party and the Liberal Party to field panellists, Baroness Sayeeda Warsi, shadow community cohesion spokeswoman, and Chris Huhne, shadow home affairs spokesman, for their respective parties, made the Labour position of 'no platform' ultimately untenable. Individual ministers, including Alan Johnson, then Home Secretary, publicly announced their refusal to debate with the BNP, however. 'I've gone 59 years without sharing a platform with a fascist', Johnson told the press, 'and I don't intend to start doing it now' (*Yorkshire Post*, 15 September 2009). Jack Straw, then Justice Secretary, was finally announced as the Labour panellist, which appeared to draw a veil over the politics of 'no platform', at least in the short term. Bonnie Greer, the black playwright and critic, joined them.

The BBC had initially approached Richard Littlejohn, a pundit, who declined an invitation and who summarized the dilemma facing those who wished to confront the BNP leader without legitimating him.

> Best case, you monster him and come across as a bully. Worst case, he challenges you to disagree with some of his views, perhaps on something as straightforward as demanding a referendum on the Lisbon Treaty, and you're immediately tarred as guilty by association . . . Once you've said he's a racist, where else is there to go? . . . We are told the programme offers an opportunity to expose the BNP. To whom?
>
> (*Daily Mail*, 20 October 2009)

Griffin's impending appearance on *Question Time* raised the issue of the 'crucial role' of the media in the rise of the *Front National* (FN) during the 1980s. Jean-Marie Le Pen, the FN leader, had been widely derided in the liberal press. This image of racist buffoonery was largely 'confounded' following his appearance on *L'heure de vérité* (*The hour of truth*), France's flagship current affairs programme in February 1984. Le Pen's appearance on this programme, broadly analogous with *Question Time*, was followed by a surge in support for the FN, from an estimated 2.5 per cent in January 1984 to 7 per cent by the end of the following month (*Le Figaro*, 28 February 1984). Le Pen's performance – he likened himself to a

'Churchillian' democract – allowed him to confound his critics, giving him an air of legitimacy that he had hitherto proved unable to attain. It confirmed him as a mainstream fixture, as well as broadening the parameters of what it was permissible to say within the public arena. Indeed, his newfound profile enabled Le Pen to re-introduce a raft of hitherto taboo subjects, such as Holocaust denial and myths about racial inequality, into the mainstream, emboldening his followers further and drawing the French political elite to the right in order to counter the growing FN appeal. *The Guardian* highlighted these parallels, serving to raise concerns that *Question Time* would function as a similar launch pad for the BNP.[6]

No doubt with this in mind, Griffin's appearance was greeted with a storm of protest from the trade union movement. The general secretaries of three major trade unions wrote an open letter condemning the Corporation's 'serious error of judgement' in inviting Griffin (*The Guardian*, 21 October 2009). By far the most serious challenge came from Peter Hain MP, then Welsh secretary, who lodged a complaint with the BBC Trust, a body that supports the Corporation and seeks to ensure its independence, arguing, incorrectly as it transpired, that, as a result of a court case against the BNP brought by the Equality and Human Rights Commission (EHRC) concerning its 'whites only' constitution, which was in breach of the Race Relations Act, the BNP was essentially an 'illegal' organization. The Trustees refused to hear Hain's appeal, however, 'because to do so would be inconsistent with the BBC's constitutional arrangements that the governing body of the BBC does not intervene in programmes before they have been transmitted, and would undermine the editorial independence of the BBC.'[7] Hain was furious, stating that the BBC had 'made one of the biggest mistakes in its proud history . . . This gift of credibility will last him [Griffin] a political lifetime'.[8]

Mark Thompson, the BBC Director-General, publicly defended the decision to invite Griffin to appear on *Question Time* as an 'editorial judgement' that he stood by as a reflection of the Corporation's central principle of political impartiality. The BNP had met the 'objective criteria' to warrant its invite as a result of its performance in the European elections, argued Thompson. Not to invite Griffin would have been a breach of the BBC charter, he stated. It was not the job of the BBC to proscribe or censor the BNP, a step that 'can only be taken by government and parliament'. Unless the BNP were proscribed, then it 'is unreasonable and inconsistent to take the position that a party like the BNP is acceptable enough for the public to vote for, but not acceptable enough to appear on democratic platforms such as *Question Time*', Thompson observed.[9]

These lofty ideals were slightly tarnished by several stories that Mentorn, the company that produced the show, had been lobbying since at least 2007, often against the wishes of both the *Question Time* production crew and the BBC itself, for the inclusion of the BNP on the programme, in the knowledge that Griffin's appearance would give the show an unprecedented ratings coup. Thompson and his deputies had reportedly vetoed the request several times, while host David Dimbleby had been 'torn' on the issue (see *Daily Telegraph*, 24 October 2009). It was the winning of two seats in the June 2009 European elections that apparently led to a reconsideration of the request, though BNP support had only increased by 1.3 per cent since 2004. Such internal politicking aside, public support for the BBC decision once it was announced rose from 63 per cent to 75 per cent prior to the broadcast (*The Sunday Times*, 24 October 2009).

Griffin was well aware of the propaganda value of the platform he had been given, not to mention the resultant furore that had accompanied the announcement. 'Thank you Auntie' for giving the BNP such a boost, he declared, while in the same breath accusing the BBC of being 'institutionally biased' against him. 'I thank the political class and their allies for being so stupid', he told *The Times* gleefully. 'The huge furore that the political class has created around it clearly gives us a whole new level of public recognition' (*The Times*, 21 and 22 October 2009). With his appearance assured, Griffin told his supporters that, although the programme would be 'political blood sport', he relished the opportunity and that it would be 'THE key moment that propels the BNP into the big time'. His appearance, he told followers, was 'history in the making'. 'Never before have we had the chance to present our patriotic, commonsense solutions to Britain's nightmare situation to the public at large in such a prominent fashion' (BNP e-newsletter, 21 October 2009).

On the eve of his appearance, Griffin had every reason to be confident. Twenty-four hours before he appeared, the BNP website had received approximately five million hits from 73,000 visitors, according to the BNP.[10] On the day of the recording, Television Centre in West London was besieged by anti-fascist protesters, twenty-five of whom succeeded in breaking through the cordon and getting into the building, before being removed by BBC security staff and the police. Griffin was taken into the building through a back entrance, surrounded by a phalanx of heavily built minders, who themselves faced the full glare of publicity in the days following revelations about their criminal convictions (*Daily Mail*, 26 October 2009).

Prior to the filming of the programme, *Question Time* presenter David Dimbleby stressed to the studio audience that it should 'not just be the Nick Griffin show' (*The Independent*, 23 October 2009). His entreaty was in vain. Questions from the audience were from the very outset aimed almost entirely at the BNP leader and his record. In the face of persistently hostile questions from the floor and broadsides from a hostile panel, Griffin delivered a less than polished performance. He was noted to be visibly shaking. When he spoke, Griffin came across as shifty and evasive and appeared visibly embarrassed, and indeed he was not exactly candid on at least one occasion when confronted with past pronouncements. BNP members in the audience offered little succour to their beleaguered leader.[11]

Griffin used his appearance to attack Islam, to brand the sight of homosexuals kissing as 'really creepy' and to state that David Duke's Ku Klux Klan was 'almost totally non-violent', a claim that was met with derision by the studio audience. His greatest gaffe, however, was when confronted about his Holocaust denial. Griffin claimed that he 'did not have a conviction for Holocaust denial', which of course was true. There is no law outlawing Holocaust denial in Britain. He does, however, have a conviction for inciting racial hatred based on material he wrote in his own anti-Semitic journal, *The Rune*, which regularly denied the Holocaust. Griffin refused to elaborate on the subject, claiming 'I cannot tell you why I said those things in the past, or why I have changed my mind', because European law prevented him from doing so. Jack Straw, the Justice Secretary, assured him that there was no such law. Griffin refused to be drawn. Griffin's persistent smirk during the exchanges led Dimbleby to ask, 'Why are you smiling, it is not a particularly amusing issue?'. His participation in the show did not moderate Griffin's conspiratorial views regarding the BBC, which he branded on air as, 'part of a thoroughly unpleasant, ultra-leftist establishment which, as we have seen here tonight, doesn't even want the English to be recognized as an existing people' (BBC, *Question Time*, 22 October 2009).[12]

From the point of view of the BBC, the programme was an unmitigated success. The programme recorded its highest viewing figures in its thirty-year history, 8.2 million viewers at its peak. More important, though, was how Griffin measured up to his own personal *L'Heure de Vérité*. The verdict of national newspapers from across the political spectrum the following morning was unanimously withering: 'BNP leader Nick Griffin is . . . a disgrace to humanity' (*Daily Express*, 23 October 2009); 'Bigot at bay' (*Daily Mail*, 23 October 2009); 'Griffin uses BBC to attack Islam and defend the Ku Klux Klan' (*Daily Telegraph*, 23 October 2009); 'I'm the most loathed man in Britain (we couldn't have put it better, Mr Griffin)' (*The Sun*, 23 October 2009); 'BNP chief Griffin is a nutter . . . even wife puts the boot in' (*Daily Star*, 23 October 2009); 'Rat run – BNP bigot scuttles away after humiliation on TV' (*Daily Mirror*, 23 October 2009); 'Question Time for BNP Leader. His answer: "I am not a Nazi"' (*The Guardian*, 23 October 2009); and 'The BBC gave him the oxygen of publicity. He choked' (*The Independent*, 23 October 2009). Simon Darby, the deputy BNP leader, sought to assure followers during this welter of negative publicity that Griffin had achieved a 'very respectable score draw', which was over-egging the pudding somewhat.[13]

Griffin claimed that he had faced a 'lynch mob' and stated that he would be writing to the BBC to complain about the changing of the format of the programme, as well as arguing that it should not have been held in London because it was 'no longer a British city', having previously claimed that the capital had been 'ethnically cleansed' of its native, white population.[14] He did his best to mitigate the hostile publicity surrounding both his performance and his remarks, attempting to normalize his appearance by claiming that he had 'struck up a rapport' with co-panellist Bonnie Greer (*The Independent*, 23 October 2009). The reality was somewhat different. Greer described sitting next to the BNP leader as, 'probably the weirdest and most creepy experience of my life . . . I spent the entire night with my back turned to him. At one point, I had to restrain myself from slapping him' (*Daily Mail*, 23 October 2009).

In the days and weeks following the furore over Griffin's appearance, newspaper coverage shifted to focus on the growing backlash against the BBC itself, following a dawning realization among some commentators that the change to the format and the hostility faced by Griffin from both the audience and panel helped cast

Griffin as the 'victim', which fed into the general BNP narrative of victimhood and 'persecution'. Indeed, within twenty-four hours, the BBC had received 357 complaints about the programme, with 243 callers supporting Griffin's claims of bias, many no doubt BNP supporters. The BBC robustly and persuasively defended itself against accusations that the show was 'rigged' against Griffin.[15]

Despite complaints about his treatment, Griffin claimed that his appearance on *Question Time* was 'the moment that changed British politics'.[16] The media circus aside, did Griffin's appearance on *Question Time* have any effect? In the wake of the programme, a YouGov poll suggested that 22 per cent, or one-fifth, of the electorate would 'seriously consider' voting for the BNP (*The Sunday Times*, 24 October 2009). On the surface, this represented an alarming rise in support for the BNP. But actual vote intention polling showed no increase in BNP support following Griffin's appearance. *The Times* confidently predicted that, 'history shows that BNP will follow Mosley's Fascists down the drain'. Did Griffin's appearance on *Question Time* mark the moment when the British far-right established itself as an insurgent force in British politics, or was Griffin's risible performance the high water mark, 'the moment when the party was seen for what it is, and crashed in flames'? (*The Times*, 23 October 2009). A brief anecdotal survey of Muslim opinion in London's East End, conducted by *The Guardian,* revealed a general indifference to Griffin's appearance and confidence that the voters would reject his arguments.[17] Griffin's appearance also generated an online game entitled 'Slap Nick Griffin', which enjoined players to voice their disapproval by giving Griffin a virtual slap round the face. Griffin was 'slapped' 20 million times before the application was taken offline – its programmers considering that the point had been made.[18]

Regardless of this frivolity, a number of commentators pointed to the fact that the Rubicon had been crossed. James Macintyre, a former *Question Time* producer and now political correspondent for the *New Statesman* current affairs magazine, warned that, regardless of Griffin's performance, 'symbolically the damage is done: there he was in his suit, tie and poppy, on a panel alongside a Cabinet minister and the best presenter in the business, gaining false respectability. The taboo of voting BNP has been lifted' (*Daily Telegraph*, 24 October 2009). Macintyre subsequently backed the launch of a campaign group entitled 'Expose the BNP', which, in the run up to the 2010 general election, provided background briefings for reporters, news editors and others in the media industry.

In the short term at least, Macintyre's fears appeared well founded. Griffin's appearance, regardless of the quality of his actual performance, had, according to the BNP, generated an unprecedented interest in the party. Prior to the programme, Griffin had claimed that he hoped his appearance would attract 'a whole crop of new, quite high-quality, serious political people' (*The Times*, 21 October 2009). The following morning, the BNP claimed that, 'On this day alone our website has had in the region of 15 million "hits" and over 2,000 new registrations for future membership before QT even started!' (BNP e-newsletter, 23 October 2009). Elsewhere, this figure was inflated on the BNP website to 'some 9,000 new people', who, the party claimed, 'had signed up as registered potential members or on our mailing lists'. The party claimed that, the following day, a further 1,000 people had registered for membership of the party when the current freeze is lifted.[19] The BNP were triumphal. 'In the Euro elections, we gained 40,000 enquiries, but spent £500,000 to do so', stated the BNP webmaster, 'on *Question Time* we spent peanuts but gained almost 25 per cent of the Euro election total in eight hours! We had to upgrade our server capacity enormously, which allowed us to cope with extra traffic'.[20]

Whether such claims were anything more than bravado, Griffin's poor performance did not appear to unduly dent his standing with BNP voters in its core areas such as Burnley, Lancashire, where the party had four borough council seats and one county councillor. Many of those questioned believed that Griffin had been the victim of a 'witch hunt' (*The Guardian*, 23 October 2009). Nevertheless, although *Question Time* may not have immediately damaged the standing of the BNP, the following year it is perhaps worth noting, without implying any particular causality, that the BNP lost two of its seats in Burnley as well as being wiped out in its electoral stronghold of Barking and Dagenham.

There were certainly dissenting voices, notably Lee Barnes, the BNP legal officer, who was critical that Griffin had failed to 'press the attack' against the 'ethnic middle class' for 'taking up the best jobs while still playing the bogus race card for every opportunity . . . Perhaps there needs to be a few "White Riots" around the country à la the Brixton Riots of the 1980s before the idiot white liberal middle class and their ethnic middle class fellow travellers wake up', he stated on his website.[21] Grumblings of discontent on far-right Internet forums were magnified into a slightly mischievous story claiming Griffin's poor performance could trigger a leadership challenge (*The Times*, 27 October 2009), though this has since become a reality, with Griffin's challenger noting his performance on *Question Time* as one of (many) reasons why a change of leadership is required.[22]

For sure, there was no significant short-term 'bounce' in BNP electoral fortunes. In the first parliamentary by-election to take place after *Question Time*, in Glasgow North East on 12 November, the BNP came fourth with 1,013 votes (4.92 per cent), compared with 920 votes (3.2 per cent) in 2005, despite newspaper reports that the party might save its deposit and come third (*The Times*, 6 November 2009). The BNP has traditionally fared badly in Scotland, though the constituency, a staunchly Labour seat, perhaps offered its best chance of success. It is one of the most socially deprived in Scotland, if not the country, as well as having the highest level of asylum seekers in the country, something the BNP campaign readily invoked. Although *Question Time* no doubt raised Griffin's profile, there is little to suggest that it echoed the effect of Le Pen's appearance on *L'Heure de Vérité*. In fact, in one post-*Question Time* poll, as many as 69 per cent of respondents still believed that Griffin remained 'at heart a Holocaust denier and only pretends to have changed his views to make the BNP appear more moderate' (YouGov poll for *Jewish Chronicle*, 27–28 October 2009). All the same, as the BNP's John Bean put it, 'QT did not sink the good ship BNP, nor drown its captain' (*Identity*, no. 102, 2010).

In the cold light of day: BNP perceptions

Irrespective of recent episodes of indulgent treatment, for many of Britain's right-extremists, the media still remain their most formidable opponent. A glance at the recent history of Britain's far-right soon reveals that what really brought home the power of the media to Britain's right-extremists was the NF 1979 general election debacle. Despite contesting over 300 seats, in the largest election push by any British extreme-right party in the twentieth century, the NF received more exposure for its platform from American and Canadian radio networks than the entire national broadcasting services in Britain. It was not the NF's policies but the violence occasioned at its campaign meetings, such as Southall, that attracted the newspaper headlines (see Renton, 2006: 150–1). Yet, rather than coverage of rioting, more damaging, the NF declared, was the media blackout of its policies. For Britain's contemporary extreme right, the overwhelming lesson from 1979 was that the mass media constituted their number-one enemy (*Spearhead*, no. 129, July 1979).

It comes as no surprise, therefore, that former Front chairman John Tyndall should have set aside an entire chapter to the supposed machinations of Britain's mass media in *The eleventh hour*, his political manifesto cum autobiography, first published in 1988. Within this canonical text, which supplied the BNP with its articles of faith until Griffin gave the party its recent ideological makeover, Tyndall gave vent to his conspiratorial predilections. According to Tyndall, the media's power is such that they represent a 'state above the state', an all-powerful institution committed to 'left-liberal' goals of internationalism, racial integration and liberal democracy. For the most part, as Tyndall described it, the power the media wield is '*negative* coercive power', a form of censorship that is 'concentrated on stopping the broadcasting of ideas it is against more than it is with promoting the ideas it favours' (Tyndall, 1998: 278). Consequently, there is, Tyndall said, no discussion of why the multiracial society does not work, racism is always presented negatively, and even the so-called 'quality' press 'steadfastly refuses to permit a word to be uttered in suggestion that conspiracy is at work in national and international affairs' (Tyndall, 1998: 275).

These last remarks are revealing, for within the inner sanctum of the mass media lie those that Tyndall had judged responsible for this invisible censorship, that is to say, a select few hidden away in the shadows, the 'dark and subterranean forces that are never exposed to the public eye and which most of the public do not even know exist' (Tyndall, 1998: 284). From here, it takes little stretch of the imagination to picture what Tyndall had seen in his mind's eye: a sinister conspiracy of privileged Jews exercising inordinate control over the mass media that, in furtherance of Zionism, internationalism and eventual one-world government, actively promote the destruction of the British nation.

Yet, despite a promise to do something about it, 'or it will destroy our country utterly and irreparably' (BNP: *The enemy within: how TV brainwashes a nation*, 1993: 2), it was January 1997 before the BNP tried bringing this supposed 'media conspiracy' to wider public attention. Through 'Operation Daylight', it hoped to drag the issue out of its dark shadows and expose it to the cold light of day. The centrepiece of the campaign was the dissemination of a booklet, *Who are the MIND-BENDERS? The people who rule Britain through control of the mass media,* authored by future BNP chairman Nick Griffin.[23] The intention was to mail this booklet to thousands of people, 'magistrates, local clergymen, sixth formers, police officers, young journalists and the like' (BNP, *Who are the MIND-BENDERS?* 1997: 24), and thereby fire up public debate. Yet no such debate ever materialized. Few booklets were circulated, not least because it fell on members to bulk purchase copies and identify recipients. Although the aim was to bring out further editions, no others were forthcoming. In any case, the campaign was ill timed: it coincided with the run-up to the 1997 general election, and the attention of party activists was elsewhere.

In truth, *MIND-BENDERS* rehearsed the arguments that Tyndall had already expounded in *The eleventh hour,* that is to say, the mass media constitute a power greater than government and manipulate news by deliberately selecting items to suit their own liberal-left ideological agenda. As a result, cases of anti-black racism are supposedly given prominent coverage, while racial violence directed against whites is ignored; the achievements of ethnic-minority sportsmen are given disproportionate coverage (supposedly to show the benefits of multiracial society); BNP activities go unreported, unless opposition leads to violence; and current affairs discussion programmes are 'rigged' insofar as 'dangerous' viewpoints are always excluded. *MIND-BENDERS* specifically asked: '*Who* are the people who determine what is watched on television and printed in the newspapers?' A 'great many of the people concerned operate in the shadows', Griffin declared, and to further call our attention to this 'eye-opener' he set it in bold: '**For this reason, very few people in Britain are aware of the huge influence over the mass media exercised by a certain ethnic minority, namely the Jews**' (BNP, Who are the *MIND-BENDERS?,* 1997: 4).

Yet *MIND-BENDERS* went further. Inspired by a similar booklet authored by Dr William Pierce, leader of the US-based neo-Nazi group, the National Alliance, Griffin was intent on showing that this statement was not just armchair speculation. Griffin did not flinch from naming names, and the remainder of the 24-page booklet was given over to disclosing the identity of those Jews who, the BNP claimed, had control in the mid 1990s over broadcasting, the press and publishing in Britain, as well as the entertainment industry both in Britain and in Hollywood. Key figures identified included Alan Yentob (director of BBC programmes), Independent TV bosses Michael Grade and Michael Green, Channel Four boss Jeremy Isaacs and the allegedly part-Jewish Rupert Murdoch, head of BSkyB and owner of numerous British newspapers, *The Times*, *The Sunday Times*, the *News of the World* and *The Sun*. Yet it need hardly be added that the methodology behind *MIND-BENDERS* was suspect. None of this was placed in context, parts were factually inaccurate, and the presence of a few hundred Jews working within the media (which employs many thousands) does not in and of itself prove that there is any such conspiracy.

It is, of course, true that Griffin penned *MIND-BENDERS* before he was elected party chairman in 1999 and before rebranding the BNP as a respectable 'modern' nationalist party. If, in 1997, Griffin had been excited by the publication of *MIND-BENDERS*, once he had become party chairman he was sure to become ill at ease with its contents. Quite simply, the subject matter of *MIND-BENDERS* jarred with Griffin's attempt to distance the BNP from its neo-Nazi past. Hot-headed talk of nefarious Jewish conspiracies would hardly mainstream or 'normalize' the BNP. At the same time, however, Griffin could not close his eyes to the booklet's existence, especially when opponents continued to draw attention to it to evidence the party's hidden agenda.

Griffin's answer was not to deny 'that certain minority groups do punch far above their weight when it comes to influence within the media', as *MIND-BENDERS,* his 'now out-of-print survey', had demonstrated. But he did abandon (publicly at least) conspiracy theory. 'The real position with regards to the mass media', as he now judges it, is that it is governed, not by some monolithic conspiracy, but by profit (*Identity*, no. 53, March 2005). To talk down Jewish conspiracy theory, it is now all too clear that the party's traditional animus against the media is being reconfigured. This is not to say that we are being offered a different reading in terms of a left-liberal elite, often controlled by 'foreign' owners, manipulating and censoring news, denying a platform to the BNP, portraying it in the worst possible light through 'lies' and 'smears', and 'smothering' debate about the alleged failures of multiracial society. But reference is now made, not to Tyndall's *Eleventh hour,* but to Noam Chomsky's *Manufacturing consent* (1998), which 'provides a detailed explanation of how news is filtered to tailor information to the needs of the powerful'. What is different is the assignment of cause: capitalism not conspiracy. Even so, none of this can disguise the fact that, within the party, a latent conspiratorial anti-Semitism remains. Hence, after John Bean, editor of *Identity,* had called on readers to reject 'Judeo-obsessivism' and the anti-Semitic extremism of the party's past, he still found it necessary to qualify it all by stressing that:

> Lest anyone misunderstand, the BNP has not 'embraced Zionism', 'sold out to the Jews', or anything like it. We remain well-aware that subversive Jews exist, that some Jews tend to have a characteristic style of (materialistic and scheming, like Karl Marx and George Soros) subversion, and we remain committed to fighting them, *when this is really the case.*
>
> (*Identity*, no. 66, May 2006)

So how would a BNP government attend to the supposedly manipulative power of the media? In order to stop the media from being used as 'a poisonous weapon which does not hesitate to distort, twist and pass off the most outrageous lies as truth' (*Identity*, no. 32, May 2003), the BNP would enact a new law that would prohibit the media from deliberately disseminating falsehoods about an individual or organization for financial or political gain (BNP, *Rebuilding British democracy*, 2005: 9; BNP, *Democracy, freedom, culture and identity*, 2010: 43). It also promised legally to proscribe the media from promoting racial integration (BNP, *Rebuilding British democracy*, 2005: 20). Besides these measures, there would be informal censorship too. Once elected to office, Griffin promised that a BNP government would hold meetings with media proprietors and would 'thrash out ways in which they would agree to ending any possibility of abuse of their power, in exchange for being left to enjoy the purely financial benefits of their ownership' (although media proprietors would be more heavily taxed) (BNP, *Rebuilding British democracy*, 2005: 9).

If all of this is far too redolent of illiberal extremism, the BNP tries to set our minds at rest with the promise that the existing right of reply through the Press Complaints Commission would be replaced with a 'truly independent body' that grants 'the victims of media falsehood the right of reply with equal prominence, plus financial compensation' (BNP, 2005: 9; BNP, 2010: 43). Furthermore, it offers an undertaking that a Bill of Rights guaranteeing freedom of speech would be enacted. Evidently, the (misleading) impression that Griffin wants to leave us with is that a BNP government would oversee Britain's transition to a 'truly democratic' state, which 'allows all sections of our society free and unfettered access to the media' and yet puts an end to the 'dictatorship of the media over free debate' (BNP, 2005: 9). The reality, however, would no doubt be tightly censored and submissive media, which would find themselves all too quickly gagged by the BNP's own version of 'political correctness'. After all, as the BNP's Paul Golding sees it (*Identity*, no. 101, 2009), journalists are *propagandists*.

Counter-strategies: the BNP response

It goes without saying, of course, that in early twenty-first-century Britain, the possibility of a future BNP government is infinitesimal. For all its recent electoral gains, the BNP remains Britain's most disliked party. A 2004 poll found, for instance, that 76 per cent of respondents 'could never vote' BNP (John et al., 2006: 8). With such widespread antipathy towards it, which is, as we have already seen, variously reproduced in the mainstream media, it is small wonder that the party's campaigning strategies should prioritize ways to both evade and disarm mainstream media opposition.

With a view to bypassing its media enemies altogether, the most significant development has been the party's zealous embrace of alternative media technologies, above all, the Internet. For Nick Griffin, the potential of this new broadcast medium is obvious: 'The great value of this medium is that it allows people to see for themselves precisely what we believe, instead of receiving their information about the BNP through the filters of the fundamentally hostile and dishonest mass media' (*Spearhead*, no. 362, April 1999). Griffin's aim is to project online an impression of the BNP and its policies that runs counter to the many negative representations that the public receives through the established media. The thinking behind the party's website, which features its own Internet TV channel, 'BNPtv', is to develop an alternative medium of its own and thereby circumvent the self-appointed 'gate-keepers' who supposedly control the information society receives and who thereby determine its concerns. One by-product of BNPtv is 'FSID' (Freedom, Security, Identity, Democracy), a DVD that has been sent out to its local groups every month to assist in recruitment. Other initiatives include investing in grass-roots alternative media: seemingly 'non-political', special-interest blogs, 'all drip-dripping the acceptability and growing support of the BNP into their own small circles'. The BNP also promises to further expand online 'social networking', 'fast becoming the ultimate internet platform for communication and socialising between vast numbers of Britons and other kindred peoples around the world'. Through developing these alternative media, Griffin believes that the controllers of the mainstream media will be 'caught between a rock and a hard place': they will either maintain their policy of supposed censorship, 'aware that an unknown, but growing number of people are now able to see the truth for themselves', or they will, for the sake of their own credibility, allow the public a glimpse of the fact that multiracialism is not working (*Moving on moving up. Why people are voting for Nick Griffin*, n.d.: 2).

If truth be told, this counter-strategy is showing some results. From modest beginnings in 1995, it was not long before the party's website had acquired a readership that outstripped the combined circulation of all its printed publications (on the BNP's early web presence, see Copsey, 2003). Although Internet traffic statistics are notoriously contentious, the BNP boasts that it had the most viewed website (www.bnp.org.uk/) of any political party in Britain by 2003, and it now claims to have the most viewed political party site in Europe. In 2009, the reach of the BNP website was four times greater than that of the Conservative Party site, and seven times greater than that of the Labour Party. Although far less than the website reach of the BBC, it compared favourably with the website reach of major provincial newspapers, and of political weeklies such as the *Spectator* and the *New Statesman*.[24] The BNP has claimed that the success of its website has led it to several denial-of-service attacks, though it has offered no proof of these assertions. As for peak traffic flows, these occur during election periods, if the party itself attracts national publicity, or else in the immediate aftermath of major race-related events, such as the July 2005 London bombings. Although hard to quantify, it now seems likely that the majority of the party's recruitment comes through website traffic. Moreover, such is the professionalism of the site, with its deceptively restrained content that is nonetheless prepared to 'tell things as they really are', any unsuspecting visitor to it would believe that the BNP lay within the mainstream of British politics. In this way, its online manifestation clearly lends support to Griffin's broader normalization strategy. That said, following a particularly acrimonious dispute with its former webmaster, the BNP website was taken down. This occurred just days before the 2010 elections, severely hampering the ability of the party to get its message across to followers and indeed potential voters.

None of this means, however, that the BNP pays no heed to how it is represented in the established media. At various times, the thinking of its leadership has been that overestimating the hostility of the media should be avoided as much as underestimating it. In other words, on a few occasions, particularly at local level, the party believed that it might obtain reasonable media coverage of its opinions and activities. Under Tyndall, local activists were encouraged to attract local media publicity by adopting certain 'tricks of the trade', such as distributing small numbers of inflammatory leaflets in an area likely to excite a response, then simply waiting for the local press to reproduce the leaflet on its front page, thereby saving the party both time and money. An alternative tactic was to 'feed' news to a journalist in such a way as to give the impression that it was from an opponent and thereby prompt the journalist to request that the party defend its point of view (see BNP, *Activists' handbook*, 1994(?): 32–5). Nonetheless, there was still an underlying assumption among the party's rank-and-file that, more often than not, any publicity would be negative, and so few branches, if any, followed this advice.

Not until Griffin's appointment as director of BNP publicity in the run-up to the 1999 European elections was any sense of professionalism brought to this side of party operations. With Griffin acting as a catalyst for it, the BNP established its own Media Monitoring Unit (MMU) in 1998. Modelled upon the Labour Party's instant rebuttal unit, it sought to combat adverse press coverage by cajoling journalists, especially at local level, to stop referring to the BNP in terms that ordinary voters would find objectionable. Where Tyndall had thought that the party could afford to be depicted as 'dangerous' and 'extremist', provided that it was not seen as a home of 'juveniles' or 'buffoons', Griffin saw things differently. He finally recognized that 'irresponsible and impractical extremism remains the political kiss of death as far as 98 per cent of people are concerned', and therefore wanted directly to challenge, wherever possible, media representations of the party as a violently racist and anti-Semitic 'neo-Nazi' or 'fascist' organization. Furthermore, rather than just leaving it all to local party branches, which now required authorization before appointing a local press spokesperson, this central unit, organized by Dr Phil Edwards (real name Dr Stuart Russell), would search out opportunities to obtain publicity for the BNP and its policies. For the most part, the MMU targeted local newspapers and radio. Not as well informed about the party, the local media could be more readily cajoled into retracting a statement, through letters of complaint, e-mails and/or telephone calls (*Searchlight*, no. 286, April 1999). Following Edwards' resignation as the BNP's National Press Officer, the MMU was superseded by 'Operation Fightback', whereby the BNP encouraged its online supporters to contact the Press Complaints Commission directly, providing a ready-made online complaints form for supporters to complete.

Although increasing professionalism has featured, Griffin's approach to obtaining media publicity is essentially opportunistic. Often, the party simply waits for an occasion to present itself. On general election night in 2001, for instance, Griffin responded to the ban on speeches at the Oldham count by wearing a gag and T-shirt with the slogan 'GAGGED FOR TELLING THE TRUTH'. This publicity stunt, alongside the fact that he had polled 16.4 per cent of the vote – which at the time was the highest vote ever for a far-right candidate in a British parliamentary election – guaranteed widespread media coverage. The BNP also wasted no time in distributing anti-Islamic leaflets, in wake of the July 2005 London bombings, with the headline 'Maybe now it's time to start listening to the BNP'.[25] It also captured headlines when distributing leaflets that published the controversial *Jyllands-Posten* cartoon of Muhammad. More recently, Griffin used his election to the European Parliament to stage an impromptu press conference on College Green at Westminster, which he was forced to abandon in front of TV cameras after anti-fascists had pelted him with eggs.

Such opportunism, a desire to respond to the circumstances of the moment, also lay behind the party's Instant Response Group. Another Griffin initiative, this was originally formed in the late 1990s in order to obtain publicity for the party by sending activists out to locations where they could respond to issues at very short notice. Given the speed with which such activities are organized, confrontation with potential opponents (and the negative newspaper headlines that typically emerge as a result) is kept to a minimum.

Perhaps unsurprisingly, with this modus operandi, activities do ebb and flow. During 2004, orchestrated by its London organizer Bob Gertner, Instant Response Group activities included a counter-picket organized outside the central London offices of the *Daily Mail*, where the BNP demonstrated against protesters who were angry at the *Mail's* repeated tirades against asylum seekers. One BNP placard, in appreciation of how the newspaper was legitimizing its message, read: 'Vote BNP, Read the *Daily Mail*'. A few weeks later, a small BNP contingent held a picket outside the headquarters of the National Union of Journalists (*Searchlight*, no. 345, March 2004: 20). But the most effective picket that year was held, not in the capital, but in its northern stronghold of Burnley. Here, on 19 February 2004, the BNP demonstrated against the visit of then Tory leader Michael Howard, who played the 'race card' when visiting the town in the run up to the European elections. On that day, the BNP claimed to have enjoyed more airtime than in any other single day in its entire history (*Identity*, no. 42, March 2004). It was surpassed, however, on the evening that Nick Griffin and fellow BNP activist Mark Collett were acquitted on charges of inciting racial hatred in February 2006. The TV coverage of flowers, cheers and flag-waving from their supporters as the two men emerged from Leeds Crown Court was rightly described by the BNP as 'our greatest publicity coup ever'. But such publicity by its very nature is sporadic. For all its counter-strategies, including the increasingly effective use of alternative media technologies, the BNP ordinarily finds itself struggling for the oxygen of publicity.[26]

During election periods, the BNP can, of course, take advantage of the long-standing practice of providing airtime to parties through the medium of a three-, four- or five-minute party election broadcast (PEB). For the BNP, a PEB represents a worthwhile financial sacrifice, as it affords the party the sole opportunity to broadcast to the nation and place its name before the electorate, if only for five minutes, as part of its strategy to build on existing support and to gain momentum for future electoral contests.[27] Even here, however, its efforts have been thwarted. At the time of the 2004 European elections, for instance, the version of the BNP election broadcast given to Channel Five focused on allegations that underage white girls, some as young as eleven, were being 'groomed' for prostitution by gangs of

'Asian' men in Yorkshire, crimes that the BNP claimed were ignored by authorities and the media. The BNP PEB was filmed to exploit the furore surrounding the Channel Four documentary *Edge of the city*, which explored a range of social problems blighting Bradford, though focusing upon allegations of 'grooming' of young white girls by 'Asian' men. Channel Five requested the BNP re-edit it before permitting transmission as it was felt that the broadcast was 'likely to stir up racial hatred' and thus breach the channel's Programme Code. The resulting broadcast was so heavily edited *by the BNP* – sections of script were obscured by bleeps and the sound of wind – it was largely incomprehensible.[28]

Conclusion

By continuing to demonize ethnic minorities, asylum seekers and refugees, the media have helped fuel the rise of the BNP. There can be little doubt that media reproduction of stereotypical bias towards certain ethnic minority groups, in particular through print journalism, has legitimated the BNP message, though this is not to imply a straightforward causal link between the two, merely to highlight that a complex relationship exists between the two parties, which would certainly benefit from further empirical research. Indeed, public hostility to immigrants, Muslims and asylum seekers is not exclusively a media-generated phenomenon, and it is equally possible that the media are simply responding to the pre-existing prejudices of their readers, or that both media attention and escalating public hostility are products of a common cause, such as the escalation in migration levels and/or terrorist attacks. Correlation – the rise in both the BNP vote and media coverage of immigration and asylum issues – is not the same as causation, but it is surely significant that references to press reports frequently recur in focus group evidence from areas where the BNP has polled well (see John et al., 2006). It is also worth noting that, according to one poll, the majority of BNP voters most often read *The Sun/Star/Express/Mail* – those newspapers that most frequently stigmatize migrants and refugees. None reads the *Guardian* or *Independent* (YouGov poll for Channel Four, 28 May to 4 June 2009).

Yet it is also true that, through a series of critical investigative documentaries and press exposés, the media (including the right-wing tabloids) have helped inform society about the true characteristics of Britain's contemporary far-right. But increasingly, as a consequence of Griffin's normalization strategy, the issue on the doorsteps is fast becoming one of 'dissonance', that is to say, when smartly dressed BNP canvassers pay a visit, negative media representations are at odds with what voters actually experience, which highlights the limits of journalistic exposés.

The relationship between the media and the BNP is far from straightforward. The media can work for the BNP and against it. It is both 'friend *and* foe' (Mudde, 2007: 248–55). Regrettably, space has precluded a study of the local press, but similar patterns emerge. In Brighton, for instance, the editor of the *Brighton and Evening Argus* believed that the best policy was to ignore the BNP and deprive it of the oxygen of publicity (*Press Gazette*, 22 April 2004). This stance was criticized by both local anti-fascists and the *Press Gazette*, the newspaper trade magazine, which indicated misgivings as to whether such a strategy really was the most appropriate use of its potential influence on political debate (*Press Gazette*, 22 April 2004). A far stronger stance was adopted by the *Yorkshire Evening Post*, which stridently exposed the BNP in Yorkshire, winning the newspaper the CRE's regional newspaper award twice in three years. Although it refused to ignore the BNP, neither did the *Yorkshire Evening Post* allow the BNP a right of reply, 'We don't allow them to spout their lies through our newspaper', its editor stated (*Press Gazette*, 22 April 2004). But this strategy may not have worked particularly well: the BNP's strongest region in the 2009 European elections was Yorkshire and Humberside, though it should be further noted that, although the overall percentage of the BNP vote rose from 8 per cent in 2004 to 9.8 per cent in 2009, its vote, numerically, declined from 126,538 to 120,139, a decrease of approximately six thousand votes. At other times, the local press has helped set favourable agendas for the BNP – in Oldham, for instance, where the local newspaper, the *Oldham Chronicle*, repeatedly drew attention to the issue of Asian-on-white crime in the town in 2001 (see Copsey, 2008: 126–30).

Of one thing we can be certain: media support for fascism remains beyond the pale. Even for those newspapers that have been most vociferous in their anti-foreigner tirades, the BNP still constitutes an unacceptable 'other', or 'Bloody Nasty People', as *The Sun* headline described them. On the other hand, for a right-wing press determined to show that Britain has a 'race problem', the growth of the BNP provides further grist to their mill. Moreover, subjecting the BNP to critical attack allows the media to reproduce racial prejudice without drawing the accusation that it is receptive to fascism. Perhaps it should come as no surprise, therefore, that when press coverage of immigration increased between 1999 and 2003, so too did coverage of the BNP (John et al., 2006: 22–3). With British society still unable to confront its own prejudices, the very existence of the BNP as the 'other' allows it to sustain the myth that Britain is a tolerant nation, and so, sadly, 'we somehow need the fascists', as Tony Kushner shrewdly put it (Kushner, 1994: 27–45).

Notes

1 Available online at: http://news.bbc.co.uk/hi/english/static/in_depth/programmes/2001/bnp_special/default.stm (accessed 13 November 2009).
2 Available online at: http://news.bbc.co.uk/1/hi/england/bradford/4294357.stm (accessed 14 August 2006).
3 Available online at: www.channel4.com/news/2003/special_reports/young_nazi_proud.html (accessed 13 November 2009).
4 Available online at: http://news.bbc.co.uk/1/hi/uk_politics/1434200.stm (accessed 13 November 2009).
5 Available online at: www.irr.org.uk/2003/january/ak000013.html (accessed 13 November 2009).
6 Available online at: www.guardian.co.uk/commentisfree/2009/oct/22/bnp-nick-griffin-le-pen (accessed 13 November 2009).

7 Available online at: www.bbc.co.uk/bbctrust/news/press_releases/october/question_time.shtml (accessed 13 November 2009).
8 Available online at: http://news.bbc.co.uk/1/hi/entertainment/8319136.stm (accessed 13 November 2009).
9 Available online at: www.guardian.co.uk/commentisfree/2009/oct/21/question-time-bbc-bnp-griffin (accessed 13 November 2009).
10 Available online at: http://simondarby.blogspot.com/2009/10/night-before-storm.html (accessed 13 November 2009).
11 Available online at: www.liberalconspiracy.org/2009/10/30/nick-griffin-not-alone-in-qt-audience/ (accessed 13 November 2009).
12 Available online at: www.bbc.co.uk/iplayer/episode/b00nft24/Question_Time_22_10_2009/ (accessed 13 November 2009).
13 Available online at: http://simondarby.blogspot.com/2009/10/to-help-socially-engineer-multicultural.html (accessed 13 November 2009).
14 Available online at: http://news.bbc.co.uk/1/hi/uk_politics/8322322.stm (accessed 13 November 2009).
15 Available online at: www.bbc.co.uk/blogs/theeditors/2009/10/nick_griffin_on_question_time.html (accessed 13 November 2009).
16 Available online at: http://vodpod.com/watch/2419571-chairman-nick-griffins-speech-at-the-trafalgar-club-dinner (accessed 13 November 2009).
17 Available online at: www.guardian.co.uk/politics/2009/oct/23/muslim-reaction-nick-griffin (accessed 13 November 2009).
18 Available online at: www.slapnickgriffin.co.uk/ (accessed 13 November 2009).
19 The BNP was, at the time of the broadcast, subject to a legal freeze on recruitment following the EHRC court hearing, which legally bound the party not to accept any new members for a three-month period until January 2010.
20 Available online at: http://bnp.org.uk/2009/10/bnp-reaps-9000-strong-enquiries-harvest/ (accessed 13 November 2009).
21 Available online at: http://leejohnbarnes.blogspot.com/2009/10/qt-and-ethnic-middle-class-arseholes.html (accessed 13 November 2009).
22 Available online at: http://eddybutler.blogspot.com/p/questions-and-answers.html (accessed 4 July 2010).
23 Although Nick Griffin authored it, Griffin's one-time associate Mark Deavin carried out the research. On Deavin and his role within the BNP, see Copsey (2008: 74, 102–3).
24 For comparisons, refer to the Alexa analytical tool; see www.alexa.com/.
25 The leaflet reads: 'WHICH DO *YOU* FIND OFFENSIVE? A cartoon of Muhammad with a bomb for a turban OR Muslim demonstrators calling for terrorist attacks on Europe and the "extermination" of non Muslims.'
26 Chairman's Introduction, British National Party, Statement of Accounts year ended 31 December 2005, p. 5.
27 It is for this reason that Martin Webster observed cheerfully, following the loss of all ninety deposits by NF candidates in the 1974 general election: 'We were laughing all the way to the bank. Where else can you get simultaneous five minute broadcasts on the BBC and ITV for thirteen and a half grand?'; see *The Guardian*, 12 October 1974.
28 Available online at: http://news.bbc.co.uk/go/pr/fr/-/1/hi/uk_politics/3757641.stm (accessed 13 November 2009).

References

Barnes, J and Barnes, P. (1990) 'Oswald Mosley as entrepreneur', *History Today*, 40 (3): 11–16.

BNP (2005) *Rebuilding British democracy. British National Party general election 2005 manifesto*, Welshpool, Powys.

BNP (2010) *Democracy, freedom, culture and identity, British National Party general election 2010 manifesto*, Welshpool, Powys.

Copsey, N. (2003) 'Extremism on the net: the extreme right and the value of the Internet', in Gibson, R., Nixon, P. and Ward, S. (eds) *Political parties and the Internet: net gain?*, London: Routledge.

Copsey, N. (2008) *Contemporary British fascism: the British National Party and the quest for legitimacy*, 2nd edn, Basingstoke: Palgrave-Macmillan.

Dorrill, S. (2006) *Blackshirt: Oswald Mosley and British fascism*, London: Penguin.

Eatwell, R. (1998) 'The dynamics of right-wing electoral breakthrough', *Patterns of Prejudice*, 32 (3): 3–32.

Eatwell, R. (2004) 'The extreme right in Britain: the long road to modernization', in Eatwell, R. and Mudde, C. (eds) *Western democracies and the new extreme right challenge*, London: Routledge.

Ellinas, A. (2010) *The media and the far right in Western Europe*, Cambridge: Cambridge University Press.

Ferguson, R. (1998) *Representing 'race': ideology, identity and the media*, London: Arnold.

Gabriel, J. (1998) *Whitewash: racialised politics and the media*, London: Routledge.

John, P., Margetts, H., Rowland, D. and Weir, S. (2006) *The BNP: the roots of its appeal*, Essex: Democratic Audit, Human Rights Centre.

Kushner, T. (1994) 'The fascist as 'other'?: racism and neo-Nazism in contemporary Britain', *Patterns of Prejudice*, 28 (1): 27–45.

Mosley, O. (1968) *My life*, London: Nelson.

Mudde, C. (2007) *Populist radical right parties in Europe*, Cambridge: Cambridge University Press.

Renton, D. (2006) *When we touched the sky: the Anti-Nazi League 1977–1981*, Cheltenham: New Clarion Press.

Thurlow, R. (1998) *Fascism in Britain: from Oswald Mosley's Blackshirts to the National Front*, London: IB Tauris.

Troyna, B. (1980) 'The media and the electoral decline of the National Front', *Patterns of Prejudice*, 14 (3): 25–30.

Troyna, B. (1987) 'Reporting racism: the "British way of life" observed', in Husband, C. (ed.) *'Race' in Britain: continuity and change*, London: Hutchinson.

Tyndall, J. (1998) *The eleventh hour: a call for British rebirth*, 3rd rev. edn, Welling: Albion Press.

5

AMBIVALENT ADMIRATION?

The response of other extreme-right groups to the rise of the BNP

Steven Woodbridge

Introduction

The rise and nature of the British National Party (BNP) have elicited a dizzying variety of largely hostile responses from other extreme-right groups in Britain. In the early 1980s, much of this critique focused on the leadership qualities of BNP founder John Tyndall (1934–2005). After the National Front (NF) and BNP had been direct rivals in the 1983 general election, the NF's national activities organizer Martin Webster wrote angrily that Tyndall was a cynical and persistent liar and a 'pompous mini-*Duce*' who went in for 'Mosley-style' speeches and marching music (*Nationalism Today*, no. 17, 1983).

Similarly, in recent years, the question of the leadership of the BNP has re-emerged as a major bone of contention on the far-right. The management qualities and personal style of Nick Griffin, Tyndall's BNP successor, have been subjected to notably strong attack by extreme-right critics. One disgruntled far-right devotee complained on the Final Conflict website forum in March 2009: 'Griffin and his cabal have destroyed a once great Nationalist party and it's plainly obvious to see that Griffin is in league with the Synagogue of Satan.'[1]

In addition to intense personal dislike of the BNP's leaders and their political credibility, the party's ideology and policies have also come under withering scrutiny from other disciples of extreme-right philosophy, especially since Griffin took the party helm in 1999. Some activists have claimed that the BNP is no longer sufficiently racist. The chairman of the NF, for example, exclaimed in 2007: 'The BNP is no longer a genuine White Racial Nationalist Party and the National Front entirely disassociates itself from it' (*Searchlight*, no. 379, January 2007). Conversely, others have seen the BNP as *too* racist. The Freedom Party (FP), founded in 2000 by disenchanted former BNP activists, showed obvious frustration at what FP members saw as the BNP's refusal to moderate its position on race. They argued that the BNP had no real understanding of 'community politics' and was not sufficiently 'populist', and that BNP strategy consisted of little more than waiting for 'society to collapse' (*Introducing the Freedom Party,* London, 2003). On the other hand, the godfather of British neo-Nazism, Colin Jordan (1923–2009), viewed the BNP's populism and search for respectability with palpable disdain. Employing a hard-line National Socialist racial perspective, Jordan argued that the party's pursuit of power through the ballot box was 'sheer illusion' in the face of an increase in the 'coloured vote' in Britain.[2] In Jordan's estimation, Griffin was a 'Trimmer', whose 'sell-out' was succeeding only because 'those who really rule behind the window-dressing of the ballot box' were exploiting the BNP leader as a 'useful instrument' for taming the BNP (*Gothic Ripples*, December 2002). From yet another point on the extreme-right political spectrum, Ian Anderson, chairman of the now-fragmented National Democrats, stated to the media that he would not touch the BNP 'with a barge-pole' (*Searchlight,* no. 354, December 2004; London *Evening Standard*, 23 April 2007).

However, despite the apparent intense unfriendliness of other parts of the extreme right towards the BNP's leaders and policies, this chapter will argue that this animosity is not as straightforward as it may seem. Existing side by side with hostility, there has also been a marked ambivalence shaping some other extreme-right attitudes towards the BNP. At times, the relationship has been, and remains, more complex and nuanced than might first appear.

Ideological purity or the lure of populism?

As with the first wave of British fascism during the interwar period, the extreme right in Britain since 1945 has been characterized by numerous internal and public divisions. Personality clashes, factional in-fighting, party splits and breakaways, together with tensions and disagreements over ideology, have all been recurring features. Rival versions of nationalism have frequently emerged within far-right circles. British extreme-right leaders have often zealously fought to protect their own miniscule empires from would-be competitors, and Richard Thurlow's description of them as 'Sawdust Caesars' remains apt (Thurlow, 1998: 278). The recent electoral success of the BNP has merely served to further stir all these haughty emotions, creating fresh turmoil and a host of new (and usually short-lived) minor parties. Parties and groups set up by, or attracting, disillusioned former BNP members have included not just the Freedom Party but also the White Nationalist Party, the Nationalist Alliance, the Wolf's Hook White Brotherhood, the British Peoples Party, the England First Party, the Britain First Party, the Democratic Nationalists and the New Nationalist Party. Intense debates have broken out within the extreme right in Britain over the appropriate strategic response to operating within the confines of a liberal parliamentary democracy. Should there still be revolutionary confrontation with the state? Or, taking the BNP's recent electioneering strategy as a role model, should there be pragmatic adjustment to the requirements of mass electoral politics?

For some British far-right activists, the revolution versus respectability dilemma has been simple: they still prefer a revolutionary strategy. The 'political soldiers' of the International Third Position (ITP), for example, have been highly critical of the BNP's rush to be 'acceptable'. The ITP commented on their Final Conflict website in 2008: 'We don't want "change". We don't want a tweak here or a new law there. *What we need is revolution.*'[3] For others, the options have been less clear. Although they have admired aspects of the BNP's new electoral professionalism, they remain opposed to anything that smacks of ideological dilution. Good examples of this quandary could be found in the statements of the British Peoples Party, shortly after it was launched in 2005. There was talk of 'very selective involvement in elections', but also a rejection of 'moderation' in favour of the movement's 'revolution'.[4]

Since its foundation by John Tyndall, such questions have also been regularly discussed in internal BNP ideological material. In fact, the ideological purity versus electoral respectability debate, sometimes framed as the street versus ballot box dichotomy, or even simply as 'boots' versus 'suits', became a major source of friction between Tyndall, who was very reluctant to alter any aspect of his 'racial nationalist' creed, and Nick Griffin, who saw potential electoral benefits from implementing major changes to the BNP's political programme. From 1999 onwards, such disagreements on policy became deeply entwined with a major personality clash between the two obstinate protagonists (*Spearhead*, no. 427, September 2004; *Searchlight*, no. 352, October 2004).

This chapter will *not* be a detailed analysis of the BNP's ideology and policies as such, but, rather, an exploration of what 'traditional' fascists and other British extreme-right acolytes have said in their propagandistic publications about both the rise and changing nature of the BNP. Although there has been some outright opposition to the BNP from other extreme-right parties, this is not the whole story. Some groups have shown a more ambivalent and opaque response to the BNP. In order to capture a sense of the multiplicity and complexity of extreme-right reactions to the BNP, the discussion will therefore provide brief analysis of three ideological variants of the non-BNP extreme right: the Mosleyites, described here as the 'originals'; the National Front, who still see themselves as the main 'rivals'; and the racial nationalists, defined here as a loose, diverse and shifting alliance of 'disaffected' activists who remain firmly committed to a more hard-line version of racial philosophy.

The first two variants, of course, put down their roots well before the emergence of the BNP and have not reacted kindly to the 'new arrivals' on the far-right scene since 1982. The third variant has consisted mainly of those who once had high hopes for the BNP, especially under Tyndall's tenure, but have since become very disillusioned by the BNP's changing stance on race under his successor, Nick Griffin. The ideologues attached to all three of the variants discussed here have also demonstrated the most striking examples of holding two conflicting emotions at the same time: they have admired aspects of the BNP's rise, but remain critical of some key policy developments in the party. The discussion of ambivalence will also help to draw out some of the main controversies that have been at the heart of the wider extreme right's ideological responses to the BNP, such as unease over the BNP's stance on Europe, struggles over who is best placed to defend the interests of the nation, distrust of the BNP's electoral populism, and recurrent complaints by racial nationalists of BNP 'betrayal' over race and immigration.

The Mosleyites: blowing hot and cold

First, we must discuss those who can be termed the original or traditional fascists: British fascists and neo-fascists, who have had a long historical pedigree, a lineage going back to the pre-war British Union of Fascists (BUF) and post-war Union Movement (UM), and still view themselves as the original pioneers of British nationalism. What views have the followers of Sir Oswald Mosley (1896–1980) and, to coin Roger Griffin's term, contemporary Mosleyite 'groupuscules' held about the BNP since it emerged in 1982 (Griffin, 2003: 27–50)?

In general, the Mosleyites have claimed to speak with more authority about present-day extreme right-wing parties such as the BNP, and have tried to retain the intellectual high ground in far-right circles. Some of the 'originals', who were effectively finished as serious electoral contenders themselves by the early 1970s (their last major effort was in the GLC elections in London in 1970), sought instead to influence what Michael Quill termed 'the thought and feeling of all parties and organizations', and warned they would no longer take part in 'the dog-fight' of present-day politics (*Comrade*, no. 6, April 1987). Quill was confident the time would come when the mass of the British people would still turn to the ideas of Mosley.

Similarly, veteran Mosleyites hoped to permeate their ideas into wider civil society through the cultural journal *Lodestar* (1985–92), which was envisaged as an intellectual successor to Mosley's journal *The European* (1953–9). But some of the Mosleyites also held hopes of one day directly re-entering the political arena, and tended to adopt an imperious and self-righteous attitude to other, more 'lowly' extreme-right parties, such as the NF and the BNP and their leaders. In particular, a key source of disagreement with the BNP concerned the question of 'Europe'.

The Mosleyites in the 1980s were an ageing and rapidly diminishing band, initially clustered around a group of die-hard UM loyalists. Although they strongly denied it, in many ways they remained old-style fascists, full of nostalgia for 'The Leader', and they viewed the new BNP with lofty distaste. Indeed, within a few months of the formation of the BNP in 1982, the Mosleyite Action Society (which was in reality the Mosley Directorate/Secretariat, effectively under the control of former UM officers Jeffrey Hamm and Robert Row) offered a largely hostile assessment of John Tyndall and his new party. They particularly focused on what they believed was the BNP's insular stance towards the world beyond Britain's borders.

In the November 1982 edition of their monthly journal *Action*, Hamm and Row acknowledged Tyndall's overriding concern for Britain and its interests. On the other hand, they were clearly upset with certain elements of the new BNP's political programme, specifically the NF-style emphasis on opposition to Europe. The *Action* article warned 'Beware of false prophets', especially 'those who are not living in the modern world'. Running through their article was a snobbish but grudging respect for Tyndall's nationalist political philosophy, but also deep alarm at how the BNP's foreign policy objectives potentially conflicted with the European dimension originally promoted by Mosley through his post-war creed of 'Europe a nation'. The *Action* editors noted: 'Tyndall is a nationalist. His slogan is "Nationalists of Britain, unite". Let us say from the start that we are all for nationalism – providing it leads forward and not back to the distant past' (*Action,* no. 305, November 1982).

This deep suspicion of the BNP's overt anti-Europeanism continued within the official remnants of the UM and the Mosley Secretariat for the next twenty or so years, first through the journal *Action* (which folded with the death of Jeffrey Hamm in 1992), and then through *Comrade*, the increasingly irregular publication of the Friends of Oswald Mosley (FOM). The FOM, founded in 1982, considered the NF and BNP to be 'racist thugs' and, according to one Mosleyite in 1995, 'We reckon we're a cut above them'. The organization saw itself as 'quietly superior, the aristocracy of the far right' (Francis Beckett: 'Still following the leader', *Independent on Sunday*, 24 December 1995). In fact, the BNP was rarely directly referred to in early FOM publications, even though Mosleyites and BNP members shared an interest in issues such as a critique of immigration levels and frustration with the mainstream establishment parties, and some senior BNP members attended FOM social events (*Searchlight*, no. 248, February 1996). Yet it was not just a case of outright ideological hostility towards the BNP. With the electoral success of the party in the early years of the new century, the tone of the FOM moderated. The FOM became more ambivalent towards the BNP and, at times, even cordial.

Admiring the struggle? Mosleyite assessments in the new century

The FOM group was primarily a dining club and social network for old Mosleyites. It had no formal membership, and on average could attract only about one hundred people to its annual commemorative dinners (*Comrade*, no. 48, February 1998). However, the younger supporters still retained a close interest in contemporary extreme-right politics, including the electoral fortunes of the BNP. In a 2001 issue of FOM's *Action News*, for example, the Mosleyites touched on the recent summer race tensions in the north of England. FOM argued that the large percentage of votes for the BNP in Oldham and Burnley in the 2001 general election were cast because the BNP 'provided an opportunity for White people to give vent to their frustrations through the ballot box'. Always on the lookout for grandiose historical parallels, *Action News* also claimed that the BNP line echoed the 'Votes Not Violence' campaign mounted by Mosley and the UM following the Notting Hill riots of 1958, which, the journal argued, had influenced the Immigration Act of 1962 (*Action News*, August 2001).

As the Griffinite BNP gained further electoral support, the FOM expressed satisfaction at how this was, in their estimation, part of a more general and welcome rise of the extreme right throughout Europe. In May 2002, *Action News*, dissecting these trends, claimed that: 'The establishment in Britain and elsewhere has been plunged into a frenzy of hysteria and disbelief at the recent successes of the BNP, Front National and similar parties throughout Europe.' Editor Rob Smyth then offered the following assessment of the BNP: 'Their performance, which is matched in other countries, is very heartening', and he proclaimed: 'An antibody is now in the system, gradually attacking the poisons and conditioning of the new world order'.

However, at the same time, this admiration and positive appraisal of the BNP's success were still tempered with a very cautious tone. Indeed, in relation to the BNP and other such right-wing parties, Smyth argued that the 'big question mark' over many of these parties was that they 'seem to have only half an ideology – nationalism'. Apart from that component, he complained, 'their policies are populist and conservative, constructed on the hoof with no underlying ideas threading them together'. Smyth warned that this was leading to pressure to change policies for short-term advantage. Pointing to Austria and Italy, he complained about how policies were being 'watered down' by far-right parties to gain respectability, and he counselled, evidently with the BNP in mind: 'We hope that other nationalist parties do not go the same way' (*Action News,* May 2002).

This ambivalence towards the emergence and nature of the BNP during the last twenty-eight years can also be detected in the publications of two other variants of contemporary Mosleyism: the secretive group the League of St. George (LSG) and the relatively new European Action (EA) pressure group. Seen by some as an elite or vanguard pro-Nazi organization, the LSG was originally founded in 1974 by frustrated members of the Union Movement who, while still loyal to Sir Oswald and his policies, wanted a more ideological and pro-active approach to contemporary politics. In 1976, for example, the League stated that they honoured 'National Socialism' and looked forward to the day when the creed would form the foundation of 'a new unity of Europe' (*Searchlight,* no. 87, September 1982). Like the UM, the LSG was resolutely dedicated to Mosley's concept of a united Europe or 'Third Force' in the world, and fervently hoped that other parts of the British extreme right would eventually convert to this vision. As its new website put it in early 2008: 'The League has never aimed to be a political party but more of a lobby group to influence and encourage established nationalist parties to embrace the *Europe a Nation* philosophy.'[5]

Although the LSG hoped it could change John Tyndall's views on the issue of Europe,[6] the veteran ideologue remained determined to pursue a strong anti-EEC line in the 1980s and 1990s, and this antagonism towards European institutions was maintained by Nick Griffin in the twenty-first century. In fact, Griffin's Europhobia increased markedly when he became one of two BNP Members of the European Parliament in 2009. The League, however, despite its obvious disappointment with the BNP's policy on Europe, took a more conciliatory view of Tyndall and Griffin's philosophy when it came to general domestic politics. The pre-eminent LSG message was the need to avoid schisms within nationalism, especially in the BNP. As *League Sentinel* put it in 2005, this is because they believe that: 'In electoral terms, the party is the best chance, at the moment, for Britons to regain control of our country' (*League Sentinel*, no. 64, 2005).

The LSG has seemingly decided that encouraging the BNP in the electoral field is a more important priority than trying to persuade the party to become more 'European' in outlook. One reason for this is that most of the original founders of the League have either died or moved on, and the people who now run the LSG view the BNP with much more sympathy and, at times, clear admiration (Edwards, 2008: 32–3), while the LSG's officers have become more adept at publicity (*Blood and Honour*, no. 42, 2009). It is also important to recognize that the League now shares much of the BNP's obsessive fears about Islam in Europe and the West (*League Sentinel*, no. 74, 2008; no. 78, 2009).

Timidity on the issue of the BNP's relationship to Europe has not been present in the EA group, another strand of Mosleyism. This small Mosleyite variant espouses its views in the newspaper *European Action*, launched in 2005. EA appears to have inherited part of the legacy of the FOM organization and, having also taken on a *groupuscular* form, wants to repackage Mosley's ideas for a younger generation of activists. The EA newspaper/group has asserted that it is 'post-fascist' and claims that fascist and neo-Nazi organizations such as the League of St. George have misunderstood Mosley's post-war attempt to move beyond left and right to create a distinct European vision (*European Action*, no. 18, September–October 2008).

Furthermore, EA has become highly critical of what it sees as the 'narrow' nationalism of certain extreme-right parties in Europe, including the BNP. When surveying the British right-wing political landscape, and in marked contrast to the conciliatory strategy of the LSG, EA has eschewed any idea of trying to unite all British nationalists in common political endeavour. In early 2007, its leading ideologue Robert Edwards, a former West London area UM organizer, commented dismissively:

> Some people are under the misapprehension that there is something called 'the nationalist movement' and that we all ought to be brothers and comrades under that political generic umbrella. We have known for long that there is no such fraternity and that wide differences of ideology will always prevent such a bonding.
>
> (*European Action*, no. 8, January–February 2007)

This attitude has inexorably shaped EA's general perspective on the BNP. From the outset, the EA group made it abundantly clear that Mosley's European vision underpinned their whole political philosophy and they had no time for 'reactionary' versions of nationalism (*European Action*, no. 1, November–December 2005; no. 5, July–August 2006). This message was also repeated in an article on the group designed to raise the EA's profile among explicitly National Socialist activists (*Blood and Honour,* no. 41, 2009). Yet, despite this strong line, and intense dislike of BNP leader Nick Griffin, EA has still provided space to BNP supporters in the letters pages of its newspaper (*European Action*, no. 19, November–December 2008). Edwards has proffered one or two olive branches to grass-roots BNP members, commenting at one point: 'At least they have the moral courage to commit themselves to what they consider to be a patriotic cause' (*European Action*, no. 20, January–February 2009).

The National Front: defending the nationalist brand?

We must now turn to a second main source of extreme-right ambivalence towards, and criticism of, the BNP and explore the tensions and rivalries that have erupted over which party of the far-right is the main rival to the BNP and thus the legitimate defender of 'race and nation'. As we noted at the outset, various small parties (consisting largely of former BNP activists) have all tried to assume such a role, with very mixed results. The England First Party (EFP), for example, which gained two local council seats in Blackburn in May 2006, saw a small trickle of disillusioned BNP activists defect to its ranks, much to the irritation of Griffin and his officers, but the EFP seemed incapable of mounting anything more than limited regional challenges to the BNP in local elections and quickly lost momentum. By 2007, its membership was no more than thirty-nine, with an additional ninety-seven 'supporting' members (*Searchlight*, no. 379, January 2007). The British Peoples Party (BPP) also stood a few candidates in the 2006 local elections, but this was more for publicity purposes rather than in any firm expectation that they could damage the BNP in direct electoral competition. Again, the BPP's membership has stood at little more than thirty to fifty in recent years (*Searchlight*, no. 379, January 2007; no. 391, January 2008).

No other party on the extreme right appeared capable of offering any serious organized threat to the BNP on a national scale. The contemporary National Front, however, still believes this mantle remains solely with itself, and that the BNP are usurpers on the nationalist scene. Rather like the Mosleyites, the NF emphasizes its members' self-proclaimed historical qualifications as long-term survivors who have kept the 'flame' pure. The NF argues that the BNP's success is faddish and 'temporary' and that, sooner or later, people will turn back to the NF, which, in the Front's estimation, remains a more dependable and authentic extreme-right party.[7] As far as the NF is concerned, the BNP has betrayed the nation and 'sold out' to the British establishment, especially since the advent of Nick Griffin to the leadership. One NF writer made this plain in the Front's newspaper, *The Flame*, in 2001:

> We in the National Front have felt for some time that the new leaders of the BNP are more interested in getting themselves elected, than fighting the nation's cause. During the past year we have received many letters from BNP members worried about the watering down of their party's policies.
>
> (*The Flame*, Oldham Riots Special Issue, 2001)

Yet, as we shall see, the NF has also displayed signs of ambivalence towards their fellow nationalists in the BNP. As the anti-fascist magazine *Searchlight* has pointed out, the National Front 'was once the "brand name" of British fascism and dominated the far right'. In *Searchlight*'s view, 'those days are long gone' and, since the 1980s, the NF 'has been completely eclipsed by the BNP' (*Searchlight*, no. 379, January 2007). Although this is a largely accurate assessment, the NF is still breathing and, in significant ways, articulates in 'micro' form some of the anxieties about the BNP held by other critics on the far-right. It is also important to recall that, during the course of the 1980s, there was a titanic struggle on the fringes of the extreme right between the NF and BNP, for the loyalty of activists and for what Nigel Copsey has appropriately called the 'ideological soul' of British nationalism (Copsey, 2008: 29). One inside account, commenting on this period, claimed that: 'The NF hated the BNP and vice versa' (Hepple, 1993: 4). A significant aspect of this struggle was a fight over the actual term 'National' and, at one point in 1982, Tyndall even contemplated naming his new party the 'National Party', which provides us with a useful insight into how certain conceptual labels can assume a sacrosanct configuration in extreme-right discourse. In some ways, albeit in minor form, this intense ideological tussle between the NF and BNP continues today.

The contemporary version of the NF can trace its origins to the mid 1990s. At that juncture, membership was languishing at 600, and some of the leadership decided the actual name 'National Front' held too many negative associations in the eyes of the public; they also began to look enviously at how extreme-right parties elsewhere in Europe were successfully 're-inventing' themselves through party name-changes in their search for legitimacy and growth. Consequently, in July 1995, the NF experienced yet another schism, with one faction of about 300 members, led by Ian Anderson, renaming itself the National Democrats, while the other (minority) faction retained the 'NF' brand name. Ironically, it is the latter group that has managed to survive. As it currently stands, the NF is a significantly smaller, more fragmented and less coherent party than the BNP, existing rather precariously in the shadow of Griffin's now much larger and more successful organization. Precise figures are hard to find but, in terms of membership numbers, in 2007 it was estimated the NF had approximately 100–150 members (*Searchlight*, no. 379, January 2007). Party accounts submitted to the Electoral Commission in the same year also indicated the national membership numbered about 150. The NF's annual Remembrance Day march and parade in London, a key public event for the party, saw attendance drop to as low as thirty people in 2007, and although this figure recovered to 300 in 2008, the Front's ability to rally its small national membership remains notably weak (*Searchlight*, no. 414, December 2009). During the course of 2009, for example, average attendance at NF regional branch meetings was between twenty and fifty members, and the NF's Remembrance Day march in November 2009 could muster only 150–200 supporters. Nevertheless, the NF has still been able, at times, to be a real thorn in the side of the BNP, at both the ideological and electoral levels. In fact, this became evident shortly after the NF's damaging 1995 internal split, when signs of renewed activity indicated that some NF activists were quickly recovering their confidence and, moreover, were determined to show they could still fly their flag, despite the increasing public awareness of the BNP. In 1997–8, for example, when the BNP tried to tap into the disparate waves of discontent being expressed at the Countryside Alliance marches, NF activists also appeared at those events. On the 1998 march, when BNP members distributed copies of a new publication entitled *The British countryman* (edited by Nick Griffin) and also handed out copies of a leaflet urging shoppers to 'Buy British beef', the NF distributed its own rival leaflets carrying very similar themes.[8]

Although there has been evidence of NF and BNP supporters occasionally working together at street level and in local elections (*Searchlight*, no. 402, December 2009; no. 420, June 2010) and of attending the same meetings dedicated to the memory of John Tyndall,[9] the BNP's national officers have generally been very unhappy about such activity, fearing it might damage the BNP's new respectability agenda. Griffin's lieutenants have carried out purges of some of the remaining Tyndallites in the party, anxious they might have secret sympathies with the NF or with other 'white nationalist' groups such as the BPP, and some of these 'purged' activists have indeed found sanctuary in the NF (*Searchlight,* no. 386, August 2007). What they have discovered, however, is a party with poor organization, a lack of resources and a very static 'racial' creed. Moreover, in contrast to the Griffinite BNP, the NF has remained chiefly wedded to a 1970s-style confrontational strategy of street marches and public protests, something the BNP now appears to regard as vulgar and not part of 'modern' nationalism (see *Identity*, no. 21, June 2002; no. 66, May 2006). In an audacious use of terminology, and in order to reinforce the BNP's claims to be a reformed party, Griffin has gleefully derided the Front as a 'neo-fascist organization', conveniently excising the story of his own formative origins in the NF (*Searchlight*, no. 379, January 2007).

For a long period, the tiny NF was held together by Terry Blackham, who viewed the BNP with open contempt and sought to keep the NF alive and active through both street marches and occasional forays into local elections. 'Race' was often a principal ideological theme underpinning this strategy. The late 1990s, for example, saw the NF take the lead among British extreme-right groups by organizing a series of street protests and marches against 'East European' asylum seekers (*The Flame*, no. 10, 1999). A succession of NF marches in the southern coastal towns of England, such as one in Dover in November 1997, were designed to raise local tensions over race and immigration, but also to remind the public and the broader extreme right that the NF was still active and that the much larger BNP did not have a monopoly on nationalism. The NF also sought to stir up local community tensions and gain further publicity in Oldham, in Greater Manchester, in May 2001, much to the alarm of the BNP, who felt the Front was intruding on natural BNP territory. When Griffin announced his intent to stand as a candidate in Oldham West and Royton, the NF declared it would also field its own candidates in the area. At one point, the NF transported fifty members into Oldham from London and Birmingham to attempt a march (the police promptly escorted them out again), and a smaller number of NF activists carried out extensive door-to-door leafleting. The Ritchie Report on the Oldham disturbances noted the NF gained 'significant publicity' from the media through its activities in the town (Ritchie, 2001: 70). Tellingly, following the summer 2001 'race riots' in Oldham, Burnley and Bradford, there was a rise in NF street activity, paid for by a slight increase in NF members and funds as a result of the tensions.

The NF has also endeavoured, on occasions, to exploit or even out-manoeuvre the BNP's 'law and order' platform in other areas of BNP growth in the north of England. Again, this has usually exhibited a racial dimension. In Manchester in 2005, for example, the NF began a leafleting campaign in a ward with notable crime problems by trying to recruit new members for what they termed the 'White Shields', or citizen anti-crime patrols. The leaflets, if genuine, were quite instructive about the NF's view of the BNP at local level. Referring to 'the softy BNP', the leaflets noted that BNP members thought they had done well in the area 'due to the softening of their repatriation policy (sell-out in our view)', and said, with public support, the NF would prove the BNP wrong.[10]

Frontism today: reclaiming the nationalist brand?

NF support and momentum nationally have ebbed and flowed, with great variation across the country and no consistent pattern. The NF has suffered financial problems and more bouts of in-fighting in recent years, especially in 2007, when Blackham left the party (*Searchlight*, no. 387, September 2007; no. 390, December 2007), and again in 2009–10. On the other hand, despite these internal tensions, the latest incarnation of the NF has managed to stay afloat and has occasionally acted as a magnet to disgruntled former members of the BNP, including some whose election campaigning skills were honed in that party, such as Ian Edward, former organizer of the BNP's North West London branch (who eventually became the new NF chairman in early 2010), and, in 2006, Tess Culnane, a former BNP European elections candidate.

Culnane's defection to the NF was viewed with particular pleasure by NF members.[11] However, by early 2009, she had rejoined the BNP. The BNP leadership evidently decided there were certain veterans with populist appeal who they could ill-afford to have on the outside of the party in a crucial elections year. There was also BNP concern that, compared with the Blackham period, the NF was beginning to adopt a glossier and more coherent electoral strategy, seeking to muscle in on potential BNP voting territory in the run-up to the 2009 European and local elections. Indeed, the NF has recently made new efforts to move into the electoral field and compete more directly with the BNP for the 'respectable' nationalist vote. This has seen some limited success. There was, for example, new confidence on display in the NF as a result of unexpectedly high votes for the five NF candidates who stood for election to the London Assembly in May 2008, two of whom saved their deposits. The Front's newspaper, *The Flame*, excitedly proclaimed this as the party's 'Best results in 30 Years', adding: 'We can take great heart in the eventual goal of winning our country back' (*The Flame*, no. 30, 2009). The NF also fielded seventeen candidates in the 2010 general election and eighteen candidates in the 2010 local elections, but none of these posed any major challenge to the BNP's own campaigns (*Searchlight*, no. 420, June 2010). During the course of early 2009, there were also clear indications of a major internal reorganization of the NF, with the creation of a new website and what the Front grandiosely termed new publicity and elections 'departments'. Again, this appeared to be further evidence of the NF adopting some techniques from the BNP's more professional electoral model. In addition, Tom Linden, a former Harrogate BNP organizer, who became the revamped NF's media spokesman, claimed in November 2009 that the Front's new weekly electronic news bulletin, *National Front News*, had reached a circulation of over 4,000. He argued 'the future looks very bright for us', adding the NF was 'a political phoenix' rising again 'from a once raging fire', showing drive and enthusiasm.[12] This new determination to sharpen up the NF's operation and political impact culminated in a 'palace coup' against the ageing NF leadership staged by younger members in early 2010, with an interesting number of these 'young Turks' being former BNP members (*Searchlight*, no. 418, April 2010).

Nevertheless, it would be a mistake to interpret this as wholesale BNP-style modernization. Despite more emphasis on better organization and more professional communication, the Front's core creed remains unaltered. In fact, it is at the ideological level where the NF has been most at loggerheads with the BNP in recent years, and the party has tried hard to carve out a distinctive nationalist and 'racial' position on the broad extreme-right spectrum in Britain. A letter in the NF newspaper, *The Flame*, in 1998 expressed this well. The author was heavily critical of the BNP, asserting: 'Our duty as members of the National Front is to maintain our independence and integrity', and argued the NF's task was to emerge 'as the main patriotic movement' in Britain. The letter added: 'The vagaries of the Nationalist political complex may sway this way or that, but we intend that the final victory which emerges will be that of our own National Front – and only the National Front!' (*The Flame*, no. 8, 1998).

Similarly, in an NF 'Questions and answers' document, the Front's claims to be a distinctive party were set out explicitly in Section 10, entitled 'Myths about the National Front'. In answer to question 87: 'Are you the same as the British National Party, you've got the same policies haven't you?', the NF's response stated: 'No, the BNP is a totally separate organization with its own policies/agenda'. Although the NF conceded some of its views were similar, the statement emphasized that 'the BNP do not have a compulsory repatriation policy like the NF has and our party chairman isn't on an ego trip'.[13]

Moreover, despite the effort to engage in a more professional electoral strategy, at the same time the NF has remained keen to describe itself as a 'racial nationalist' party, asserting that: 'The National Front is a political movement based on the principle of racial nationalism', and its current leadership still openly adheres to what it has called the 'philosophy' of 'racial nationalism', which 'involves pride in one's own race and nation . . .' (Section 2, questions 17 and 21, in: 'National Front: 100 questions and answers'). Such language is designed to reassure potential supporters that, in contrast to the BNP's Griffinite policy of ethno-nationalism, the NF retains authentic and unchanged racial principles.

Another favourite NF ideological tactic, devised to put clear water between itself and Griffin's party, has been a renewed attempt to wrestle the 'National' label back from the BNP. In 2003, for example, *The Flame* urged people to 'Join the NF, a "Real" British Nationalist Party' (*The Flame*, no. 21, 2003). Again, in 2007, no doubt to reinforce their claim to be the original brand on the nationalist landscape, the NF, both in its newspaper and on its website, capitalized strongly on the fortieth anniversary of the creation of the original Front in 1967. Rather like the Mosleyites, the NF was eager to play the longevity card. In one typical piece in *The Flame*, the writer pointed out to readers that the NF 'is the longest serving national party in the UK and the only one which truly represents the British nation'. In an obvious jibe at the BNP, the author claimed that the NF 'has stuck rigidly to its original principles, without compromising itself to our nation's enemies in return for an easy time' (*The Flame*, no. 28, 2007). Predictably, this message was repeated in mid 2009, when the NF's relaunched website carried the following boast from an NF stalwart: 'After 42 years we are the best known Nationalist party in Europe. Everyone has heard of the NF.'[14]

Crucially, however, despite all the above, and in a fashion similar to some Mosleyite assessments, the current NF has also displayed, at times, a notably complex 'dual' posture towards the BNP in its ideological output since the mid 1990s. On the one hand, NF activists have tried to ensure that the Front is in a strong position to take full advantage of any internal wrangles within the BNP and mop up any disaffected members of Griffin's party. This was particularly the case after Griffin was forced to change the membership criteria of the BNP's constitution in November 2009 to comply with the Equalities Bill. Capitalizing on this, when three BNP members defected to the NF in December 2009, the NF's website carried the defectors' explanatory statement, which included the question: 'What is the point of the BNP if you admit foreigners?'.[15] On the other hand, some BNP policy themes have been looked at with close interest by the NF's ideologues in recent years.

In early 2008, for example, the London section of the NF placed a 'Message to the disillusioned' on its website, which undoubtedly sought to exploit the tension and discontent within the larger BNP that had broken out in late 2007, especially among some of Griffin's elected councillors. The NF's statement told potential BNP defectors that it was 'absolutely imperative' that they stayed within 'Nationalist politics, whether it be within your current party or elsewhere'. It urged such people not to drop out or give up. But perhaps the most significant part of the NF's message to the elected councillors among any potential BNP dropouts was the Front's advice that they should at least continue with 'community politics'. The NF's statement suggested that: 'If you continue the community politics within your wards (regardless of what nationalist party you represent), you will achieve the desired/increased vote necessary for victory.' However, at the same time, the message still urged all 'sincere nationalists' to join the NF, pointing out the NF 'is another vehicle to further our cause to save our race and nation'.[16]

The NF's reference to 'community politics' was subtly revealing, as it indicated that the Front's key activists were increasingly recognizing the value of BNP-style localized electioneering to disseminate their policy ideas and perhaps sought to emulate such tactics. Moreover, the NF was intent on somehow detaching 'genuine' nationalists within the BNP from their 'corrupt' leaders, a message increasingly returned to by the NF's new officers.[17] It is also a refrain that has been expressed regularly by other ideologues on the extreme right, especially by those who set up the White Nationalist Party in 2002, then later the *Spearhead* Support Group, and eventually formed the BPP.[18] Unsurprisingly, in 2010, the NF began to emphasize how John Tyndall was 'now its spiritual leader', putting his photographic image on to the party's website.[19]

The racial nationalists: rallying the disaffected?

A third main source of both criticism and ambivalence towards the BNP has emerged through a strand of far-right ideology and activism that has been termed 'racial nationalism'. In essence, racial nationalism purports to be a form of nationalism where the 'nation' is defined in terms of race, genetics and biological determinism. This discourse has ranged from the 'moderate' and less intense version articulated by the NF, which, after all, still wants to engage in a form of 'respectable' electioneering, through to the more explicit criticisms of the BNP espoused by parties that merely dabble with electioneering and prefer strongly to proclaim their belief in 'white nationalism' or 'national socialism', such as the BPP (which has recently adopted the late Colin Jordan as its spiritual mentor) and the November 9th Society (N9S). It culminates in the ideas of hard-line groups that draw their inspiration directly from National Socialist racial philosophy and fantasize about revolution and 'race war'. The main theme voiced by all these activists is a critique of the BNP's adoption of the trappings of mainstream politics at the apparent expense of a commitment to 'race'. Kevin Quinn, leader of the tiny N9S, exemplified this attitude when he dismissed the BNP in 2006 as 'Conservatives on steroids' (*Jewish Chronicle,* 17 November 2006).

Defence of 'race and nation' can still act as a major litmus test of a leader's credibility for many such far-right activists, and, since 1999, BNP leader Griffin has been increasingly viewed as having failed this test by the 'white nationalist' and openly neo-Nazi factions on the British extreme right (Sykes, 2005: 147–8). The BNP's adoption of 'ethno-nationalism' in 2006, with a new emphasis on cultural identity rather than racial hierarchy, was received with particular dismay by racial nationalists (*Searchlight*, no. 367, January 2006), and this consternation was reinforced by the BNP's change to its membership criteria in 2009 to allow members from the ethnic minorities to join the party (*Searchlight*, no. 414, December 2009; no. 418, April 2010).

Criticism of the BNP's stance on race has sometimes gone hand-in-hand with more complex reactions. A good example of NF ambivalence towards the BNP on the issue of race was the NF website's notably sympathetic coverage of Simone Clarke, who was a leading ballerina for the English National Ballet but, after an undercover investigation by *The Guardian* newspaper, was also revealed to be a member of the BNP. The NF, shaping its coverage through a racial perspective, argued that 'Marxists and Zionists' had hounded Miss Clarke, and 'no doubt' had 'an African or Asian ballerina already lined up to take the lead in future "English" National Ballet productions'. According to the NF, the lesson here was that: 'The aim of left-wing movements is to wipe out the white British nation, while humiliating it in the process'. Moreover, Clarke's 'half-caste' child with her former partner was not her own fault, but was down to 'too few' of her parents' generation taking the trouble 'to counter the nation-wrecking and genocidal propaganda which was being broadcast'. However, despite this outbreak of NF sympathy for Clarke, the Front could not resist a side-swipe at Richard Barnbrook, her new BNP boyfriend at the time. In the NF's view, Barnbrook had used a 'watered down version of the original BNP policy' on mixed marriages, and had even later retracted this statement. In the Front's estimation, Barnbrook 'will not help us win our country back by collapsing into bleatings of surrender whenever he comes up against the enemy'.[20]

Significantly, when the NF was reorganized in 2009, despite the party's move towards greater BNP-style electoral professionalism, a new statement entitled 'Who stands for Britain?' re-emphasized the party's continuing ideological commitment to white nationalism, which suggested that a 'boots' versus 'suits' type of debate was still taking place in the party. The article asserted there was to be 'no weakening' on the key issues of immigration and multiracialism, and that repatriation remained paramount. The NF was urged not to discard the symbols and slogans of a 'white nationalist' movement, because the party's basic principles are 'immutable – they cannot be changed!'. Referring to the reactions of the 'populist brigade' in the party, the authors asserted that the NF should be proud to stand tall and defend Britain's whites.[21]

The NF critique of BNP racial policy has been shared strongly by other veteran activists on the broader British extreme right, who also emphasize 'immutable' principles on race. In particular, much of this discontent centred for a while on the 'Tyndall loyalists', an uneasy and highly schismatic alliance of activists who all looked back with longing on John Tyndall's leadership of the BNP and his apparent greater commitment to deterministic racial doctrine. Through the *Spearhead* Support Group and e-bulletins such as *Nationalist Week*, the Tyndallistas tried to persuade the former BNP leader formally to break with the BNP and found a new 'White Nationalist' party, but he was adamant this would be a mistake (*Spearhead*, no. 434, April, 2005).

The mantra of the Tyndall loyalists and other associated activists who were very disillusioned with the BNP was an almost religious adherence to the so-called 'fourteen words' ('we must secure the existence of our people and a future for white children'), a phrase invented by the American neo-Nazi David Lane (1938–2007), a member of the infamous group The Order, and this has continued to function as a kind of rallying phrase for many of those who argue that the Griffinite BNP, in its relentless drive for votes and mainstream respectability, has lost touch with its original 'racial nationalist' ideological roots. This type of critique can especially be seen in the prolific writings of Eddy Morrison, who has been a member of a whole series of extreme-right groups during his career.[22]

One of the most prominent indicators of far-right ideological disaffection with the BNP regarding 'race' was the reaction to Griffin's apparent softening of the BNP's hostility to Israel and the Jewish community. This created numerous complaints on far-right Internet forums (especially by British extreme-right contributors to the United States-based neo-Nazi 'Stormfront' site) and, as far as many non-BNP activists were concerned, was irrefutable evidence that the BNP had 'sold out' to ZOG (the 'Zionist Occupation Government'). The acronym 'ZOG' is conspiratorial shorthand for the claim that liberal democracy is subject to underhand Jewish control. Such a view of the BNP's new approach was exemplified in statements by the International Third Position groupuscule. The ITP argued that the BNP 'has been openly courting the Jewish vote and pumping out material which confirms what most of us knew years ago: the BNP has become a multi-racist, Zionist, queer-tolerant anti-Muslim pressure group'.[23]

In similar vein, Griffin's critics have sought directly to link the BNP's electoral strategy to the hidden hand of 'ZOG'. The BPP, for example, noted in 2006 that the 'big buzzword' in nationalist circles was 'respectability', but asked provocatively: 'What in the final analysis is this "respectability"? It is another word for acceptance'. In the BPP's estimation, respectability in reality meant acceptance by the media, acceptance by the establishment and 'Acceptance by ZOG!'. According to the BPP, white people on the sharp end of 'the struggle' in the front-line inner cities 'do not give a damn' about who is respectable or not: 'They want to back a party which is tough, no nonsense, doesn't hide the truth and stands up for them. They want a party that puts white people first'.[24] Likewise, in 2007, the BPP placed an article on the Internet entitled 'You choose! BNP or BPP?'. This consisted of two stark columns comparing BNP policy with that of the BPP and invited nationalist activists to decide which party placed the 'white people' first. The article claimed the BNP were 'pro-Zionist', supported Israel and offered no support to Holocaust revisionists, whereas, in contrast, the BPP believed 'World Zionism to be the root cause of many of the world's problems', considered Israel to be a 'bandit' state and were 'pro-revisionist'. It also alleged the BNP had 'no other strategy but constantly standing in elections as the way to power', whereas the BPP had a 'planned phased strategy to achieve power' and promised: 'No grovelling in the dirt for a handful of votes at the risk of what we believe in'.[25]

The same message of profound disaffection with the BNP over the subject of 'race' was also contained in an important BPP-sponsored text by Eddy Morrison, a former BNP activist who was for a while a leading light in the BPP. In his autobiographical *Memoirs of a street soldier*, distributed originally through the BPP,

Morrison gave an inside account of life in the BNP and attacked what he saw as the 'radical policy shifts' that Griffin had initiated in the party. He claimed that this was why he had left the party in disgust. He argued that Griffin was a 'chameleon type character', and bemoaned that 'to sacrifice our very basic Racialist beliefs for the sake of a handful of crumbs from ZOG's table in the shape of a few Council seats and votes was out of the question' (Morrison, 2005: 48–9).

Some of the most negative and outspoken criticisms of the BNP's contemporary stance on race have been expressed, however, by activists who still very much locate themselves on the explicit National Socialist and 'revolutionary' side of the 'boots' versus 'suits' ideological divide. In particular, the damning comments of Steve Cartwright, of the Scottish wing of the Blood and Honour movement, have been disseminated extensively on far-right Internet discussion forums and especially among a diverse range of openly neo-Nazi groupuscules. In early 2008, in response to Griffin's annual 'New Year message', Cartwright complained bitterly about the BNP leader's 'Stalin-like' purging of people in his party and argued that the 'corrupt Griffin is in danger of destroying all the good work the Party has achieved over the last few years'. As far as Cartwright was concerned, 'Nowadays Griffin much prefers to surround himself with Yes men, Kosher flag-wavers and sexual degenerates than serious, racial militants.' Cartwright was once close to Griffin. He had first met him in the mid 1990s and claimed that, at the time, Griffin pushed all the right buttons, 'emphasising militancy as well as paying due respect to the nationalists and National Socialists of the past'. While Griffin spoke, even at this point, of the need to repackage and modernize the BNP, Cartwright and his National Socialist colleagues nevertheless felt that Griffin kept the militants 'on side' and was a 'kindred spirit'. This was reinforced by Griffin's anti-Semitic writings. Cartwright revealed: 'When "Who are the mindbenders?" was published we thought "Our man" had balls'. However, Cartwright then alleged that, in due course, he began to see the writing on the wall. Griffin's 'political Ju-Jitsu' apparently made Cartwright and others increasingly uncomfortable. Thus, in Cartwright's estimation: 'Over the last few years Griffin has made a headlong flight from genuine racial nationalism' and 'has betrayed many of the people who helped get him where he is today in the BNP'. Not mincing his words, Cartwright proclaimed that, in his opinion, Griffin 'is a traitor, a liar and a charlatan. He is the perfect example of power corrupting and absolute power corrupting absolutely'.[26] There is some evidence that Griffin has courted such condemnation from the more extreme groups as part of his legitimation strategy. Tellingly, in 2009, the media-savvy BNP leader argued in a newspaper interview: 'The BNP has changed enormously, and in the course of changing enormously I've made myself literally the most unpopular person with Britain's neo-Nazis in the entire world' (*Independent On Sunday*, 14 June 2009).

Staying with the hard-liners, even where there is much less ambivalence towards the BNP, pragmatism and a 'peg on the nose' attitude have still influenced the stance of some racial nationalists when it comes to the question of whether or not to vote for the BNP. Despite a loathing for Griffin, the recognition that even a 'watered-down' BNP could still damage the hated mainstream political parties arguably moulds this rather contradictory inclination. Prior to the 2009 European elections, for example, Eddy Morrison, who had rejoined the NF but still very much identified with the overt racial-nationalist strand of far-right philosophy, revealed: 'I have spoken to a good number of non-aligned white nationalists recently and despite the fact we are not members we will be voting BNP. Let's hope this tremendous effort gives ZOG a real shock to its rotten core!'[27] Even the Blood and Honour movement, hardly a friend of the BNP, urged its supporters to 'get out and vote in June' as a BNP seat 'in the cash cow of Europe' could 'finance our defence for all we hold dear' (*Blood and Honour*, no. 42, 2009).

Conclusion

As we noted at the outset, the extreme right in Britain has been characterized by numerous rival versions of nationalism, and even within extremist groups it is clear there are 'centrists' as well as 'radicals', and this has been evident in the ideological variants discussed here. The groups analysed above all claim to be the authentic defenders of British identity, and, in turn, this has invariably shaped how they have viewed the rise, policy changes and general activities of the BNP. Brief case-study examination of just three far-right ideological strands in operation since the rise of the BNP (the originals, the rivals and the disaffected) helps to capture in condensed form some of the wider praise, ambivalence and criticisms made of the BNP by numerous other ideologues on the far-right. Exploration of how these extreme-right ideologues and activists have responded to the growth and nature of the BNP points to recurrent patterns in general extreme-right views of the party.

Thus, although in some ways the parties and groupuscules scrutinized here do not sit comfortably with other extreme-right groups and their philosophies, in other important ways they *share* views when it comes to their complex and ambivalent responses to the BNP's leaders and their discursive verdicts on the BNP's ideology. In particular, the recent policy changes and electoral progress under Griffin's stewardship of the BNP have placed the extreme-right activists considered here in an acute political dilemma: do they persist in holding the BNP at arm's length (the FOM stance), or provide open encouragement to fellow nationalists (the LSG attitude), or continue fiercely to snipe at the BNP from the sidelines (the EA position)? Or should they take on the BNP in direct electoral and ideological competition, perhaps offering a firmer and less 'tainted' nationalist creed (the NF alternative)? Such quandaries also preoccupy other factions on the far-right: should they stick to 'pure' principles, such as racial nationalism and/or revolution (the BPP, N9S, ITP, Blood and Honour movement, and so on), or try to pursue some form of BNP-style 'populist' election campaign themselves (as attempted by the Freedom Party and the EFP)? These questions are not unique to the British context. In a sense, they echo those faced by extreme-right parties elsewhere in Western Europe (Hainsworth, 2008: 132).

A key theme raised in the chapter therefore concerns the role of ambivalence. Despite the discontent, the ideological soul-searching and the hostility of the Mosleyites, the NF, the racial nationalists and various other groups on the extreme right regarding the BNP, at the same time there have also been markedly mixed emotions at work, including, on occasions, empathy, furtive regard and even open admiration. This is an important consideration in any attempt to map the extreme-right landscape in Britain since the early 1980s and in the development of new perspectives on the BNP's role in that story.

Notes

1 'BNP removes race-mixing video', Final Conflict news blog, 10 March 2009 (comments section). Available online at: www.politicalsoldier.net (accessed 20 March 2009).
2 'Democracy is death' (n.d.). Available online at: www.heretical.com/British/jordan.html (accessed 23 April 2009). Jordan also referred to 'the Griffinite perversion of the BNP'. See: www.bpp.org.uk/colinjordan (accessed 3 June 2008).
3 '"Change" or revolution: time for nationalists to sweep clean', Final Conflict news blog, 16 August 2008. Available online at: www.politicalsoldier.net (accessed 18 August 2008). This sceptical stance towards electioneering has been a consistent theme in ITP publications over the years. See, for example, *Final Conflict*, no. 13, 1997: 10–11.
4 Eddy Morrison: 'White nationalism now!' (2005). Available online at: www.bpp.org.uk/wnnow (accessed 16 August 2008). See also: 'Nationalism in Britain – populism or white nationalism?' (2007). Available online at: www.bpp.org.uk/nationalisminbritain (accessed 30 June 2008).
5 'Welcome!' (2008). Available online at: www.leaguestgeorge.com (accessed 30 June 2008).
6 See, for example, *Patterns of Prejudice*, 13 (1) January–February 1979: 15–16.
7 One NF activist commented in relation to the BNP: 'We need to target them, show them that the NF are the originals, we were here first, the BNP are frauds'. See: 'Worth joining the NF?', National Front Forum. Available online at: www.britishnationalfront.com (accessed 1 September 2008).
8 NF support for the Countryside Alliance marches especially pleased one rural Scottish supporter who, after one march, passed around the NF's leaflets the following week. See: *The Flame*, no. 8, 1998: 3.
9 A good example occurred in mid 2008: 'John Tyndall Memorial Meeting', 5 August 2008. Available online at: www.londonnationalfront.org.uk (accessed 23 June 2009).
10 'National Front tries to recruit vigilante patrols', *The Guardian*, 8 October 2005: 9. Such tactics have been repeated more recently by the British Peoples Party in the Manchester area. See *League Sentinel*, no. 78, 2009: 4.
11 'Tess speaks in London', 21 January 2008. Available online at: www.londonnationalfront.org.uk (accessed 23 June 2009).
12 Tom Linden: 'The National Front goes from strength to strength!', 12 November 2009. Available online at: www.national-front.org.uk/nationalfront (accessed 25 June 2010).
13 Section 10, question 87, in: 'National Front: 100 questions and answers'. Available online at: www.natfront.com (accessed 30 June 2008).
14 'BNP leader ashamed of his party', 12 July 2009. Available online at: www.national-front.org.uk (accessed 20 July 2009).
15 'Disbandment of reform group', 20 December 2009. Available online at: www.national-front.uk/chrisj (accessed 25 June 2010).
16 'A message to the disillusioned', 2 January 2008. Available online at: www.londonnationalfront.org.uk (accessed 20 June 2008).
17 See, for example, Tom Linden: 'Our nationalist future', 2009. Available online at: www.national-front.org.uk/ournationalistfuture (accessed 17 June 2010).

18 See: *Nationalist Week,* no.1, 1 May 2004. Available online at: www.bpp.org.uk/nw1 (accessed 26 August 2008). See also the statements of the BPP, especially: 'Our plans for the new year', 16 November 2005. Available online at: www.bpp.org.uk/futureplans (accessed 30 June 2008). Also useful is: 'How dare we criticize the BNP?', *Nationalist Week*, no. 175, 21 June 2008. Available online at: www.bpp.org.uk/latestnw (accessed 30 June 2008).

19 Tom Linden: 'The National Front 2010', 7 May 2010. Available online at: www.national-front.org.uk/nf2010 (accessed 17 June 2010).

20 'Once proud Britons', 2008. Available online at: www.natfront.com/Occupation (accessed 30 June 2008).

21 'Who stands for Britain?', 2009. Available online at: www.national-front.org.uk (accessed 20 July 2009).

22 See, for example, Eddy Morrison: 'BNP or NF? Time to choose', 2009. Available online at: www.national-front.org.uk/choose (accessed 10 October 2009).

23 'Which is the most Zionist party?', Final Conflict news blog, 11 April 2008. Available online at: www.politicalsoldier.net (accessed 15 August 2008).

24 'Respectability? Who needs it?', 2006. Available online at: www.bpp.org.uk/respectability (accessed 30 June 2008).

25 'You choose! BNP or BPP?', 2007. Available online at: www.bpp.org.uk/youchoose (accessed 30 June 2008).

26 'Rock against Griffinism: new year's message response by Steve Cartwright', Final Conflict news blog, 9 January 2008. Available online at: www.politicalsoldier.net (accessed 22 August 2008).

27 'An exciting prospect', 19 January 2009. Available online at: www.britnationalist.blogspot.com (accessed 20 January 2009).

References

Copsey, N. (2008) *Contemporary British fascism: the British National Party and the quest for legitimacy*, 2nd edn, Basingstoke: Palgrave-Macmillan.

Edwards, R. (2008) *The enemy within*, Ramsgate: European Action.

Griffin, R. (2003) 'From slime mould to rhizome: an introduction to the groupuscular right', *Patterns of Prejudice*, 37 (1): 27–50.

Hainsworth, P. (2008) *The extreme right in Western Europe*, London: Routledge.

Hepple, T. (1993) *At war with society*, London: Searchlight Publications.

Morrison, E. (2005) *Memoirs of a street soldier: a life in white nationalism*, London: British Peoples Party.

Ritchie, D. (2001) *Oldham Independent Review Panel Report*, Oldham: Oldham Independent Review Organization.

Sykes, A. (2005) *The radical right in Britain*, Basingstoke: Palgrave-Macmillan.

Thurlow, R. (1998) *Fascism in Britain: from Oswald Mosley's Blackshirts to the National Front*, London: I.B. Tauris.

6

FROM DIRECT ACTION TO COMMUNITY ACTION

The changing dynamics of anti-fascist opposition

Nigel Copsey

Introduction

All too often, accounts of the far-right, whether in Britain or elsewhere, overlook the dynamics of anti-fascist opposition. Of the four major academic studies of the National Front (NF) in the 1970s (Billig, 1978; Fielding, 1981; Taylor, 1982; Husbands, 1983), only Taylor's study engages meaningfully with organized opposition to the NF (see Taylor, 1982: 141–70). When it comes to the British National Party (BNP), a similar pattern emerges. Although there is a growing literature on the BNP, far too little attention is being paid to its opposition. This is regrettable. As anti-fascist opposition has shown significant effects on the BNP's developmental trajectory, the relationship between the BNP and its opposition should not be ignored.

Organized anti-fascism has been understood as a *reactive* phenomenon, that is, the nature of the anti-fascist response has been determined by the nature of the stimulus (Copsey, 2000: 189). Although still essentially reactive, what emerges from this chapter is a rather more nuanced understanding of an interaction through which the anti-fascist movement and the BNP have exerted effects upon each other. At the outset, as we shall see, this interaction was characterized by direct forms of 'contact interaction'. Over the longer term, once the BNP abandoned its physical struggle for control of the streets, so the anti-fascist movement was forced to come to terms with a different type of interaction – an interaction 'at distance'. This introduced an entirely new dynamic to the relationship and gave cause for the anti-fascist opposition to respond. The consequence has been the recalibration of opposition strategy, characterized by an obvious shift from direct action to community action. This chapter provides an account of that shift, which, we can further reveal, was evident across both militant and 'liberal' wings of the anti-fascist movement.

Militant anti-fascism: a 'footnote in history'?

By the close of the 1980s, and the point at which the BNP became Britain's premier far-right party, the most significant anti-fascist group was Anti-Fascist Action (AFA) – a militant organization dedicated to driving fascists off Britain's streets. In common with all militant anti-fascists, AFA advocated the use of physical violence. As one AFA activist put it:

> Militant anti-fascism has a single goal – to forcefully disrupt the fascists going about their business. Our aim is to prevent them selling their papers, distributing their leaflets, putting up their stickers and posters. Our intention is to make it impossible for them to stand candidates in elections, and where they do manage to stand, disrupt their campaigns at every stage. Ultimately, our aim is to crush them completely, to wipe them off the face of the earth.
>
> (*Fighting Talk*, journal of Anti-Fascist Action, no. 7, n.d.)

For AFA, there could be no place for armchair anti-fascism. To justify itself, it recited the words of Hitler – quoted as saying: 'Only one thing could have stopped our movement – if our adversaries had understood its principle and from the first day had smashed, with the utmost brutality, the nucleus of our new movement.' This was the principle that 'the left always pays lip service to, but never learns from', AFA remonstrated (*Fighting Talk*, no. 1, September 1991). 'We say no platform for the fascists – no meetings, no marches, no paper sales, no leafleting – and we mean it . . . Our aim is to cause maximum disruption to fascist activities' (*Fighting Talk*, no. 5, n.d.). The object of militant anti-fascism was a simple one: to destroy, through direct physical action, fascist infrastructure and morale, 'to go through the fascist ranks like a rat through cheese'. And this was no empty talk. 'The worst of the lot', one BNP activist lamented, 'total scum. When you bump into them, you know it's a fight for survival; some of them are even skinheads!' (Hepple, 1993: 21).

As the latest incarnation of Britain's physical-force anti-fascist tradition, AFA traced its inheritance back through the Anti-Nazi League (ANL) squads of the late 1970s, the 62 and 43 Groups, to those who fought Mosley on the streets in the 1930s, and to the volunteers who fought Franco in Spain (on Britain's anti-fascist traditions, see Copsey, 2000). Originally founded in 1985, AFA's formation occurred at a time when, following the collapse of the ANL in the early 1980s, Britain had no co-ordinated anti-fascist opposition (on the ANL, see Renton, 2006). By the mid 1980s, even though the NF and the BNP posed no electoral threat, racist attacks were increasing significantly. The situation in London was deemed most serious, especially in the East End (see the Evrigenis Report, 1985: 53). There was also concern that the dearth of anti-fascist opposition had emboldened fascists to such an extent that they now felt able to attack left-wing activities with impunity. This was brought to the fore in June 1984, when a sizeable group of seventy to eighty far-right skinheads attacked an open-air festival for the unemployed, organized by the Labour-controlled Greater London Council.

The far-right's nemesis was Red Action (RA), a working-class militant offshoot from the Socialist Workers' Party (SWP). Often heavily built types, RA paper sellers regularly invited 'worried looks and the squeal of "but you look like the National Front"' (*Red Action*, no. 75, 1997). With the fascists 'getting bolder', at liberty to attack 'large left-wing activities in broad daylight', a resolute RA 'decided this had to be dealt with' (*Fighting Talk*, no. 21, April 1999). Few in number, and thus lacking the capacity to act independently, RA initiated behind-the-scenes discussions with several other groups interested in giving concrete existence to a new anti-fascist front. A conference was finally convened in July 1985 at London's Conway Hall. At this conference, which brought together hundreds of anti-fascists, Anti-Fascist Action was formally launched (see Fekete, 1986).

In the beginning, AFA was a relatively broad-based, non-sectarian organization. Even if some larger radical-left organizations did not elect to join (SWP, Militant, Communist Party), AFA still succeeded in drawing together numerous militant left and anarchist groups within its ranks (Red Action, Class War, Workers' Power, the East London Direct Action Movement), along with more moderate black and ethnic minority (BME) organizations that campaigned against racist violence, such as East London's Newham Monitoring Project (NMP) and the Refugee Forum. The National Union of Students also affiliated to AFA, as did several Labour Party branches, trades councils and individual trade union branches. 'One of the mistakes of the anti-fascist movement in the past has been to play up differences between direct action, mass community mobilisation and educational and propaganda work', explained the NMP's Unmesh Desai, a founder member of AFA's national secretariat, 'But you can't have just one strategy, but a number of strategies that compliment [sic] each other. Everyone has a part to play in AFA' (*Searchlight*, no. 136, October 1986). Laudable perhaps, but AFA's founding principles – to oppose fascism both physically and ideologically, while also recognizing the rights of ethnic minorities to defend themselves from racist attacks – were portents of an organizational mismarriage.

AFA's militant wing saw in fascism a reactionary, anti-working class system. Class rather than race was its compass point. Yet, at the outset, moderate anti-racists from the NMP held the upper hand. The way to defeat fascism, the NMP opined, was not through class-based militancy but through challenging popular support for racist ideas. At AFA's launch, militant anti-fascists, believing that fascists would attack the conference, had spent the entire time outside the conference hall on stewarding duties. As a result, 'from the very outset the political orientation was being dictated by others. Political naivety played a part as well, the militants wrongly assuming that regardless of what was decided in meetings everything could be rectified on the streets' (*Fighting Talk*, no. 21, April 1999). Despite acknowledging that BME communities had a fundamental right to defend themselves against racist attacks – in other words to physically oppose racism and fascism – anti-racists from the NMP were dismissive of what David Renton dubbed 'professional anti-fascists' (Renton, 1999: 114), that is, squads of anti-fascist fighters preoccupied with giving fascists 'a good kicking'. Not surprisingly, this position jarred with AFA's combative wing. Several RA militants, former activists in the original ANL, had been expelled from the SWP in the early 1980s for 'squad-ism' – precisely the type of direct action that AFA's more 'liberal' wing objected to (see Hann and Tilzey, 2003: 87–9). Although AFA's moderates saw the value in militants ensuring that AFA meetings could take place without being attacked, they felt ill at ease with 'taking on the fascists' in sporadic and isolated street battles. Sure enough, within five years, AFA's original coalition unravelled.

Yet, in spite of these internal differences, which had already come out in the open by the time of AFA's first national conference in 1986, early AFA could still lay claim to some success. In 1986, following an attack by AFA on an NF march in Bury St Edmunds in Suffolk, a beleaguered NF leader (and future BNP leader), Nick Griffin, thought it best not to hold further demonstrations. 'We abandoned large-scale demonstrations because we felt that they were counter-productive', another member of the NF's directorate explained, 'we are now following instead a policy of trying to persuade people that our ideas were right in a behind-the-scenes and low-profile kind of way'.[1] Also in 1986, in the largest anti-fascist demonstration since the 1970s, over 2,000 anti-fascists mobilized against the NF's annual Remembrance Day parade in London. This made the front page of the *Daily Mail*, but AFA then struggled to sustain further press interest. According to one former activist:

> The liberals had manoeuvred themselves into positions of authority in AFA, and as a consequence the organization was dying on its feet, stifled by an ineffective leadership that thought the best way to fight fascism was to appeal for Parliament to do something about the problem.
>
> (Hann and Tilzey, 2003: 123)

By 1989, the Remembrance Day march had occasioned an organizational split. AFA's 'liberal' wing called another march, which in the event attracted some 300 people (as opposed to 2,000 in 1986); 500 militants meanwhile occupied the fascists' assembly point at London's Victoria, which delayed the NF march for nearly an hour. Confident of an increasingly receptive audience for militant anti-fascism, RA, which constituted the largest single group in AFA and comprised the majority of its active membership, seized the initiative. In September 1989, ahead of the Remembrance Day march, it relaunched AFA as the militant wing of the anti-fascist movement. RA now insisted that AFA propaganda should disseminate a class message that defended the interests of the working class (*Fighting Talk*, no. 12, November 1995). The anarcho-syndicalist Direct Action Movement (DAM) rejoined, as did the Trotskyist Workers' Power (WP). Meanwhile, AFA's 'liberals', who in 1987 had proposed a change of name to Anti-Racist Anti-Fascist Action (in a bid to put race above class), walked out. An alternative organization for anti-racists, the London Alliance Against Racism and Fascism was formed, but this initiative came to nothing.

Thereafter, AFA operated from a radical (working-) class position. This was disambiguated through reference to a set of core beliefs: first, that the primary objective of fascism, once in power, was the subjugation of the working class, and, hence, only the working class could oppose it; second, that fascists did not just play the 'race card' – on issues such as housing and unemployment, they appealed to the genuine concerns of ordinary working-class voters; third, that fascist success was often grounded in discontent with Labour-controlled councils, and therefore AFA had to reclaim space in working-class areas for a radical alternative to both Labour and fascism. Fourth, that this alternative entailed organizing opposition to the capitalist system, as this was the system that gave rise to fascism in the first place. And what further followed from this radical analysis was AFA's insistence that the state had no positive role to play in the fight against fascism whatsoever. This position clearly differentiated AFA from 'liberal' anti-fascists, who advocated non-violent, legal campaign methods, including calls for the authorities to take action against fascists. 'If you seriously oppose the fascists in a way which is effective, you are operating against the state. This is a fact of life' (*Fighting Talk*, no. 7, n.d.).

In organizational terms, AFA was a decentralized federation. By 1996, there were twelve groups listed in the north, twelve in the south, four in the Midlands, three in Scotland, and one in Wales. London AFA, which produced its magazine, *Fighting Talk*, was an alliance of RA, WP and the DAM. To the north, although RA dominated AFA in Manchester and Glasgow, elsewhere it was anarchists, often from the DAM, who constituted the main body of activists (see Anon., 2007). AFA also extended its reach overseas, where its intention was to end the international isolation of militant anti-fascist groups. In October 1997, AFA called an international conference for militant anti-fascists in London, with anti-fascists from no less than twenty-two groups attending, including delegates from North America, Scandinavia, Germany, France, Spain and the Netherlands. A militant international anti-fascist network was subsequently launched (*Fighting Talk*, no. 18, December 1997; no. 19, April 1998). As for size of membership, this was never disclosed, and we know precious little about it. According to one press report, most AFA members came from the same constituency that the BNP targeted, that is, street-hardened, white, working-class youth (*The Guardian*, 25 November 1994). Yet membership was open to both men and women, regardless of their capacity for physical confrontation. Despite a reputation for being just a group of left-wing thugs who took pleasure in a good row, AFA operated across a much wider canvas, organizing fundraising events, carnivals, concerts, public meetings, pickets and demonstrations. The object of such work was primarily ideological: to 'explain why fascism exists, whose interest it serves, and point people towards an alternative' – in other words, to create space for 'progressive' ideas to reach into working-class areas (Anti-Fascist Action, 'Introduction to London AFA', 1991).

Nonetheless, physical-force anti-fascism remained AFA's lifeblood – even more so once competition emerged within the anti-fascist arena. By 1992, AFA had to contend not only with the re-emergence of the SWP-dominated Anti-Nazi League, but also with new (and often better-funded) organizations, such as the Anti-Racist Alliance (ARA), an organization formed by Labour Party black activists (on the relaunch of the ANL and on ARA, see Copsey, 2000: 167–74). AFA's response was to differentiate itself from this competition by further emphasizing its physical mettle. 'Any militant anti-fascists who may have joined them in the hope of actually fighting fascism should stop wasting their time', AFA sneered, 'The difference here is while the ANL and ARA set out to simply protest at the fascists' presence, we set out to stop them' (*Fighting Talk*, no. 3, 1992). In view of that, just how successful was AFA's form of anti-fascist direct action? And what effects did militant anti-fascism have on the BNP's developmental trajectory?

By the mid 1990s, AFA was claiming that it had fought the BNP to a standstill. In the north west, Midlands and Scotland, seldom could the BNP stage a public event without disruption from AFA. Yet it also remained true that the BNP retained a visible presence in East London, especially in Millwall, where it had gained a foothold, culminating in the election of the BNP's first local councillor in 1993 (on the BNP's Millwall victory, see Copsey, 2008). AFA had prioritized this area between 1990 and 1992 in an intervention that encouraged the BNP to establish a stewarding group, Combat 18 (*Independent on Sunday*, 1 February 1998). After 1992, however, as AFA candidly admitted, it had lost its grip on the area. Two reasons were given: first, the local intervention of the ANL, which had made it more difficult to organize against the BNP; second, divisions within London AFA, which saw Workers' Power, intent on radicalizing the ANL, 'jump ship' (*Fighting Talk*, no. 10, January 1995). There was undoubtedly a third reason. In September 1992, in the largest fascist–anti-fascist confrontation since Lewisham in 1977, AFA had ambushed scores of neo-Nazi Blood and Honour skinheads at London's Waterloo station. This confrontation 'assumed the status of a "cultural icon" for AFA members' and became 'an emblem of its capacity to confront and defeat fascism at street level' (Hayes and Aylward, 2000: 58). But it also had the effect of distracting AFA from physically confronting the BNP in East London.[2]

Militant anti-fascism left an indelible impression on the BNP. The decisive moment came in 1994, when the BNP abandoned its old 'march and grow' strategy in favour of a new 'hearts and minds' approach, that is, a Millwall-style approach characterized by local electioneering and community politics. This reconfiguration of strategy was announced at a BNP organizers' conference on 29 January 1994 (see *British Nationalist*, March 1995). It was certainly not Griffin's doing, as he did not resurface in the BNP until later. In any case, as late as 1996, Griffin was still trying to put a stop to the 'over-moderation' of the BNP, declaring it more important for the BNP 'to control the streets of a city than its council chamber' (*Spearhead*, no. 324, February 1996).

Following an encouraging 20 per cent poll for the BNP in a local by-election in Millwall in October 1992, the BNP chairman John Tyndall had issued a memorandum to national officers and local party leaders urging a new approach. Tyndall had stressed the need for the BNP to distance itself from 'street-gang politics and to stake its claim to a place in the serious political arena' (*Spearhead*, no. 299, January 1994). His deputy, Richard Edmonds, agreed. Recently arrested on a charge of violent disorder resulting from a confrontation with anti-fascists in East London's Brick Lane in September 1993, Edmonds had spent nearly three months in prison before being released on bail. According to Tyndall, the Brick Lane incident, which had been filmed by TV cameras, had resulted in the media once again adopting

> the convenient tactic of lumping 'left-wing extremism' together with 'right-wing extremism' protesting that both were equally bad, and that everything would be fine in the Brick Lane area had those horrid people of the BNP not chosen to make the area a battleground between themselves and their opponents.
>
> (*Spearhead*, no. 297, November 1993)

For the moment, both Tyndall and Edmonds counselled against 'march and grow' tactics. But their counsel was entirely expediential. Tyndall would seek a return to 'march and grow' in 1995, and he later confessed that he 'did not share the view of what was probably a majority of my colleagues at the time that these (marches and public demonstrations) were politically counter-productive, and I still do not share that view' (*Spearhead*, no. 367, September 1999). In the run up to the 1994 local elections, 'Now that the BNP was enjoying much higher levels of support, it was important', Edmonds said, 'to behave in a responsible and restrained manner, to prove that the BNP was a serious political party worthy of electoral support' (*British Nationalist*, March 1994). This position sat well with BNP modernizers, in particular National Elections Officer Eddy Butler, the architect of the Millwall 'rights for whites' campaign, and Tony Lecomber, the BNP's East London organizer. Both Butler and Lecomber wanted to normalize the BNP. Their aim was to neutralize the 'old "Nazi" jibe' through 'community politics', through doorstep campaigning 'right in amongst white communities'. 'We must avoid engaging in aggro', one BNP modernizer exhorted, 'not through fear of the reds as some would emotionally have it, but because it is strategically for the best' (*The Patriot*, no. 2, 1997).

In withdrawing from the physical arena, by turning its back on the confrontational strategy of its past, at one fell swoop the BNP denied militant anti-fascists the opportunity for direct action. This would drain AFA of its lifeblood, while also denying the 'controlled media' the opportunity to hold the BNP responsible for violent disorder. Anti-fascists had, the BNP believed, scored a spectacular own goal when they had attacked the party's bookshop in Welling, in South East London, in October 1993, provoking a riot between anti-fascists and the police. Over sixty people had been hospitalized, and *The Sun* tabloid, in a predictable media backlash, had offered a £1,000 reward for information on the rioters. Soon after, a Granada TV documentary (*World in action*) turned on anti-fascist militancy and presented AFA as a full-blown paramilitary conspiracy (*Fighting Talk*, no. 7, n.d.). Meanwhile, the BNP emerged from this episode relatively untarnished because, on the face of it, the BNP had acted with restraint. 'The reason for abandoning confrontational street politics was because it hindered our political progress', Tony Lecomber explained, 'and was the only thing holding our extreme opponents together' (*Spearhead*, no. 346, December 1997).

'It takes two to tango', AFA recognized, so what of its 'reason for being if the BNP decide that they don't want to play anymore'? (*Fighting Talk*, no. 12, November 1995). Faced with something of a Hobson's choice, RA proposed filling the vacuum left by the alienation of the working class from the Labour Party, to ensure that an alternative to the far-right exists in working-class communities. 'It cannot be left to the far-right to organise the resistance to Labour in working class communities. To allow the likes of the BNP the opportunity to graft racist solutions on to legitimate working class grievances would be fatal' (*Fighting Talk*, no. 18, December 1997). In other words, militant anti-fascists should mimic the BNP, engage in conventional politics and root themselves in community-based activism within run-down, working-class neighbourhoods. As the vehicle for this, RA proposed a new political organization to complement AFA – the Independent Working Class Association (IWCA). Founded in October 1995, the IWCA was established to both uphold and advance the political independence of the working class. The fly in the ointment, however, was that many from AFA's anarchist wing were ideologically resistant to electoral politics and simply refused to have the IWCA imposed on them. Furthermore, as soon as RA prioritized the IWCA, so its activists retreated from militant anti-fascism. Instead of revitalizing AFA, it went into decline. As Lecomber said, 'Not to adapt leaves them impotent and in decline, but to adapt will take time and leave them considerably weaker.' By the end of 1997, a gleeful Lecomber could write that the BNP's radical opponents had become 'a footnote in history' (*Spearhead*, no. 346, December 1997).

Looking back, was there even any need for militant anti-fascists to make such a tactical switch? Although the BNP had withdrawn from the physical arena, it did not withdraw from the streets altogether. AFA might still have harassed the BNP when its activists canvassed on the doorsteps, but the spread of CCTV and the increasing powers of the police to stop and search in anticipation of violence (1994 Criminal Justice Act – Part 4, Section 60) had become a major disincentive. According to AFA, by the mid 1990s, its activities were becoming increasingly exposed to hard-line policing. In one incident, riot police broke an activist's leg in five places; in another, a plainclothes police squad arrested ten AFA militants (*Fighting Talk*, no. 21, April 1999). Yet, regardless of whether or not one condones militant anti-fascism, without it the BNP was given space to operate freely and it then used that space to finesse its operations. What's more, the IWCA hardly constituted the most effective anti-fascist response. Although it gained a foothold in some areas, such as Oxford, in none of these areas was there a direct challenge from the BNP.

For sure, militant anti-fascists were not without influence. Yet their effects stand out as radically different to those intended. Contrary to expectations, far from destroying the BNP in a war of attrition, militant anti-fascism actually *encouraged* its modernization. Moreover, when the BNP changed tack, militant anti-fascists were left with little alternative but to follow suit:

> And AFA was hamstrung. The strategy of confrontation that had been so devastating against the old BNP way of doing things proved impotent

> against the new. If indeed the new (fascist) politics mean success and the old failure, then AFA too must take this on board, otherwise in ten years time it is us who may also share in the experience of seeing them at every turn.
>
> (*Fighting Talk,* no. 15, November 1996)

The result of all this was that, by the time Nick Griffin took charge of the BNP in 1999, he had little militant anti-fascist opposition to contend with. It was 2004 before militant anti-fascists from a variety of anarchist organizations had regrouped under a new national and international umbrella federation known as 'Antifa'. But to this day, what's left of militant anti-fascism is a mere shadow of its former self. Lacking AFA's numbers and engaging in random, small-scale physical actions, Antifa surely belongs to another time and another place. Its flat refusal to acknowledge that the BNP has grown to the point where it can no longer be contained by physical force is unfortunate. 'We cannot accept that militancy against the fascists is not an effective strategy', one of its activists declared stubbornly, 'as we know it can and does work'.[3] Yet, in August 2008, when Antifa militants attempted to smash the BNP's annual Red, White and Blue festival in Derbyshire:

> After emerging from a field dressed in anarchist black . . . Antifa were dealt with – severely and quickly – by riot police. Assessed simply against their own aim – that of stopping the festival – the group's expedition to Derbyshire can only be seen as a complete failure.
>
> (*The Guardian*, 3 September 2008)

'Liberal' anti-fascism: a new way forward?

RA was not alone in thinking that the BNP could only be defeated through local grass-roots activity. After Millwall, on the movement's 'liberal' wing, the anti-fascist magazine *Searchlight* also turned towards community initiatives. This was evidenced by the publication of *When hate comes to town: community responses to racism and fascism* in 1995 – an instruction manual for community-based anti-fascist self-organization. The major drawback with national anti-fascist/anti-racist organizations, the handbook said, was their inability to put down local roots, and, though not always, 'All too often they are seen by local people as "parachuting" into areas with serious problems of racial violence, gaining some publicity and moving on again' (Searchlight Educational Trust, 1995: section 3.1–4). Furthermore, *Searchlight* had also paid heed to how community groups, led by local Anglican churches, had raised turnout and defeated the BNP in Millwall in 1994 (see Holtam and Mayo, 1998). That same year, in neighbouring Newham, local community groups had united behind the NMP's anti-BNP campaign, which saw more than one hundred community, religious and political groups endorse the NMP's campaign to 'vote for equality not for hatred'. In January 1995, to maximize anti-BNP turnout at a council by-election in Newham, NMP volunteers had even visited BME residents in their homes and transported them to polling stations (see Newham Monitoring

Project, 1995: 17–21). For *Searchlight*, one object lesson from Millwall was that BNP electoral success occurred on small majorities. Raising anti-BNP turnout could make all the difference. This was further borne out during 2002–3, when Griffin's BNP first began to capture local council seats. In almost all cases, the BNP's margin of victory was less than 150, and often it was less than 50. It followed that smaller left-wing parties (such as the IWCA) should steer clear of any areas where the BNP was a contender. Otherwise, *Searchlight* insisted, it would take votes from Labour and run the risk of BNP victory (Searchlight, STOP THE BNP conference pack, 2003).

Although political parties, churches and BME organizations could play an important role in defeating the BNP, *Searchlight* maintained that trade unions should head up local campaigns. It had traditionally enjoyed a close relationship with trade unions, often campaigning alongside them for the expulsion of fascists from the workplace. This relationship was strengthened further still with the launch of 'Trade Union Friends of Searchlight' in 1996, followed three years later by 'Communities combating hate' – an ongoing series of local and regional trade union workshops geared towards developing community-based anti-fascist responses. For *Searchlight*, trades councils were best placed to build broad, non-sectarian coalitions with other local anti-fascist forces, as several hundred trades councils existed across the country. Furthermore, as trades councils could call on the most committed and experienced activists, many veterans of anti-NF campaigns of the 1970s, they had the wherewithal to co-ordinate the most effective local responses. In Oldham, for instance, in response to the electoral threat of the BNP, the local trades council established Oldham Trade Unionists Against Racism and Fascism in September 2001; in Bradford, the trades council, through its anti-fascist committee, co-ordinated the local response to the BNP (on the anti-fascist campaign in Oldham, see Lowles, 2007: 147–62). In the meantime, *Searchlight* would offer a guiding hand, providing advice, assistance, intelligence and materials to these local anti-fascist groups.

Tactically, the community campaign strategy that *Searchlight* mapped out saw some significant departures. Too often, it said, national anti-fascist groups, such as the ANL, were looked upon as outsiders, parachuted in at election time only to disappear shortly afterwards. So, in the first place, *Searchlight* insisted that anti-fascist groups establish their own local identity. Anti-fascist literature should bear the imprint of the community in which it was distributed. A series of customized, community-style newsletters, carrying a masthead that local people could identify with, was deemed most effective. Such a tactic had been pioneered in Newham in the mid 1990s, when the NMP had worked alongside local residents to distribute *Docklands Voice*. In February 2003, Ribble Valley Against Racism incorporated the image of a local railway viaduct into its anti-BNP 'Heart of the Valley' newsletter; in Oldham, local anti-fascists distributed the *Oldhamer* (nine editions by 2007); in neighbouring Failsworth, it was *Failsworth Voice*; in Burnley, the local trades council circulated the *Burnley and Padiham Gazette*; in Bradford, it was the *Bradfordian*, which for the 2003 local elections also included a special issue, *Queensbury Focus*, targeted specifically at the neighbouring town of Queensbury. Such targeting even narrowed down to a customized version for different areas of the same ward. In January 2003, for instance, during the Mixenden by-election in Halifax, a local anti-BNP newsletter, *Mixenden Matters*, was circulated to residents on the run-down Mixenden housing estate. A different version of the newsletter, *The Tablet*, was targeted at Mount Tabor, the more affluent area. This title deliberately played on local biblical connections because residents did not identify with the Mixenden name (Searchlight, STOP THE BNP conference pack, 2003).

As Griffin's BNP had also traded skinheads for suits, simply labelling the BNP as 'Nazi' or 'fascist' would no longer suffice either; nor would waiting for the BNP to organize a demonstration, because 'then we are likely to be waiting for a very long time' (Searchlight, STOP THE BNP conference pack, 2003). Mirroring the localized publicity material of the BNP, anti-fascist literature, *Searchlight* insisted, should engage with local issues and debunk the BNP's 'plausible untruths', that is, false rumours spread locally by the BNP concerning plans to house asylum seekers, build mosques, the frequency of anti-white racial crime and so on. Anti-fascist groups were also urged to seek endorsement from respected people in the local community, such as a local vicar for example, or perhaps the secretary of the local residents' group, but not necessarily people associated with party politics, as BNP voters typically held mainstream political parties in contempt. Further critical elements included voter-ID: identifying anti-BNP voters through telephone or door-to-door canvassing and targeting these voters with follow-up material that stressed the importance of turning out to vote. An effective media strategy, in which anti-fascists 'made friends not enemies' of the local press, was also recommended. Also, in what proved to be one of its more controversial instructions, anti-fascists were told not to demur from attacking religious fundamentalism, an issue that anti-racists traditionally avoided for fear of giving credibility to the BNP. 'If such (Islamist) groups have a high profile locally then our literature should condemn them' (Searchlight, STOP THE BNP conference pack, 2003). Needless to say, the efficacy of this community campaigning strategy – originally geared towards containing the BNP in its northern England strongholds – hinged on local trade union strength. Where this was deficient, community responses were not always possible.

This, then, was the state of affairs between 2002 and 2003, when Griffin's BNP first started winning council seats: small teams of community activists busy trying to contain the BNP, 'fire fighting' from one election to the next, operating independently of any political party. It was not until the end of 2003, the point at which the BNP had already garnered seventeen council seats, that a new, national anti-fascist organization was formed. This was 'Unite Against Fascism' (UAF), a broad-based national campaign group initiated by the National Assembly Against Racism (NAAR – the successor to the Anti-Racist Alliance), the ANL (SWP), various faith groups, such as the Muslim Council of Britain, the TUC and numerous MPs/MEPs (*Socialist Worker*, 6 December 2003). Not aligned to any particular party – its original sponsors included Conservative MPs Michael Howard, David Cameron and Sir Teddy Taylor – the leadership of UAF was split between two joint secretaries: Weyman Bennett of the SWP and Sabby Dhalu of the NAAR. Notwithstanding the fact that there was 'no secret that we have long-standing tactical differences with some of the component parts of UAF' (*Searchlight*, no. 344, February 2004), *Searchlight* still affiliated to UAF's steering committee. Before long, however, tactical differences came to the fore. *Searchlight's* position that anti-fascists should not shirk from confronting the difficult issues that anti-racists normally avoid soon rubbed up against UAF's insistence that anti-fascists should never make concessions to racism. In 2005, *Searchlight* resigned from UAF following allegations of 'pandering to racism'.[4]

Chaired by former London mayor Ken Livingstone, UAF's central aim has been to maximize anti-BNP turnout. It wanted to mobilize the anti-fascist majority in British society through an alliance of trade unionists and those parts of society traditionally vilified by the extreme right: blacks, Asians and Muslims, Jews, gays, the disabled and all democrats. In 2004, by claiming to have doubled voter turnout in the north west, UAF insisted that it had played a pivotal role in preventing the election of Nick Griffin to the European Parliament (Unite Against Fascism Newsletter, Autumn 2004). According to its analysis, the rise of the BNP has gone 'hand in hand' with falling voter turnout. It follows that 'reversing that trend is critical to defeating the BNP' (Unite Against Fascism, Briefing Paper, no. 1, 2005). Therefore, UAF campaigns 'have to work out how to mobilize every single voter who will not vote for the BNP as the higher the turnout, the greater the threshold the BNP has to climb to get elected' (Unite Against Fascism, Briefing Paper, no. 4, 2005). Since 2004, UAF has distributed millions of anti-BNP leaflets – 2.5 million alone at the 2009 European elections. In 2009, as in previous campaigns, UAF's message to voters has been a consistent one: 'that the BNP was a fascist party, that there was a serious danger of them winning seats, and that they could be stopped if enough people turned out to vote against them' (Unite Against Fascism, 'Tackling the rise of the BNP', July 2009). But, at the 2009 European elections, turnout fell to 34.7 per cent, a fall of 3.82 per cent on 2004, when, if truth be told, the extension of postal voting and the combination of elections (local and European), more so than the intervention of UAF, had boosted voter turnout.

In too many respects, UAF represents an anti-fascism that has stood still. Although the formation of local UAF groups has seen it localize its campaigns to an extent, UAF still harks back to the 1970s. Its protests, rallies, leafleting, 'Love music hate racism' concerts and carnivals, and re-runs of 'no platform' and 'pull the plug on the fascist thugs' media campaigns are all too reminiscent of strategies deployed against the 1970s NF by the ANL and Rock Against Racism. Admittedly, in the 1970s, anti-fascists had hammered home the message that the National Front was a Nazi Front. Today, the critical factor that must be accepted, however reluctantly, is that negative campaigning, when it is countered by the BNP with door-to-door contact, becomes ineffective, if not counter-productive. As the BNP appreciates, face-to-face contact does much to dispel the 'far-right extremist' message of anti-fascist opponents. As Nick Griffin sees it:

> Note that it's not the canvassing itself that has this effect, but the gap between expectation and reality. It is this gap that breaks the conditioning and makes

> the voters think for themselves . . . and once they conclude that our opponents have been lying to them about us, such negatives as they hear in future are likely to be water off a duck's back.
>
> (*Identity*, no. 83, October 2007)

What is more, to vote 'ABF', that is to say 'anyone but fascists', as UAF urges, does little to address the underlying concerns of a growing minority of disgruntled and alienated BNP voters who feel abandoned by Westminster's political class. 'The time will come', Griffin predicted, 'when this process of setting us completely apart from what is doomed to become an utterly discredited political elite will be seen to have been the single most important factor in our rise to power' (*Identity*, no. 77, April 2007).

Reflecting on the limitations of negative campaigning, in July 2005 *Searchlight* called on anti-fascists to focus 'not so much on what we are campaigning against but on what we are campaigning for' (*Searchlight*, no. 361, July 2005). It wanted anti-fascists to offer a positive message of hope – hence the slogan 'Hope not hate', which adorned a *Searchlight* campaign bus that toured the country in 2007, 2008, 2009 and once again in 2010. It was also obvious that the BNP could no longer be 'contained' by small teams of trade union and community group activists. In local elections in 2004, the BNP had stood over 300 candidates; by 2007, this figure had leapt to over 700. As local anti-fascists struggled to cope with the proliferation of BNP candidates, *Searchlight* now argued for a long-term political solution. This meant rebuilding the bridge between people and the local democratic process, especially in traditional working-class neighbourhoods, where the BNP had established itself as a rival to Labour. But, unlike the IWCA, this did not mean offering a radical alternative to Labour. On the contrary, it now meant working closely with mainstream political parties, especially Labour, bringing the Labour Party and the trade unions together in local campaigns against the BNP. To this end, it established 'Labour Friends of Searchlight' in June 2005 – an organization chaired by Holborn and St Pancras MP, Frank Dobson, with Dagenham MP Jon Cruddas as vice chair. Labour Friends of Searchlight was specifically designed to help local Labour parties defeat the BNP (on Labour's response to the BNP in Burnley, see Copsey, 2005: 189–98).

By 2007, *Searchlight* was co-operating closely with local Labour parties and trade unions across many of the BNP's target wards, particularly in West Yorkshire and the West Midlands. At the 2006 local elections, of the thirty-three council seats that the BNP had won, twenty-eight had been previously held by Labour. At the 2007 local elections, over 80 per cent of its target wards were Labour wards. Cause and effect are hard to measure, but, where co-ordinated community campaigning took place, it appears to have made a difference. The BNP's share of vote fell in many of its core areas in 2007, tellingly in both the West Midlands and West Yorkshire. In a grudging reference to *Searchlight's* 'Hope not hate' campaign, which had found a major sponsor in the form of the *Daily Mirror*, the BNP's Mark Collett conceded that: 'No doubt thousands upon thousands of pounds were spent on this campaign and it was used in an attempt to steal just enough votes from us to peg us back in key wards' (*Identity*, no. 78, May 2007). The BNP further conceded, in June 2007, that Labour had undergone a 'paradigm shift' in organization: 'They and their union allies are now capable of out-organising us in a limited number of places, thereby cutting off our support spike' (*Identity*, no. 79, June 2007). Such campaigns could work to good effect in other ways too, particularly when it came to re-invigorating Labour's grass-roots organization. As *Searchlight's* Nick Lowles and Paul Meszaros (2007: 27–8) tell it:

> The first example of where this new form of politics worked was in Dagenham, east London. In the run up to the 2005 general election . . . rather than ignoring this threat, as was then the norm within the party, Dagenham CLP and its local MP Jon Cruddas took the BNP on . . . While Dagenham Labour Party used the threat of the BNP to energise its activists and rebuild its organisation, the opposite was true for (neighbouring) Barking CLP. The result was that the BNP polled 16.7% in Barking, its highest vote in the country, whilst gaining only 9.8% in Dagenham . . . The BNP recognised the resistance being put up in Dagenham and subsequently switched their focus to Barking, where they went on to gain 11 councillors the following year.

It is clearly not clutching at straws to suggest that, if it can convince sufficient 'working class people that it is Labour, and not the BNP, that is fighting their corner' (Rusling, 2007: 37), the Labour Party might re-integrate itself into those working-class communities left out in the cold by Westminster's political elite. In Barking, where Nick Griffin stood as a parliamentary candidate in the 2010 general election, the scale of victory for the sitting Labour MP Margaret Hodge (by 8,883 votes in 2005; 16,555 votes in 2010), combined with the fact that Labour won all fifty-one seats on the local council, underscores the extent to which an intense, co-ordinated, local anti-BNP campaign could revitalize a once moribund and divided local Labour party. With some choice words, a jubilant Hodge could proclaim: 'The lesson from Barking to the BNP is clear: Get out and stay out, you're not wanted here and your vile politics have no place in British democracy. Pack your bags and go!' (*Independent*, 7 May 2010).

Conclusion

Having surveyed the trajectory of the anti-fascist movement from the mid 1980s to the present day, what conclusions can we draw? The history traced here reveals a number of things. First, the most obvious point to emerge from this chapter is that, by helping to occasion a historic shift in BNP policy, militant anti-fascism did factor in the BNP's modernization (even if a more significant factor was that the BNP had reached a political dead-end under Tyndall). For that reason, the modernization of the BNP should not be considered in isolation from its opposition. Second, if we accept that this modernization is at least partly responsible for the

BNP's rise, it follows that militant anti-fascism, although perhaps successful in the short term, has had a deleterious effect over the longer term. Even if the BNP tired of physical confrontation before the opposition did, in the long run the BNP understood that 'many of those who oppose the BNP will become disarmed if there is no open target to aim at' (*The Patriot*, no. 2, 1997). Once disarmed, the moment that Anti-Fascist Action wound down its activities, vital breathing space opened up for the BNP to develop its appeal on the doorstep at a time when further political space opened up for it as a consequence of the decline of local Labour parties and the rising saliency of the BNP's favoured issues. Then, by the time militant anti-fascists had regrouped, the BNP had already secured election of a number of its candidates to public office and had thereby passed an important credibility threshold. The BNP has clearly moved on since the 1980s and 1990s, but anti-fascist militants have not. Approaches of this kind simply fail to appreciate that small-scale, sporadic physical confrontations can no longer render the BNP inoperative. If truth be told, militant anti-fascism, especially when the BNP is seen to act in legitimate and law-abiding ways, only risks widening sympathy for the BNP's cause. It gives a more media-savvy BNP carte blanche to project itself as the victim of unfair persecution.

When the BNP turned to community politics, so the anti-fascist movement followed. Since the BNP's victory in Millwall, a marked shift by anti-fascists towards local-level, community engagement has taken place, and, as we have seen, this recalibration of strategy has been apparent across both wings of the anti-fascist movement. Even Unite Against Fascism, which takes most inspiration from national campaigns against the 1970s NF, has attempted to localize some of its activity. For *Searchlight*, empowering local communities has meant seeking a political solution to the BNP in Labour. But it is Labour that is the crux of the problem for anti-fascist militants: the 'total ineptitude and the tangible contempt that exists in some areas between Labour and its former constituency has locally and nationally begat the BNP'. In simple language, 'it is the politics of the Labour Party that has created the BNP' (*Fighting Talk*, no. 12, November 1995). Hence, for the IWCA, *Searchlight's* position 'is not anti-fascism, it is anti-extremism' – a sterile politics that is committed to stopping the BNP without disturbing the political equilibrium.[5]

We have, of course, far from reached the end of the story. With the election of the BNP's Nick Griffin and Andrew Brons to the European Parliament in 2009, a new chapter in the history of anti-fascism opened up. Among anti-fascists, there was now reluctant recognition that the political landscape had changed, and the BNP had finally established some kind of mainstream presence. As *Searchlight's* Nick Lowles said:

> Firstly the BNP has MEPs and whether we like it or not Nick Griffin and Andrew Brons will appear more regularly on television. No platform agreements between political parties were already breaking down before the election, with only Labour holding to them, and this process is likely to quicken now.
>
> (*Searchlight*, no. 409, July 2009)

For Lowles, the immediate priority was to build anti-fascist groups 'in every community in the country'. The basis for these community groups would be the one in 470 adults that engaged in its 2009 'Hope not hate' campaign, which saw 3.4 million newspapers and leaflets delivered (in some parts of the country, more material than that delivered by the mainstream parties). According to figures returned to the Electoral Commission, *Searchlight* spent over £137,000 funding this anti-fascist campaign (over £50,000 more than UAF). Meanwhile, after surveying the new landscape, UAF urged the mobilization of the largest possible mass movement to drive the BNP out of the political mainstream (Unite Against Fascism Supporter Letter, July 2009). Elsewhere, a new campaign group – 'Nothing British' – arrived on the scene. An online group linked to the Conservative Party, it called for responsible opposition to the BNP. Originally founded in March 2009 by former *Sunday Times* journalist James Bethell and Tim Montgomerie, former chief of staff to Iain Duncan Smith, Nothing British rejects the unconditional policy of no platform, appealing to traditional 'British' values of liberty, decency and tolerance (see www.nothingbritish.com).

Revealingly, in an open letter to the left, the SWP, one of the main constituent bodies of UAF, predicted that the 'Nazis' success will encourage those within the BNP urging a "return to the streets". This would mean marches targeting multiracial areas and increased racist attacks. We need to be ready to mobilise to stop that occurring' (*Socialist Unity*, 10 June 2009). And the recent emergence of the anti-Islamist English Defence League (EDL), formed in late June 2009, would seemingly lend credence to such a prediction. Without doubt, far-right extremists have been attracted to the EDL, a street-activist group that, along with its Scottish and Welsh partner leagues, has staged a series of confrontational anti-Islamist protests across numerous British cities since the second half of 2009. Yet the EDL is not the BNP, and, even though there is evidence of some links between organizations, Griffin has officially proscribed and condemned the EDL, claiming (conspiratorially) that it is being manipulated and directed by 'Zionists' in order to create a 'race war' on Britain's streets. As Eddy Butler made clear in the BNP's official statement on the EDL, 'The BNP does not march in the streets but rather campaigns in an ordinary democratic fashion in elections, door-to-door canvassing and leafleting.'[6] Nonetheless, it is still tempting for anti-fascist opponents to conflate the EDL with the fascist BNP, not helped by former Labour Communities Secretary John Denham's rather crude comparison of the EDL with Mosley's Blackshirts. All this only increased the possibility that the SWP would press UAF into radicalizing its activities. In March 2010, at one demonstration in Bolton, more than seventy people were arrested as a result of violent clashes between UAF and the EDL. It was reported that fifty-five of those arrested were from UAF. This figure included UAF joint secretary Weyman Bennett, who was charged with conspiracy to organize violent disorder (*Daily Mail*, 21 March 2010).

In the wake of the BNP's election to the European Parliament, Bennett had (rather disingenuously) endeavoured to locate UAF in Britain's militant anti-fascist tradition: 'The BNP should be physically confronted wherever it tries to organise', the SWP's Bennett declared (*The Times*, 13 June 2009). But this clearly misses the point that Griffin's major concern is 'to minimise the chances of confrontation with opponents – it's normality and friendliness we need to portray, not conflict' (*Identity*, no. 94, September 2008). Moreover, such 'fighting talk' by Bennett simply enables Griffin to cast the BNP as a victim of 'human rights abuses', denouncing, in his maiden speech to the European Parliament, UAF as a violent organization of 'far-left criminals'.

Rather than physical confrontation of the BNP, the experience of the 2010 general election in Barking and Dagenham (and in Stoke-on-Trent) further supports the argument that intensive, moderate and co-ordinated local campaigns are more effective. In both Barking and Dagenham, while local Labour parties worked hard to reconnect with ordinary voters on the doorsteps, a concentrated 'Hope not hate' anti-fascist campaign in the weeks leading up to polling day saw delivery of some 92,000 anti-BNP newspapers and some 55,000 leaflets. Specific literature was targeted at women (less likely to vote BNP than men), pensioners (invoking the memory of the Second World War), BME and first-time voters. A dedicated worker was employed to raise anti-BNP turnout among faith communities; a dedicated press officer played down the BNP's chances of victory (in 2006, it was felt that Hodge had given the BNP a credibility boost when she told the *Sunday Telegraph* that eight out of ten of her white constituents were threatening to vote BNP). Thousands of phone calls were made to identify anti-BNP voters, and, on polling day itself, 176 volunteers knocked on some 6,000 doors in key wards (see *Searchlight*, no. 420, June 2010; *Searchight Extra*, June 2010).

It also seems likely that, by knocking on doors and distributing thousands of leaflets, Barking and Dagenham UAF complemented this local anti-fascist operation. In a novel departure, 'A crucial component of the UAF campaign was to engage with those who were tempted to vote BNP and challenge their arguments' (UAF, *Stopping the Nazi BNP in the 2010 elections*). Its canvassers estimated that around 4,500 conversations were held on doorsteps across the borough. For Margaret Hodge, UAF formed 'part of the winning strategy', but whether a central factor in defeating the BNP was labelling the BNP as Nazis, as Labour MP Peter Hain proposes, remains a moot point. 'It's great to see UAF organising like the Anti-Nazi League', Hain, a key figure in the 1970s ANL declared (UAF, *Stopping the Nazi BNP in the 2010 elections*). But there are clear pitfalls in drawing too much from the 1970s experience, for it is surely only through a monumental lack of judgement that the BNP would recommission the jackboot. As Griffin said:

> No high-laced boots, combat trousers or flight jackets. No tattooed faces or old-lady-frightening skinheads (if unavoidably bald, please wear a hat). No scruffy 'designer' stubble. I'm sorry if this list offends anyone, but we're going out there to break damaging stereotypes, not to reinforce them.
>
> (*Identity*, no. 94, September 2008)

Notes

1 Patrick Harrington, unedited interview transcript, 1988. Originally consulted at Modern Records Centre, University of Warwick, MSS. 321/Box 2.

2 That said, the BNP's successful candidate, Derek Beackon, did apparently experience one unfortunate incident several days prior to his election, when he was confronted by some AFA members in an East London park; for details of this episode, see Bullstreet (2001: 24).

3 Antifa, *What we think: Antifa activists interviewed by Sean Matthews from the Workers' Solidarity Movement, Ireland*, (n.d.), p. 4.

4 On the *Searchlight*/UAF split, see http://whatnextjournal.co.uk/pages/Politics/UAF.html (accessed 17 August 2009).

5 See 'Labour got what it deserved – and so did the BNP'. Available online at: www.iwca.info/?p=1014 (accessed 18 August 2009).

6 http://bnp.org.uk/2009/09/the-english-defence-league-a-statement-from-the-bnp%E2%80%99s-national-organiser/ (accessed 7 January 2010).

References

Anon. (2007) *Anti-Fascist Action – an anarchist perspective*, London: Kate Sharpley Library.

Billig, M. (1978) *Fascists: a social psychological view of the National Front*, London: Harcourt Brace Jovanovich.

Bullstreet, K. (2001) *Bash the fash: anti-fascist recollections 1984–93*, London: Kate Sharpley Library.

Copsey, N. (2000) *Anti-fascism in Britain*, Basingstoke: Palgrave-Macmillan.

Copsey, N. (2005) 'Meeting the challenge of contemporary British fascism? The Labour Party's response to the National Front and the British National Party', in Copsey, N. and Renton, D. (eds) *British fascism, the Labour movement and the state*, London: Palgrave-Macmillan.

Copsey, N. (2008) *Contemporary British fascism: the British National Party and the quest for legitimacy*, 2nd edn, Basingstoke: Palgrave-Macmillan.

Evrigenis, D. (1985) *Committee of Inquiry into the Rise of Fascism and Racism in Europe*, Brussels: European Parliament.

Fekete, L. (1986) 'The anti-fascist movement: lessons we must learn', *Race and Class*, 28: 79–85.

Fielding, N. (1981) *The National Front*, London: Routledge & Kegan Paul.

Hann, D. and Tilzey, S. (2003) *No retreat: the secret war between Britain's anti-fascists and the far right*, Lytham: Milo Books.

Hayes, M. and Aylward, P. (2000) 'Anti-Fascist Action: radical resistance or rent-a-mob?', *Soundings*, 14: 53–62.

Hepple, T. (1993) *At war with society*, London: Searchlight Publications.

Holtam, N. and Mayo, S. (1998) *Learning from the conflict: reflections on the struggle against the British National Party on the Isle of Dogs, 1993–94*, London: Jubilee Group.

Husbands, C. T. (1983) *Racial exclusionism and the city: the urban support for the National Front*, London: George Allen & Unwin.

Lowles, N. (2007) '2001: pavement politics', in Lowles, N. (ed.) *From Cable Street to Oldham: 70 years of community resistance*, London: Searchlight Publications.

Lowles, N. and Meszaros, P. (2007) 'Beating the BNP: a practical approach', in Rusling, M. and Grindrod, F. (eds) *Stopping the far right*, London: Fabian Society.

Newham Monitoring Project (1995) *The enemy in our midst*, London: Newham Monitoring Project.

Renton, D. (1999) *Fascism: theory and practice*, London: Pluto Press.

Renton, D. (2006) *When we touched the sky: the Anti-Nazi League 1977–1981*, Cheltenham: New Clarion Press.
Rusling, M. (2007) 'Conclusion: Labour at the forefront of anti-racism', in Rusling, M. and Grindrod, F. (eds) *Stopping the far right*, London: Fabian Society.
Searchlight Educational Trust (1995) *When hate comes to town: community responses to racism and fascism*, London: Searchlight Educational Trust.
Taylor, S. (1982) *The National Front in English politics*, London: Macmillan.

7

THE BNP IN LOCAL GOVERNMENT

Support for the far-right or for community politics?[1]

Karin Bottom and Colin Copus

Introduction

To date, the British National Party (BNP) has failed to secure parliamentary representation at Westminster, yet it has – with varying intensity – been a presence in local government for more than a decade. At the local council elections in June 2009, the party fielded 465 candidates (enough to secure a party political broadcast for the local elections alone), while 69 candidates fought the accompanying European Elections (*BBC News*, 11 May 2009). The party secured three county councillors on separate councils: Lancashire, Leicestershire and Hertfordshire – the first time the party has held seats at this level – and took two seats in the European Parliament – again for the first time – one for the Yorkshire and Humber region (Andrew Brons); the other, for the North West, where the party leader, Nick Griffin, was elected. The BNP also held one seat on the London Assembly. Prior to the May 2010 local elections, the BNP had fifty-six council seats (though two resigned on the eve of the election) across more than twenty-five councils and, on some, numerically at least, it constituted a substantial bloc of opposition, such as in Barking and Dagenham Borough Council, where it was the main opposition party. In contrast to party expectations, however, the May 2010 elections – national and local – did not see the BNP consolidate and build on what it considered to be a trajectory of success. Nationally, it increased its share of the vote, but failed to secure an MP, while, locally, the party experienced significant losses, including all its councillors in Barking and Dagenham, and lost representation on eight councils (Election 2010, *BBC News*). The BNP also failed to take a seat in the Barking and Dagenham council by-election less than three months after the elections (*BBC News*, 8 July 2010). A comparison of BNP representation across English councils is displayed in Table 7.1.

TABLE 7.1 A comparison of BNP council seats in England in 2009 and immediately after the May 2010 local elections

	Council	*2009 seats*	*2010 seats*
1	Hertfordshire CC	1	1
2	Lancashire CC	1	1
3	Leicestershire CC	1	1
4	Barking and Dagenham	12	0
5	Redbridge	1	0
6	Havering	1	0
7	Stoke-on-Trent	8	5
8	Thurrock	1	1
9	Bradford	2	2
10.	Calderdale	1	1
11	Kirklees	1	0
12	Leeds	1	0
13	Rotherham	1	1
14	Sandwell	2	0
15	Solihull	1	0
16	Amber Valley	2	2
17	Boston	1	1
18	Burnley	4	2
19	Charnwood	1	1
20	Epping Forest	4	1
21	North West Leicestershire	2	2
22	Nuneaton and Bedworth	2	1
23	Pendle	2	2
24	Redditch	1	0
25	Sevenoaks	1	1
26	Staffordshire Moorlands	1	1
27	Three Rivers	1	1
	Total	57	28

Note: The table needs to be read with some caution. All local elections held in 2010 were among councils that have elections by thirds, where only one councillor per ward would be seeking re-election. Consequently, not all of the BNP's seats above would have been contested in May 2010.

Source: Local Council Political Positions.

Despite recent years seeing the BNP undergo a change of image in order to increase its catch-all potential and thus electability – similar in many respects to Labour under Tony Blair and the Conservatives under David Cameron – questions remain as to whether such modernization has been genuine or whether the BNP continues to be an anti-system, far-right party with goals and ideology that are incompatible with a liberal–democratic political system (see Copsey, 2007). Indeed, it must be asked, whether the party's elected members use their democratic mandate to conduct council business in the same way as other parties, or simply use their representation to develop the image of the party as respectable, while generally acting in ways that would be unacceptable for a councillor? We suggest that these questions are particularly pertinent right now, while the party seeks to determine its short- and long-term post-election strategies.

Here, we examine these questions in relation to BNP councillors and, using a selection of results from recent and ongoing research, ask how the party has impacted upon politics at a local level? Though not exclusively, this chapter concentrates on the period prior to the 2010 elections and, in doing so, captures the party at the height of its success to date. The party's organization within councils is explored, as is how its councillors conduct council business, how they perceive their role as councillor and how they carry it out. It asks the controversial question of whether these councillors are intrinsically different to their colleagues, or whether they are similar on any or indeed all levels? It then proceeds to examine how other parties have responded to the arrival of BNP councillors, finally presenting some findings that suggest BNP councillors do indeed display a number of features that can also be found in their more mainstream counterparts. First, however, the chapter sets out the recent history of the party in local government.

The BNP and local government

The BNP won its first council seat in 1993, when Derek Beackon took the Millwall ward of Tower Hamlets council. Since then, its fortunes have been mixed and inconsistent (Eatwell, 2004; Copsey, 2004), and, despite strong and highly visible reactions to the party's successes, it is yet to make real breakthrough at a local level, that is, capture control of a local council. Nevertheless, it has managed to steadily, if slowly, raise its local profile, fielding over 600 candidates in the May 2008 local elections, nearly a threefold increase on 1997. These elections saw it gain thirteen seats and extend its presence into eight more councils, though none of the results were particularly substantial. Table 7.2 shows the BNP's representation on principal councils before the 2010 local elections; seats and the party's seat percentages on each council are displayed. It is clear that, with the exception of Barking and Dagenham, Stoke-on-Trent, Burnley and Epping Forest, BNP representation, even before 2010, was relatively minimal. Representation is, in the main – though not exclusively – urban, and the majority of seats were found on district councils, where a particularly influential factor in BNP success has been its ability to embed itself within local communities and articulate a relatively banal form of community politics, which has then become legitimized in that particularly locality (Rhodes, 2009).

Compared with other small parties in local government, the BNP is a minor force in most respects. Prior to the 2010 elections, small parties, independents and political associations held 1,370 seats[2] (7.5 per cent) in England, and, of those, the BNP was responsible for just over 4.2 per cent (Local Council Political Compositions). This figure fell only marginally after the 2010 elections, and yet the BNP saw its share of the non-mainstream seats decrease by more than half (Local Political Compositions).

Numerically, the BNP is indeed a minor party. Though also minor, the Greens, with over 100 councillors, currently sit on more councils than the BNP. They

TABLE 7.2 British National Party seat percentages in England (May 2008–May 2009)

	Council	*BNP seats/seat percentage*	*Council control*
County councils			
1	Hertfordshire	1/1%	C Maj
2	Lancashire	1/1%	C Maj
3	Leicestershire	1/2%	C Maj
District councils			
4	Amber Valley	2/1%	C Maj
5	Boston	1/3%	I Maj
6	Burnley	4/9%	LD Min
7	Charnwood	1/2%	C Maj
8	Epping Forest	4/7%	C Maj
9	North West Leicestershire	2/5%	C Maj
10	Nuneaton and Bedworth	2/4%	C Maj
11	Pendle	2/2%	NOC
12	Redditch	1/3%	C Maj
13	Seven Oaks	1/2%	C Maj
14	Staffordshire Moorlands	1/2%	C Maj
15	Three Rivers	1/2%	LD Min
London borough			
16	Redbridge	1/2%	C Maj
17	Barking and Dagenham	12/24%	L Maj
18	Havering	1/2%	C Maj
Metropolitan boroughs			
19	Bradford	2/2%	C Min
20	Calderdale	1/2%	C Min
21	Kirklees	1/1%	L & LD Maj
22	Leeds	1/1%	C & LD Maj
23	Rotherham	1(2)/2%(3%)	L Maj
24	Sandwell	2/3%	L Maj
25	Solihull	1/2%	C Maj
Unitary councils			
26	Stoke-on-Trent	8/13.3%	I Maj
27	Thurrock	1/2%	C Min

Notes: C = Conservative; L = Labour; LD = Liberal Democrat; I = Independent; NOC = no overall control; Maj = majority; Min = minority.

Source: Local Council Political Positions; Council Websites; Hope Not Hate Complete List of BNP Councillors [12.05.2009; 22.05.2009].

also enjoy representation on a number of principal Welsh councils, as opposed to the smaller community ones that the BNP sits on, hold two seats in the London Assembly, whereas the BNP held one, and, in May, the party secured its first Member of Parliament, Dr Caroline Lucas (Brighton Pavilion). In fact, the majority of non-mainstream seats are held by independent and local party councillors (approximately 75 per cent)[3] (Local Council Political Compositions), and, in many respects, it is they, not the BNP, who tell the most important local stories: the success of groups such as 'Independent Health Concern' in Kidderminster (IHC) and the 'Boston Bypass Independents' (BBI) are significantly more dramatic,[4] despite being geographically concentrated.

The excessive level of interest in the BNP can be explained by its ability – much like the rest of the far-right party family – to exert what Herzog (1987) refers to as a 'mobilization potential', in that its power to affect the political agenda and influence debate is disproportionate to its size. In this sense, it acts as a local opinion-former, its relevance being in its ability to attract attention and shape the direction of competition. In keeping with classic small-party theory, the BNP brings new issues to the public, acting as a 'trial balloon' for the mainstream (see Fisher, 1980: 611–2), often forcing it to respond to issues that would otherwise be considered too controversial to address. In every sense, the BNP galvanizes popular discontent with the ruling political elite in such a way that it cannot be ignored (see Clark et al., 2008).

Media reporting has perpetuated this negative picture at a local level, stating that the majority of BNP local councillors can neither organize nor cohere while they behave in a manner inconsistent with the responsibilities of office.[5] Yet disreputable behaviour is not solely the domain of the BNP, as the complaints and investigations undertaken by 'Standards for England' (formerly the Standards Board) show. Councillors from all parties can behave in a less than ethical fashion,[6] yet concerns regarding the BNP remain, run deep and eclipse those that may arise about councillors from other parties. Unlike other organizations, the core of the BNP, the very ideology upon which it is based, provokes questions that just do not apply to others, because the party exists outside the liberal political orthodoxy and thus must be subjected to extensive investigation and questioning. Unacceptable behaviour is the expected norm for the BNP, and, consequently, we are not surprised when it takes place; rather, it serves to vindicate received wisdom. In contrast, inappropriate behaviour by councillors from other parties is considered *pathological* and appears to be interpreted as an aberration, because the party concerned reflects core democratic values and is supportive of a democratic, pluralistic system.

In sum, the BNP is judged by different standards to other parties because the party's origins invite – even demand – scepticism. What can often been seen as an over-reaction to BNP successes feeds into the rhetoric employed and the positioning developed by the BNP as the champion of the excluded underdog and itself a victim (as the recent BBC *Question Time* appearance of BNP chairman Nick Griffin emphasized). Indeed, other candidates leaving the platform when victorious

BNP candidates are speaking and the reaction of anti-fascist organizations to its European success have publically highlighted the 'exceptionalism' with which the BNP is treated and also served to paint the party as a victim. As a Unite Against Fascism (UAF) demonstrator was reported as saying at Nick Griffin's attempt to hold a press conference outside Parliament: 'I believe in free speech, but not for fascists' (*Sunday Telegraph*, 7 June 2009)!

Here, we examine the BNP through a less exceptionalist lens, investigating it as we would any other party to provide a picture of the party's councillors and how they behave in office. What we do here is examine the work of BNP councillors and compare them with those of other parties in order to present a picture of the BNP in local government.

The overwhelming majority of councillors across Britain come from one of the three main parties – almost 92 per cent of councillors in England are Conservative, Labour or Liberal Democrat, the remainder, often – and unhelpfully – termed as 'others', comprising the local branches of small but nationally based parties, various types of local organization and independent politicians (Clark et al., 2008). These councillors are, however, too diverse to be grouped together. The nature of their roles and responsibilities forces them to determine a division of loyalty among those that they represent, the party or organization of which they are a member – if indeed they are – and the council upon which they sit (Copus, 2004: 14), the nature of the tension being very much dependent upon the organizational ties that constrain him or her. This tension is far reaching and important: it informs a councillor's representative role (and council members vary in terms of their perceived representative responsibilities) (Newton, 1976), levels of activity (Gyford et al., 1989), contact with the local bureaucracy (Corina, 1974), community emphasis (Copus, 2004), attitudes towards the importance of party (Copus, 2004) as well as campaigning techniques (Copus, 2007); indeed, there is no such thing as a typical councillor.

Councillor role analysis

Councillor role analysis has predominantly concentrated on two features: policy-making and councillors' relationships with their constituents. Eulau et al. (1959) distinguished between representative style and focus: the former referred to the criterion of judgement used by the representative, and the latter to the body or group to which the representative gave preference. They drew attention to how representatives act as *free agents*, or trustees of the electorate's interests; *delegates*, who place the wishes of the voter at the centre of their political attention and, in some cases, may even act as though bound by those views; and, *politicos*, who act as a trustee where possible or a delegate when required.

Rao (1998) indicates that distinguishing between various aspects of representation enables us to tell whether the councillor functions more as a delegate or a trustee. This enables us to judge whether the councillor acts in the interest of the community, as a constituency servant or mentor, or as a servant of the party.

Yet, as Jones (1975) has noted, such distinctions are difficult to disentangle, as the councillor may also act as a representative of a broad section of the community, a particular organized group, another local authority or individual citizens.

Newton (1976: 122–4) divided councillors into five role types: the *parochial*, who focuses on his or her ward and individuals within it; the *people's agent*, who also focuses on the problems of individual constituents, but has a broader, city-wide perspective; *policy advocates*, who express a preference for broad policy issues and governing the council; *policy brokers*, who also focus on the council as a whole, but act as mediators in the policy process; and *policy spokesmen,* who see themselves as speaking on behalf of the electorate on general policy issues. Gyford (1976: 133–41) saw councillors as 'tribunes' of the people, focused on individual or ward casework, or as statesmen, focused on broader policy and party concerns. Copus (2004) also draws our attention to the pastoral role of the councillor, which involves focusing on the collective needs of a ward and the citizens within it.

Heclo (1969) saw the councillor as a *committee member*, specializing in the business of the council, a *constituency representative* focusing on local concerns, or a *party activist* who approaches council work with the interests of the party at the forefront. Corina (1974) developed a five-way typology to explain the nature of the councillor's relationship with his or her party: the *party politician*, *ideologist*, *partyist*, *associate* and *politico-administrator*, each of whom varied in the connection and closeness they had with the party and in how they interpreted its role and purpose within the conduct of council affairs. Simply put, some councillors are more inclined to place party and ideology above all else, while others see the party as assisting them in some aspect of council work.

Councillor role analysis enables us to explore councillor activities in specific settings and in relationship to players within local democracy: the council as a politically representative institution; the community and individuals represented; and the party. This chapter now explores whether what we already know about councillor focus and role enables us to understand BNP councillors in the same way as it does other councillors – thus challenging 'exceptionalist' interpretations of the BNP in council. The chapter examines whether the existence of BNP councillors fundamentally alters councillor role analysis. To do this, we examine BNP councillors' activities in council, their relationship with the communities they represent, and the way they act as a party within council. Finally, the chapter draws conclusions about whether or not BNP councillors represent a threat to established democratic practices and local representative democracy, or whether that threat is more crudely and simply to the seats held by other parties.

BNP in council

Meetings of full council, or overview and scrutiny and regulatory committees, represent the formal, open, public theatres of representation. They are the places where councillors can articulate their views; express party positions; give voice to the opinions expressed within the communities they represent; explore policies and decisions of the local political leadership; hold to account and challenge the council bureaucracy over public services; and deliberate local and national political concerns – all this, of course, for those councillors elected as a candidate of a political party, will be done through the filter of party ideologies and party interest and advantage.

The image presented may be a somewhat romanticized version of council meetings, meetings that have been challenged on countless occasions for being too formal and routine, as well as being dominated by agendas and the needs of running a large, bureaucratic machine, rather than providing a chamber for political discourse. Furthermore, the party group and the meetings of the majority party group have long replaced council as the place where debate and deliberation take place and policy and decisions are formulated to be ratified in formal council settings (Copus, 1999a; 1999b; 2001). Yet these settings provide an opportunity to examine the conduct of local politics and to examine party behaviour.

Despite much commentary to the contrary, when it comes to council meetings, the attendance of BNP councillors does not appear to be overly different from that of councillors from other parties, especially given their comparatively small numbers. Indeed, part of the 'bad councillor mythology' that has been developed around the BNP is that they do not attend council meetings. Over the municipal year May 2008–May 2009, BNP councillors in England attended the majority of full council meetings for which they were eligible, 23 displaying 100 per cent attendance, the lowest recorded attendance being 36 per cent, and average attendance 84 per cent. Indeed, attendance figures in the four councils that see the BNP with relatively significant and thus more comparable representation – Burnley, Barking and Dagenham, Epping Forest and Stoke-on-Trent – again demonstrate that councillor attendance was not particularly different from the average of those from other parties. Table 7.3 displays the data rounded up to the nearest full attendance number and percentage.

Such attendance figures go some way in dispelling perceptions of BNP poor attendance at council. Indeed, where attendance is relatively low (Barking and Dagenham), this is also the case for the mainstream. In fact, it could be argued that councillors who do exhibit poor attendance records are deploying their resources well if they sit in small groups. When considering the small size of most BNP groups – twelve was the largest – any absence, for whatever reason, has a greater impact on the *presence* of that group in a meeting than for a larger group; particularly so in committee, where the group may have only one or two members. Generally speaking, the notion that BNP councillors 'don't attend' is somewhat overexaggerated: while some exhibit lower levels of attendance, the majority simply do not, and, being engaged in council work, BNP councillors begin to display the same role orientations as other councillors. Within BNP groups – keeping in mind that most are less than four members – a share of policy-focused councillors is also evident. This demonstrates a wish to influence policy development and, in some cases, spokespeople have emerged for particular policy causes. Indeed, reference to council minutes evidences this;[7] furthermore, party groups appear – in most

TABLE 7.3 BNP councillor attendance at full council in Burnley, Epping Forest, Barking and Dagenham and Stoke-on-Trent (May 2008–May 2009)

Council attendance		BNP attendance	Non BNP average	All councillor average attendance
District councils				
1	Burnley	9/11 (82%)	9/11 (82%)	9/11 (82%)
2	Epping Forest	6/7 (86%)	6/7 (86%)	6/7 (86%)
London borough				
3	Barking and Dagenham	6/9 (66%)	7/9 (77%)	7/9 (77%)
Unitary council				
4	Stoke-on-Trent	11/12 (92%)	11/12 (92%)	11/12 (92%)

Note: Attendance and percentage figures calculated to the nearest full number.

Source: Council websites; Local Council Political Compositions.

instances – to vote cohesively and vote with other party groups in order to pass motions or legislation. In an interview, one BNP group leader expressed confidence that the party would control the council after the next elections and emphasized that the BNP group was 'learning as many of the ropes' as possible for when it took power. Indeed, the group's members needed to be expert in policy work, as intense political opposition was expected, as was obstructionism from council officers and problems with the law, if the group took control. Though this councillor's predictions did not materialize, his/her comments clearly demonstrate that the local party in question had a clear operational strategy for the future.

Attendance at council meetings rests on opportunities to attend, and that depends on allocation of members to various overview and scrutiny and regulatory committees. Of fifty-six BNP councillors elected before 4 June 2009, forty-nine sat on committees; eight were not allocated any committees; three sat on over ten; and average committee membership was three: the smaller the group, the greater the strain on resources in terms of committee membership and full council attendance. When it comes to committee membership and attendance, the BNP seems no different from other small council groups: they experience resource problems; the committees on which they serve are the gift of the ruling group; a small number of members may have to cover a wide range of responsibilities and attendance demands; and the group may – like any group – have members who did not expect to win, or stood after being promised that they would be a paper candidate and had no chance of winning – in other words, reluctant councillors.

Only two councils saw BNP councillors with chairing or vice-chairing responsibilities, four on Stoke-on-Trent and one on Epping Forest. Yet not a single

BNP councillor on Barking and Dagenham – where the BNP held the largest number of the party's seats and formed the official opposition group – held a chair or vice-chair. At that time, Labour on Barking and Dagenham had a majority of two over the BNP and the two Conservatives; Stoke-on-Trent was a hung council, where sixty councillors divided into nine groups, with no single group having an overall majority; Epping Forest had five groups, plus a lone Labour councillor and an overall Conservative majority of eight seats. So, what we saw was a majority Labour council denying opposition groups committee chairs or vice-chairs; a hung council allocating chairs and vice-chairs among all groups; and a council with a majority party but a number of other groups granting those other groups vice-chairs. In any circumstances, all these scenarios would be unremarkable as, in the main, distribution of such positions is specified by council culture and council rules. Indeed, an interview with Independent Community and Health Concern (ICHC) in 2008 confirms this. Though ICHC then sat as the official opposition, with almost 24 per cent of seats, the ruling Conservative group denied it any full chairing responsibilities (Bottom and Crow, 2008). ICHC now holds fewer seats, but continues to be denied chairing responsibilities. Consequently, we have to presume that the inclusion and exclusion of the BNP – as described above – are, in many respects, unremarkable.

Part I of the Local Government Act, 2000, introduced an ethical framework and a rigorous code of conduct within which councillors operate. Councillor conduct is monitored by a standards committee that each council is required to form; all were to be policed by the 'Standards Board' (now 'Standards for England'), which had the power to investigate complaints against councillors and impose sanctions, including removal from office. In research projects conducted by the authors, councillors have often complained that referrals made by fellow councillors and by officers are used as a tactic for silencing or intimidating opponents, where little real ground for complaint exists. Although the officers of the Standards for England are practiced in weeding out frivolous and vexatious complaints, the process, as a complaint moves through the system to rejection, is an unsettling time for a councillor. However, the accession of BNP to elected council has heightened concerns relating to the maintenance of standards. Dr Robert Chilton, the Chair of Standards for England, has stated that local authorities believe that the BNP's lack of established discipline, its proclivity to pursue a narrow agenda as opposed to wider council duties, and its tendency to instigate adversarial politics in chamber that can lead to insult throwing 'undermine public confidence in local democracy' and collectively pose a potential risk to standards in local government (cited in Drillsma-Milgrom, 2009: 2).

Similarly, a chief executive for a council where the BNP held representation stated that he/she believed that the party's councillors are keen to 'push the standards regime to the limit' and do not mind being censured by it (cited in Drillsma-Milgram, 2009: 1). Reference to council minutes does indeed support this view. Though some members are recorded as speaking neutrally on topics, examples of inflammatory rhetoric and ensuing heated debate can also be found.[8] However, it must be recognized that such inflammatory rhetoric and heated debate cannot just be associated with BNP councillors. We must understand that elected representatives from all parties do not always conduct themselves with decorum, and, when in a very small group, making a loud noise may be the only way to get heard; this is not to excuse, but rather to explain such activity. Indeed, these authors have considerable experience of conducting research among the councillor population, and one of the constants that has been noted is the lengths elected members will go to in order to create obstacles for their opponents. This includes not just the tone – and extent – of behaviour they are willing to engage in, but also allegations they are willing to make: examples include aggression, bullying, inappropriate activities, interrupting council meetings, arrogance and verbal abuse, and even staged walkouts are not entirely unknown.

To date, Standards for England does not provide detailed information on complaints against any councillor, and though details are made available on those conducted through to conclusion, records are only kept for limited periods. For these reasons, it is not possible to ascertain an accurate longitudinal picture of BNP councillors' behaviour in comparison with that of their party colleagues, or indeed the rest of the councillor population. Nothing short of a comparative and representative study that compares the demeanour and language of *all* councillors' rhetoric and behaviour will ascertain whether more incidences can be found in the BNP. However, what we can and do argue here is the following: it is not *what* the BNP does that makes them exceptional, rather, it is the matter on which they base their politics.

In a more general sense, the responses from councillors – of all political hues – to the election of BNP colleagues sit on a continuum that runs from verbally violent denunciations of the party, including personal attacks on their calibre, honesty, integrity, intelligence and in some cases even odour and personal hygiene, to a reluctant resignation to working with BNP councillors, driven by the realities of council work and composition; indeed, the dynamics and interactions of council politics are often related to a council's political composition and the respective size of the council groups, as opposed to any other factor (Copus, 2004). In a fractured council, particularly where no group has a majority, it is far less easy for councillors to be choosey about with whom they work; in contrast, where a party has a sizeable majority, opposition can be marginalized and ignored.

Notwithstanding this, the vocalized attitudes of main party councillors – interviewed for this research – were in many respects predictable: they do not like BNP councillors and take it as an affront to decency and dignity that they are required to work with them. The following quotation illustrates this; it is not unrepresentative:

> It sickens me we have to work with them . . . I'd keep them off everything; but we've made it as hard as possible for them to ask questions or use scrutiny. I'm sick of looking at them [*sic*] smug, nasty faces.
>
> (Labour councillor)

Beyond such comments though, deeper concerns were expressed regarding the reasons for BNP council election success. Evident was a palpable fear that portions of the electorate – beyond those that had voted BNP – were rejecting the broad liberal, multicultural diversity agenda shared by the main parties; in other words, voters were rejecting the political orthodoxy. Moreover, there was a growing awareness that the BNP was beginning to find support among, primarily though not exclusively, the white working class, simply because the needs of this group had been downplayed or ignored.[9]

BNP councillors as elected representatives

Taking Eulau et al.'s (1959) notion of representative style and focus as a starting point, along with what is known about councillor role orientations, we can start to examine the nature of BNP councillors as elected representatives and ask how they approach the notion of representation. All councillors experience a tension between the demands of governing a council area and the promotion and defence of the interests of the wards from which they were elected, particularly when such interests may clash (Copus, 1999a; 1999b; 2004). In other words, when the 'general good' as defined by a council leads to a 'specific bad' for some, the councillor must choose to govern or represent. Moreover, in the allocation of scarce resources and policy development, councillors must decide on winners and losers and thus will promote what they consider to be their main focus of concern.

The representative style and focus of BNP councillors have been criticized by other parties in the research and generally. The key concerns here relate to parties' attitudes towards those they represent. That councillors tend to feel an affiliation for certain sections of their electorate, indeed may even be, or consider themselves to be, part of a specific group (Maud, 1967; Jones, 1975) has not, in the main, provoked any real anxiety in the past: councillors are expected to behave responsibly, acknowledge overall responsibility for the whole community and represent the broad interests of their wards or divisions. Although councillors may choose to concentrate on policy, monitoring roles, representative responsibilities, community leadership or indeed the party (Snape and Dobbs, 2003: 51), it is taken that one group of society will not be excessively valued or devalued over others, certainly not to the point of overt neglect. However, given the BNP's racist and anti-immigrant policies, as well as the irresponsible, violent, polemic and populist politics with which it is associated, it is frequently argued that the party's councillors are unable and unwilling adequately to serve all voters.

The BNP and 'representation' were examined in an exchange between Nick Griffin and the broadcaster Bill Turnbull, on *BBC News* on Monday 8 June 2009. Turnbull implied that Griffin would not represent Muslim constituents; Griffin responded that he would represent anyone who approached him, but suggested that the interests of Muslims in his constituency were served by the Labour Party, and that other ethnic minorities – whose issues he would be happy to respond to – had been ignored by Labour. Griffin's response that it would be to the Labour

Party that the Muslim community would turn indicates, in one sense, that all parties have their preferred constituents, and that, given the choice, constituents would approach the representative whose political affiliation they favour – nothing exceptional here. On the other hand, it could equally be argued that more than a preferred constituency was being referred to in that statement; rather, that implied – and overtly exclusionary – advice existed in the words 'the Labour Party is there for them' (*BBC News*, 8 June 2009).

In interviews, no BNP councillor stated that he or she would refuse to address the problems of ethnic minority constituents, but neither had any of those interviewed been approached by someone from an ethnic minority requesting assistance, the key theme of responses being: 'we would not refuse but we do not expect to be asked' – pertinent and indeed shrewd responses as, in most cases, constituents not wishing to approach the BNP have the option not to do so. However, between 2008 and 2010, the BNP held a full complement of seats in one Stoke-on-Trent ward and a majority in two, all three with populations that were reported as being over 98 per cent 'white British' in the 2001 UK Census (Office for National Statistics).[10] Though this is no longer the case, the representation options that were available at that time to non-white residents in these wards require further investigation. Furthermore, future research would do well to examine the representational behaviour of the party's three county councillors. Given the single-member divisions in which they sit, these councillors are more likely to experience an approach from an ethnic minority constituent before borough councillors and MEPs.

Although the party may no longer voice the position espoused by its first elected councillor, Derek Beackon (Millwall), who explicitly refused to represent Asian members of his community, and rejects all suggestions that it is racist on its website,[11] and figures such as Richard Barnbrook (Greater London Assembly member) draw attention to the various representative activities that he undertakes for non-white Londoners, blaming the state not immigrants for a multiracial Britain (*BBC News*, 4 September 2008),[12] the party continues to be associated with distinctly racist politics. It voices greater commitment to representing what it describes as the 'indigenous population' on its website and is associated with inciting racial hatred (Griffin himself being convicted of this offence in 1998). Its members are regularly accused of making statements perceived to be racist,[13] and party literature continues to promote what appears to be a thinly veiled policy of voluntary repatriation. Although the party may argue that it articulates and provides an inclusive representation policy, it is clear that much of its activity mitigates against this image; indeed, a substantial body of evidence seems able to refute the party's claims. Ultimately though, what is really required is empirical evidence that proves 'approach and refusal' or 'less than assiduous attention' to a specific case; this would be difficult to prove though, as not all councillors pursue case-work in the same fashion.

So, are BNP councillors exceptional, in terms of the questions that have been raised here over their willingness to 'represent', in the broadest terms, or conduct pastoral work? Councillors from the main parties have, themselves, displayed exclusive attitudes towards those they do and do not represent – the white, middle-aged, middle-class (male) a particular target of jibes and insults common among Labour councillors. Indeed, demonizing of the white, male, middle aged and middle class is commonplace among much discourse concerned with representation, and all parties have an enemy and a core-client group whose interests they seek to promote. Using here a deliberate caricature to make the point: would a Labour or Conservative councillor refuse to pursue the interests (or pursue them less diligently) of a part of the ward where they knew they received few votes and which contained their political enemy? Or would a Labour or Conservative councillor refuse to take up case-work from someone whose background they took to be 'not one of them' or whom they believed did not vote for them. The answer in both cases should be 'No', although let us conject that exceptions are bound to exist for more extreme-minded members of the two parties. So, if we can assume that councillors of the main parties keep their exclusive 'anti' attitudes towards their class opponents to discourse only, and do not act on them when dealing with individuals or when acting as a representative; or, that they reflect views about local concerns that cut across party lines and are not ideologically-based, and that they do not refuse to take up case-work for those they perceive to be 'other'; then should we not judge BNP councillors by these same assumptions? Indeed, we should be able to, and yet our ability to do this is mitigated against by BNP policies and rhetoric that suggest that, instead of seeking to favour one group in society above another, the party actively excludes the other, to the extent that – in many respects – it gives the appearance of ignoring and rejecting the basic tenets of liberal democracy.

To summarize, the BNP councillors interviewed and studied display the same spread of focus towards policy, ward representation and case-work as have been noted in councillors from other parties (see Copus, 1999a; 1999b; 2004; 2007). Those studied sat easily within the role definitions of the *delegate*, *trustee* or *politico*, and they expressed a broad belief that their election had given them a mandate to act on behalf of their community as a 'trustee' of its best interests. They did not feel mandated on each and every issue before the council – even on the particularly complex and contentious issues. But in regard to the latter, the general view among those interviewed was that they would seek to find out the balance of opinion on issues by approaching community groups, tenants' and residents' associations and their own networks – all networks held by any councillor of any party are exclusive and self-selected and self-maintained, of course. BNP councillors expressed the view that acting as a trustee allowed them to use their own judgement, which in turn allowed them to put distance between themselves and the voter and fill that void by reference to the party and the BNP group – much like any party councillor.

While BNP councillors may not refuse case-work from any constituents, the question of policy raises another issue of representation. The pursuit of policy objectives and the solution of social, moral and political problems by the development of policy rest on two factors, much like pastoral care: the perceived general good and the particular set of interests to be promoted. Here, like other councillors, the BNP has a vision of the general local public good and of a specific group whose interest they seek to promote, much like other parties. The point of divergence for the BNP from other parties comes from whether or not the interests that policy seeks to promote are mutually exclusive or can have an inclusive element. The question remains: does any policy promoted by any party have an all-encompassing embrace, or are there always winners and losers within the locality? BNP councillors answered this question by indicating that they had the interests of the wider community at heart in policy development, but that they also wished to defend those interests through appropriate policies for the communities whose interests, they argued, were under threat. They also wished to redress the preferential treatment they believed had been granted to minorities. In local policy then, the BNP can be seen to be exclusive, as indeed are all parties when it comes to giving preference their natural constituency. However, the issue here is that the BNP's understanding of the 'general good' is more ideologically limited and selective than that of its modern-day opponents, mainstream or otherwise. Consequently, it is not exclusion per se that is the issue; it is the nature and extent of that exclusion that is the issue.

What we see with BNP councillors is a Burkean approach to representation that is also adopted and preferred by most councillors (Copus, 1999a; 1999b; 2001). In other words, when it comes to local issues and policy, BNP councillors will, as all councillors, listen to their constituents, but not be bound by them. In so doing, the party looms larger in councillors' frame of reference than the community – again, not exceptional. One BNP councillor summed up the position of many of his/her colleagues when he/she stated:

> I joined the party (BNP) to fight for what I believe in. I always listen to what people say and do what I can to help out. But, being a councillor is a chance to show our policies and fight for what we believe in and if people don't like it, well, we won the seat so we'll back the party.
>
> (BNP councillor)

Such expressions of party loyalty are not unique to the BNP and are reflected across the three main parties (see Copus, 2004). The difference is that the BNP does not control any councils and, if it did, the question would have to be asked: how would its party groups react to public opposition to a council decision – emerging from the normal run of council business – that they had presided over, for example school closure or grant permission for planning development? Our research leads us to conclude that BNP councillors would react much the same as other councillors and back the party (this discussion is developed in the next section).

However, councillors that place the party first do so in the knowledge that it will – probably – protect and cushion them. Yet all BNP councillors have, to date, operated in small groups, some exceptionally small. Though such groups experience the same need to cohere in public as larger ones, they are not insulated from 'events' or the fall-out that may result from factionalism; consequently, councillors prioritizing re-election – for whatever reason – will be more inclined than those in larger groups to feel mandated by ward opinion, though rarely to the extent of rejecting their own and their party's views. What this research uncovered was the emergence of two types of BNP councillor, each exhibiting a distinctly different relationship with the party, and it is to this we now turn.

BNP councillors and the party

The Local Government (Committees and Political Groups) Regulations 1990 require all political groups formed on councils to register with the council; a group must have two or more members to be officially recognized and to be able to claim proportional allocation of committee seats. BNP council groups will be formed as any other party groups, so what we explore here is the journey of the BNP member to the council, taking into account their recruitment to the party, as well as the motivations that encouraged them to stand for election; second, we examine how BNP groups operate on council, and whether they display the same characteristics as other party groups.

Different categories of activist can be found in the BNP's membership, and this also applies to the party's councillors. Two types have been identified. The first can be described as the *party ideologue*, or the *party-person* (Copus, 2004). That is, a party activist who joined the BNP – or any other party for that matter – with a clear commitment to its core beliefs and policies and an affinity for the party, based on values, coupled with a desire to promote and advance the interests of the party and those values. Such a motivated individual will fit easily into the expectations and demands of party membership and will find their own appropriate level of activity within the party. Whether or not the party person holds any office in the party, at any level, party activity becomes almost like an obsessive hobby, and such individuals are at the centre of the continued existence of any local party. They keep the machinery going, organize and administer the party, ensure it has a local public profile and, above all, are publicly loyal to its policies, positions and decisions – irrespective of private reservations. It is only in moments of crisis that the party-person will publicly break rank with the party, or leave it; such crises do not occur often. The BNP ideologue that joined the party will experience the same motivations to political activity experienced by members of other parties – it is simply beliefs that differ.

Not all BNP councillors are party ideologues or party persons. Rather, some joined the party through a different route and hold a different set of motivations and relationships, not only to the BNP but also to party politics more broadly. It is here that the BNP, in recruitment and councillor activity, share some of the practices of the Liberal Democrats (see Copus, 2007). Some BNP councillors, in common party parlance, had been 'recruited on the doorstep'. One councillor summarized this in interview:

> They (BNP) came round with leaflets a few times and knocking on doors. I told them what was wrong here [she referred to a range of issues that

> described the run-down nature of the area and did not mention race throughout this interview]. They came back and told me they'd got in touch with the council. After a bit they asked if I'd join and stand for the council . . . I thought they were serious about getting things done and none of the other parties bothered to come round, so, in the end I did it.
>
> (BNP councillor)

The BNP is, in some but not all wards they hold or have targeted, employing the type of community politics that has been so successful for the Liberal Democrats (see Copus, 2007). Moreover, BNP branches are recruiting council candidates on the doorstep. It is difficult to assess how widespread this tactic is, but it clearly links to a broader community politics approach that rests on nurturing a particular ward, including regular leaflet/newsletter delivery, locally orientated campaigns, petitions and the development of a high local profile for individuals who will become council candidates. Community politics rests on a collective and individual pastoral approach – pursuing grievances and promoting and defending the interests of a ward or communities within it – and it extends far beyond the usual six weeks of intensive election campaigning. Voters may turn to the BNP because of the work the party has done in particular areas and, more often than not, because the other parties have not responded in kind to the community politics adopted by some BNP branches.

A BNP councillor commented in interview:

> The people of the area put their trust in me to sort out what needs doing around here and that's what I'm going to do: I'll put this ward first. The old parties have let everyone down; they don't care; you never see them. That's not going to be what I do.
>
> (BNP councillor)

Community politics and the recruiting of candidates from local networks have the potential to enhance electoral success for any party willing to spend the time in such work. Indeed, it is well suited to smaller parties, because it does not rely on large numbers, but rather on small groups of people – most obviously two or three who will become the candidates and a small group of workers from inside and outside the party. What community politics and the recruitment of candidates on the doorstep do, however – and this is so for the Liberal Democrats – is to bring into the party a number of individuals who do not have an orientation towards party politics and do not necessarily place priority on or even value party loyalty, discipline and cohesion. It also results in councillors being elected that have not been educated at the school of hard-knocks politics and have not experienced the rough-and-tumble of party political life.

BNP council groups can consist of the *party ideologue* and the *community councillor.* The existence of these two types can generate problems for group cohesion in council meetings, with the community councillor feeling less inclined to follow a line with which he or she disagrees. Here again, we see similarities with Liberal Democrat groups, whose fissiparous tendencies are often exacerbated by an underlying dislike of party discipline – despite most Liberal Democrat groups generally cohering in public. None of the BNP interviewees admitted knowledge of any nationally produced group standing orders (again, many Liberal Democrats interviewed for other research have been unaware of the national standing orders produced by the Association of Liberal Democrat Councillors). The small size of most BNP groups makes strict adherence to such rules unnecessary – although no doubt other parties would pounce on any public disagreements between BNP councillors, as they do with public disagreements between councillors of any party.

Clearly, it is no longer possible to consider all BNP councillors as party ideologues dedicated to pursuing particular political ideals. Rather, we must be cautious in considering the nature of BNP groups and the approach their councillors take to local politics, as well as their relationship with the wider party. Given the party's relatively short period of office and the comparative newness of its community-orientated element, it is hard to predict how the party will develop; for example, whether the ideologues will marginalize the community-orientated faction of the party, or indeed vice versa. Numerous factors, including the 2010 elections results – national and local – will influence the way in which the BNP now chooses to meet its current challenges, but as a primarily vote-winning organization it will pursue the policies and actions that its decision-makers believe will maximize rewards at the ballot box. Now that the party has lost the majority of the – very tenuous – legitimacy it was beginning to build, a return to extreme, radical ideology may well prove all too attractive.

Conclusion

The BNP has yet to make a major breakthrough into councils across the country; its progress has been very slow and recently it has experienced significant setbacks. Yet the party has become a feature of the local political landscape in many localities – its presence extending far beyond seats in council – and it can no longer easily be dismissed as an aberration. So, is the BNP exceptional? It would be fair to conclude that assertions suggesting that its councillors are poor meeting attendees; do not take a full part when they do turn up; do not understand council procedures; are badly behaved; and are successfully isolated and ignored by other parties to such an extent that they can and do not achieve anything as councillors have been exaggerated, to some extent. Although some BNP councillors do behave in this way, our research suggests that, equally, some do not, and, in the absence of extensive research across all councils where the party is represented, a conclusive answer cannot be provided on this.

Like their contemporaries, BNP council groups have their policy- and governing-focused specialists, who take a keen interest in broad policy agendas. They have councillors who are pastoral in nature and focus on the collective well-being of their wards and of individuals within them. While others look to the party, ideology, core values or a key constituency when it comes to making decisions, others look to their ward or groups within it. Here, BNP councillors reflect the style and focus adopted by councillors from all parties. In terms of broad representation, BNP councillors pursue the interests of those they perceive to be their core constituents. All parties seek to protect and promote the interests of a core constituency and reach beyond that constituency for two reasons: first, a genuine desire to promote a wider set of interests; and second, as a catch-all election ploy to obtain political office.

When it comes to ward representation, BNP councillors have displayed the loyalty and concern for – the majority of – their patch that would be expected of any councillor. Dealing with the problems of individuals within that patch is a more ambiguous area, given that ethnicity plays a part. Personalities also have a stake in the complex relationships between elected representatives and those who seek their assistance on individual issues. We would suggest that a watching brief is kept on the development of this – but, as we write, BNP councillors are providing advice surgeries and advertising them to all comers on council websites. Yet, given the understandable reticence many non-white ward members may have in terms of attending these surgeries, the absence of an overt effort by the party to quell such concerns should be perceived as significant.

Finally, we conclude that there is little that evidences BNP exceptionalism as a group of councillors if they are considered in isolation. Rather, what has been found to be exceptional – compared with other parties – is the way in which their particular ontology appears to sit with accepted norms, and the reactions that their representative presence has provoked: from councillors from other parties, the media and political pressure groups. However, the party does not exist in a vacuum. Consequently, it must be evaluated within the context in which it operates. When it is, the BNP appears somewhat more exceptional, not so much in its conduct of council activities, but rather in the nature of its preferred constituencies and the responses it generates. Indeed, it seems to be here that we find the kernel of BNP 'exceptionalism' in local government.

Notes

1 Research for this chapter was undertaken with the assistance of research grant F.094.AP 'Small parties: influence and effect on democratic engagement and local politics', from the Leverhulme Trust.
2 Figures are subject to change and were taken on a given day.
3 Exact figures are difficult to ascertain, as most groupings of 'others' include all organizations and individuals that are not common and identifiable small parties (see Clark et al., 2008).
4 ICHC secured power on Wyre Forest District Council in 1999 and remains there, having participated in a number of administrations; currently, it constitutes the official opposition. Its MP, Dr Richard Taylor, was returned to his second term at Westminster in 2005; in 2010, he lost to the Conservative candidate. The Boston Bypass Independents took twenty-five of the thirty-two seats on Boston Borough Council in 2007. Though somewhat depleted in numbers, the group still holds a majority and, at the time of writing, runs the Council.

5 For example, Richard Barnbrook, former BNP councillor for Barking and Dagenham and member of the London Assembly, was suspended for a month from his local council for making incorrect comments on local knife crime, which he refused fully to retract (Drillsma-Milgrom, 2009: 1).

6 For example, refer to English Standards (formerly Standards Board for England), which provides information relating to this. Other examples include accusations (though also acquittal) of electoral fraud in Birmingham (*BBC News*, 4 April 2005); ballot fraud accusations (though acquittal) in Tower Hamlets, BBC London (*BBC News*, 3 October 2005); and Labour bullying in Coventry (*BBC News*, 21 October 2004).

7 Here we refer to Burnley, Epping Forest, Barking and Dagenham and Stoke-on-Trent councils.

8 Council minutes, however, must be read with some caution, as they do not always provide a narrative explanation of council meetings and are often decisional minutes only.

9 See Hazel Blears' (then Communities Secretary) comments about mainstream parties abandoning sections of the white working class (*The Daily Telegraph*, 22 November 2008). Refer also to a recent publication by Communities and Local Government that draws attention to these issues, highlighting working-class perceptions of unequal distribution of resources; see Communities and Local Government, *Sources of resentment, and perceptions of ethnic minorities among poor white people in England*, Crown Copyright (2009). See also Hazel Blears' comments about white working-class 'fears' (*Telegraph View*, 2 January 2009).

10 All three in Bentlee Townsend ward (two councillors post-2010 local elections); two out of three in Weston and Meir Ward North (one councillor post-2010 local elections); and two out of three in Abbey Green ward, where the BNP had previously held all three seats until one stepped down to sit as an independent in January 2010 (one councillor post-2010 local elections; the ex-BNP, now Independent, councillor remains) (Stoke-on-Trent City Council).

11 See, most recently, Nick Griffin's appearance on *Question Time* (22 October 2009).

12 Barnbrook has also voiced a commitment to representing the 'real [one must assume white] people of London' (*BBC News*, 4 September 2008).

13 For example, the party's link between Islam and Pakistan and British communities experiencing problems with hard drugs. Deputy Party Leader Simon Darby accused the Archbishop of York John Sentamu of interfering in British politics, suggesting that if 'foreigners' meddled in Uganda they would be attacked with spears (*The Guardian*, 6 May 2009). Since his election to the European Parliament, Griffin has suggested the sinking of boats containing illegal immigrants might disincentivize attempts to enter Britain (*BBC News*, 8 August 2009).

References

Bottom, K. and Crow, A. (2008) Interview, Independent Community and Health Concern, Wyre Forest District Council.

Clark, A., Bottom, K. and Copus, C. (2008) 'More similar than they would like to admit? Ideology, policy and populism in the trajectories of the British National Party and Respect', *British Politics*, 3: 511–34.

Copsey, N. (2004) *Contemporary British fascism: the British National Party and the quest for legitimacy*, Basingstoke: Palgrave-Macmillan.

Copsey, N. (2007) 'Changing course or changing clothes? Reflections on the ideological evolution of the British National Party 1999–2006', *Patterns of Prejudice,* 41 (1): 61–82.

Copus, C. (1999a) 'The party group: model standing orders and a disciplined approach to representation', *Local Government Studies,* 25 (1): 17–34.

Copus, C. (1999b) 'The councillor and party group loyalty', *Policy and Politics,* 27 (3): 309–24.

Copus, C. (2001) 'Citizen participation in local government: the influence of the political party group', *Local Governance*, 27 (3): 151–63.

Copus, C. (2004), *Party politics and local government,* Manchester: Manchester University Press.

Copus, C. (2007) 'Liberal Democrat councillors: community politics, local campaigning and the role of the political party', *Political Quarterly*, 78 (1): 128–38.

Corina, L. (1974) 'Elected representatives in a party system: a typology', *Policy and Politics,* 3 (1): 69–87.

Drillsma-Milgrom, D. (2009) 'BNP members need careful handling', *Local Government Chronicle*, 1 October.

Eatwell, R. (2004) 'The extreme right in Britain: the long road to modernization', in Eatwell, R. and Mudde, C. (eds) *Western democracies and the extreme right challenge,* London: Routledge.

Eulau, H., Whalke, J., Buchanan, W. and Ferguson, L. (1959) 'The role of the representative: some empirical observations on the theory of Edmund Burke', *American Political Science Review*, 53: 742–56.

Fisher, S. L. (1980) 'The "decline" of parties' thesis and the role of minor parties', in Merkl, P. (ed.) *Western European party systems,* London: The Free Press.

Gyford, J. (1976) *Local politics in Britain,* London: Croom Helm.

Gyford, J., Leach, S. and Game, C. (1989) *The changing politics of local government*, London: Unwin- Hyman.

Heclo, H. (1969) 'The councillor's job', *Public Administration,* 47 (2): 185–202.

Herzog, H. (1987) 'Minor parties: the relevancy perspective', *Comparative Politics*, 19 (3), 317–29.

Jones, G. W. (1975) 'Varieties of local politics', *Local Government Studies,* 1 (2): 17–32.

Maud, Sir J. (Chair) (1967) *Committee on the Management of Local Government, Volume 1: Report*, London: HMSO.

Newton, K. (1976) *Second city politics: democratic processes and decision-making in Birmingham*, Oxford: Clarendon Press.

Rao, N. (1998) 'Representation in local politics: a reconsideration and some new evidence', *Political Studies,* 46, (1): 19–35.

Rhodes, J. (2009) 'The Banal National Party: the routine nature of legitimacy', *Patterns of Prejudice*, 43 (2): 142–60.

Snape, S. and Dobbs, L. (2003) 'The scrutineer: the impact of overview and scrutiny on councillor roles', *Public Policy and Administration,* 18 (1): 46–62.

PART III

International perspectives

8

ASSESSING THE POLITICAL RELEVANCE OF ANTI-IMMIGRANT PARTIES

The BNP in comparative European perspective

Anthony M. Messina

> The . . . population agreeing with positive statements and disagreeing with negative ones about the [National Front] . . . varied between 8 and 20 per cent and averaged 15 per cent. On the basis of this latter figure, and subtracting the 6 per cent of actual and potential voters, this gives an estimate of an additional 9 to 10 per cent of the population with covert sympathy for the NF in Britain . . .
>
> (Harrop et al., 1980: 282)

> Our evidence suggests that a significant minority, as many as 18 to 25 per cent of the population, would consider voting for the British National Party.
>
> (John et al., 2006: 5)

> In 1979 the NF . . . got 191,719 votes, a similar total to the BNP today, although it only represented 0.6% of those who voted, compared to the BNP's 0.74% in 2005 . . . By these figures the BNP is not much stronger than the NF was at the end of the 1970s.
>
> (*Searchlight*, no. 360, June 2005)

Introduction

The surge of subnational electoral support for the British National Party (BNP) since 2002 poses an enigma. On the one hand, the BNP is the most successful far-right party in British electoral history (Goodwin, 2007: 241; Renton, 2003; 2005); on the other hand, compared with many of its contemporary European counterparts, the BNP is an electoral pigmy (Ignazi, 2006: 186; John and Margetts, 2009: 502; Mudde, 2002: 40). Which is the more pertinent fact when assessing the current political influence and forecasting the likely electoral trajectory of the BNP?

This chapter filters the above questions through the prism of the comparative politics of anti-immigrant groups and parties in Western Europe. Within this context, two overarching questions are addressed. First, how politically relevant are Western Europe's ubiquitous anti-immigrant groups? Second, to what degree have their presence and activities influenced mainstream politics and state immigration and immigrant policy? The general insight this chapter offers is that, far from posing a universal threat, few anti-immigrant groups in Western Europe can and do significantly influence domestic politics and policy; moreover, even these do so only in very specific political circumstances. The majority of anti-immigrant actors, including the BNP, are currently and indefinitely confined to the fringes of domestic politics and policy-making (Statham and Geddes, 2006: 256).

Drawing upon evidence from a variety of sources, this chapter specifically assesses the BNP's influence on public attitudes towards immigration and settled immigrants, major party political discourse and national public policy. Our central argument is that, owing to the BNP's illiberal origins and the circumscribed opportunity structure of British domestic politics, the BNP *does not currently exercise, and for the foreseeable future is unlikely to enjoy*, significant influence on national immigration politics or policy.

Post-Second World War anti-immigrant groups and parties

Anti-immigrant groups and political parties across post-1980 Western Europe generally share three major characteristics (Messina, 2007: 95). First and most obviously, they are hostile towards settled immigrants and opposed to all new immigration (Zaslove, 2004: 100). Second, much of their modest political and/or electoral success during the past two decades springs from their exploitation of the social tensions accompanying the settlement of post-Second World War immigrants (Betz, 1994: 67; Bjørklund and Andersen, 2002: 128–9; Rydgren, 2004: 187). Finally, the major anti-immigrant groups have fostered a climate of public hostility towards immigrants that, in turn, has created a more favourable political context for them (Schain et al., 2002: 6; Williams, 2006).

However, anti-immigrant groups are far from equal; rather, they significantly vary in form, ideological orientation, political strategy and potential for electoral success. Indeed, Western Europe's major anti-immigrant groups can be usefully clustered into five major families.

Generic groups

Generic or 'pure' anti-immigrant groups, such as Ireland's Immigration Control Platform and the now defunct *Bevara Sverige Svensk* (Keep Sweden Swedish), have several common features. First, they are *exclusively* obsessed by an animus towards settled immigrants and new streams of immigration. Generic anti-immigrant groups are not inspired by grand world-views or political ideologies. Most do not adopt

TABLE 8.1 Families and select examples of post-1980 anti-immigrant groups in Western Europe

Generic right	*Neo-fascist right*	*Opportunistic right*	*New radical right*	*Ethno-national right*
Stop the Foreigners	British National Party	*Freiheitliche Partei*	*Front National Österreichs*	*Lega Nord*
Vigilance	National Democrats	*Movimento Sociale Italiano*	*Fremskridtspartiet*	*Vlaams Belang*
Bevara Sverige Svenskt	*Nederlandse Volks-Unie*	*Schweizerische Volkspartei*	*Fremskrittsparti*	*Alsace d'Abord*
Mouvement contre l'insécurité et l'immigration abusive	*Deutsche Volksunion*			*Ligue Savoisienne*
Stop Immigration	*Die Republikaner*			
An Feachtas um Smacht ar Inimirce	*Partido Nacional Renovador*			

economic or other policy programmes unrelated to their obsession with state immigrant and immigration policy. A second distinguishing feature of all generic anti-immigrant groups is their lack of formal organization. To the extent their supporters 'support' the group, they do so through their modest financial contributions, volunteer labour and/or spontaneous attendance at the group's public rallies or events. Because generic anti-immigrant groups primarily exist to achieve a negative end, they are more ephemeral protest vehicles than permanent organizations. A third characteristic of these groups is their adoption of unorthodox strategies to represent and disseminate their views. Rallies, public marches and various other unconventional activities are favoured by generic anti-immigrant groups to attract public attention to their cause. Lacking substantial financial and human capital, generic anti-immigrant groups exploit the free publicity their provocative activities command within the media.

Neo-fascist groups

Unlike generic anti-immigrant groups, neo-fascist groups *are* inspired by an overarching ideology. Neo-fascist groups embrace the core tenets of classical, pre-Second World War fascism, although most distance themselves in their public discourse from their infamous ideological forerunners. Like their pre-war predecessors, neo-fascist groups value social and political order and hierarchy, are wary if not explicitly contemptuous of capitalism, reject multiculturalism and are aggressively nationalistic. Where neo-fascist groups part company from their more radical predecessors is with respect to their grudging adherence to the rules of democratic politics (Renton, 2005: 44). Although hostile towards liberal democracy, neo-fascist groups in Western Europe, virtually without exception, rhetorically concede its legitimacy.

For neo-fascist groups, then, antagonism towards post-war immigrants automatically follows from their core ideological orientation, which validates racial hierarchy and, thus, the inevitability of inter-ethnic and racial conflict. This said, neo-fascist groups are also hostile towards settled immigrants for instrumental reasons. Specifically, they are disposed to adopt a highly visible anti-immigrant posture in order to appeal to the widest possible political constituency, and certainly to a broader one than their core authoritarian positions and ideas would otherwise attract (Betz, 1994: 80–1).

Neo-fascist groups are formally organized. Most have regular, albeit usually a modest number of, dues-paying members; convene annual meetings or conferences; allocate routine, if ill-defined, leadership roles and responsibilities; and maintain a national headquarters. Several neo-fascist groups in Western Europe, including the BNP, have operated for a decade or longer. The formal organization of neo-fascist groups is inspired by their lofty political ambitions. Unlike generic anti-immigrant groups, neo-fascist groups are not exclusively preoccupied with short-term questions of racial or ethnic conflict. They are generally less interested than generic anti-immigrant groups are in altering the course of current public policy or influencing the attitudes of mainstream political elites (Williams, 2006). As their ultimate objective is to capture national political power, neo-fascist groups create and maintain a formal organizational structure in order to be able to prevail politically over the long term. Thus motivated, it is fairly common for neo-fascist groups to participate in local and national elections.

In some of the aforementioned ways, neo-fascist groups resemble mainstream conservative political parties. Nevertheless, they differ from such parties in several important respects. First, few neo-fascist groups are committed to contesting elections as the sole means of achieving power. In addition to other considerations influencing their commitment to the electoral process, neo-fascist groups pragmatically recognize that their latent support within the national electorate is highly circumscribed. As a result, they also pursue extra-electoral strategies to achieve their political ends. A second difference is that neo-fascist groups are generally unavailable to join electoral coalitions. Their unavailability stems from the reluctance of mainstream parties to ally with them, as well as their ideological aversion to political compromise. A third difference is that, unlike mainstream conservative parties or even the opportunistic right, new radical right (NRR) or ethno-national right, neo-fascist groups disproportionately draw their support from 'protest voters', for whom issues of race and immigration are of paramount importance (Taylor, 1982: 100–1). Although less dependent than generic groups are on immigration-related issues for their institutional survival, neo-fascist groups nevertheless must be able to draw from the pool of *mobilizable* xenophobic and/or racist voters in order to advance politically.

Opportunistic right

On the surface, 'opportunistic-right' groups, such as Austria's *Freiheitliche Partei Österreichs* (FPÖ, Austrian Freedom Party) and *Schweizerische Volkspartei* (SVP, Swiss' People's Party), have a great deal in common with neo-fascist groups. Like the latter, the opportunistic right has inherited or adopted much of the *Weltanschauung* of pre-Second World War fascism. Like neo-fascist groups, the opportunistic right is formally organized. As their more extremist counterpart does, the opportunistic right regularly contests elections. However, a number of important differences distinguish the opportunistic right from neo-fascist groups, thus allowing the former to exercise greater influence over the domestic politics of immigration.

Perhaps the most distinguishing feature of the opportunistic right is that its anti-immigrant and anti-immigration postures are primarily driven by a calculated political strategy to win votes. Unlike neo-fascist groups, the opportunistic right is not inspired by an obsessive, race-centred ideology. Rather, its hostility to state immigrant and immigration policy is folded into a broader populism that pragmatically weaves immigration-related issues into a larger critique of the existing political and, very often, the socio-economic order (Kitschelt, 1995: 162). In contrast to neo-fascist groups, the opportunistic right will trim its illiberalism on immigration-related issues if it repels too many voters.

A second feature distinguishing the opportunistic right is its malleable ideology. Opportunistic-right political parties, at various points in their history, will ideologically waver between the extreme and the more moderate political right (Betz, 2002). Thus, where an opportunistic-right party is situated along the ideological spectrum at a given point in time depends upon a confluence of political variables, including the personal ideological disposition of its leaders and the political opportunity structure.

The opportunistic right can also be distinguished from neo-fascist groups with regard to its orientation towards the mainstream parties of government. Unlike neo-fascist groups, the opportunistic right is not permanently constrained, either by ideology or by the content of its policies, from allying with mainstream political parties or being embraced by them. As a result, the opportunistic right is very much a player in the formation of governments and parliamentary coalitions.

New radical right

Like the three previously cited anti-immigrant groups, NRR parties are inspired by a right-wing authoritarianism that situates them at the forefront of the domestic political backlash against immigration. Like neo-fascist parties and the opportunistic right, NRR parties have dues-paying members, regularly contest elections and aspire to govern. As with the opportunistic right, many of the electoral appeals of the NRR strike a populist chord. However, despite sharing several characteristics and ambitions with its ideological cousins, the NRR is a distinctive anti-immigrant actor.

Especially distinguishing the NRR is the unique manner in which it combines a neo-liberal commitment to capitalism and individual economic freedom with illiberalism towards immigrants, immigration, materialism and contemporary democracy (Kitschelt, 1995: 19–20). For the NRR, the social conflict engendered by immigration serves as a catalyst that crystallizes 'right-wing extremism on the level of party competition if political entrepreneurs can embed xenophobic slogans in a broader right-authoritarian message for which they find a receptive audience' (Kitschelt, 1995: 3). Although NRR parties are hostile towards immigrants and opposed to all new immigration, they are *not* politically over-invested in these positions. Immigration-related social conflict provides an opportunity for the NRR to mobilize citizens who are primarily disillusioned with the broader sociopolitical and economic order.

Its racism and xenophobia have made the NRR hitherto ineligible to join mainstream parties in electoral pacts or government. Mainstream conservative parties cannot easily embrace the NRR without incurring a risk of alienating a critical number of their core, predominantly politically moderate voters. Although some confusion reigns about which parties can be appropriately subsumed under this category, the French *Front National* and the Danish and Norwegian Progress Parties stand out as important examples of this genre of anti-immigrant political actor.

Ethno-national right

In many important respects, the ethno-national right overlaps with the opportunistic right. Like the latter, the ethno-national right 'appropriates' anti-immigrant and anti-immigration positions in order to win votes (Kitschelt, 1995: 175). Like the opportunistic right, the ethno-national right can accentuate or submerge immigration-related appeals as the political opportunity structure and/or short-term electoral circumstances dictate. As for its counterpart, the ideological orientation of the ethno-national right is flexible, thus allowing ethno-national parties an opportunity periodically to reassess their core tenets and redefine them in line with their current policy preferences. Moreover, the ethno-national right is formally organized, regularly contests elections and aspires to attain political power through conventional political and electoral institutions. However, in contrast to the opportunistic right and every other right party, bar pure anti-immigrant groups, ethno-national parties are primarily single-issue oriented.

The core theme energizing the ethno-national right is, of course, ethno-nationalism (Leslie, 1989: 45), the most politically salient issue for its supporters and the cleavage without which the ethno-national right could not long politically survive. The fact that the ethno-national right is primarily organized around ethno-nationalism not only relegates its anti-immigration posture to a secondary status but also prevents it from becoming too prominent in its rhetoric or electoral appeals. Just as the NRR cannot completely abandon its pro-market positions or overly emphasize its anti-immigration posture, so too the ethno-national right is similarly constrained with respect to its commitment to ethno-nationalism. Indeed, anti-immigration appeals merely complement the ethno-national right's traditional agenda by linking the economic, cultural and political 'penetration' of the periphery (i.e. the traditional regions) by the metropole (i.e. central government) with its simultaneous human 'invasion' by undesirable and unwanted immigrants. Although many ethno-national groups operate across contemporary Europe, only the Italian *Lega Nord* (Northern League), the Belgian *Vlaams Belang* (VB, Flemish Interest) and a handful of others properly belong to the ethno-national right.

Longevity and ideological commitment

Although anti-immigrant groups self-evidently foster and exploit popular anti-immigrant sentiment, it is less clear if, and to what extent, they exercise significant political influence (Minkenberg, 2001; Perlmutter, 2002; Pettigrew, 1998). According to Williams (2002; 2006), the political impact of these groups can be empirically investigated along three dimensions: influence on the political agenda; impact on other parties within the party system; and effect on public policy, particularly legislation. In employing multiple empirical methods, Williams (2002) discovers that, in Austria, France and Germany, anti-immigrant parties exercise far more influence on agenda setting and public policy than they do on the positions mainstream parties adopt on immigration-related issues.

Adopting a more subjective approach to the question of influence, we return to our aforementioned categories to gain insight into the perseverance of anti-immigrant groups within the domestic political arena and to evaluate their respective propensities to advocate *forcefully* and advance *successfully* an anti-immigration and anti-immigrant policy agenda. Informed by our earlier discussion, the five categories of anti-immigrant group can be aligned along the axes of longevity (i.e. the tendency of anti-immigrant groups to endure as key actors in the political and/or party systems) and ideological/political commitment (i.e. the level or intensity of a group's commitment to an anti-immigration and anti-immigrant policy agenda) as represented in Figure 8.1. In this figure, the higher a group is on the axis of political longevity and the further right it is located on the axis of ideological/political commitment, the more influence, *ceteris paribus*, it is likely to exert on domestic immigration and immigrant politics and policy.

What Figure 8.1 suggests is that the NRR is potentially the most influential anti-immigrant actor within Western Europe (Williams, 2006). It is the most influential in the sense that, of the five families of anti-immigrant groups, the NRR is best positioned to intervene in the domestic politics of immigrant and immigration policy in a manner that is likely to affect the course of politics and public policy. Moreover, NRR groups can sustain such influence over the medium to long term.

The NRR is so located because, in contrast to generic and neo-fascist groups, it combines a relatively high degree of permanence within the political and the party systems with an unwavering ideological and political commitment to

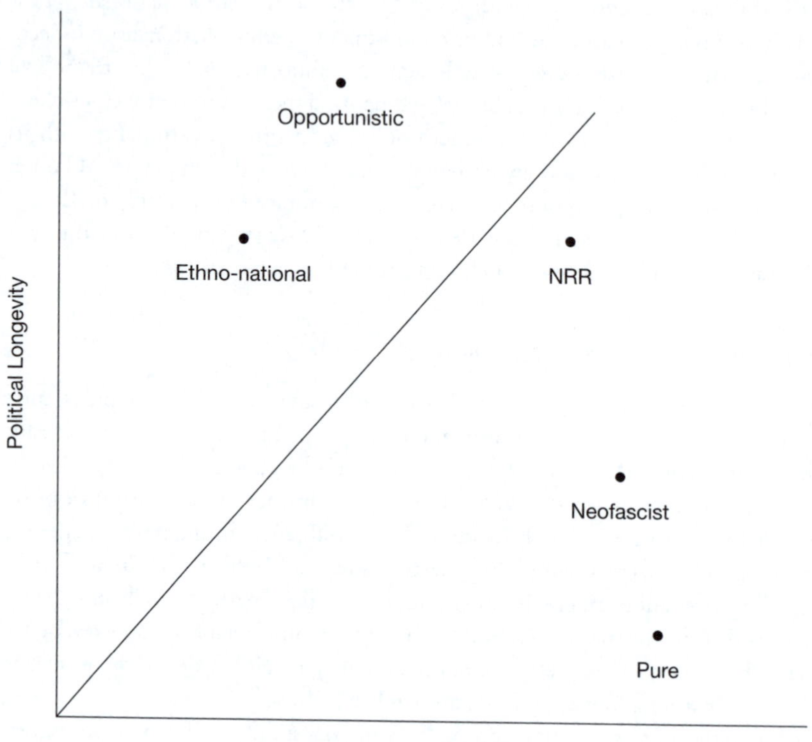

FIGURE 8.1 Political influence of anti-immigrant groups

promoting an anti-immigrant policy agenda. Unlike its illiberal counterparts, the NRR combines a deep commitment to an anti-immigration policy agenda with a considerable capacity to project its ideas and prescriptions into the political mainstream over time. Generic anti-immigrant groups and, within some countries, neo-fascist groups are more hostile towards settled immigrants than the NRR. Conversely, by virtue of its demonstrated political longevity and ability to straddle successfully the boundary between the hard and moderate political right, the opportunistic right occupies a more secure foothold within the political/party system. However, what privileges the NRR in the domestic politics of immigration is its unique ability to appeal to voters who are not particularly racist or xenophobic while, simultaneously, keeping these issues at the forefront of its public political agenda (Husbands, 1981). Because it can attract substantial political and electoral support from citizens across the socio-economic spectrum without compromising its commitment to an anti-immigration and anti-immigrant agenda, the NRR is able to bring to bear substantial, effective *and* sustained political pressure on policymakers and mainstream political parties, as the example of the *Front National* in France especially well demonstrates (Schain, 2002; Williams, 2006).

Origins, supporters and electoral potential of the BNP

Where does the BNP fit into the above analysis? Before addressing this question, we will very briefly sketch the BNP's political origins and electoral history.

As has been recounted numerous times, organized political opposition to immigration in Britain surfaced relatively early during the post-Second World War period (Copsey, 2004; Messina, 1989). Uniting the original post-war British National Party and the League of Empire Loyalists, the National Front (NF) was founded in 1967, primarily in response to the neglect of race-related issues by Britain's major political parties. Although the party inherited the ideological baggage of anti-Semitism and opposition to Britain's post-war decolonization, it was the immigration issue that ultimately energized the coalition of right-wing actors that gave birth to the NF (Walker, 1978: 58).

It is often forgotten that, at the peak of its popularity, the NF enjoyed significant support within the British electorate. Indeed, from 1972 to 1978, it was not unusual for NF candidates to receive between 8 and 16 per cent of the vote in local elections and parliamentary by-elections. Steed (1978: 29) estimates that NF candidates averaged 5.2 per cent of the vote in twenty-five by-election contests between 1968 and 1978. Moreover, in one public opinion survey conducted after its electoral support had waned, 21 per cent of all respondents agreed that it would be 'good for Britain' if the NF were represented in the House of Commons (Harrop *et al.*, 1980). Even at the nadir of its popularity during the 1970s, 303 NF candidates garnered 191,000 votes in the 1979 general election (Table 8.2).

With the National Front's organizational implosion during the early 1980s, however, the current iteration of the BNP gradually emerged (Copsey, 2004: 100–23). Competing in its first general election against a rump National Front in 1983, the new BNP sponsored fifty-four candidates and attracted fewer than 15,000 total votes. As Table 8.2 indicates, the BNP's performance in general elections has been poor both before and after Nick Griffin's ascent to the leadership of the BNP in 1999. During the 1997 general election, the party fielded fifty-seven candidates, saving three deposits and winning almost 36,000 votes. Four years later, it put up thirty-three candidates and attracted 47,000 votes, with the election's high point occurring in the constituency of Oldham West and Royton, where the BNP won 16.4 per cent of the vote, after racial tensions had precipitated rioting within the constituency. In the 2005 general election, the BNP sponsored 119 candidates and garnered a total of 192,750 votes. Although little improved over the NF's performance in the October 1974 general election, the BNP's total vote in 2005 increased fourfold over 2001. In the 2010 general election, the BNP fielded a record 339 candidates, who garnered more than a half million combined votes, thus making it the best ever performance for a far-right party in a British general election. This said, the average vote per BNP candidate in 2010 increased only modestly over 2005 (Table 8.2).

As has been extensively chronicled (Rhodes, 2006; 2009a), the BNP's greatest electoral gains in recent years have not occurred in general elections, but rather

TABLE 8.2 Performance of neo-fascist parties in British general elections, 1970–2010

Political party	*Candidates*	*Votes*	*% vote*	*Average vote per candidate*	*Retained deposits*
National Front					
1970	10	11,449	0.0	1,145	0
1974 (F)	54	76,865	0.2	1,423	0
1974 (O)	90	113,843	0.4	1,265	0
1979	303	191,719	0.6	633	0
1983	60	27,065	0.1	451	0
1987	–	–	–	–	0
1992	14	3,984	0.0	285	0
National Democrats					
1997	21	10,829	0.0	516	1
National Front					
1997	6	2,716	0.0	453	0
2001	5	2,484	0.0	497	0
2005	13	8,029	0.0	618	0
2010	17	10,784	0.0	634	0
British National Party					
1983	54	14,621	0.0	271	0
1987	2	553	0.0	277	0
1992	13	7,005	0.0	539	0
1997	57	35,832	0.1	629	3
2001	33	47,129	0.2	1,428	7
2005	119	192,706	0.7	1,620	34
2010	339	564,331	1.9	1,665	76

Sources: BBC News, 2010; Kavanagh and Butler, 2005: 204; London: House of Commons.

in low-turnout, subnational and European elections. The party's initial electoral breakthrough occurred in 1993, when Derek Beackon was returned as councillor for Millwall (in London), a seat he subsequently forfeited. The BNP's next electoral milestone occurred in the Lancashire towns of Burnley and Oldham, where, in November 2001, the party secured a relatively high share of the vote in three ward by-elections, following race riots there the previous summer. In the subsequent English local elections in 2002, sixty-seven BNP candidates polled 30,998 votes in twenty-six local authority districts. Since 2002, the BNP has fielded ever more candidates at the local level and, as a result, it has garnered an increasing number of local council seats. By 2008, the BNP had fifty-five local councillors; moreover, when parish, town and community councillors are included, the party held over 100 seats. However, the BNP achieved its most significant electoral breakthrough to date when it won two seats in the European Parliament in June 2009. For the first time, the party captured seats in a national election, with Nick Griffin winning a constituency in the North West region, after Andrew Brons prevailed in Yorkshire and the Humber. Capitalizing on the MPs' expense scandal during the election campaign, but mostly benefiting from a haemorrhaging of the Labour Party's traditional support, the BNP received 6.2 per cent of the national vote, a modest increase of 1.3 per cent on the support it received in the 2004 European elections.

BNP electorate

What primarily motivates BNP voters? Like all neo-fascist, anti-immigrant parties across Western Europe, including its predecessor the NF, the BNP draws a disproportionate share of its support from politically disaffected voters for whom immigration-related issues are especially salient (Deacon et al., 2004: 13; Harris, 2010: 13; Rhodes, 2006: 17; 2009a). As John et al. (2006: 8) explain:

> Those respondents in our [2004] poll who had supported the BNP were more likely to believe that immigration was the most important issue. In the European election exit polls, 77 per cent of BNP voters give this option, 24 per cent of Conservative supporters . . . 24 per cent of Liberal Democrats and 10 per cent of Labour supporters.

Indeed, the preoccupation of BNP voters with immigration-related issues very much unites these voters with a party that is obsessed with immigration. Along these lines, almost 90 per cent of BNP parliamentary candidates cited the issue of immigration/asylum in their 2005 general election campaign literature, a theme that intersects law and order (78 per cent), Europe (72 per cent) and security/terrorism (67 per cent), or other issues that were cited frequently by BNP candidates (Robinson and Fisher, 2005: 22).

This said, the BNP's supporters are *not* especially invested in the party; indeed, almost half of BNP voters primarily identify with another political party (Harris, 2010: 8). Rather, unlike the supporters of several NRR parties across Western Europe (Simmons, 1996: 182), very many BNP voters support the party – as the NF's voters did during the 1970s (Taylor, 1993: 180) – in the spirit of an ephemeral protest (Deacon et al., 2004: 20), that is, as a way of communicating their displeasure with the major political parties' neglect of immigration-related and other issues (Cruddas et al., 2005: 14). As John et al. (2006: 12) report:

> Even in Barking and Dagenham, where the BNP has polled well, the party is disliked and distrusted. The BNP was seen as a racist, anti-immigrant and deceitful party and voting for it as an aberrant or embarrassing act . . . a 'kick up the backside', or a wake-up call, for the major parties.

Moreover, unlike France's *Front National* and other more electorally successful anti-immigrant parties, few of the BNP's voters are formal members of the party.

One estimate early in this decade put the BNP's paid membership at only several thousand, or approximately a sixth of the membership claimed by the NF during the 1970s (Renton, 2003: 84). The BNP now claims a membership of approximately 13,000. By comparison, France's *Front National* could boast 75,000 formal members at its peak. Moreover, during the early 1990s, the Austrian FPÖ is reported to have had 40,000 members and, at the height of its popularity during the late 1990s, the *Deutsche Volksunion* (DVU, German People's Union) had 20,000 members.

Circumscribed political opportunity structure

Another impediment to the party's political advance is that, even when immigration-related issues are salient and anti-immigrant sentiment surges within the British electorate, the BNP cannot presume it will profit. This is so for at least two reasons. First, because most British voters view the BNP extremely negatively and its electoral supporters are not especially invested in the party, the BNP's *potential* vote is highly circumscribed; indeed, contrary to some speculative reports (John and Margetts, 2009), there is little reason to believe that it currently exceeds the upper limit of the NF's potential vote during the 1970s (Harrop et al., 1980: 282). Without a strong ideological or partisan glue to bond its supporters to the BNP, a critical number of the former tend to abandon the party from one election to the next. Indeed, in losing twenty-six council seats in the 2010 local elections, including all twelve that the party had gained in Barking and Dagenham in 2006, the BNP reconfirmed its inability to make further electoral inroads in localities where it has previously gained council seats (Renton, 2005: 43–4).

A second reason why the BNP's electoral potential is circumscribed is that the Conservative Party has historically exercised a high degree of political ownership over immigration-related issues (Mudde, 2002: 41), especially at the national level. Having asserted its ownership of immigration-related issues early in the policy attention cycle during the post-Second World War period and cultivated the relatively small anti-immigrant vote sufficiently well during this time, the Conservative Party has politically 'crowded out' all anti-immigrant parties, including the BNP (Copsey, 2004: 28, 48). Consequently, whenever the Conservative Party emphasizes immigration-related issues (Tables 8.3 and 8.4), as it did during the 2005 general election (*The Economist*, 2005a; Smith, 2008: 423), the BNP's electoral potential wanes. In politically articulating the general public's hostility to immigration and immigrants since the late 1970s (Eatwell, 2004; Messina, 1989: 126–49), the Conservative Party has largely precluded other groups within the domestic political marketplace from politically exploiting these themes successfully for very long.

Political influence of BNP

Irrespective of its prospects for further political and electoral growth, to what extent has the BNP impacted British politics and public policy? As Williams (2006) did

TABLE 8.3 Candidates mentioning immigration/asylum in their 2005 general election literature (percentage)

Party	*Mentions issue*	*Positively*	*Negatively*
Conservative	84	11	80
Labour	21	5	17
Liberal Democrat	4	3	0
BNP	89	0	89

Source: Robinson and Fisher, 2005: 13, 22.

TABLE 8.4 Issue priorities of major parties in 2005 general election (percentage)

Issue	*Conservative*	*Labour*	*Liberal Democrat*	*Mean issue emphases (S.D.)*
Health**	14	16	13	15 (1)
Education**	17	31	33	27 (7)
Crime*	25	9	5	13 (9)
Immigration*	14	5	1	6 (6)
Defence	3	2	22	9 (9)
Pensions	4	1	9	5 (3)
Economy**	6	28	5	13 (11)
Unemployment	1	3	0	2 (1)
Taxation	14	3	10	9 (5)
Europe	1	1	1	1 (0)

Notes:
* Issue 'owned' by the Conservative Party
** Issue 'owned' by the Labour Party

Source: Green and Hobolt, 2008: 7-8.

in her study of anti-immigrant groups elsewhere, we can investigate – albeit using different measures – the extent to which the BNP has influenced: general public opinion; the policy positions of the major political parties; and public policy, including national legislation.

Public opinion

For obvious reasons, the question of whether or not the BNP has influenced British public attitudes on immigration-related issues is difficult to investigate. This said, it is reasonable to presume that in the *absence* of a shift in public opinion on immigration-related issues since the allegedly more modern and professional BNP emerged at the beginning of this decade (Copsey, 2004: 100–8; Rhodes, 2009b) and, perhaps more importantly, *after* the traumatic events of 11 September 2001 in the United States and the 7 July 2005 London bombings, it can be confidently affirmed that the party and its activities have *not* significantly influenced public opinion.

That immigration-related issues have become more salient in Britain, particularly since the traumatic events of 11 September 2001, is irrefutable (Clarke et al., 2006: 6). Since 2001, the salience of immigration-related issues has soared, increasing more than twofold on the monthly average. To underscore the sea change that has occurred in public opinion: 30 per cent or more of respondents identified immigration-related issues as among the 'most important' in thirty-seven of seventy-six monthly surveys between September 2001 and December 2007. In contrast, these issues failed to achieve a comparable level of salience in *any* month during the previous twenty-seven years (Ipsos MORI, 1974–2008) (see Figure 8.2).

Have Britons become less tolerant of immigration and immigrants as immigration-related issues have become more salient? The survey evidence suggests not. As Table 8.5 reveals, the public's view of whether or not there are 'too many immigrants in Britain' has remained relatively constant: robust majorities agreed with this sentiment both *before* and *after* 2001. Indeed, the distribution of responses to a survey conducted in 2007 was very similar to what it was in 1989 and 2000. Compared with the 1960s, when more than four in five persons opined that too many immigrants had been admitted into Britain (Messina, 1989: 12), contemporary British attitudes toward immigration and immigrants seem tolerant and relaxed.

Further evidence of continuity in British public opinion is contained in Table 8.6. When asked to choose between five statements about immigration policy, large majorities preferred the option of making immigration laws 'much tougher'. Yet the size of this majority has varied little, even slightly shrinking from 2003 to 2007.

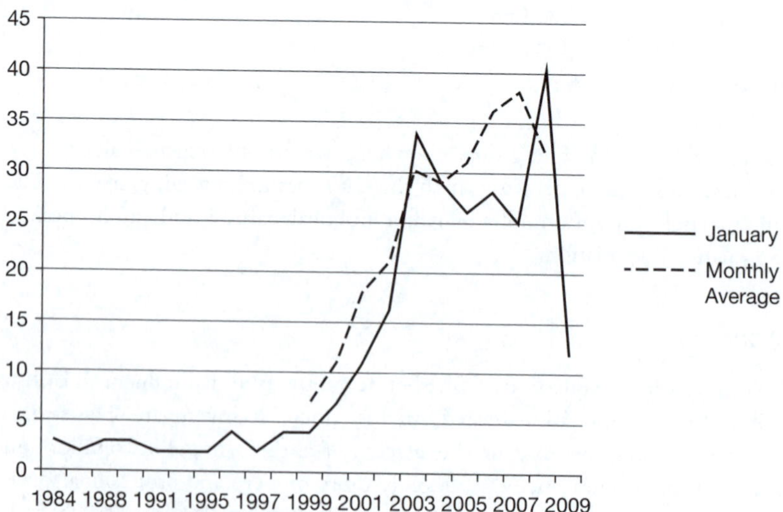

FIGURE 8.2 Race/immigration/immigrants 'most important' issue, 1984–2009 (percentage)

Source: Ipsos MORI.

TABLE 8.5 Opinion on whether or not 'there are too many immigrants', 1989–2007 (percentage)

	Total agree	*Total disagree*	*Neither/nor**	*Don't know*
1989	63	18	18	1
1994	64	33	–	3
1997	61	35	–	4
1999	55	33	–	13
2000	66	17	13	3
2001	54	31	10	5
2007	68	22	8	2

Note:
* 1994–9 data from surveys using self-completed questionnaires with no 'neither/nor' option and, except in 1999, no 'don't know' option.

Source: Ipsos MORI.

TABLE 8.6 Opinion on immigration, 2003–7 (percentage)

Laws on immigration should:	*2003**	*2005*	*2006*	*2007*	*Net change 2003–7*
be abolished . . .	2	2	1	2	0
be relaxed	4	8	5	5	+1
remain as they are	12	19	17	13	+1
be much tougher	67	58	63	64	–3
be stopped altogether	13	11	12	12	–1
don't know	3	2	2	3	0

Note:
* Face-to-face survey

Source: Ipsos MORI.

Fairly constant too is the percentage of respondents advocating that 'immigration should be stopped altogether'. Somewhat surprisingly, given the negative political environment for immigration purportedly generated by the aforementioned terrorist events and the BNP's local electoral inroads, the view that all immigration should be curtailed never exceeded 13 per cent between 2003 and 2007.

As the survey data reported in Table 8.7 indicate, more targeted public attitudes on immigration from the Middle East and North Africa too have not significantly changed. Although the percentage of respondents citing immigration from the aforementioned region a 'good thing' declined between 2002 and 2007, a *majority* of the British public nevertheless remained positive. Moreover, the minority citing migration from the Middle East and North Africa as a 'bad thing' actually *decreased* over this period. Among six West European populations with significant experience of Muslim immigration, only Swedes were less hostile than Britons to migration

TABLE 8.7 Opinion on migration from Middle East and North Africa, 2002–7 (percentage)

	Britain				*France*			
	2002	*2005*	*2006*	*2007*	*2002*	*2005*	*2006*	*2007*
Good Thing	53	61	57	51	44	53	58	53
Bad Thing	40	30	32	34	53	45	41	44
Don't Know	7	10	11	15	3	2	1	2
Trend	Positive				Positive			

	Spain			*Germany*				*Italy*	*Sweden*
	2005	*2006*	*2007*	*2002*	*2005*	*2006*	*2007*	*2007*	*2007*
Good Thing	67	62	44	33	34	34	26	20	57
Bad Thing	26	33	45	59	57	59	64	67	28
Don't Know	7	5	11	8	8	7	10	14	15
Trend	Negative			Negative					

Source: Pew Research Centre.

from the Middle East and North Africa in 2007. In a different poll, conducted across eleven countries in 2005, only 14 per cent of Britons held an 'unfavourable view of Muslims', the lowest among Europeans.[1]

What can be concluded about the above-cited survey data? Most obviously, the BNP has not measurably influenced British public attitudes on immigration-related issues since the party's recent electoral local breakthroughs. Despite the traumas of 11 September 2001 and 7 July 2005 and the BNP's attempts to exploit them politically (Copsey, 2004: 135), the British public has not become more negatively inclined towards immigrants and immigration, including migration from the Middle East and North Africa. Unlike the *Front National,* which first brought immigration-related issues to the political fore in France during the 1980s and, since then, has dominated public discourse on these questions (Schain, 1995; Williams, 2006), the BNP has *primarily reacted to, and not shaped,* British public attitudes on immigration.

Content of major party discourse

Granted that the BNP has not demonstratively influenced public opinion on immigration-related issues, has it nevertheless foisted these issues on to the respective agendas of the major political parties?

There is little doubt immigration has assumed a more prominent place in British political discourse since the late 1990s (Messina, 2007: 119–22), i.e. before the BNP's local electoral surge. To the chagrin of even some of its core supporters, the Conservative Party made asylum and immigration, and particularly the Labour government's purported failure to control immigration flows, much more of an issue in its general election campaign in 2005 than it did in 2001 (*The Economist*, 2005b; Geddes, 2005: 284). As Table 8.3 indicates, more than 80 per cent of Conservative parliamentary candidates mentioned immigration in their election addresses, and, for the vast majority, the issue was negatively framed. Indeed, on both scores, Conservatives were only marginally different from the BNP's candidates.

This said, to conclude that the Conservative Party's emphasis on immigration in 2005 was a reaction to the BNP is unwarranted. Rather, having established its ownership of immigration at least two decades previously, the Conservative Party was predictably trying to raise the issue's already high salience within the electorate in order to exploit its advantage over Labour (Table 8.4). As Green and Hobolt (2008: 13) have observed:

> central to the issue ownership model is the claim that owned issues benefit parties the greater their salience. We should [therefore] find that increasing the salience of an issue on which a party has a relative advantage is consistent with vote-maximising behaviour.

Rather than defensively reacting to the BNP's agenda or to the potential threat of voter defections to the BNP during the general election campaign, the Conservative Party deliberately embraced immigration to exploit its ownership of the issue (Geddes, 2005: 288) and deflect the electorate's attention away from the issues 'owned' by the Labour Party (Table 8.4).

Moreover, further undermining the thesis that the Conservatives emphasized immigration in the 2005 general election in response to pressure from the BNP is the fact that Conservative candidate addresses were no more likely to frame immigration negatively in marginal than in safe parliamentary seats, despite the fact that immigration was of great concern to voters in marginal constituencies (Geddes, 2005: 289). In contrast, Conservative parliamentary candidates were more negative about the European Union in marginal than safe seats (Robinson and Fisher, 2005: 17). On the basis of these facts, Robinson and Fisher (2005: 18) have concluded that the Conservative Party adopted a 'principled stance' on immigration 'rather than playing the "race card" in tight electoral contests' during the 2005 general election.

The Labour Party emphasized immigration much less than the Conservatives during the general election campaign (Table 8.4), choosing instead to campaign primarily on the salient issues it owned: education, the economy and health (Green and Hobolt, 2008: 7). Exceptions to this general rule were the speeches of Labour's leader, Tony Blair, which addressed the immigration issue more frequently than either the party's election broadcasts or campaign press releases (Green and Hobolt, 2008: 8). However, in downplaying the immigration issue during the general election and highlighting its positive, economic dimension, while largely ignoring its cultural, identity and social implications in its election manifesto, it is likely that the Labour Party did not perceive the BNP as an especially serious electoral threat.

Volume and content of national legislation/policy initiatives

What of the BNP's possible influence on the volume and content of national legislation and other policy initiatives on immigration? As Table 8.8 makes clear, successive Labour governments made immigration and immigrant policy a priority for formal legislation after 1997. Indeed, as Somerville observes, since 2001, Labour's 'rate of lawmaking [on immigration] surpasses that of every social policy area. In addition, legislation has been supplemented by a number of major policy proposals and plans'.[2] Yet, on the basis of the evidence, it is highly doubtful the proliferation of immigration-related initiatives after 1998 is a direct response to the BNP.

First, although several key initiatives represented in Table 8.8 clearly reflect the Labour governments' priorities to control immigration and enhance border security – also the BNP's core concerns – the emphasis of Labour's 'post-1997 immigration regime was managing immigration for macroeconomic purposes, a commitment that facilitated *more rather than less* immigration. Given its obvious expansionary bias, it is difficult to see how this regime supports the thesis that Labour governments were under significant pressure from anti-immigration public opinion and/or the BNP in realigning Britain's immigration policies during the past decade. Second, as Table 8.8 makes clear, Labour's post-1997 restriction of some immigration streams, and particularly asylum, began well before the BNP's local electoral surge. The 1999 Immigration and Asylum Act predated the surge by more than two years. Moreover, the 2001 Anti-Terrorism, Crime and Security Act, crafted well before the BNP's local electoral ascent and formally introduced into Parliament in the same month as the Burnley and Oldham by-elections, was obviously a hasty response to the spike in public concern about domestic security in Britain following the 11 September 2001 attacks on New York. Finally, the embrace of anti-discrimination legislation and community cohesion policies by successive Labour governments self-evidently situated them on the opposite side to the BNP on the race relations/immigration integration priority spectrum. Indeed, these recent initiatives were very much in keeping with the progressive thread of Labour's traditional immigrant policies (Messina, 1989: 42).

TABLE 8.8 Select immigration policies and national legislation, 1998–2008

Policy/legislation	*Type*	*Year*	*Overview*
Fairer, Faster and Firmer: A Modern Approach to Immigration and Asylum	White Paper	1998	Instituted new controls and a 'covenant' with asylum seekers; emphasized need for administrative overhaul.
Human Rights Act	Parliamentary Act	1998	Incorporated European Convention on Human Rights into UK law, giving human rights the status of 'higher law'.
Immigration and Asylum Act	Parliamentary Act	1999	Created a 'covenant' with asylum seekers, but generally restrictive; made provisions for a new welfare support system (the National Asylum Support Service).
Race Relations (Amendment) Act	Parliamentary Act	2000	Broadened anti-discrimination legislation to police and immigration service and created 'positive duty' for race equality on public authorities.
Antiterrorism, Crime and Security Act	Parliamentary Act	2001	Suspected immigrant terrorists could be interned (potentially on a permanent basis). The Special Immigration Appeals Commission (SIAC) reviews decisions, but the act does not permit judicial review of the SIAC.
Secure Borders, Safe Havens: Integration with Diversity in Modern Britain	White Paper	2002	Established comprehensive reform, including the goal of 'managed migration'.
The Nationality, Immigration and Asylum Act	Parliamentary Act	2002	Increased asylum restrictions (breaking previous 'covenant') and new enforcement powers, but supported economic immigration.
Highly Skilled Migrant Program	Change to regulations	2002	Created immigration scheme based on points aiming to attract high-skilled migrants.
Asylum and Immigration (Treatment of Claimants, etc.) Act	Parliamentary Act	2004	Further reduced asylum appeal rights and other restrictive measures.

continued . . .

TABLE 8.8 . . . *continued*

Policy/legislation	*Type*	*Year*	*Overview*
Controlling our Borders: Making Migration Work for Britain	Five-Year Departmental Plan	2005	Set out strong measures to regain control of borders and manage migration through a new points system.
Improving Opportunity, Strengthening Society: The Government's Strategy to Increase Race Equality and Community Cohesion	Policy Strategy	2005	A race–equality strategy designed to cut across government, complemented by a cross-cutting, race–equality target, and overseen by a board of senior public figures.
Integration Matters: The National Integration Strategy for Refugees	Policy Strategy	2005	Strategy to integrate refugees, including new 'integration loans' and piloting a one-to-one caseworker model. Founded on strategy formulated in 2000.
A Points-Based System: Making Migration Work for Britain	Policy Strategy	2006	Proposed five-tier economic migration system: high skilled; skilled with job offer; low skilled; students; and miscellaneous.
Immigration, Asylum, and Nationality (IAN) Act	Parliamentary Act	2006	Mainly focused on immigration (rather than asylum), it included restrictions on appeal rights, sanctions on employers of unauthorized labour and a tightening of citizenship rules.
Fair, Effective, Transparent and Trusted: Rebuilding Confidence in Our Immigration System	Reform Strategy	2006	Created arm's-length Border and Immigration Agency, replacing the Immigration and Nationality Directorate on 2 April 2007.
Enforcing the Rules: A Strategy to Ensure and Enforce Compliance with Our Immigration Laws	Policy Strategy	2007	Called for secure border control built on biometric visas and greater checks.

continued . . .

TABLE 8.8 . . . *continued*

Policy/legislation	*Type*	*Year*	*Overview*
UK Borders Act	Parliamentary Act	2007	Gave police powers to immigration officers and requires foreign nationals to have a Biometric Immigration Document (BID).
Criminal Justice and Immigration Act	Parliamentary Act	2008	Provides special immigration status for terrorists and serious criminals who cannot be removed from the UK for legal reasons.

Source: *Migration Information Source*; Ministry of Justice.

Conclusion

Whatever their respective policies, ideological orientation, organizational form or core political strategy, anti-immigrant groups across Western Europe are united in carving out, securing and/or advancing their position within the domestic political order by opposing new immigration and the presence of settled immigrants. In staking out this illiberal political ground, these groups often fill the lacuna created by mainstream political parties that are unwilling or unable to address the anxieties of a critical mass of so-called native citizens.

In Britain, this familiar pattern has not been faithfully replicated, however. To the contrary, because the Conservative Party has historically exercised a high degree of political ownership over immigration-related issues and it has been especially visible in opposing new immigration, the BNP and its predecessor, the NF, have been historically relegated to the margins of politics – particularly at the national level. Moreover, because challenges to the Conservative's ownership of immigration-related issues in Britain typically have been generated by neo-fascist groups – groups viewed by a super majority of Britons as beyond the pale and to which few would offer their enduring allegiance – the latter have little influenced public opinion, the major parties' positions or national policy. All things being equal, there is little reason this state of affairs will change.

Although at first glance this 'optimistic' conclusion is seemingly contradicted by the BNP's recent electoral gains at the subnational level and the steady ascent of the UK Independence Party (UKIP) in European elections, it is nevertheless consistent with the factual circumstances. On the first score, it must be remembered that the BNP has experienced considerable difficulty making further electoral inroads in localities where it has previously polled well (Renton, 2005: 43–4). Although there are numerous local environments within which the BNP could potentially make new inroads, as a party with few formal members, a poor public reputation, a narrow electoral base and fickle and negatively motivated supporters, the BNP is badly positioned to exert influence over politics and policy in the medium to long term, even at the local level. Moreover, as argued above, encouraging subnational electoral results for Britain's anti-immigrant parties generally do not translate into national political influence or electoral support.

John and Margetts (2009: 496) have recently argued that the potential vote for the extreme right in Britain nevertheless remains considerable, as the UKIP's supporters 'provide another source of latent support [for the BNP] due to linkages perceived by the electorate between the BNP and the UKIP', especially on matters of immigration. Although space constraints do not permit a comprehensive response to John and Margetts' provocative claim, several of its problems can be briefly stated.

First, like several analysts of the NF's vote during the 1980s (Harrop et al., 1980; Husbands, 1983: 142–3), John and Margetts and others (Ford et al., 2010) advance the dubious assumption that the latent, *mobilizable* anti-immigrant vote is much greater than its actual vote and imply that anti-immigrant voters might eventually be brought under the umbrella of a single anti-immigrant political party. The history of the failed, neo-fascist NF suggests it is safer than not to be sceptical of these suppositions until events demonstrate otherwise.

Second, they conspicuously neglect to consider the Conservative Party's ability to outflank the anti-immigrant right whenever the former's core electoral interests are at risk, especially during general elections (Messina, 1989: 126–49). Although the Conservative Party cannot banish the BNP from the British political and electoral landscape, its *demonstrated* influence on the fortunes of the anti-immigrant right and its historical ownership of immigration as a national issue are perhaps as great as, or greater than, any mainstream centre-right party in contemporary Western Europe (Mudde, 2002: 41).

Third, John and Margetts underestimate the inherent and inevitable volatility of immigration's salience with the British electorate and its obvious negative implications for the BNP. As Figure 8.2 demonstrates, the national salience of immigration-related issues, although currently at historically high levels, has markedly fluctuated during the current economic crisis, much like it did during previous periods. Although a decline in the salience of immigration-related issues may have less effect on subnational than national political or policy outcomes, it is clear that the performance and influence of Britain's anti-immigrant parties, and especially pure and neo-fascist groups, are negatively impacted by it (Messina, 1989: 121–5).

Fourth, and most importantly, they misleadingly conflate popular and electoral support for the predominantly anti-immigrant BNP with support for the predominantly anti-EU UKIP. The UKIP formally claims to be non-racist, non-sectarian and democratic. Indeed, its constitution contains a clause that commits UKIP to racial non-discrimination; moreover, the party's rules require its candidates to declare they have no previous or current association with far-right organizations. Given the past association of UKIP with several far-right political figures, the aforementioned claims should not be accepted, of course, at face value. Nevertheless, unlike the BNP, UKIP is clearly not a neo-fascist party; nor is it broadly a party of the extreme right (Abedi and Lundberg, 2009: 76). Rather, because of its obsession with Britain's membership in the EU, often to the subordination or exclusion of all other issues including immigration (Hayton, 2010: 27; Usherwood, 2008), UKIP more closely resembles the generic or ethno-national right. This distinction matters because, in order to advance its anti-EU agenda successfully, UKIP, unlike the BNP, is likely to submerge the more strident features of its anti-immigration posture and, in the process, further diminish its already limited influence on British immigration politics and policy (Abedi and Lundberg, 2009: 75). As Ford et al. (2010: 19) persuasively argue, if UKIP chooses to over-privilege issues of immigration and racism, 'it may alienate many of its strategic supporters, who are primarily motivated to defect from the Conservatives by their Euroscepticism'. In short, although UKIP is currently opposed to new immigration, there is no evidence its voters are *primarily* inspired by anti-immigrant sentiments (Ford et al., 2010: 13); perhaps more pertinently, a large majority of UKIP voters view the BNP negatively (Hayton, 2010: 31). In this respect, UKIP's supporters have more in common with Eurosceptical Conservatives than BNP voters (Ford et al., 2010: 12; Usherwood, 2008). Conversely, although the BNP is hostile to Europe and European integration, immigration, not Europe, is its supporters' greatest concern, and less than half of them view the BNP postively (Hayton, 2010: 31). As a result, a political or electoral coalescence of the much circumscribed British anti-immigrant political right, often predicted but hitherto unrealized, is unlikely to occur any time soon.

Notes

1 See Pew Global Attitudes Project, 'Islamic extremism: common concern for Muslim and Western publics' (2005). Available online at: http://pewglobal.org/reports/display.php?ReportID=248 (accessed 14 May 2009).

2 See W. Somerville, 'The immigration legacy of Tony Blair', *Migration Information Source*. Available online at: www.migrationinformation.org/Feature/display.cfm?ID=600 (accessed 14 April 2009).

References

Abedi, A. and Lundberg, T. C. (2009) 'Doomed to failure? UKIP and the organizational challenges facing right-wing populist anti-political establishment parties', *Parliamentary Affairs*, 62 (1): 72–87.

BBC News (2010) 'Election 2010'. Available online at: http://news.bbc.co.uk/2/shared/election2010/results (accessed 14 July 2010).

Betz, H.-G. (1994) *Radical right-wing populism in Western Europe*, New York: St. Martin's Press.

Betz, H.-G. (2002) 'The divergent paths of the FPÖ and the Lega Nord', in Schain, M., Zolberg, A. and Hossay, P. (eds) *Shadows over Europe: the development and impact of the extreme right in Western Europe*, New York: Palgrave-Macmillan.

Bjørklund, T. and Andersen, J. G. (2002) 'Anti-immigration parties in Denmark and Norway: the progress parties and the Danish People's Party', in Schain. M., Zolberg, A. and Hossay, P. (eds) *Shadows over Europe: the development and impact of the extreme right in Western Europe*, New York: Palgrave-Macmillan.

Clarke, H., Sanders, D., Stewart, M. and Whitely, P. (2006) 'Taking the bloom off New Labour's rose: party choice and voter turnout in Britain, 2005', *Journal of Elections, Public Opinion and Parties*, 16 (1): 3–36.

Copsey, N. (2004) *Contemporary British fascism: the British National Party and the quest for legitimacy*, Basingstoke: Palgrave-Macmillan.

Cruddas, J., John, P., Margetts, H., Rowland, D., Shutt, D. and Weir, S. (2005) *The far right in London: a challenge for local democracy?*, York: The Joseph Rowntree Reform Trust.

Deacon, G., Keita, A. and Ritchie, K. (2004) *Burnley and the BNP and the case for electoral reform*, London: Electoral Reform Society.

Eatwell, R. (2004) 'The extreme right in Britain: the long road to "modernization"' in Eatwell, R. and Mudde, C. (eds) *Western democracies and the new extreme right challenge*, New York: Routledge.

Economist (2005a) 'A new, improved race card', 7 April.

Economist (2005b) 'The Tories tough stance on immigration shifted few votes', 25 May.

Ford, R., Cuts, D. and Goodwin, M. J. (2010) 'Strategic Eurosceptics, polite xenophobes or angry men? Support for the UK Independence Party (UKIP) in the 2009 European parliament elections', unpublished paper.

Geddes, A. (2005) 'Nationalism: immigration and European integration at the 2005 general election', in Geddes, A. and Tonge, J. (eds) *Britain decides: the UK general election 2005*, Basingstoke: Palgrave-Macmillan.

Goodwin, M. J. (2007) 'The extreme right in Britain: still an "ugly duckling" but for how long?', *The Political Quarterly*, 78 (2): 241–50.

Green, J. and Hobolt, S. B. (2008) 'Owing the issue agenda: party strategies and vote choices in British elections', *Electoral Studies*, 27 (3): 1–17.

Harris, G. (2010) 'The British National Party and the new issue agenda: issue preference and policy evaluation in far right support', unpublished paper.

Harrop, M., England, J. and Husbands, C. (1980) 'The bases of National Front support', *Political Studies*, 28 (2): 271–83.

Hayton, R. (2010) 'Towards the mainstream? UKIP and the 2009 elections to the European Parliament', *Politics*, 30 (1): 26–35.

Husbands, C. T. (1981) 'Contemporary right-wing extremism in Western European democracies: a review article', *European Journal of Political Research*, 9 (1): 75–99.

Husbands, C. T. (1983) *Racial exclusionism and the city: the urban support of the National Front*, London: George Allen and Unwin.

Ignazi, P. (2006) *Extreme right parties in Western Europe*, Oxford: Oxford University Press.

John, P. and Margetts, H. (2009) 'The latent support for the extreme right in British politics', *West European Politics*, 32 (3): 496–513.

John, P., Margetts, H., Rowland, D. and Weir, S. (2006) *The BNP: the roots of its appeal*, Colchester: Democratic Audit.

Kavanagh, D. and Butler, D. (2005) *The British general election of 2005*, Basingstoke: Palgrave Macmillan.

Kitschelt, H. (1995) *The radical right in Western Europe: a comparative analysis*, Ann Arbor, MI: University of Michigan Press.

Leslie, P. M. (1989) 'Ethnonationalism in a federal state', in Rudolph, J. R. and Thompson, R. J. (eds) *Ethnoterritorial politics, policy and the Western world*, Boulder, CO: Lynne Rienner.

Messina, A. M. (1989) *Race and party competition in Britain,* Oxford: Oxford University Press.

Messina, A. M. (2007) *The logics and politics of post-WWII migration to Western Europe*, New York: Cambridge University Press.

Minkenberg, M. (2001) 'The radical right in public office: agenda setting and policy effects', *West European Politics*, 24 (4): 1–21.

Mudde, C. (2002) 'England belongs to me: the extreme right in the UK parliamentary election of 2001', *Representation*, 39 (1): 37–43.

Perlmutter, T. (2002) 'The politics of restriction: the effect of xenophobic parties on Italian immigration policy and German asylum policy', in Schain, M., Zolberg, A. and Hossay, P. (eds) *Shadows over Europe: the development and impact of the extreme right in Western Europe*, New York: Palgrave-Macmillan.

Pettigrew, T. F. (1998) 'Reactions toward the new minorities of Western Europe', *Annual Review of Sociology*, 24: 77–103.

Renton, D. (2003) 'Examining the success of the British National Party: 1999–2003', *Race and Class*, 45 (2): 75–85.

Renton, D. (2005) 'A day to make history? The 2004 elections and the British National Party', *Patterns of Prejudice*, 39 (1): 25–45.

Rhodes, J. (2006) 'The "local" politics of the British National Party', *Sage Race Relations Abstracts*, 31 (5): 5–20.

Rhodes, J. (2009a) 'The political breakthrough of the BNP: the case of Burnley', *British Politics*, 4 (1): 22–46.

Rhodes, J. (2009b) 'The Banal National Party: the routine nature of legitimacy', *Patterns of Prejudice*, 43 (2): 142–60.

Robinson, E. and Fisher, F. (2005) *General election 2005: what the voters saw*, London: New Politics Network.

Rydgren, J. (2004) *The populist challenge: political protest and ethno-nationalist mobilization in France*, New York: Berghahn Books.

Schain, M. A. (1995) 'The National Front and agenda formation in France', unpublished paper.

Schain, M. A. (2002) 'The impact of the French National Front on the French political system', in Schain, M. A., Zolberg, A. and Hossay. P (eds) *Shadows over Europe: the development and impact of the extreme right in Western Europe*, New York: Palgrave-Macmillan.

Schain, M. A., Zolberg A. and Hossay, P. (eds) (2002) *Shadows over Europe: the development and impact of the extreme right in Western Europe*, New York: Palgrave-Macmillan.

Schain, M. A., Zolberg, A. and Hossay, P. (2002) 'Introduction', in Schain, M. A., Zolberg, A. and Hossay, P. (eds) *Shadows over Europe: the development and impact of the extreme right in Western Europe*, New York: Palgrave-Macmillan.

Simmons, H. G. (1996) *The French National Front: the extremist challenge to democracy*, Boulder, CO: Westview Press.

Smith, J. (2008) 'Toward consensus? Centre-right parties and immigration policy in the UK and Ireland', *Journal of European Public Policy*, 15 (3): 415–31.

Statham, P. and Geddes, A. (2006) 'Elites and the "organised public": who drives British immigration politics and in which direction?' *West European Politics*, 29 (2): 248–69.

Steed, M. (1978) 'The National Front vote', *Parliamentary Affairs*, 31 (3): 284–5.

Taylor, S. (1982) *The National Front in English politics*, London: Macmillan.

Taylor, S. (1993) 'The radical right in Britain', in Merkl, P. H. and Weinberg, L. (eds) *Encounters with the contemporary radical right*, Boulder, CO: Westview Press.

Usherwood, S. (2008) 'The dilemmas of a single-issue party – the UK Independence Party', *Representation*, 44 (3): 255–64.

Walker, M. (1978) *The National Front*, Glasgow: Fontana.

Williams, M. H. (2002) 'What's left of the right? Measuring the impact of radical right-wing parties in Western Europe on institutions, agendas, and policy'. Paper presented to the American Political Association Annual Meetings, Boston, 28 August–1 September.

Williams, M. H. (2006) *The impact of radical right-wing parties in West European democracies*, New York: Palgrave-Macmillan.

Zaslove, A. (2004) 'Closing the door? The ideology and impact of radical right populism and immigration policy in Austria and Italy', *Journal of Political Ideologies*, 9 (1): 99–118.

9

ALIEN INFLUENCE?

The international context of the BNP's 'modernization'

Roger Griffin

The apple never falls far from the tree[1]

In his youth, John Tyndall had few inhibitions about being photographed sporting a Swastika[2] and made no secret of his neo-Nazi convictions concerning the need to defend the British branch of the 'Aryans' from the alleged agents of racial decay. In 1965, he wrote in his journal, *Spearhead*:

> with the numbers of murdering asocials [a term taken from Nazi racial policy] and perverts on the increase, as a result of our sick society, there will be an unanswerable case when the day for the great clean up comes, to implement the final solution against these sub-human elements by means of the gas chamber system.[3]

Two decades later, in his novel-length party programme, written when he was leader of the BNP, *The eleventh hour. A call for British rebirth* (Tyndall, 1988: 589), a poor man's *Mein Kampf*, he was stressing that the purging of decadence cannot be delivered by working within the existing constitutional system:

> If we are seriously to grapple with the chaos of the present day and formulate a creed and movement for national rebirth, our thinking must begin with *an utter rejection of liberalism* and a dedication to the resurgence of authority [. . .] It must entail the embrace of a political outlook which is, in relation to the present, *revolutionary*. Nothing less will suffice.

Since Nick Griffin succeeded him in 1999, the language of the BNP has been scrupulously purged – at least in the public arena – of references to the need for a process of cultural and eugenic 'clean up', spearheaded by cadres determined to carry out Hitler's mission in the streets of Britain. The struggle for rebirth is now officially presented in its literature as the fight, not for a new order, but for the preservation of England's (or is it Britain's? – the terms remain confusingly interchangeable in BNP literature) unique civilization and sense of belonging. The BNP's fight for whites on occasion can now give rise to assertions that, taken out of context, imply that the BNP is not even a political party, but a movement of moral and religious renewal that had put the paganism and public disorder of Tyndall's party far behind it: its magazine *Identity*, in February 2008, states 'Christianity is so large a part of our identity that to give it up would mean giving up that identity. If we gave it up, we might still exist, but we would no longer be ourselves'.[4]

Yet a more ancient stratum of political thought lying just below the newly laid turf of 'identity politics' is exposed when, in his chairman's message for the same issue, Nick Griffin makes it clear that his central concern is far from being the salvation of the human soul. It is the salvation of the 'home people' (or 'folk', as he calls it elsewhere, with historical connotations far removed from simple morris dancing) from the dark forces conspiring to undermine its ethnic cohesion, now that the 'true' British folk-community has been transformed into a multi-ethnic and multi-faith society in the grip of terminal disintegration:

> Old certainties are being replaced by insecurity and the destruction of all we hold dear by a rolling neo-Marxist revolution of Political Correctness. Waiting in the wings to impose 'order', an ever more confident Islam is recognized by more and more people as a mortal threat to their traditions, liberties and even their lives. Old alliances crumble and a new political age dawns. Our time is coming and you and I know it.[5]

It is clear that Griffin's allusion to a 'new dawn' here does not reflect the millenarian fantasies of Christian fundamentalists, but rather that of all white supremacists, who feel besieged and threatened by the forces of globalization and mass migration. Given the politics of his predecessor, Griffin's phrase 'our time will come' still carries a covert message of hope to unreconstructed fascists who see themselves not as citizens or voters, but as part of an elite of political soldiers waiting for the day when the shackles of democracy can at last be thrown off. For, as is increasingly recognized by political scientists and historians, the defining hall-mark of fascism as an ideology is that its most fanatical believers see their nation or race in the grip of accelerating decadence, which is destined imminently or eventually to give way – after a process of enforced regeneration and 'creative destruction' – to a new era (what I have termed elsewhere a *palingenetic* form of ultra-nationalism) (Griffin, 2007: ch. 6).

This chapter seeks to illuminate a comparatively neglected layer of causation shaping the way the BNP, under Griffin, has been able to evolve into an organization widely treated as no longer beyond the pale of 'normal' democratic politics, and sufficiently legitimate and media-genic to be debated with on prime-time TV, something unthinkable when Tyndall was its leader. To do this, it proposes to concentrate on how the international context of fascism's adaptation to the transformed historical conditions encouraged Nick Griffin first to abandon party politics altogether and then to re-enter the arena as the leader of a party committed, not to neo-Nazism, but to a strategy that has come to be known as 'neo-populism'. In stark contrast to classic fascism, a revolutionary bid to create a new order, neo-populism (also known as radical right-wing populism or the populist radical right: see Mudde, 2007), attempts to implement its xenophobic policies along with other policies critical of 'the system', in a way reminiscent of the growth of reformist socialism out of the failures of revolutionary Marxism in the nineteenth century. Instead of advocating the 'utter rejection of liberalism', neo-populism concentrates on preserving the benefits of liberal democracy for the 'home' people, a position summed up in the *Front National* slogan '*Les Français d'abord, métèques dehors*', or the *Republikaners'* '*Deutschland den Deutschen, Ausländer raus*'.[6] The issue this chapter thus seeks to illuminate is the sincerity of Nick Griffin's claim to have turned his back on the party's neo-Nazism for a reformist, constitutional form of xenophobia, given his readiness to chop and change ideologies in the past to assure himself a dominant role in the politics of British white supremacism. In doing so, it will also highlight the paradox that, though the BNP presents itself as a quintessentially British party embodying the national 'genius' and defending its 'aboriginal' ethnic traits,[7] the course it has taken under Griffin has been plagiarizing foreign trends in racist politics. More importantly, it has done so in a purely cosmetic way that prevents it from achieving its goal of a substantial electoral following and legitimacy within the party-political system.

The post-war evolution of fascism

On the surface, Nick Griffin would seem to be a much more original thinker than John Tyndall, who was stuck firmly to a neo-Nazi analysis of post-war Britain, with a smattering of Mosleyite fascism (e.g. in the call for referendums) thrown in for good measure. Certainly, he has shown himself far more alive to the need to address the problems of updating and 'marketing' a political programme that, in the wake of the Second World War and the horrors of the extermination camps built to purge the New Europe of degeneracy, could only induce repugnance in mainstream civil society. That is certainly the image he is keen to project: the innovator, the modernizer, the Tony Blair (or now the David Cameron) of the neo-Nazi right, the creator of the 'new BNP'.

Once the post-1945 evolution of the form of revolutionary nationalism known as 'fascism' away from its interwar variants is taken into account, a different narrative emerges. Within a few years of the war's end, the seeds of a 'fascist international' had already been sown – long before the World Wide Web made global networking so easy – recruited mostly from activists who deplored the Allied victory and saw civilization itself being threatened by the cold war, the establishment of Soviet Russia as a second superpower, and the rise of communist China, not to mention the perpetual presence of the mythicized Jew. One of the first to recognize that the situation called for a new world-view and a new strategy was Francis Yockey, a Chicago-born convert to Nazism and rabid anti-Americanism during the war. His career as a self-appointed undercover agent for the new fascist Europe, a creed that he espoused in *Imperium* (1948), provides a fascinating case study in how rapidly Nazism could evolve into a new political species within months of Hitler's death, in the hands of a genuine, if perverse, visionary. Yockey's book helped persuade a new generation of fascists that their struggle now had to transcend narrow nationalism by forming an international movement to fight the globalizing forces of capitalism and communism.

In the home of fascism itself, the revolutionary right 'Traditionalist' thinker Julius Evola, highly marginalized till 1945, provided revolutionary nationalists a new sense of direction and purpose with three key works, *Revolt against the modern world* (Evola, 1995 [1934]), *Man among the ruins* (Evola, 2002 [1953]), and *Ride the tiger* (Evola 2003 [1961]). Thanks to such books, post-war fascists could cast themselves in the role of an elite of warrior-priests who had remained true to the primordial, spiritual 'Tradition' and were prepared to stave off the total collapse of a rotten civilization – not just in Italy but in the 'West' – still mired in what Evola identified as the '*Kali Yuga*', the Hindu term for the final age of decadence that preceded the new golden age. He not only had a major impact on fascist intellectuals struggling to find an exit strategy from both the present world order and 'classic' national socialism or fascism, but in Italy provided the rationale for 'black' terrorist groups during the years of the 'Strategy of Tension' (Bull, 2007).

The spread of Evolianism was only one component of an explosion of ideological activity in Italy in the 1960s, as a younger generation of far-right intellectuals sought to create a 'right-wing culture' to meet the challenge of the highly evolved left-wing culture that was then in the ascendancy as the main opposition to the hegemony of Christian Democracy. Its proponents, such as Marco Tarchi and Gianfranco de Turris, produced an outpouring of conferences, magazines, newspapers, articles, and books, some of them displaying a genuine passion for political theory and history unimaginable in Britain (Ferraresi, 1984). The perverse effect of the creation of a 'fascist culture' was that the sporadic episodes of black terrorism that swept Italy from the 1960s till the early 1980s were based, not on the crude neo-Nazism of the type adopted by the likes of John Tyndall, but on an abstruse 'philosophy of history' (Sheehan, 1981).

By the time Italian neo-fascists were holding seminars on the new right at a mountain retreat in the Abruzzi (named Camp Hobbit in homage to Tolkien's *Lord of the rings,* which they read as an allegory of the struggle between evil materialism and the spiritual forces of the 'Tradition'), Armin Mohler had long since published his influential *The conservative revolution in Germany* (Mohler, 1972 [1949]). Written as a PhD thesis under Karl Jaspers, while Germany was still occupied and in ruins, it offered a highly tendentious *catalogue raisonné* of the vast subculture of thought and literature in pre-Nazi Germany that, in different ways, suggested the need for a right-wing revolution to save the nation and the West from spiritual decadence and social collapse. It exerted considerable influence, in and outside

Germany, on a new generation of nationalists and racists, repelled by both communism and liberalism, but intent on developing a critique of the present that was free from the taint of Nazism.

It was France, however, that boasted the most powerful and sustained contribution to the revitalization of the far-right after the catastrophe of Nazism. Its rich compost heat of decaying fascist ideology was sufficiently fertile to produce, in Maurice Bardèche's *Qu'est-ce que le fascisme?* (Bardèche, 1961), an influential rethinking of fascism's rationale along post-war Europeanist lines that underscored the bankruptcy of narrow, nation-state-based chauvinism and the language of biological racism. Instead, it outlined the 'true fascist' mission, namely to save Europe (and, hence, civilization itself) from the evils of US and Soviet imperialism, a cause he claims the Third Reich only embraced in the last two years of the war, when it created the International Brigades of the Waffen SS.[8] Following in the same vein, the radical rethinking of fascism after the loss of the Algerian war also produced two even more important ways of being a non-Nazi fascist after 1945.

The first of these was elaborated largely thanks to the voracious intellectual appetite of Alain de Benoist to get a grip on the root causes of modern decadence and offer, not just a diagnosis, but a prognosis on which to conceptualize the transition to a new, spiritually healthy Europe. It was a quest that took him on an eclectic reading odyssey through art, science, history, philosophy, sociology, psychology, and politics, fuelled by an urgent sense of the bankruptcy of interwar fascism's commitment to biopolitical racism, narrow nationalism, and paramilitarism. The drive for a new synthesis was intensified in the 1960s by France's loss of the Algerian War and the domination of Parisian life by left-wing militants and intellectuals. Abandoning conventional politics or concessions to populism, it based its tactics on the Gramscian concept of 'cultural hegemony' ('*gramscisme de droite*'), rather than violence, as the key to political power, and drew considerable inspiration from Nietzsche and the Conservative Revolution. The result was the *Nouvelle Droite* movement of radical cultural critique 'beyond left and right' (though fundamentally 'right-wing') that, spreading out from France to create local national variants, has played such a profound role in creating an international metapolitical right, the 'European New Right' (ENR). It is 'metapolitical' (Griffin, 2000) in the sense that its activists stay aloof from party politics and overt acts of political violence. Instead, they constitute a permanent think tank, providing books, articles, and websites to supply a largely virtual community made up of those who find the existing world order repugnant and are nostalgic for a Europe made up of 'organic' ethnic societies, freed from the plagues of multiculturalism, materialism, and globalization, and believe the true mission of fascism, Nazism, and their emulators was to create such a Europe (Taguieff, 1994; Bar-On, 2007).

The second area of fascist self-reinvention to which French, or rather Francophone, activists made a major contribution was Third Positionism (TP), a term given to a wide gamut of far-right movements that seek to go beyond the dichotomy of right and left by synthesizing the 'best' of the anti-capitalist tradition of communism with the most vital forms of a Europeanized ultra-nationalism.[9]

It is a strategy that aligns TP ideologues with some struggles being fought out in the developing world against US hegemony or the Fukuyaman 'new world order', thereby producing some strange ideological bedfellows. The pioneers of this particular permutation of neo-fascist ideology included Francis Yockey, as well as the Frenchman René Binet, who converted from Trotskyism to Nazism as a German prisoner of war.

Another was the Belgian Jean-François Thiriart, a collaborationist during his country's occupation by the Nazis, who, after the loss of the Congo in the 1960s, attempted to adapt his wartime National Bolshevism – a variant of German fascism popularized by Ernst Niekisch under the Weimar Republic – to the realities of post-war Europe. Nicolas Lebourg (Lebourg 2006) has painstakingly reconstructed the tadpole-like habitat of TP groupuscules that have existed since the 1980s on the shadowy margins of mainstream French and Belgian politics, with names such as *Troisième Voie* and *Nouvelle Résistance* and ideologues such as Christian Bouchet and Luc Michel. Each advocates a different cocktail of right-wing and left-wing values that, in one way or another, perpetuate the mission established by Binet or Thiriart.

Most of the minute far-right groupings that have mushroomed since 1945 so prolifically, though mostly ephemerally and inconspicuously, outside the arena of parliamentary politics in continental Europe have exhibited two outstanding features of neo-fascism's adaptation to the transformed, and generally hostile, habitat in which organic, revolutionary nationalism has had to survive. These are metapoliticization (or the renunciation of *Realpolitik* to focus on cultural and ideological battles) and Europeanization (the transcendence of chauvinistic nationalism). Both traits set them apart from the paramilitarized electoral party under a charismatic leader that was revolutionary nationalism's vehicle of choice in the 'fascist epoch', as exemplified by the *Partito Nazionale Fascista* (PNF) and NSDAP. Thus, while most of those concerned by the prospect of a fascist resurgence scanned the skies for signs of a renaissance of the NSDAP in a new guise, small pockets of fascist radicalism were able to survive and evolve under the radar, in 'uncivil society' (Umland, 2008), by avoiding high-profile party-political activity altogether and fighting a 'battle of ideas' to combat the forces of communism and liberalism.

Nick Griffin and the Third Position

Griffin's career as a fascist activist was to be profoundly affected by such continental developments. He had come of age politically in the late 1970s, when the National Front was still making waves, and rose to become the organizer of its student organization. His first impulse was not to leave the ship when it seemed to be rapidly sinking after Thatcher's victory, but to help give the party a new sense of direction after its poor results in the 1979 general election. Once elected to the NF's new governing body after Tyndall was forced out following the defeat, he helped launch *Nationalism Today*, which, together with another new NF publication, *Rising* (1982–5), set about translating the party's neo-Nazism into Third

Positionism, producing a dialect of neo-fascism that must have been utterly strange to ears of the neo-Mosleyite and neo-Hitlerite party faithful. In 1985, Griffin was praising Louis Farrakhan's black separatism and, in 1988, he went on a fund-raising trip to Libya to meet Iran-backed Colonel Gaddafi. He was not a loner in treading this path, but part of a faction of neo-fascist young radicals searching for a revolutionary rather than electoral route to power that avoided waking the ghosts of the Second World War. Its other main personalities were Patrick Harrington, Phil Andrews, Derek Holland, and Troy Southgate, all of whom were convinced that the time had come in Britain for an overhaul of NF ideology as radical as that undertaken by Alain de Benoist twenty years before in France.

There may well have been a personal factor behind Griffin's adoption of an Italian, Evolian variant of Third Positionism. Both he and his NF colleague Michael Walker had close dealings with Roberto Fiore, who, as former head of the Italian terrorist group *Nuclei armati rivoluzionari* (NAR), had been accused of involvement in the Bologna bombing of August 1980 and fled to London.[10] Inspired by the writings of Julius Evola and dedicated to the cause of black terrorism, NAR had close links to the extensive TP political subculture in Italy.[11] *Searchlight* revealed in 1984 that Griffin, Walker, and Fiore were running a company called Heritage Tours together from Michael Walker's flat in London, which suggests a high degree of intimacy and trust. But for this personal link, it is difficult to see how esoteric Italian neo-fascist ideas about the political soldier, the pan-European struggle against ('Jewish') communism and capitalism, and the need for European nationalists to ally themselves with movements in developing nations opposed to US, Soviet, and Israeli interests could come to be adopted by the most dynamic faction of what had, till recently, been the UK's foremost neo-Nazi party.

In 1989, Griffin left the NF to help set up a new group, International Third Position (ITP), conceived as an umbrella organization for TP groups all over the world.[12] In the meantime, Michael Walker had long since abandoned party politics to dedicate himself to being Britain's main spokesman of the European New Right through his magazine *The Scorpion* (founded in 1981 as *National Democrat*), which blended Evolian ideas with the ideology of Alain de Benoist and other Francophone new right thinkers. It was a sign of how intensely marginalized electoral neo-fascism had become to British political life that, by 1990, all the NF's most radical ideological innovators had abandoned party activism for the realm of 'metapolitics'. This they pursued, not in a high-profile national movement, but as part of the shadowy groupuscular subculture that has played such an important role in keeping extremism of the left and right fascist alive in the post-war era (Griffin, 2003).

However, in contrast to his companions in the ideological war they had declared on 'the West', Griffin's subsequent career suggests that his commitment to the core TP world-view was skin deep. In 1993, shortly after leaving ITP, he was speaking at meetings of the BNP, which Tyndall had reformed in 1982, and writing under a pseudonym for its publications. In 1995, he officially joined the party and, despite his record as a leading light in the TP faction that had abandoned the NF's neo-Nazism as a superseded form of fascism, was appointed by Tyndall as editor of *Spearhead*. Both in this role and as editor of another hard-line, anti-Semitic journal, *The Rune* (produced by the Croydon BNP), Griffin seems to have reverted back to his default neo-Nazism, embracing anti-Semitism, Holocaust denial, hostility to multiculturalism, and the belief in a homogenous British people and identity. It was an article he published in this journal that led to his successful prosecution for incitement to racial hatred in 1998.

Without any attempt to justify his abrupt change of tack, Griffin had put his commitment to ITP behind him and no longer courted tactical alliances with Islamic countries.[13] Symptomatic of his renewed allegiance to traditional neo-Nazism is the pamphlet *Who are the MIND-BENDERS?*, published in 1997. Based on *Who Rules America?*, by William Pierce, author of *The Turner diaries* (1978), it follows the tradition of anti-Semitic conspiracy established by *The protocols of the elders of Zion* in accusing the Jews of controlling society through their manipulation of the entertainment and news media. After his stint in the ITP underground, this was business as usual for a former NF official. Yet, as the famous Cook Report 'sting' operation against Griffin revealed in 1997, it was in the period that he edited *The Rune* that he was already planning to transform the BNP into the English clone of Le Pen's *Front National*. In September 1999, Griffin was elected leader of the BNP, taking full advantage of the party's internal crisis after another pathetic election result under Tyndall. Thus the secret blueprint for the party's makeover could be put into action.

Griffin's crash course in neo-populism

The planned makeover was based on neo-populism. Precisely because of its moderate success in ridding the BNP of its neo-Nazi image, Griffin's imposition of neo-populist trappings has been thoroughly scrutinized by academics (e.g. Copsey, 2007; 2008). Symptoms of the process were the replacement of Tyndall's *Spearhead* by the glossy *Identity* as the party monthly, the banning of overt anti-liberal, neo-Nazi, anti-Semitic, or nationalist revolutionary language by party officials, and the promotion of a racism couched in the careful language of 'differentialism' or 'ethno-pluralism', which stresses the threat posed by multiculturalism to all racial identities and the need to conserve the 'difference' between races, thus abandoning the white supremacist discourse of racial hatred and calls for the enforced repatriation of non-Anglo-Saxon Britons. While links to Combat 18 or other violent elements within the neo-Nazi subculture were played down or concealed, a concerted attempt was made to woo Labour voters who felt their jobs or traditional communities were under threat because of the influx of migrants, particularly from Eastern Europe, as well as Conservative voters of a xenophobic disposition, who might have begun to feel like strangers in their own country, but who would never knowingly vote for a fascist party. The obvious value of neo-populism to the hard-core fascist right who remained at the heart of the BNP's activism was that it allowed it to exploit the public anxieties generated by the rise in immigration and by Islamist attacks on Western society in the public forum of legitimate debate, and not just in the shadowy world of right-wing groupuscules, even if to do so forced it to cultivate elaborate euphemisms to conceal its neo-Nazi instincts.[14]

Clearly, the need for the BNP to adopt the tactics of neo-populism did not come to Nick Griffin in a 'Damascus moment' of conversion. Rather, it seems he became convinced of the need to abandon both neo-Nazism and ITP delusions about a creating a new elite of (partially Gaddafi-backed) political soldiers and to seek power through the ballot box instead, as advocated by a modernizing faction within the BNP made up of individuals such as Eddy Butler, Mike Newland, and Tony Lecomber. These drew the lesson from the BNP's success in getting Derek Beackon elected as local councillor for Millwall in 1993 that the party should redirect its focus towards local community politics. The modernizers pushed this strategy – which they labelled 'Euronationalist', acknowledging the shift towards the party's 'Europeanization'.

What stands out in the present context about Griffin's shift of tactics since 1997 is that, once again, an alien form of extremist politics has been imported by British racists with a minimum of intelligent adaptation to the national context. Neo-populism first emerged as a mainstream form of politics in France, when the *Front National*, having shed any obvious links to its fascist origins, established itself in the 1980s as a party-political outlet to populist concerns about a variety of threats to 'Frenchness' and the French way of life. In the interwar period, such concerns would have mostly been channelled into support for ultra-nationalist or fascist groups. By the mid 1990s, with the cold war over, the space for extremist politics shrinking, disaffection with traditional parties growing, and mass immigration rising, significant neo-populist parties had emerged in Belgium, Austria, Scandinavia, Switzerland, Russia, and Italy, each adapted to the unique historical, political, and cultural context in which it sought to find political space to grow into a mass electoral force. None of them was a direct emulation of the *Front National*, but rather a product of a parallel conjuncture of conditions, just as the Romanian Iron Guard was not an imitation of the NSDAP or PNF, but an original product of a structurally similar but unique domestic crisis in Romania.

The success of any European neo-populist party breaking into the political mainstream depends on the degree to which it can be viewed by a critical mass of voters in the general public, repelled by neo-Nazism in particular and revolutionary nationalism in general, as an integral, 'organic' part of their national culture. It does so when a critical mass is achieved in the populist (minority, but widely diffused) perception that the party is defending the nation from the negative impact that 'foreigners' (whether from abroad or indigenous) or 'globalization' (e.g. EU or US norms of existence) are allegedly having on jobs, housing, education, crime, and cultural identity. They are especially well placed to exploit such anxieties when mainstream parties are seen as failing to address, or actually aggravating, them with their 'liberal policies' or their support for the EU.

Le Pen was able to become a major player in French politics partly because, under him, the *Front National* was able to build on a deep indigenous tradition of extreme-right concerns with the decadence of liberalism and the need to defend national identity that flowered in the 1890s, the 1930s, under Vichy, and during the Algerian War in the 1950s and early 1960s. It was significantly helped in developing a sophisticated form of differentialist racism by selectively adopting the cultural discourse of identity being disseminated in the numerous publications of the French new right, from the late 1960s onwards, to reinforce its pillorying of 'foreigners' as the main source of the country's social problems, such as crime and unemployment. It has also been helped by proportional representation and by unique constellations of immediate sociopolitical factors that enabled it to break through in 1986 with thirty-five seats. The peak of the party's notoriety came in the days before Le Pen's run-off against Jacques Chirac in the presidential elections in 2002, which unleashed a wave of domestic and international concern that Le Pen would give the president a run for his money (see Shields, 2007). It was not to be, and, despite establishing strongholds in municipal politics in a few regions, in terms of becoming the dominant force in national politics the FN and its splinter groups continue to be a failure. Since its spectacular success in 1986, it has only held two seats in the National Assembly. Its national vote declined from 14.95 per cent in the 1997 elections to 4.29 per cent in 2007, and its number of seats in the European Parliament fell from seven to three in the 2009 elections. Nevertheless, it has established itself as a permanent factor in French politics. This is because its neo-populism is not cosmetic but expressed a deep-seated conviction that the benefits of the French Republic should be enjoyed by a 'French people', a community imagined in such a way as to exclude its seven million Muslims.

A study of the changing fortunes of *Freiheitliche Partei Österreichs* (FPÖ, Austrian Freedom Party), superficially comparable with the new BNP, suggests that it has been able to survive the defection of its leader Jörg Haider in 2005 and his subsequent death in 2008 because it emerged spontaneously from within the domestic political system as a wholly Austrian party. It had no need to model itself on Le Pen's party, but represented widespread and deeply felt popular grievances about immigration, the EU, the remoteness of mainstream parties, the excessive tax burden, and the way Austria's imperial and Nazi past had been officially confronted. Jörg Haider's particularly media-genic personality enabled it to enter a coalition government with the People's Party in 2000, but it was also because the FPÖ was not a neo-fascist party (despite the charges of neo-Nazism levelled in the international socialist press) and generally avoided the language of overt xenophobia, let alone overt racial hatred, that it was able to gain a high national profile. It thus developed a 'reputational shield' (Ivarsflaten, 2006) from attacks on it as a racist party, which the BNP's neo-Nazi past and core fascist activists preclude it from establishing.

Given the situation Nick Griffin confronted as successor to Tyndall in 1999, he might have done better to take as his role model, neither the FN nor the FPÖ, but Gianfranco Fini's *Alleanza Nazionale* (AN). In January 1995, the AN emerged from the dissolution of the intransigently neo-fascist *Movimento Sociale Italiano* (MSI), which had failed to enter mainstream politics in over forty years of intense nationwide activity. In taking this radical step towards respectability, Fini was astutely seizing the unique opportunities offered by the meltdown of the republic's old party system and the dissolution of *Democrazia Cristiana* (DC) under the impact of the *Tangentopili* scandals and the *'Mani Pulite'* (Clean Hands) operation, which left him one of the few political leaders not tainted by corruption. A key to the AN's success in making the transition to a 'post-fascist' party was its first programme of 1995, known as 'The Fiuggi Theses'. This, while officially 'post-fascist' and designed to appeal to many of those on the 'centre-right' who had been accommodated in the now defunct DC, contained a subtext capable of appealing both to nostalgic Fascists and neo-fascists (Griffin, 1996).

Nevertheless the change of course was sufficiently radical for most hard-core fascists to leave the new party to form their own formations. With its new name, programme, and identity, the party went on regularly to obtain between 11 and 16 per cent of the national vote as a component of the Berlusconi's 'House of Freedoms' alliance, alongside the *Lega Nord* and *Forza Italia*, the embodiment of a 'postmodern' political formation tailored to the age of multiple, media- and consumer-driven realities. The radicalism of its ideological ancestry utterly spent, it finally merged with Berlusconi's *Forza Italia* in 2009 to form the *Popolo della Libertà*. Meanwhile, its leader, Fini, has held the posts of deputy prime minister, foreign minister, and, since 2008, president of the Chamber of Deputies, and in 2010 was being widely tipped to succeed Berlusconi as the next president of the republic.

Such a degree of respectability and penetration into national life Griffin can only fantasize about. What stands out, in contrast with the 'new BNP', is that the AN was not only deeply rooted in Italy's unique history and political system but, in 1995, underwent a genuine transformation to a populist radical right party that had burnt its bridges with a fascist past that extended deep into Mussolini's Italian Social Republic. It has since become ever less radical. As a result, it soon developed a strong 'reputational shield' and became absorbed into the heart of a right-wing coalition government, leaving overt anti-immigration policies to the *Lega Nord*. Griffin, however, seems unwilling even to contemplate such a radical break with his party's core neo-fascist identity and thus condemns himself to permanent marginalization and pariah status, however many times he appears on national television alongside conventional politicians. Fini's refined rhetoric in parliament and media interview and the absence of any trace of racial hatred or nostalgia for a racially pure Italy (almost as nonsensical an idea as that of a pure British race) show up the inadequacies of Griffin's performance on the political stage.

All successful neo-populism is, to use Fini's own eloquent term, 'post-fascist', perhaps containing disturbing echoes of interwar fascism for political scientists and the radical left, but the product of an age in which, in stark contrast to the 1920s and 1930s, liberal democracy itself, however corrupt or corruptible, has no immediate prospect of being overthrown by a revolutionary force from within. Because it was genuinely post-fascist, the AN could genuinely modernize itself in a way impossible for a fascist or post-fascist party. The idea of the PNF or NSDAP transforming itself into a fully electoral party, with no links to paramilitarism or revolutionary aspirations, and then into a stable partner of a right-wing coalition, before losing its identity altogether in a merger with a party (in the case of Berlusconi's *Forza Italia*, a party embodying the worst excesses of apolitical consumerism), is unthinkable, something the BNP 'modernizers' do not seem to have realized.

Neither fish nor fowl: Griffin's identity crisis

The relative success of Le Pen, Haider, and Fini in their role as neo-populist (or in Fini's case now 'post-populist') politicians is in no small part due to the fact that their leadership roles were not based on dissimulation. They were based on a solid political identity in which any residual extremism in their nationalism or reactions to immigration was channelled into mainstream democratic politics, whatever some extremists of a revolutionary disposition on the fringes of the party might have wanted. Griffin's career as a political activist, however, suggests an element of play-acting in whatever guise he adopts. Thus, in 2008, a spokesman for the far-right British Peoples Party endorsed the BBC's description of him as a 'political chameleon', commenting

> he has changed stance so often on various issues, both political and tactical, that many have been baffled when it comes to ascertaining what he really stands for – or indeed whether in fact he stands for anything at all beyond his single-minded personal ambition.[15]

Similarly, a member of the English ITP (which Griffin helped found) pointed out:

> He has been a conservative, a revolutionary nationalist, a radical National Socialist, a Third Positionist, a friend of the 'boot boys' and the skinhead scene, a man committed to respectable politics and electioneering, a 'moderniser'. Which is he in reality? Perhaps he has been all these quite sincerely – in which case his judgement is abysmal; or *perhaps he has been none of them sincerely – which speaks for itself!*[16]
>
> (my emphasis)

Certainly, the BNP has raised its profile since the end of Tyndall's leadership. Nick Griffin's decision to give it a populist radical right façade came at a time when a series of challenges to traditional British identities and democratic institutions in the new millennium has enlarged the political space for xenophobic politics: the influx of political and economic asylum seekers, the mass immigration of new EU citizens, the rise of Islamism, and the soaring unemployment triggered by a severe structural crisis in the British and international economy. The year 2009 saw Nick Griffin and Andrew Brons elected as MEPs under the EU's proportional representation voting, and an appearance on the BBC's *Question Time* alongside Jack Straw gave Griffin unprecedented public exposure. Yet, in the general election of 2010, the party failed to win a single seat, despite fielding more candidates than ever before, and came third in Barking behind Labour and the Conservatives, gaining some 18,000 votes fewer than Margaret Hodge, the victorious Labour candidate.

In an e-mail to supporters on the eve of the ballot, Griffin had written:

> This election, regardless of the results, is the watershed for this party . . . This is the last election the British National Party fights as a large small party – we are now a small large party. What's more, our enemies know this . . . The BNP has arrived and will be knocking on the doors of power sooner than some ever imagined!

The reasons for the failure of Griffin's attempted modernization of the BNP to bring about the breakthrough into mainstream politics Griffin so desperately desires are doubtless complex. They include the lack of a PR system of voting and the rise of the UK Independence Party as a competitor for the political space available for anti-EU and anti-immigration policies, as well as repeated exposure of the BNP's unreconstructed racist and fascist activists by the media and by anti-fascist activists in the streets and in the press. What this chapter has attempted to highlight are two additional factors that might be usefully taken into account when analysing the fortunes and misfortunes of the BNP.

First, the attempts by fascists to adapt their revolutionary struggle for a reborn national or racial community to the realities of the post-1945 era, after the Allied victory in the Second World War and the exposure of the full horrors of the Third Reich, have been systematically marginalized by mainstream democracy. Even in Italy and Germany, the homelands of the two fascist regimes, neo-fascist parties attempting to play the game of democracy in order to overthrow it have systematically failed to mobilize mass support, no matter how grim the political or financial crisis, while paramilitary fascism and 'black' terrorism, even at their peak, have succeeded only in killing innocent people and spreading a sense of public revulsion and fear, without precipitating a revolutionary situation. Nor has the growth of an international 'white music' scene, using the power of rock music and ballads to mobilize a youth culture that existed only embryonically before the 1960s, had any discernible impact on mainstream society.

Meanwhile, the 'metapolitical', ideological permutations of the original fascist Utopianism found in the International Third Position and the European New Right may have created an influential political subculture in some countries (notably France, Germany, Italy, and Russia), but the paradigm shift to a new hegemony for right-wing schemes to bring about an 'organic culture' have remained stubbornly on the page. The shrivelling on the vine of Britain's National Front in the 1980s and the pathetic performance of the BNP under Tyndall are thus, beyond any continent domestic factors, symptomatic of the chronic structural weakness of post-war fascism as a whole in the modern era. Griffin's attempt to rebrand it as a neo-populist and, hence, a non-fascist party in order to achieve a mass following is thus based on a correct reading of the need to abandon the image of the BNP cultivated by *Spearhead* (to which he was a leading contributor).

In addition, recent history has shown that neo-populism can indeed have a major impact on national politics. Under the more 'charismatic' leaders such as Le Pen, Jörg Haider, Gianfranco Fini, Umberto Bossi, and Christoph Blocher, some neo-populist parties have, at times, found themselves forcing traditional parties to respond to their policies, either by mobilizing popular support to resist the threat they pose or by making concessions to their demands and even entering into coalition with them. In the Netherlands, first Pim Fortyn and then Geert Wilders have transformed the Dutch political scene since 2002, placing concerns over national identity, immigration, the viability of multiculturalism, and the threat posed by Islamism at the top of the national agenda. In June 2010, it was only a concerted blocking manoeuvre by the Christian democrats that prevented Wilders from securing a cabinet post in a coalition government, after gaining 1.5 million votes and twenty-four seats (nearly a sixth of the Dutch 150-seat parliament) in a populist campaign against immigration and the building of new mosques and for imposing a tax on Muslim headscarves. Contemporaneously, in neighbouring Belgium, long-simmering tensions between the Flemish and Walloon communities had reached a pitch where there was serious speculation that the nation would split along ethnic (or 'regional-separatist') lines. If there ever was a schism in Belgium on the lines of Czechoslovakia's peaceful division into two sovereign states in 1993 (an event also brought about by populist 'ethno-regionalist' movements), then the years of campaigning by the *Vlaams Belang* (formerly the *Vlaams Blok*) for a separate Flemish nation could no longer be dismissed as a futile episode of xenophobic 'extremism', but rather as the preparation for a new status quo.

In the context of the new BNP, the crucial point that stands out about the success of neo-populism in each case, however, is that it has not served as a camouflage for 'nostalgic fascism' or neo-Nazism, nor as an elaborate exercise in euphemism and 'doublethink' of the sort openly acknowledged by Nick Griffin. The contrast between Fini's creation of the AN from the MSI in 1995 with Griffin's 'modernization' of the BNP since 1999 is striking. There has been no official name change, no Bad Godesberg-style renunciation of revolution,[17] no purge of hard-liners, no caesura with the past, no changing of the guard. It is the constant slipping of the mask of Griffin and his activists to reveal unreconstructed racist and neo-Nazi attitudes beneath the photo-opportunistic smiles that has doomed to failure the BNP's bid to establish itself as a British democratic neo-populist party or 'ethnocratic liberal' whose avatar is the *Front National* rather than the British Union of Fascists (BUF). The party's modernization is thus not authentic, but a botched cosmetic defascistization in which the taste of highly seasoned fascist mutton continually makes nonsense of the democratic lamb-dressing.

It is this lack of authenticity in Griffin's choice to cynically adopt a neo-populist New Speak without undergoing any radical revision of his historical understanding or ideological convictions that lies at the heart of Griffin's utter failure to gain a foothold in legitimate politics. In existentialist terms, what undermines his bid for power is his inability to be a sincere, radical-right democrat. He is thus forced into 'bad faith' by a chameleon-nature that condemns him to ape positions that express racism in a non-revolutionary, non-fascist sense. As a result, the 'watershed' or 'turning-point' in the party's fortunes predicted by Griffin on the eve of the 2010 general election is destined to remain an ever-receding mirage. It will doubtless continue knocking vigorously on the doors of power, just as he told the party faithful, but has no prospect of being let in. The present impasse is destined to remain permanent as long as he remains party leader, because of a fundamental dilemma. If Griffin's neo-populism is faked, it will not convince more than a marginalized minority of the electorate. If it were ever sincere, he would cease to be a fascist and thus would be forced to abandon a core part of his personality that seems to define his public persona and private being.

Ultimately, then, it is Griffin's fractured personal identity and not some mythic 'British identity' that is a key to the continued failure of BNP to usher in a new dawn. As long as he continues to treat neo-populism like an alien form of politics to be donned like a disguise, in what he considers at bottom to be the masquerade of party politics, he will be incapable of taking the radical steps needed to purge his party of its neo-Nazi past. He thus condemns himself to perpetuate the right-wing tradition established by the BUF and the National Front before him: that of relying on foreign imports for its core ideas and style, while in constant denial about the hopeless prospects for any breakthrough. If this analysis is right, the BNP will remain, not even a large small party, but a small small party.

Notes

1 German proverb.
2 http://www.thebnp.org/ (accessed 17 June 2010).
3 *Spearhead*, February 1965.
4 The article is by Tim Heaydon and was downloaded from the BNP's impressively 'glossy' website: www.identitymagazine.org.uk/pdf/200802iii.pdf (accessed 13 August 2008). The site is a showcase for the 'modernized' (i.e. euphemized) BNP's user-friendly, family-oriented electoral image.
5 Nick Griffin, *Identity* (2008) Available online at: www.identitymagazine.org.uk/pdf/200802i.pdf (accessed 13 August 2008).
6 For the general context of this transition, see Griffin (2001).
7 '"No one is to maltreat the Abos in any way . . . If there's anybody watching", went the Monty Python Australian sketch and, taking us to be the 'Abos' (which, *in a very real sense,* we British Aborigines are), that's exactly the situation today' [my emphasis] Nick Griffin, *Identity* (2008). Available online at: www.identitymagazine.org.uk/pdf/200802i.pdf (accessed 18 August 2008).
8 For the general context of French fascism's makeover, see Algazy (1984), which documents the extraordinary vitality of mostly Europeanized and de-Nazified neo-fascism in France between 1945 and 1980.
9 The large collection of articles on a wide gamut of cultural and political themes made available by former NF activist and currently 'national anarchist' Troy Southgate on his website (www.rosenoire.org/) provides an insight into the dynamic process of synthesis that can occur in neo-fascist circles that have rejected neo-Nazism in the search for an alternative world-view.

10 See 'Profile of Nick Griffin' on the 'Hope not Hate' website. Available online at: www.stopthebnp.org.uk/uncovered/pg03.htm (accessed 24 September 2009).

11 After the Italian bombing, NAR member Giorgio Vale became head of yet another well-known TP group, *Terza Posizione*, while Fiore headed another Evolian TP *groupuscule* called *Forza Nuova*.

12 In 2001, the ITP changed its name to England First and became a part of the European National Front.

13 A leading ideologue of the British metapolitical extreme right commented on this episode thus:

> The worst thing about Griffin, I think, is not the fact that one can point to various periods of his career and show how they appear to be diametrically opposed. People do evolve, after all, including myself – but once he left the reactionary politics of the 1970s and early-1980s NF and became a political soldier revolutionary, he then decided to turn round and go back down the same road during the early-90s. This, I think, is what people such as myself find so unacceptable. It smacks of careerism and opportunism, rather than any kind of principled effort or rational strategy.
>
> (Private e-mail of August 2008, cited with permission of the author)

14 For a blatant example of how deliberate this strategy is, see the now notorious YouTube clip from a talk Griffin gave to US fascists, available online at: www.youtube.com/watch?v=04QolIvfQEw. See also the BNP's *Language and concepts manual*, April 2009 version, available online at: http://sim-o.me.uk/wp-content/uploads/2009/04/language_discipline.pdf (accessed 24 September 2009).

15 See http://aryanunity.com/griffinfile.html (accessed 18 August 2008).

16 Cited on the 'Stop the BNP' website. Available online at: www.stopthebnp.org.uk/uncovered/pg03.htm (accessed 18 August 2008).

17 The German SDP formally renounced its commitment to Marxist revolutionary principles at its Bad Godesberg Congress in 1959.

References

Algazy, J. (1984) *La Tentation neo-fasciste en France: De 1944 à 1965*, Paris: Fayard.

Bardèche, M. (1961) *Qu'est que le fascisme?*, Paris: Les Sept Couleurs.

Bar-On, T. (2007) *Where Have All the Fascists Gone?*, Aldershot, Hampshire: Ashgate.

Bull, A. C. (2007) *Italian neofascism. The strategy of tension and the politics of nonreconciliation*, Oxford: Berghahn.

Copsey, N. (2007) 'Changing course or changing clothes? Reflections on the ideological evolution of the British National Party, 1999–2006', *Patterns of Prejudice*, 4 (1): 61–82.

Copsey, N. (2008) *Contemporary British fascism. The British National Party and the quest for legitimacy*, 2nd edn, London: Palgrave-Macmillan.

Evola, J. (1995 [1961]) *Revolt against the modern world*, Rochester, VT: Inner Traditions International.

Evola, J. (2002 [1953]) *Men among the ruins. Post-war reflections of a radical traditionalist*, Rochester, VT: Inner Traditions International.

Evola, J. (2003 [1961]) *Ride the tiger. A survival manual for the aristocrats of the soul*, Rochester, VT: Inner Traditions International.

Ferraresi, F. (1984) *La destra radicale*, Milan: Feltrinelli.

Griffin, R. (1996) 'The "post-fascism" of the Alleanza Nazionale: a case-study in ideological morphology', *Journal of Political Ideologies*, 1 (2): 123–45.

Griffin, R. (2000) 'Between metapolitics and apoliteía: the new right's strategy for conserving the fascist vision in the 'interregnum', *Modern and Contemporary France*, 8 (2): 35–53.

Griffin, R. (2001) 'Interregnum or endgame? Radical right thought in the "post-fascist" era', in Freeden, M. (ed.) *Reassessing political ideologies*, London: Routledge, 116–31.

Griffin, R. (2003) 'From slime mould to rhizome: an introduction to the groupuscular right', *Patterns of Prejudice*, 37 (1): 27–50.

Griffin, R. (2007) *Modernism and fascism. The sense of a beginning under Mussolini and Hitler*, London: Palgrave-Macmillan.

Ivarsflaten, E. (2006) 'Reputational shields: why most anti-immigrant parties failed in Western Europe, 1980–2005'. Available online at: www.allacademic.com/meta/p_mla_apa_research_citation/1/5/1/3/2/p151322_index.html (accessed 20 June 2008).

Lebourg, N. (2006) 'Les Nationalismes-révolutionnaires en mouvements: idéologies, propagandes et influences (France: 1962–2002)', PhD (history) thesis, University de Perpignan.

Mohler, A. (1972[1949]) *Die Konservative Revolution in Deutschland 1918–1932. Ein Handbuch*, Darmstadt: Wissenschaftliche Buchgesellschaft.

Mudde, C. (2007) *Populist radical right parties in Europe*, Cambridge: Cambridge University Press.

Pierce, William, (1978) *The Turner diaries*. Available online at: www.jrbooksonline.com/PDF_Books/TurnerDiaries.pdf (accessed 29 September 2009).

Sheehan, T. (1981) 'Italy: terror on the right', *New York Review of Books*, 27 (21 and 22) (January 22 1981).

Shields, J. (2007) *The extreme right in France: from Pétain to Le Pen*, London: Routledge.

Taguieff, P.-A. (1994). *Sur la Nouvelle Droite: Jalons d'une analyse critique*, Paris: Galilée, Editions Descartes et Cie.

Tyndall, J. (1988) *The eleventh hour: a call for British rebirth*, London: Albion Press.

Umland, A. (2008) 'Toward an uncivil society? Contextualizing the decline of post-Soviet Russian extremely right-wing parties'. Available online at: http://svonz.lenin.ru/books/Andreas_Umland-Toward_an_Uncivil_Society.pdf (accessed 20 August 2008).

10

LOCAL EMBEDDING AS A FACTOR IN ELECTORAL SUCCESS

The BNP and NPD compared

Graham Macklin and Fabian Virchow

Introduction

The rise of extreme-right and right-wing populist parties in several European countries in recent decades has produced a range of studies, each seeking to identify the factors necessary for the success or failure of such parties (Hainsworth, 2000; Minkenberg, 2002; Ignazi, 2003; Mudde, 2005; Norris, 2005). In seeking to assess the dynamics necessary for extreme-right parties to achieve an electoral breakthrough, Roger Eatwell (1998) has elaborated a model that highlights the interrelation between the micro, meso and macro determinants of success and failure. As alluded to previously in this volume, Eatwell calls our attention to three integrated factors that make individual voters react positively to the extreme right: 'first, individuals need to feel a sense of personal *efficacy*; second, they need to view the insurgent right as possessing some form of *legitimacy*; third, they need to feel a sense of declining *trust* in the socio-economic system' (Eatwell, 1998: 5; emphasis in original).

In order to understand how parties such as the *Nationaldemokratische Partei Deutschlands* (NPD, German National Democratic Party) and the British National Party (BNP) have been able to construct legitimacy, raise voters' sense of efficacy and extract advantage from declining system trust, this chapter will examine how both parties have embedded themselves in local neighbourhoods and networks as a precursor to electoral breakthrough (see Warmenbol, 2008). This case study takes as its starting point the NPD in the eastern German *Länder* (states) of Saxony and Mecklenburg–Pomerania, formerly part of the *Deutsche Demokratische Republik* (DDR), which are compared and contrasted with the British National Party (BNP) in Stoke-on-Trent in the West Midlands in central England. Although these two geographical areas are not strictly comparable, i.e. two large German states with one English city, they were selected both because of the ideological symmetry of the two political parties themselves, which have a long history of mutual collaboration, and also for the broad structural similarities of these two post-industrial areas, both of which have profound socio-economic problems. Direct comparison is made more complex, however, as a result of the different institutional and party systems in Britain and Germany and the differing impacts and constraints these have upon extreme right activism in either country. In Germany, for instance, there is a 5 per cent clause that militates against small-party representation in both the Bundestag and *Länder* parliaments.

The decision to focus upon Stoke-on-Trent rather than the wider West Midlands was dictated in part because the BNP, despite the votes polled across the area at election time, is only intermittently active elsewhere in the region. It is also the only town in the West Midlands where the BNP is represented on the local council in any great number. The BNP recently lost its councillors on Sandwell and Dudley council and retains only one councillor apiece on Nuneaton and Bedworth council and Staffordshire Moorlands council. Moreover, Stoke-on-Trent has been the sustained focus of BNP activism in the West Midlands for a number of years and thus represents the best opportunity to examine the extent to which the party has been able successfully to embed itself in local politics.

However, even here, as the 2010 local elections have recently revealed, the extent to which the extreme right has been able to sink roots into local communities has its limits. The BNP in Stoke-on-Trent, in the short term at least – its vote squeezed by the fact that local elections took place on the same day as the general election, which mitigated against the BNP – appears to be following the pattern established by the BNP in Burnley in the North West, whereby initial breakthrough and consolidation are followed by stagnation and decline. These recent events aside, this chapter explores how extreme-right parties embed themselves locally utilizing a transnational prism in order to discern whether or not a common strategy or 'strategic frame' exists that can perhaps serve as a template for future case studies. Particularly valuable would be case studies that compared and contrasted instances where one extreme-right party was successful versus another that was not, despite similar socio-economic conditions. This would, of course, serve to sharpen our overall understanding of how the extreme right seeks to construct local legitimacy, as well as the factors that detract from this quest. This chapter represents a contribution to this ongoing debate.

As noted earlier, the BNP and NPD have a long history of mutual collaboration stretching back several decades. Leading members of the BNP, including party chairman Nick Griffin and Leeds BNP activist Chris Beverley have long maintained close political and personal ties to the NPD. Beverley, who speaks fluent German, has attended a range of NPD events in the last decade, acting as a translator for Griffin's speeches when the BNP leader graces NPD events. The BNP has tried, without any noticeable sign of success, to persuade the NPD to pursue a strategy of 'modernization' similar to the BNP's and ditch its strategy of staging confrontational demonstrations. Activists from the youth groups of both organizations have also staged joint events, together with a number of activists drawn from the youth group of the Swedish *Nationaldemokraterna* (ND, National Democrats), with which the BNP also has strong fraternal ties.[1]

Both parties have made limited political inroads at a local level in recent years, following a long period at the very margins of the electoral system. They have thus failed to capture the greater scholarly interest shown in larger, far more successful far-right parties, such as the *Front National* in France or the *Freiheitliche Partei Österreichs* (FPÖ, Austrian Freedom Party) (Goodwin, 2008).

Local embedding and the electoral breakthrough of the NPD

Founded in 1964, the NPD achieved its first major electoral success in the second half of the 1960s when it entered several federal state parliaments (Kühnl et al., 1969; Hoffmann, 1999). Although many political observers expected otherwise, the NPD failed to win any seats in the 1969 federal elections, polling 4.3 per cent of the vote, below the 5 per cent threshold necessary for representation. Defeat and demoralization caused a serious schism within the NPD, plunging the party into a long-standing crisis for several decades (Dietzsch, 1988; Mecklenburg, 1996). The extreme right in Germany greeted the dissolution of the communist DDR and the reunification of Germany in 1989 and 1990 enthusiastically, as a first step to a Greater German Empire. However, electoral success at a federal state level in the 1990s proved ephemeral, not least because its representatives often performed amateurishly.

The NPD was unsuccessful in the 1990 national elections, its failure compounded by its choice of campaign themes: the imagined threats of a multicultural society and historical revisionism or Holocaust denial, which failed to resonate with the electorate. When Udo Voigt became NPD chairman in 1996, the party reorganized its structure and fixed its strategy to the so-called 'three pillar concept', which consisted of 'the fight for the streets', 'the fight for hearts and minds' and the 'fight for votes'. This reorganization of party priorities occurred simultaneously with the opening of NPD ranks to the growing neo-Nazi subculture. Several long-standing neo-Nazi activists, several of whom had played prominent roles in organizations banned by the state authorities during the early 1990s, joined the NPD, giving the organization 'street credibility' and thereby making it attractive for the extreme right and action-oriented subculture. The party recruited through 'White Noise' music events and a growing number of rallies all around Germany (Virchow, 2006), which contributed to its image as a 'young', action-orientated party focusing on non-parliamentary activities that, as Copsey notes elsewhere in this volume, stands in stark contrast to the strategy pursued in recent years by the BNP.

In 2004, the NPD added another pillar to its strategic concept, the 'fight for the organized will'. This aimed to create (temporary) alliances between the NPD and other extreme-right forces, in order to avoid situations in which two parties of the extreme right would compete in the same election, splitting the vote to the detriment of each. The so-called 'Pact for Germany' between the NPD and *Deutsche Volksunion* (DVU, German People's Union) in 2005 was accompanied by some more informal arrangements between the NPD and a network of neo-Nazi groupuscules that comprise the militant *Freie Kameradschaften,* which operate outside, though often in tandem with, extreme right-wing party political structures. This contrasts with Britain, where the BNP does not currently seek electoral pacts with other domestic extreme-right organizations, from whom it is keen to distance itself.

In the early 1980s, the NPD had recognized the strategic importance of embedding itself within the local community as a precondition for parliamentary success, at both the federal state level and at the national level. In 1981, the party produced a policy document entitled '*Kommunalpolitik Alternativ*' ('Local politics – the other way'), though this contained few if any programmatic messages concerning local and municipal politics. Instead, racist and nativist demands were combined with populist slogans contra 'the bureaucracy'. Thus the NPD, already beset by severe setbacks, proved incapable of translating these ideas from the drawing board into practical reality, causing a further deterioration in party morale in the process. Indeed, it was not until the late 1990s that the party executive compiled a further document elaborating its ideas on how its politicians should be supported at a local level once elected.

The fulcrum of NPD activity since the reunification of Germany has centred upon the eastern part of the country, seen as a 'more German Germany' by the NPD because of the missing cultural, political and economic 'Americanization', which the party perceived had infected the western portion of the country, rendering it less authentically 'German'. Civil society was also far weaker in eastern Germany following the collapse of the DDR, largely because there were fewer alternatives such as churches, trade unions and NGOs to challenge extreme-right activism, which has also benefited from a lack of activity by the mainstream political parties. These factors, within the overarching context of the economic difficulties in the east of Germany, made the region a far more fertile recruiting ground for the extreme right than the remainder of the country.[2]

In an attempt to engineer an electoral breakthrough in eastern Germany, the NPD leadership merged two approaches: the tactical renunciation of the party's name in order to disguise the role played by the party, which ran in tandem with an increased focus on grass-roots campaigning. In Dresden, the NPD and other extreme-rightists drawn from outside its official political structures began the 'National Alliance Dresden', which proved successful in the June 2004 local elections in Saxony. Just a couple of months later, the NPD polled 9.2 per cent of the vote in state elections, winning the party twelve representatives to the Saxon state parliament, the *Landtag*.

This development highlighted a significant realignment on the German extreme right. Throughout the 1990s, the preeminent extreme-right parties had been *Die Republikaner* (REP, the Republicans), with its middle-class base (Funke, 1989; Obszerninks, 1999), and the DVU, which served as a tailor-made vehicle for its millionaire leader, Gerhard Frey (Obszerninks and Schmidt, 1998; Holtmann, 2002). Despite their earlier successes in federal state elections, both parties found themselves marginalized in the first decade of the new century. In 2010, the NPD was the only extreme-right party in Germany with members of parliament at the federal state level.

This was the result of several factors, of which the strategy of local embedding was the overarching one. The NPD, through a 'bottom-up' grass-roots activism, has steadily increased both the number of its voters and its proportion of the vote, in order to develop a hard core of support that has became increasingly entrenched at a local level with each successive electoral contest. This gives the party a solid base from which to launch further electoral challenges.

Mapping NPD success at a local level

In 2008, the NPD succeeded in gaining representation on every county council in Saxony's elections, earning between three and six seats on each council, with a total of 5.1 per cent of the vote, a considerable improvement on the 1.4 per cent that the party polled in 2004 (Jennerjahn, 2008). It was a pattern that was repeated in local elections across eastern Germany in 2009, where the NPD won seats in every state in which it stood candidates, gaining representation on councils in Leipzig, Dresden, Rostock and Erfurt for the first time. In Thuringia, the NPD vote increased from zero to 3.1 per cent, while in Saxony the party tripled its support to gain 2.3 per cent. The state of Mecklenburg–Western Pomerania saw the NPD vote increase from 0.8 per cent to 3.2 per cent, placing twenty-six extreme-right-wing candidates in municipal-level positions. In the wake of the elections, *Der Spiegel* commented that, although the results did not rival its success in the 2006 state parliamentary elections, 'the 2009 municipal elections are a symbol that the NPD is at least establishing itself across the east'.[3]

The process of electoral breakthrough and consolidation by the NPD is best followed in the east German *Länder* of Saxony and Mecklenburg–Pomerania, in the north-eastern corner of the country, where grass-roots campaigning has not only paid off at the local level but also at the federal state level too. Both states have witnessed an acceleration of local embeddedness in recent years. Saxony has become a laboratory for the NPD's grass-roots campaign. The party has transferred party offices and the staff of its newspaper to the region, which has also seen a number of long-standing party activists from western Germany move into the region in order to boost local structures. This localized focus has paid dividends. The NPD polled 23,895 votes in the 2004 local elections in Saxony. This figure nearly quadrupled to 107,694 in 2009. A similar rise could be observed in the county council election results. In 2004, the NPD polled 1.4 per cent of the vote, a figure that had risen to 5.1 per cent in September 2008 (Jennerjahn, 2008).

With regards to the latter result, the NPD had begun its campaign in 2007 concentrating on the distribution of two issues of a youth magazine, each with a circulation of 30,000. In addition, NPD cadres circulated 'white noise' CDs to teenagers at schools and marketplaces in a bid to shape youth culture. On the eve of the poll, the NPD deluged the area with election posters, even in areas where it had not been active, in order to give the appearance of a widespread, dynamic organization. More than a million copies of a propaganda paper were distributed; it focused on local affairs, though these were mingled with general slogans such as 'East Germany polls German'.

Several localities emerged as NPD strongholds in Saxony. In 2008, in Reinhardtsdorf-Schöna, a small Saxon town with approximately 1,600 residents close to the German–Czech border, the NPD again gained 25.2 per cent of the vote, a figure it had first polled in 2004, putting it ahead of all of the mainstream parties: the Christian Democrats (21.7 per cent), the Socialists (15.6 per cent), the Liberals (4.2 per cent), the Social Democrats (3.7 per cent) and the Greens (2.8 per cent). Only a local citizens' alliance (marginally) outpolled the NPD, with a vote of 26.8 per cent. Thus, over 50 per cent of the vote in Reinhardtsdorf-Schöna went to parties standing outside the political mainstream.

Individual activists, particularly those who are well known and respected locally, play an important role in the process of local embedding for the NPD (for instance, driving instructor Uwe Leichsenring in Königstein, or plumber Michael Jacobi in Reinhardtsdorf-Schöna). They are involved with local soccer clubs and parents' councils and act as honorary jurors, creating what Copsey has termed a 'cognitive dissonance' between the perception of what voters expect and the reality of doorstep or other such encounters, which helps to normalize and legitimize the extreme-right party to which they belong (Copsey, 2008: 140).

The local political climate is also of relevance in some localities. In the Saxon city of Colditz, for instance, the actions of the mayor served to limit the activities of anti-racist activists. In one instance, anti-racist organizers of a soccer tournament were informed that they would be liable for any damage to the sports field that might be caused, in the fortnight before as well as after the event. The police also made it clear that it could not protect the event, although it had been officially announced two months ahead. When, finally, the anti-racists staged a public meeting in the town centre, they were confronted by neo-Nazis and required a police escort.[4]

In Mecklenburg–Western Pomerania, a rural region bordering Poland that includes the constituency of Chancellor Angela Merkel, similar developments have taken place. The NPD slowly increased its share of the vote, building up a solid level of support in several areas of a region in which unemployment ran at more than 18 per cent, the highest in the country. In 2004, the NPD had polled 15,255 votes, gaining ten seats at a local level. In June 2009, however, this vote quadrupled to 60,908, giving the party twenty-six seats. Particular strongholds emerged in towns on the German–Polish border, where the NPD had clearly beaten the Greens and the Liberals. Even when it performed poorly in the national elections in September 2009, the NPD was still able to achieve between 5 and 10 per cent of the vote in several Pomeranian areas.

In September 2006, the NPD polled 7.3 per cent at the Mecklenburg–Western Pomeranian federal state elections, surpassing the 5 per cent needed to enter the state parliament and returning a six-strong parliamentary group to the seventy-one-seat parliament. This vote represented a significant increase on its last showing at the polls, when the party polled less than 1 per cent of the vote.[5] In Britain, the BNP hailed the vote a 'tremendous victory' for the 'modernisation and mainstreaming' of 'nationalist' forces across Europe, which it believed validated its own local strategy and which the party website was keen to stress Nick Griffin had urged the NPD to adopt.[6]

Ironically, Mecklenberg–Western Pomerania was not, historically speaking, an area in which the NPD had had a particularly strong local organization. Instead, it had been the neo-Nazi groupuscules that had campaigned continuously and had been able to get some support from the local population. The NPD achieved its success in the state largely because it co-opted the structures, strategies and personnel of the neo-Nazi groupuscules prior to its electoral breakthrough in 2006.

The island Usedom, on the Baltic Sea on the border between Germany and Poland, serves as an example of this process of political embedding outside traditional political structures. In 2003, neo-Nazi groupuscules staged a rally protesting against the travelling 'Crimes of the *Wehrmacht*' exhibition, which offered visual testimony to the crimes committed by the German *Wehrmacht* during the Second World War and against which the NPD had protested since it began touring in 1997. The extreme right campaigned against the exhibition under the slogan 'My grandpa was o.k.', winning them some sympathy among the older population. Supportive feedback raised the neo-Nazis' self-confidence. This was followed by the foundation of a political group called the 'Initiative for the Enlightenment of the People', which began distributing a free publication called *Island Courier* across the island. It had a circulation of approximately 30,000. *Island Courier* focused on regional issues, such as the forthcoming selling of a hospital, security issues in case of a stormy flood or the expected reform of the administrative machinery, rather than overtly ideological topics, allowing the neo-Nazis to open a channel of communication with the local population (Janowski, 2008).

Later that year, local neo-Nazis belonging to 'Aryan Warriors' and 'National Teutonic Brotherhood' founded another political group called 'Living better and securer in Ueckermuende'. The main activity of this group was a campaign against the proposed building of accommodation for asylum seekers in the town of Ueckermuende, across the Stettiner lagoon from Usedom. By camouflaging and concealing their extreme right-wing allegiances, the founders of this group were able to collect 2,000 signatures for a petition demanding an end to the plan. The town itself only had a population of 10,000. Local neo-Nazis had thus been successful in mobilizing one-fifth of the town in support of this particular venture. Support for the group was also voiced by a local freesheet, which repeated the group's racist statements without any critical comment (Fischer, 2008). Two of the leading neo-Nazi activists of the group – Michael Gielnik and Tino Müller – later ran as candidates for the NPD. Müller became a member of the state parliament in Mecklenburg–Pomerania in 2006, when the NPD polled 7.3 per cent. NPD electoral campaigns in Mecklenburg–Western Pomerania relied heavily upon neo-Nazi groupuscules and cadres. In return for their support, prominent neo-Nazi activists received promising places on the NPD party list. The neo-Nazis became party members and ran the election campaign.

The result of this grass-roots campaign, led by neo-Nazis and which took place over the course of a year, was a precondition for the NPD's success in the federal state elections in September 2006. In particular, the NPD had proved successful in mobilizing fears of further marginalization and downward social mobility. The NPD's slogans offering job opportunities and financial assistance to German families in need, by excluding migrants from the social security systems and the labour market, clearly resonated with a growing number of voters. The NPD organized parties for families and acted like the proverbial 'nice guy' who cared about his neighbours, which served to give the NPD's slogan 'People's community instead of dog-eat-dog society' some credibility. In localities such as Postlow and Bargischow, small villages with only a few hundred inhabitants each, the NPD gained a relative majority of the votes. Two leading members of the neo-Nazi groupuscules, Birger Lüssow and the aforementioned activist Tino Müller, became members of the federal state parliament in 2006.

In the Mecklenburg–West Pomerania local elections held in June 2009, the NPD gained sixty elected representatives. The party now has representatives on nine county councils, four town councils that are an administrative district in their own right and twenty-eight city councils across this federal state. The strongholds are mainly in the east of the state, with four NPD representatives in the county councils of Uecker-Randow and Ostvorpommern, where the NPD polled 9.1 per cent and 7.6 per cent of the vote, respectively. In several cases, mainstream political parties have proved unable to prevent the election of NPD representatives to higher office once they have been elected. In the small town of Bargischow, an NPD activist has been elected as the vice mayor. Such positions confer local legitimacy upon the NPD, conveying the impression that it is a party just like any other.

NPD political activism does not operate in a vacuum. A major factor in the NPD's success has been frustration regarding the severe economic situation. The city of Anklam, with its population of 14,000, remains dominated by unemployment, which runs at 21.2 per cent. The city has lost one-third of its population over the last two decades owing to migration. Many of those who have stayed do not expect any positive contribution from the established parties or even the political system. For them, democracy has become simply a mechanism for the administration of shortages. The turnout for the 2009 local elections stood at 43 per cent.

The NPD has been quick to capitalize on this crisis of local democracy. NPD activist Michael Andrejewski was re-elected as a city councillor and ranked fifth out of twenty-five councillors with regard to the number of votes he obtained. Andrejewski, a lawyer formerly active in a racist group in Hamburg, moved eastwards to Anklam in 2004. He moved to eastern Germany, 'because the ruling system is weaker here and easier to defeat. You have to attack an enemy where it is weak'.[7] Although Andrejewski behaves unobtrusively in the city council and the county council, he attracts attention in the federal state parliament through heckling and using bad language. As a result, he has earned eighteen calls to order and has been excluded from parliamentary meetings twice. However, to focus on his performance in the council chamber is to distract attention from the local impact that NPD activists such as Andrejewski have outside traditional political structures, which helps build their legitimacy regardless of their actual performance on the democratic stage. As Andrejewski told a BBC News reporter:

> First, we have another concept for another society. Second, we help in daily problems, we listen to people and help them with admin and social services. I have street credibility with them because I have been unemployed myself. I have shared their sorrows.[8]

Activities and sentiments such as these, which exist outside neatly quantifiable assertions regarding the success or failure of extreme-right-wing political parties, help to embed and indeed entrench support for the extreme right at a local level.

Mapping BNP success in the West Midlands – the case of Stoke-on-Trent

Since 1999, when Nick Griffin assumed leadership of the party, the BNP has placed a considerable emphasis on local community politics as a means of embedding itself within local communities and in local democratic structures. Most attention, both journalistic and scholarly, has focused, unsurprisingly, on the rise of the BNP in Burnley in the North West, which now appears to be stagnating, and in Barking and Dagenham in outer East London, where the party gained twelve councillors in 2006 (for instance, Deacon et al., 2004; Joseph Rowntree Reform Trust, 2005; Rhodes, 2009). Considerably less attention has been paid to the performance of the BNP in the West Midlands and, in particular, its attempt to embed itself in the city of Stoke-on-Trent, once the heart of the Potteries, world-famous for the manufacture of fine ceramics. This industry has now all but disappeared, as have its coal and steel industries. Gone too are the jobs associated with these industries. The city's deep-seated socio-economic problems, the fragmentation of party politics and the resultant frustration and civic disengagement were compounded by its unique governance arrangements. Under the terms of the Local Government Act 2000, a council manager and a directly elected mayor ruled Stoke-on-Trent city council. This executive model of governance, unique among local authorities, whereby the elected mayor and his chief executive manager took all policy decisions, which were only subsequently scrutinized by the rest of the council, became a source of friction that in turn fuelled dissatisfaction with, and disengagement from, local politics. The Stoke Governance Commission, the body established by the Secretary of State for Communities and Local Government, in consultation with the council, in October 2007 to examine Stoke's political system and make recommendations for its future, concluded that there was a 'deep-seated malaise' as a result of which the city's electorate had been 'short-changed'.[9] The mayoral system was subsequently scrapped following a local referendum, but the deep-seated socio-economic problems that the BNP capitalized upon persist.

During the June 2009 European elections, 121,967 people voted for the BNP in the West Midlands (8.63 per cent), a higher proportion of the vote than in the North West, where BNP chairman Nick Griffin was elected as an MEP. Although not enough to elect a BNP MEP in the West Midlands, the vote signalled a further 1.13 per cent regional rise in support for the party on the 107,794 votes the party polled in the 2004 European elections. This itself represented an increase of 5.8 per cent on its 1999 vote. In Stoke-on-Trent, the BNP polled 8,706 votes (17.62 per cent), coming fourth behind the Conservative Party in a poll in which only 26.73 per cent of residents of Stoke-on-Trent turned out to vote, the lowest turnout across the West Midlands. The BNP were buoyed by the result, an increase on the 15.3 per cent it had polled in 2004, stating that 'it's really promising for the future of our party in the city' (*The Sentinel*, 8 June 2009).

The principal beneficiary of the European elections was not the BNP, however, but the United Kingdom Independence Party (UKIP). UKIP polled the most votes in Stoke-on-Trent, 10,885 votes (22 per cent), an impressive result for the party, considering its complete lack of representation on the local council. UKIP also polled the most votes in neighbouring Newcastle-under-Lyme and returned two MEPs for the region. The Labour Party, which until recently had dominated the political landscape of Stoke, was relegated to second place with 10,144 (20.5 per cent), further adding to its woes in the West Midlands that saw it lose all but three of its seats on Staffordshire county council in the local elections, which ran in parallel with the European elections in many areas.

The Labour Party once dominated Staffordshire politics, holding all sixty seats on Stoke council only a decade or so ago. However, the implosion of the local Labour Party during these years provided the BNP with ample opportunity to attempt to embed itself in the town. This process was reflected in the party's gradual electoral progress, which reached its zenith with nine councillors in 2009. This number was reduced to seven at the beginning of 2010, when two councillors resigned from the party following an internal dispute. However, even with this reduced number of councillors, ahead of the 2010 local elections, many feared that the BNP still had a realistic chance of emerging as the largest single party on the council.

This is all the more surprising given that, until comparatively recently, the BNP in Stoke-on-Trent was a marginal force in the city. It was not until 1991 that the party formally constituted a group within the city. For many years, the party was virtually a one-man band associated with long-term activist Steve Batkin, then an unemployed pipe fitter. In 1994, Batkin was noted to be the organizer of an attempt by local racists, BNP activists and members of the militant neo-Nazi group Combat 18 to storm a local mosque, which failed, resulting in a tense confrontation between local Muslims and the extreme right (*Sunday Mercury*, 13 October 2002).

Batkin had also begun to test Stoke's electoral waters in 1993, when he stood in the Fenton Green ward, polling ninety-nine votes (4.3 per cent). The following year, he polled 170 votes (5.61 per cent), though in 1995 this had fallen to

92 votes (3.58 per cent). Standing in the ward again in 2000, Batkin polled 159 votes (9.3 per cent), which represented a healthy increase in his vote in Fenton Green following a five-year hiatus. In the 1997 general election, Batkin polled 568 votes (1.23 per cent) in Stoke-on-Trent South, though this was more than the 288 votes (0.62 per cent) polled by the National Democrats, a National Front splinter, which also stood in the constituency. Fellow BNP activist Michael Coleman stood in Stoke-on-Trent Central, polling 606 votes (1.51 per cent). The prospect of electoral success for the BNP appeared slight.

The party's prospects appeared to change in 2001, in line with a general upswing in party fortunes elsewhere in the country in the wake of widespread racial riots in the northern England towns of Oldham, Burnley and Bradford. Indeed, Stoke experienced its own wave of serious racial unrest on 14–15 July 2001 in the Cobridge area of the city, which resulted in forty-nine arrests, following rumours that the National Front was planning to march through the city.[10] A former BNP press officer later stated that the BNP deliberately fuelled these rumours, in the hope that the party would benefit from any resulting confrontation between the white and Asian populations (Smith, 2003: 125).

The real breakthrough for the BNP came in 2002, however, largely as a result of a strident campaign against 'asylum seekers', which combined with factors relating to the internal democratic governance of the city revolving around its unique system of a directly elected mayor. The BNP stunned observers when its candidate, Steve Batkin, came third, with 8,213 votes (18.67 per cent), more than the Conservative and Liberal Democrat candidates combined. At the time, the BNP had no more than thirty activists in the city (*Searchlight*, no. 331, January 2003). Batkin's electoral publicity depicted Stoke-on-Trent as a 'proud, decent English city' that had been 'abandoned, neglected and betrayed'. This decline was framed in explicitly racial terms, with publicity photos of Batkin standing outside a local public house, 'once a favourite with Longton drinkers, now it's a home for refugees from Afghanistan'.[11]

BNP literature circulating through the city at the time blamed the Labour and Conservative Parties for the decline of the Potteries and for allowing local skills to be degraded and local industry destroyed, swamped by cheaper, inferior pottery from abroad. 'Stoke should have been a priority in Labour's regeneration plans', argued the BNP, 'but instead of providing for the people of the city to rebuild their community, they are in the process of pushing them out and replacing them with economic migrants from South-Eastern Europe and the Third World' (*Voice of Freedom*, no. 31, October 2002). It was to prove an increasingly potent message, which the BNP attempted to exploit in a subsequent campaign against asylum seekers, hysteria about which forced the Mayor's office to publish a booklet entitled *Asylum seeking in Stoke-on-Trent: the facts. Report of the elected mayor's enquiry into asylum seekers in the city of Stoke-on-Trent,* in February 2003, in an attempt to assuage fears and challenge myths and misperceptions.

Such overtly anti-immigrant politicking by the BNP was combined with a far greater emphasis on local community campaigning, with close attention to cultivating the electorate at ward level through the dissemination of locally tailored *Patriot* leaflets that responded to local concerns, as well as contact with local activists such as Batkin, who, being unemployed, had the time to assiduously work target areas in the ward. The tactic paid dividends, and in 2003 Batkin was elected as the first BNP councillor in Stoke, in Longton North ward in the south of the city. He retained the position until 2007. The party came second in three other seats, including Chell and Packmoor, where the criminal record of the candidate proved no bar to him gaining 28.6 per cent of the vote (*The Sentinel*, 26 April 2003).

Unlike the NPD, whose success in areas such as Mecklenberg–Western Pomerania is underwritten by its alliance with overtly neo-Nazi groupuscules and activists, the BNP in Stoke has sought to embed itself in local communities largely through presenting a moderate face to its electorate. Shortly after his election as a local councillor, Steve Batkin, once the face of the BNP in Stoke, was 'officially reprimanded' and effectively marginalized within the local and national party, following a series of anti-Semitic comments questioning the Holocaust as a historical fact, in the wake of a public anti-fascist meeting addressed by a Holocaust survivor (*Sunday Sentinel*, 13 April 2003).

In 2003, Jenny Holdcroft, an independent councillor (who later stood on a BNP ticket), organized an anti-immigration protest. Although BNP members took part in the march, the party did not openly associate themselves with such initiatives because, as we have seen elsewhere in this volume, unlike the NPD, the BNP leadership had long dispensed with the strategy of 'march and grow' as detrimental to its public image because of the negative aura of violence that prevailed when its members were confronted by anti-fascists. In line with the strategy pursued by the local party, Stoke BNP activists tried to shake off the party's 'reputation for criminal behaviour by choosing candidates without criminal records who dress smartly in jackets and ties and declare that they are not racists'. They had also attempted to 'court pensioners at their weekly bingo meeting', at which 'they were careful to limit their attack on asylum seekers and fears over crime'. They were, however, 'given a rough reception by the pensioners who accused them of forgetting the lessons of Hitler's policies' (*Sunday Sentinel*, 16 March 2003).

This tension between the local party and the extremist image of its national parent was evident in September 2003, when the BNP contested a by-election in Stoke's Abbey Green ward, which five years later they would completely control. Among the canvassing team was Young BNP leader Mark Collett, shortly after his appearance on the documentary *Young, Nazi and proud,* in which he was filmed praising Nazism and making racist and anti-Semitic remarks. The local candidate was clearly displeased by Collett's presence, telling the local press: 'If I had known his history I would not have had him here . . . I don't want him in any ward where I stand again. I want the party to have a better image and to be taken seriously' (*Stoke Sentinel*, 24 September 2003). This is not to say that the local activists were any less extreme than activists from the national party, as remarks from a number of local activists attest, merely that, on the whole, they were better at concealing their views – BNP group leader Alby Walker was noted for his reluctance to talk about the implications of party policy – while many others were recent converts to the party and thus lacked the historical baggage attached to many of its long-standing activists.

This strategy appears to have been conducive to rapid growth. In 2004, the BNP polled an average of 28 per cent of the vote across eight wards in the city. The anti-fascist magazine *Searchlight* sounded the alarm, stating that Stoke represented the BNP's 'best prospect' in the West Midlands (*Searchlight*, no. 355, January 2005). Several months later, it reported that the party had 'grown substantially' in the city (*Searchlight*, no. 357, March 2005). This expansion was despite Batkin's negligible influence in the council chamber, where he spoke only twice, once to ask what 'abstain' meant (*Searchlight*, no. 358, April 2005). His actual contribution to the running of the council was almost beside the point. Batkin's achievement was proving that the BNP was a viable, electable option in Stoke-on-Trent. The BNP too began to report 'dramatic growth' in the city. Deputy BNP leader and West Midlands regional organizer Simon Darby argued that Stoke could be the first city to elect a BNP MP, though the party's subsequent performance in the 2005 general election proved the party was still a long way from this goal (*Voice of Freedom*, no. 58, February 2005).

However, the principal focus of Stoke BNP in 2005 was not the general election but the 2005 mayoral election. Batkin, who again stood on an anti-asylum seeker platform, almost doubled his 2002 vote, polling 15,776 votes (19.0 per cent) to come fourth. As the BNP website noted on 6 May, the day after the contest, 'This demonstrates that the support base cannot, as the hostile media have attempted to do so, be dismissed as just a tiny hard core *minority*, but is city-wide and resistant to the hostile smear campaigns used against Clr. Batkin.'[12]

The BNP in Stoke also increasingly began to seek legitimacy through campaigns against 'Islam', hardly a topic of any real salience in a city in which, according to the 2001 census, only 3.2 per cent of residents defined themselves as 'Muslim', as opposed to the 74.7 per cent who described themselves as 'Christian' and 13.4 per cent who responded that they had 'no religion' at all – figures that were broadly in line with the national average.[13] Ahead of the 2006 local elections – in which the BNP contested eight wards, winning in three and coming second in four – local activists delivered 5,000 copies of the BNP leaflet reproducing the Danish cartoon of the prophet Mohammed wearing a turban shaped like a bomb, an image used as an excuse for rioting and murder in several parts of the world. The local press noted that 'the Potteries is believed to be one of the first places in the country where the leaflet – which is now being reviewed by Staffordshire Police – is being circulated'. The BNP campaigned against the construction of a local mosque in Regent's Road, Hanley, with leaflets depicting minarets towering above council houses under the banner 'is this what you want in Stoke?'. The party also sought to prevent the construction of the mosque by offering the council £100,000 for the land, which it had already agreed to lease to the local Muslim community (*The Sentinel*, 28 February 2006).

The BNP also sought to make political capital from the manslaughter of one of its activists, who was stabbed to death in July 2007 following a domestic row with a Muslim neighbour with whom he had been in dispute for a number of years. His death featured heavily in BNP campaigning in the city, with Nick Griffin attending his funeral, feeding into its campaign against 'anti-white' racism, exemplified in the party publication *Racism cuts both ways*, which portrays whites as the principal victims of racial violence. Brown's death failed to resonate outside the BNP, however, with one right-wing tabloid publishing a stinging rebuke of the BNP for trying 'to create a "white martyr" for their own grubby ends' (*Daily Mail*, 31 May 2008). The BNP subsequently staged a rally in the city on 20 September 2008, which, as *Searchlight* observed, also served to launch their campaign for control of the council (*Searchlight*, no. 400, October 2008).

The 2007 local elections saw the BNP contest ten wards, gaining a further three seats in Abbey Green, Bentilee and Townsend and Weston and Meir North wards, the three wards in which they had won in 2006, though victory was tempered by the loss of Batkin's Longton North seat. In 2008, the BNP won a further three seats, including victories in Abbey Green and Bentilee and Townsend, making the BNP the sole political representative in two Stoke council wards. The victories seemingly corroborate the 'contagion effect' thesis, as well as highlighting the success of the BNP in consolidating its success at ward level following an initial breakthrough, though such an observation requires qualification following the 2010 election results, in which the BNP lost several seats.

The increasing level of BNP representation on Stoke council meant that attempts by the mainstream parties to block BNP councillors from positions of influence on council committees, which had been in place since 2004, were no longer tenable. They finally collapsed in 2007 when BNP councillor Mark Leat was appointed to chair of the council's Health and Well-Being Scrutiny and Overview Commission, prefiguring the normalization of BNP appointments to council committees. The BNP have also sought to broaden this legitimacy by campaigning against local school closures and positioning themselves, with mixed success, for election as school governors, which would bestow a further level of legitimacy upon them.[14]

This went hand in hand with the slow, steady electoral progress made by the party in enclaves of the city. Once elected, BNP councillors tried to embed themselves more deeply within a number of wards by consciously prioritizing ward-level case work over and above the more overtly political work on the local council. The latter is often seen as remote from the immediate concerns of voters with whom the party is seeking to forge a direct and ultimately entrenched bond, and Stoke BNP councillors have shown little interest in grappling with it. Indeed, BNP council group leader Alby Walker and his wife, fellow BNP councillor Ellie Walker, represented a model of local embedding strategy. Both were involved in community activities seemingly unconnected to the 'negative' racial themes of the party, conducting bingo in a local retirement home as well as other initiatives. This included using their councillor budgets to part-fund the revamp of a local park, which helps underscore the 'positive' legitimacy that the party is attempting to construct locally.[15] As Stoke Labour MP Rob Flello observes: 'They are adopting a much more localised, practical, day-to-day, we're-on-your-side approach to hide what the party fundamentally stands for.'[16]

This can be contrasted with its performance in the council chamber, where 'the BNP don't contribute at all'. The limits of pursuing a 'community politics' strategy to the detriment of wider politics was astutely observed by one local commentator:

> Alby & Ellie [Walker] have taken over £32,000 in allowances and I honestly cannot remember the last time either of them spoke at full council whether that is to support or oppose an issue. I have yet to hear them put anything forward as an alternative . . . They have simply just sat there and had their attendance mark and then left as early as they could. It is not good enough. The people that they represent deserve better. Don't they have a duty to try and improve the City as well as serve their wards? . . . A BNP councillor may be willing to provide luncheon clubs, dog walking and gardening services for the elderly but there is more to representing the WHOLE community and indeed the city at large.[17]

Even the limited successes of this community strategy were thrown into question in December 2009, when Alby Walker, the 'backbone' of Stoke BNP, suddenly resigned, without warning or indeed reference to either his local or national party, leading to speculation that the BNP bubble had burst. Walker's departure as group leader certainly damaged the local legitimacy of the BNP because:

> As BNP Group Leader he [Walker] has instilled in his fellow far right councillors the need to be effective and hands on in the wards that they represent . . . The Walkers have brought credibility to the BNP in this city as they are far from the stereotypical BNP profile. They are a fashionable clean cut couple who are very camera friendly, but criticism has been aimed at them for never talking openly about their parties' policies which in turn has served to insulate them from criticism associated with the espousal of views often held by BNP members concerning race and immigration.[18]

Walker's departure appears to have thrown the local BNP into disarray. Indeed it came close to derailing the launch of the party's general election manifesto, at which the BNP announced its intention to stand Simon Darby, the deputy BNP leader, in the Stoke Central seat, while Walker simultaneously announced that he would also be standing in the seat. This made the dispute within the local BNP even more acrimonious, as Walker publicly denounced 'a vein of Holocaust denying within the BNP', as well as stating that senior BNP members had, what he described as, 'Nazi, Nazi-esque sympathies'.[19] To illustrate the point, Walker revealed a photograph of BNP councillor Steve Batkin standing with neo-Nazi activists from the group Blood and Honour, who were both sieg-heiling.[20] Failing to distance himself adequately from the 'genuinely patriotic men' giving the Nazi salute in the photograph, Batkin was asked if he was a Holocaust denier, to which he responded: 'I've always believed about 300,000 people died in the Jewish holocaust, not 6 million . . . there's no way, there was that many Jews in Europe at that time who could have sustained that amount of deaths.'[21] The photograph, and indeed Batkin's response, served to tarnish the hard-won local legitimacy that the BNP had previously built up.

In the event, Walker's intervention made little difference to the BNP vote. Darby polled only 2,502 votes (7.7 per cent), compared with the 2,178 votes (7.8 per cent) that the party had polled in 2005. Walker meanwhile polled a mere 255 votes (0.9 per cent). Although the other two general election candidates fared little better, polling 3,196 votes (8 per cent) in Stoke North and 3,762 votes (9.4 per cent) in Stoke South, the local electoral failure of the BNP could be seen most starkly at a local level, which reflected the damage Walker's departure had done to the party. The BNP only managed to stand six candidates in the local elections, two of whom were standing for re-election, compared with eleven candidates in 2008. This despite hopes that they would stand fourteen or more. This 'candidate drought' appears to have been a response by many potential candidates to Walker's treatment by the national party and sections of his own local group (*Stoke Sentinel*, 12 April 2010). Not only did the BNP fail to gain any new councillors, the two councillors defending their seats (one in Bentilee and Townsend and another in Weston and Meir North) were both defeated, as was Alby Walker, who stood for re-election in Abbey Green as an independent. Although Labour won the ward, the BNP vote fell only slightly, from 858 in 2008 to 835 in 2010, though its percentage of the overall vote was squeezed by the increased turnout. Walker came a poor fifth, which perhaps suggests that his own efforts to embed the BNP within the city played second fiddle to the BNP 'brand name' with which they were associated.

The electoral defeat of the BNP was mirrored across the country, most spectacularly in the party stronghold of Barking and Dagenham, which saw the loss of all twelve BNP councillors. This served to mask the fact that the BNP in Stoke-on-Trent still returned strong votes in the city, reflecting a level of entrenched and indeed embedded support for the party in Stoke. Once heralded as the 'jewel in the crown' of the BNP by party leader Nick Griffin, the BNP in Stoke-on-Trent, in the short term at least, appears to be following the pattern of Burnley, with the party falling back after its initial breakthrough and a period of consolidation. This, of course, raises the reverse of the question that this chapter set out to answer: what factors contribute to the decline of support for far-right parties? The extent to which the BNP can or cannot recover from the political mauling of 2010 will be tested in the all-out elections of 2011, in which the remaining five BNP councillors will face the electorate. However, even if all five are defeated, one suspects that this is far from being the end of the line for the BNP in Stoke.

Factors of electoral success

This brief overview of the NPD in eastern Germany and the BNP in the West Midlands over the last decade has revealed several factors that can act in favour of a political breakthrough and the consolidation of social and political support for an extreme right-wing party. However, these factors are not necessarily the same in both countries and, in some cases, can be the polar opposite. The following factors are of particular salience:

(a) Situations of real or imagined socio-economic crisis do not lead to electoral success of extreme-right parties, unless the party itself offers a clear picture of how it intends to influence policy, particularly in relation to immigration, thereby raising voters' sense of *efficacy*.

(b) There is an interaction between the micro- and the meso-level. Sustained grass-roots campaigning leads to embedding and electoral success in the local context, and such embedding is needed to break through to the next level, that is the federal state/regional level. In the case of Germany – though not Britain – representation can generate state funding, as a result of gaining members of parliament at the federal state level. This funding can then be used to reinforce areas where local embedding is weak, through initiatives such as the increased distribution of propaganda or the opening of 'citizen's offices', something that the BNP has also recently begun to replicate in towns such as Burnley.

(c) Continuity in extreme-right campaigning is relevant. It does not necessarily matter if this is done under the name of the party that finally runs in the election. As the case of Mecklenburg–Pomerania demonstrates, a party can also profit from the grass-roots activities of other forces, so long as the campaigning content is similar. Free papers represent an instrument the German extreme right makes use of extensively.

(d) Chances of success for the extreme right are enhanced if there is a highly controversial 'big issue' and the party is able to adopt the correct strategy to maximize its potential. In Germany, the NPD and neo-Nazi groupuscules were particularly successful in 'nationalizing the social question' (Virchow, 2007a; 2007b) during the radical overhaul of the German social security system. Part of the respective campaigning profile is the attempt to show itself as the 'carer' for people in need. The BNP has pursued this strategy at a far more local level in Stoke, though these concerns are linked to 'national' campaign themes, such its campaign against 'asylum seekers' and 'Islam'.

(e) The 'quality' of the party personnel is also relevant. Extreme-right parties benefit from capable, respected and well-known activists living locally, though in this respect they are no different to any other political party.

(f) Frustration with mainstream political incumbents and with the political system as a whole contributes to the willingness of voters to support the extreme right, particularly where local politics is in crisis, as in Stoke. In other words, a decline in system *trust* is a necessary, if not sufficient, factor.

(g) The local political culture, especially the tolerance or intolerance towards far-right activities, plays an important role in making the extreme right a *legitimate* political protagonist.
(h) With regards to the efficacy of combining with other extreme-right groups for electoral advantage, the evidence is contradictory. The British case shows that groups such as the BNP have been more successful when they have succeeded in distancing themselves from overtly extremist political tendencies or individuals. The opposite appears true in Germany, where the NPD often relies on the activism of the so-called 'free nationalists' to operate in some localities.

Using our comparative case study of Germany and Britain, we have identified a set of factors that influence the probability that the extreme right will successfully mobilize voters. And we find much to support Eatwell's three-dimensional approach to extreme-right electoral breakthrough, that is to say, a combination of legitimacy, personal efficacy and declining system trust. But our analysis also raises a number of challenges to this approach. In some cases, even committing acts of violence, which one would naturally expect to hinder 'legitimacy', has not, at least in the case of the NPD, repelled the electorate from casting their vote for a right-extremist party. Further light should be shed on the significance of wider levels of antipathy (and indeed apathy) towards the democratic system and its procedures. In other words, more consideration needs to be given to the relative importance of declining system trust, as this can, both directly and indirectly, impact on voter perceptions of the legitimacy of extreme-right parties, as well as their ability to strengthen perceptions that voting for them does not constitute a 'wasted vote'. One final factor of relevance in the extreme right's quest to overcome its limited legitimacy and thus genuinely embed itself at a local level has been the performance of extreme-right local incumbents themselves, once elected. One repeated pattern, at least with the BNP, is for several councillors to be elected at one round of local elections, perform relatively poorly and then get removed the next time round. If extreme-right councillors performed well, would this help bolster legitimacy? Historians and political scientists studying the British political hinterland in particular have not yet been confronted with this conundrum.

Notes

1 http://bnp.org.uk/2009/02/bnp-youth-wing-attends-european-youth-conference/ [Accessed 4 January 2010].
2 http://news.bbc.co.uk/1/hi/programmes/crossing_continents/7105445.stm [Accessed 4 January 2010].
3 http://www.thelocal.de/politics/20090609-19809.html [Accessed 4 January 2010].
4 http://www.netz-gegen-nazis.de/artikel/wenn-rechtsextreme-politik-bestimmen-7726 [Accessed 18 January 2010].
5 http://news.bbc.co.uk/1/hi/world/europe/5349696.stm [Accessed 4 January 2010].
6 http://www.bnp.org.uk/news_detail.php?newsId=1139 [Accessed 20 September 2006].

7 http://news.bbc.co.uk/1/hi/programmes/crossing_continents/7105445.stm [Accessed 4 January 2010].
8 http://news.bbc.co.uk/1/hi/programmes/crossing_continents/7105445.stm [Accessed 4 January 2010].
9 http://news.bbc.co.uk/1/hi/england/staffordshire/7423094.stm [Accessed 8 August 2010]
10 http://news.bbc.co.uk/1/hi/uk/1439588.stm [Accessed 4 January 2010].
11 *Making your Mark in History: Voting for Stoke-on-Trent's first Elected Mayor including Election Addresses by Candidates for Mayor* (Stoke-on-Trent City Council 2002), pp. 24-5.
12 http://www.bnp.org.uk/news_detail.php?newsId=300 [Accessed 7 May 2005].
13 http://www.stoke.gov.uk/ccm/navigation/council-and-democracy/census/ethnicity-and-religion/ [Accessed 8 August 2010].
14 http://www.thisisstaffordshire.co.uk/news/BNP-loses-school-governor-election/article-1017264-detail/article.html [Accessed 4 January 2010].
15 http://vodpod.com/watch/1596920-bnp-making-a-difference-in-stoke?pod=simonben [Accessed 4 January 2010] and http://vodpod.com/watch/1596917-the-sunshine-club-abbey-hulton?pod=simonben [Accessed 4 January 2010]. See also: http://www.thisisstaffordshire.co.uk/news/Park-revamp-agenda/article-711031-detail/article.html [Accessed 4 January 2010]
16 http://news.bbc.co.uk/1/hi/uk_politics/7687826.stm [Accessed 4 January 2010].
17 http://pitsnpots.co.uk/blog/2009/11/bnp-councillor-value-money [Accessed 4 January 2010].
18 http://pitsnpots.co.uk/blog/2009/12/wol-alby-and-bnp [Accessed 4 January 2010].
19 http://news.bbc.co.uk/1/hi/england/staffordshire/8579023.stm [Accessed 8 August 2010].
20 http://www.nothingbritish.com/05/nazi-saluting-friends-are-patriots-says-bnp-councillor-and-school-governor/ [Accessed 8 August 2010].
21 http://pitsnpots.co.uk/news/2010/05/stoke-bnp-councillor-responds-nazi-salute-photo [Accessed 8 August 2010].

References

Copsey, N. (2008) *Contemporary British fascism: the British National Party and the quest for legitimacy*, 2nd edn, Basingstoke: Palgrave-Macmillan.

Deacon, G., Keita, A. and Ritchie, K. (2004) *Burnley and the BNP and the case for electoral reform*, London: Electoral Reform Society.

Dietzsch, M. (1988) 'Zwischen Konkurrenz und Kooperation. Organisationen und Presseder Rechten in der Bundesrepublik', in Jäger, S. (ed.) *Rechtsdruck. Die Presse der Neuen Rechten*, Berlin & Bonn: Dietz.

Eatwell, R. (1998) 'The dynamics of right-wing electoral breakthrough', *Patterns of Prejudice*, 32 (3): 3–31.

Fischer, B. (2008) 'Die Kümmerer. Die Kommunalpolitik der extremen Rechten in Vorpommern', in Regionale Arbeitsstelle für Bildung, Integration und Demokratie (RAA) Mecklenburg-Vorpommern e.V. (ed.) *Rechts oben. Vorpommern als Modellregion der extremen Rechten*, Waren: RAA.

Funke, H. (1989) *'Republikaner' – Rassismus, Judenfeindschaft, nationaler Größenwahn*, Berlin: ASF.

Goodwin, M. J. (2008) 'Backlash in the 'hood: determinants of support for the British National Party (BNP) at the local level', *Journal of Contemporary European Studies*, 16 (3): 347–61.

Hainsworth, P. (ed.) (2000) *The politics of the extreme right: from the margins to the mainstream*, London: Pinter.

Hoffmann, U. (1999) *Die NPD. Entwicklung, Ideologie und Struktur,* Frankfurt/Main: PeterLang.

Holtmann, E. (2002) *Die angepassten Provokateure. Aufstieg und Niedergang der rechtsextremenDVU als Protestpartei im polarisierten Parteiensystem Sachsen-Anhalts*, Opladen: Leske + Budrich.

Ignazi, P. (2003) *Extreme right parties in Western Europe,* Oxford: Oxford University Press.

Janowski, F. H. (2008) 'Wählen, wo andere Urlaub machen', in Regionale Arbeitsstelle fürBildung, Integration und Demokratie (RAA) Mecklenburg-Vorpommern e.V. (ed.) *Rechts oben. Vorpommern als Modellregion der extremen Rechten*, Waren: RAA.

Jennerjahn, M. (2008) 'Kreistagswahlergebnisse der NPD 2004 und 2008 in Sachsen: Verfestigung oder Schwächung der Partei?', in NIP-Redaktionskollektiv and Heinrich Böll Stiftung (eds) *Die NPD im Sächsischen Landtag. Analysen und Hintergründe 2008.* Dresden. NIP-Redaktionskollektiv and Heinrich Böll Stiftung.

Joseph Rowntree Reform Trust (2005) *The far right in London: a challenge for local democracy,* York: JRRT.

Kühnl, R., Rilling, R. and Sager, C. (1969) *Die NPD. Struktur, Ideologie und Funktion einerneofaschistischen Partei*, Frankfurt/Main: Suhrkamp.

Mecklenburg, J. (ed.) (1996) *Handbuch Deutscher Rechtsextremismus,* Berlin: Elefantenpress.

Minkenberg, M. (2002) 'The radical right in postsocialist Central and Eastern Europe: comparative observations and interpretations', *East European Politics and Societies,* 16 (2): 335–62.

Mudde, C. (ed.) (2005) *Racist extremism in Central and Eastern Europe*, London: Routledge.

Norris, P. (2005) *Radical right: voters and parties in the electoral market*, Cambridge: Cambridge University Press.

Obszerninks, B. (1999) *Nachbarn am rechten Rand. Republikaner und Freiheitliche Partei Österreichsim Vergleich*, Münster: Agenda.

Obszerninks, B. and Schmidt, M. (1998) *DVU im Aufwärtstrend – Gefahr für die Demokratie?,* Münster: Agenda.

Rhodes, J. (2009) 'The political breakthrough of the BNP: the case of Burnley,' *British Politics,* 4 (1): 22–46.

Smith, S. (2003) *The rising storm*, Imladris eBook.

Virchow, F. (2006) 'Dimensionen der "Demonstrationspolitik" der extremen Rechten inder Bundesrepublik', in Klärner, A. and Kohlstruck, M. (eds) *Moderner Rechtsextremismus,* Hamburg: Hamburger Edition.

Virchow, F. (2007a) 'Volks-statt Klassenbewegung. Weltanschauung und Praxologie der extremen Rechten in der Bundesrepublik Deutschland seit 1990 am Beispiel der "sozialen Frage"', in Hofmann, J. and Schneider, M. (eds) *ArbeiterInnenbewegung und Rechtsextremismus,* Leipzig: Akademische Verlagsanstalt.

Virchow, F. (2007b) 'Die extreme Rechte als globalisierungskritische Bewegung?', in Niederbacher, A. and Bemerburg, I. (eds) *Die Globalisierung und ihre Kritik(er),* Wiesbaden: Verlag für Sozialwissenschaften.

Warmenbol, L. (2008) 'The embedding of populist radical right parties in local networks: an ethnographic study at the neighbourhood level in Antwerp (Belgium)'. Paper presented at the ECPR Graduate Conference, Barcelona, 25–7 August.

CONCLUSION

Further avenues for research

Graham Macklin

The final section of this book represents not so much a conclusion as an opening for new beginnings. This volume, as its subtitle denotes, brought together a number of scholars, both new and established, at the cutting edge of their respective disciplines, to offer some 'contemporary perspectives' on the nature of the BNP. The extent to which the authors, and indeed the editors, have been successful in broadening the parameters of debate with regards to the cultural and ideological politics of the BNP, responses to it, and international perspectives on the party will ultimately be reflected in the research that this volume engenders. What has emerged since the idea first for a symposium on the BNP, staged at Teesside University in September 2008, and subsequently for the publication of papers presented at this workshop has been an awareness that research into the BNP is still in its infancy. It is hoped that the present volume will act as a stimulus towards further research into the nature of the contemporary far-right in Britain.

Readers who will have looked to this book for insights into gender and the far-right in contemporary Britain will have been disappointed. This is not due to lack of trying on the part of the editors. When we staged our original symposium, we searched in vain to solicit contributions from academics working on gender and the far-right, only to find, to our surprise, that no one was presently working on the topic of women and British fascism in contemporary Britain, though there have been several superlative historical studies (Gottlieb, 2003; Durham, 1998). Hopefully, this volume will motivate someone to pick up the cudgels.

Ford and Goodwin (2010) have demonstrated that BNP support in the electorate remains overwhelmingly male, while Mudde (2007: 90–118) has made a number of similarly insightful observations regarding the 'populist radical right' as a whole being *Männerparteien* (male parties). That said, insofar as the British case is concerned, women have played an increasingly prominent role within the party itself, particularly with regards to the 'modernization' process. Since 2006, the party has made a point of adopting female candidates and appointing women to prominent roles, in an attempt to 'soften' its thuggish image. Defending the decision, Nick Griffin outlined the reasons underpinning the strategy in 2007:

> Let me make it absolutely plain that this is not some BNP version of Politically Correct sex and disability quotas. It has nothing to do with who we would actually like to sit in Parliament for us; in many cases – almost certainly the majority, for that would simply reflect the realities of inborn human nature – that would be well educated and already successful white males. It is simply about having as many candidates as possible who, simply by being what they are, will help 'soften' our rough image and so help to open the hearts and minds of more ordinary people to us.
>
> (*Identity*, no. 83, October 2007)

This strategy was dealt a grievous blow only six months later by newspaper revelations of the extreme misogynistic views espoused by the London BNP organizer Nick Eriksen, who stated, among other things, that women were more troubled by bag theft than rape and that, since rape was 'simply sex', which women enjoy, 'rape cannot be such a terrible physical ordeal' (*Evening Standard*, 1 April 2008). Although Eriksen was eventually sacked, albeit following some prevarication, his remarks will likely continue to haunt the BNP.

Such attitudes aside, the lack of research into the role played by women as voters, supporters and indeed party activists is all the more curious, given what we know about the participation of women in the party as elected representatives, even if Griffin's own comments appear to dismiss them as little more than window dressing. Immediately prior to the 2010 local elections, the BNP had fifty-six councillors (reduced to fifty-four on the eve of the election), plus a seat on the Greater London Assembly, out of a national total of over 12,000. Eleven of the fifty-six BNP councillors were women (21.42 per cent of the total), though this percentage takes into account the fact that there are actually twelve positions filled by women – Sharon Wilkinson sits as both a district and county councillor for the BNP in Burnley. Indeed, two of the three BNP county councillors are female. Females have occupied, and continue to occupy, key roles within the party, including the positions of party manager, chairman's personal assistant, European office manager and membership secretary, as well as occupying briefly, during 1999–2000, the position of deputy leader. These examples aside, the BNP leadership remains dominated by men, who make up a disproportionate number of its membership compared with women. This we know as a result of a membership list that was leaked onto the Internet (the second in the space of year), which indicated that, as of 15 April 2009, the BNP membership of 11,811 consisted of 9,526 men and 2,034 women (*The Guardian*, 20 October 2009). Females can thus be calculated to represent 17.22 per cent of BNP membership. This is lower than the number of women said to have supported Sir Oswald Mosley's British Union of Fascists (BUF) during the 1930s, who comprised 25 per cent of its membership (Gottlieb, 2003: 1).

How does one explain this gender divide and, indeed, its historical disparities? How closely does this gender divide correspond to the gender balance of far-right parties in continental Europe? What is it about the party and its policies that appeals specifically to women, and does this differ from the appeal it exerts over their male counterparts? Indeed, given the party's adamant opposition to feminism and abortion and its pledge to pay financial incentives to encourage women to leave employment and return to home and hearth, a study of the appeal of BNP ideology to women would be particularly timely.

We know, from accounts that have appeared in newspapers, much more about the nature of the BNP membership, but key questions remain: who are these activists, why do they join, why do they stay and, less remarked upon, why do they leave? In relation to the continental extreme right, we know the answers to some of these questions, thanks to several innovative studies (see, for instance, Klandermans and Mayer, 2006). With regards to the BNP, however, we know far less about its activist base, though the research by Goodwin (2010) provides some answers, as presumably will his forthcoming (2011) volume *New British fascism: the rise of the British National Party*. The issue of BNP membership turnover was raised by a comparison of the first leaked list and the second, which was rather usefully tabulated by *The Guardian* newspaper.[1] In response, Nick Lowles, editor of the anti-fascist magazine *Searchlight,* observed:

> what happens is the membership flow acts like a bath with running water and the plug missing. People join the party, because they're angry, agitated or curious, but they leave in equal numbers out of the bottom. We believe their turnover rate is far higher than any other political party.[2]

Lowles' comment echoed that of *Guardian* journalist Martin Walker, who had made a similar observation about the National Front (NF) three decades previously, stating that its membership 'is rather like a bath with both taps running and the plughole empty'. For Walker, to regard NF members as dedicated and committed 'ideologues' would be 'to overstate the case'. Recruitment to the NF was said to be 'fitful', and its 'surges' tended to mirror renewed national interest in the question of immigration, such as in 1972 with the arrival of the Ugandan Asians (Walker, 1977: 9). Why is it that far-right parties in Britain have been unable to retain members and activists? Some two-thirds of BNP members apparently fail to reach twenty-four months continuous membership (eddybutler.blogspot.com). What does this tell us about the membership patterns of far-right parties in Britain?

While the topics of anti-Semitism, race and the question of its assault on Islam were all dealt with in the ideological section of the book, there were two glaring omissions. In the first place, we did not discuss the economic ideas of the BNP. Beyond its vague commitment to distributist economics, ethno-socialism and national autarky, encapsulated by its slogan 'British jobs for British workers', the economic programme of the BNP is a relatively unknown quantity that has been subject to scant academic scrutiny. Nor did we discuss its environmental ideology, which, while always an important component in British fascist ideology, has come to the fore within the BNP through its claims that it is the 'real green party' (BNP *County Council Elections Manifesto*, 2009) and therefore distinct from the 'watermelon' politics of the actual Green Party – green on the outside, red on the inside – which it regards as an anathema. Nick Griffin has taken up this ideological baton with particular gusto since his election as an MEP in June 2009 and his subsequent appointment to the European Parliament's Environmental Committee (ENVI), through which he was part of the delegation to the COP-15 summit in Copenhagen. Griffin used this as a platform from which to denounce global warming as a conspiracy aimed at creating a New World Order. More interestingly, however, has been the increasing attempt by the BNP to 'green' its opposition to immigration by framing arguments in terms of ecological 'sustainability' and 'diversity', arguments drawn from the *Nouvelle Droite*. To what extent this strategy resonates with the electorate has yet to be determined, though in many respects it represents a logical extension of its attempts to reframe its arguments as non-racist 'common sense'. While the historical dimensions of far-right environmental ideology in Britain have been the subject of considerable scholarly attention (for instance, Moore-Colyer, 2004), its contemporary manifestations have so far received very little sustained attention.

There are, of course, many other avenues for enquiry with regards to the racial politics of the BNP. How, for instance, has a more generalized attack on ethnic minorities in the round come to be replaced by an assault on one particular faith community, Islam? What does this say about the 'new' extremism of the BNP? What is the relationship between the BNP's anti-Islamist drive and the BNP's embrace of Christian religion? An equally important omission has been a sustained study of how wider trends in anti-Muslim prejudice within British society have helped to 'normalize' BNP Islamophobia, allowing to go unchallenged many party pronouncements about Muslims and 'Islam' that would be simply unthinkable if made in respect of blacks, Jews or others.

With regards to the responses to the BNP, the book has covered media responses to the party, the role of the BNP in local government, the evolution of anti-fascist opposition and indeed the 'ambivalent admiration' of other parties on the far-right that, for a mixture of personal and political reasons, stand opposed to the BNP and its current leadership. Each of these chapters generates more questions than they have answered, for the editors of this volume at least. The chapter on media responses to the BNP covered the subject from two distinct angles, that of national media coverage of the party and the BNP's perception of the media. Of late, as we have seen, the BNP has diluted its ideological mantra that the media are controlled by the Jews to its claim that it is misrepresented by the 'controlled media'. While the overarching ideological framework remains unchanged, the latter claim has a wider resonance with those critical of 'corporate media', which its overtly anti-Semitic overtures did not. The positive and indeed negative roles that the media play in framing public perceptions of the party, particularly at a local level, could provide an interesting case study of the role of the media in the rise (or indeed decline) of the far-right, though, in the absence of detailed polling data and survey research, one should be careful to eschew a causal determinism with regards to its role to the expense of other factors.

What the chapter in this volume did not address in any depth was the interaction between the media and the far-right at a local level. What is needed to complement studies of far-right electoral breakthroughs and, we would argue, to fully understand them, are studies of the interaction between the BNP and the media in localities where, it has been claimed, the media have been charged with facilitating the rise of the far-right. The obvious instance of this would be Barking and Dagenham in 2006. A detailed local study could confirm, deny or indeed return a neutral verdict on the power of the media in constructing local legitimacy for the far-right and thus, in part at least, contributing to (or hindering) its breakthrough at a local level. Indeed, given that the history of the BNP in Barking and Dagenham has been (since 2010) one of rise and fall, the factors that contributed to the party's dramatic fall-back in the area are as important to examine as the factors that contributed to its rise, as they suggest that it may be possible to combat the BNP's emergence and establishment in a local area. Comparative local studies would help to develop a more nuanced picture of the role played by the media in this equation, not to mention the role of anti-fascist groups, which was the focus of Copsey's chapter.

More academic work is also needed to examine, not just what the BNP thinks about the mainstream media, but, more importantly, how the party has used new technology to construct its own legitimacy and in doing so to try and circumnavigate the 'gate keepers' of the 'controlled media', whom it believes are retarding its progress as part of an overarching conspiracy to keep it from the levers of power. It is in this spirit that the BNPtv website, the BNP's online video initiative, declares 'we don't need the Mainstream Media we are becoming the Mainstream Media'.[3] The BNP website, meanwhile, claimed to be the most visited party political website in Britain, before it was taken offline during an internal party feud on the eve of the 2010 elections. What does this mean, and how is its impact felt? Who are the people visiting the website, and for what reasons? What is their response to the ideological message contained therein? How can we judge whether the BNP's alternative media strategy is any more successful as a recruiting strategy than the paper sales of days gone? More importantly, perhaps, is this even the point? Is the diffusion of its ideological message through the Internet a 'slow burner' – the impact of which cannot be measured by membership numbers alone? This question of how the far-right is using new media technologies as a tool of communication, recruitment and radicalization is one that is applicable to the wider far-right in Britain and Europe, both in terms of 'traditional' party politics and indeed terrorist activity and thus certainly requires more sustained academic attention than it has hitherto been given.

The 'ambivalent admiration' of other groups outside the BNP also highlights the fact that far-right politics is not solely an electoral threat. One of the ironies of the BNP 'modernization' strategy has been the alienation of numerous party cadres who have been enraged by each successive step that the party has taken, since 1999, towards an accommodation with the machinery of democracy. One of the unintended consequences of BNP 'modernization' has been the radicalization of many members, who have moved towards more openly extreme groups, out of the realms of parliamentary participation and into the realm of violent and *in extremis* terrorist activity. This is not to maintain that the BNP has become a moderate voice within the far-right. A number of younger activists and supporters appear to have internalized references to immigrants, increasingly militarized in party propaganda, which refers to them as 'colonizers' and 'invaders', not to mention the frequent allusions to the looming 'civil war', and have decided to take matters into their own hands, only to be arrested, tried and sentenced, for conspiring to commit acts of terrorism. Two examples include Robert Cottage, a Burnley BNP candidate, jailed for two and a half years in 2006 for stockpiling chemicals in anticipation of 'civil war', and, more recently, Terry Gavan, a Yorkshire BNP member who was jailed in January 2010 for eleven years after his 'strong hostility' to immigrants led him to stockpile firearms and nail bombs.

On the farther shores of the far-right, figures such as the London 'nail bomber', David Copeland, a former BNP member whose terrorist campaign killed three people, including a pregnant mother, and injured hundreds more in 1999, continue to be lionized on far-right online forums as an example to be emulated. Numerous activists, often portrayed in the media as 'lone wolves' but who actually appear to have had some level of contact with far-right groups or racist propaganda, have attempted to do just this, but so far the authorities have successfully apprehended them before they have been able to perpetrate their atrocities. Times change, however, and whereas Copeland targeted blacks, Asians and homosexuals, the latest targets for far-right terrorism, as the examples of Cottage, Gavan and others suggest, are more likely to be 'Muslims' or those perceived as such (Githens-Mazer and Lambert, 2010: 20–6, 42–3). The point being made is that the relationship between the far-right, violence and indeed terrorism is underexplored in the academic literature on British fascism, not to mention lamentably under-reported by the mainstream media, particularly in comparison with its focus on Islamist terrorism.

Both Islamist and far-right extremism are examined at length in Eatwell and Goodwin's book (2010), which investigates the causes and consequences of extremist mobilization and which will hopefully provide the necessary spur to further interdisciplinary research into the subject. Similarly lacking, at the other end of the spectrum, is any examination of modes of de-radicalization and disengagement among far-right extremists, particularly those inclined towards violence, compared with some of the work published by our continental colleagues (Bjørgo et al., 2008).

This issue of far-right political violence was brought to the fore again during 2009 and 2010 as a result of the continuing activities of the English Defence League (EDL), an organization opposed to 'radical Islam' that claims to be both 'anti-racist' and 'anti-fascist', but that, since its inception, has staged dozens of provocative marches in towns such as Luton, Harrow and Birmingham, at which the racist element is writ large. These marches have frequently degenerated into violence amid running battles with the police and anti-fascist protesters, resulting in mass arrests. John Denham, the secretary for communities and local government, compared the group to Mosley's BUF. Although Denham's statement appears somewhat overblown, the threat to public order and community relations posed by the EDL has led to its investigation by the National Extremism Tactical Coordination Unit, a countrywide police unit set up to combat domestic extremism (*Daily Mail*, 2 January 2010).

The reaction of the far-right to the rise of the EDL has been mixed. Many far-right activists are appalled by the multiracial nature of the group, which includes black football hooligans and others of mixed race within its ranks. Others, drawn from groups such as the NF and the British Freedom Fighters, have joined its demonstrations as a means of furthering their own, overtly racist political agendas. For its part, the BNP has conspiratorially disavowed the EDL as a 'Zionist' front group, which, they claim, is aimed to discredit the party by associating it with violence, an image it has struggled hard to shed and has no particular desire to reacquire. Thus, the BNP has 'completely proscribed'[4] the EDL. In reality, however, the relationship between the two is rather more complex. Individual BNP activists appear to have been intimately involved in its activities (*Searchlight*, no. 411, September 2009), and its leader, 'Tommy Robinson' (real name Stephen Yaxley-Lennon), was recently outed as a former BNP activist convicted and imprisoned in 2005 for assaulting an off-duty police officer (*Searchlight*, no. 421, July 2010). Other BNP activists, particularly in Stoke, have, however, bitterly condemned the organization (and indeed the police handling of the demonstration), stating that they wouldn't touch the organization 'with a barge pole'.[5] Copsey's chapter on the evolution of anti-fascist strategy from direct action to community action highlights the basic contours of the strategic response of both the BNP and anti-fascists, which, as the emergence of the EDL shows, is continuing to evolve and which might be used as a point of departure for those desiring to commit themselves to further research on this topic.

Such denunciations aside, it appears that this emerging 'anti-extremist' extremism is worthy of further study, arguably by using it to test the 'cumulative extremism' thesis (Eatwell, 2006), or indeed by focusing on their activists (*pace* Goodwin, 2010; 2011, forthcoming; Ford and Goodwin, 2010) in order to gain a greater understanding of the nature of groups such as the EDL and how they function in relation to other political groupings and youth cultures, including football 'firms'.

While Copsey's chapter provided an overview of the main developments in anti-fascist politics, it also exposed the need for further research into mainstream opposition to the BNP since the party itself became a largely electoral threat, rather than one that was to be confronted on the streets. More work is needed on the response of the Labour, Conservative and Liberal Parties in confronting the politics of the BNP at both local and national levels.

The parliamentary constituency of Barking, a local BNP stronghold, is a case in point. Here, the incumbent MP, Margaret Hodge, the former culture minister, who faced BNP leader Nick Griffin in the 2010 general election, was accused of simply 'copying' the BNP in her call for tougher rules on migrants receiving benefits ahead of the election (*Daily Mail*, 4 February 2010 and *Evening Standard*, 4 February 2010). Here, the impact of the far-right is clearly making itself felt, pushing the local MP further to the right in her attempt to outmanoeuvre the extreme-right challenge, critics allege. An altogether different strategy for tackling the BNP appertained in the neighbouring Dagenham and Rainham constituency, where Jon Cruddas was the sitting MP, however. A study of these two contrasting approaches could, for instance, tell us much about the ideological heterodoxy within the Labour Party with regards to its anti-fascist platform, which, historically speaking, has never been uniform. Indeed, in the wake of the general election results, such a case study of local anti-fascist strategy could be particularly revealing for those focused on tackling the 'new extremism' through public policy.

Griffin's appearance on BBC *Question Time* was seen by the BNP, and indeed many other commentators, as sounding the death knell for the 'no platform' policy that had successfully militated against the far-right for decades. If this is true, then a study of the evolving nature of mainstream political responses to the nature of the BNP and the ideology it espouses will be particularly noteworthy.

The Bottom and Copus study of the BNP in local government will make for difficult reading for some. Of particular salience is its conclusion that many of its elected representatives no longer conform to the earlier and well-deserved sobriquet of 'do nothing' councillors, which certainly applied to the majority of its initial wave of elected representatives. Does this assessment speak perhaps to the continued modernization and metamorphosis of the party from its origins to a new plane in which it could conceivably attract a more competent and committed calibre of candidate, whose performance could help to entrench the party further at a local level? Further case studies could provide answers to such questions. But this overview of the BNP at a local level poses a number of further questions. For instance, can the election in June 2009 of three county councillors – particularly that of Sharon Wilkinson in Burnley – in areas in which the BNP already had borough council representation be viewed as part of an upward trend, or does this merely confirm the 'white enclave' thesis, where residual pockets of hardcore support remain essentially isolated from the wider body politic? In this sense, is the BNP the proverbial 'canary in the coalmine' (Wilks-Heeg, 2008), providing us not just with a salutary warning about the perilous state of local democracy in some localities, but also 'an indicator of the advanced decay of local political parties'?

Such an observation appears particularly germane when considering the fragmentation of the political landscape in Stoke-on-Trent, a town dominated by Labour only a decade or so ago. How does one assess the emergence of the BNP in the local political arena? Is it a case of far-right 'success' or local democratic 'failure' (the one not necessarily the result of the other), and what does this tell us about the dynamics of a far-right breakthrough? The results of the 2010 local elections prompt a further question: for instance, does the resurgence of Labour in Stoke and Barking suggest that the emergence of the BNP can function as the jolt to local politics necessary to reverse the decay? If so, what factors have driven the turnaround? Are the electoral reverses permanent or, as the BNP allege, merely a manifestation of the more sophisticated electoral machinery employed by mainstream parties with which groups such as the BNP simply cannot compete?

Clearly, further local case studies of the BNP in local government are much needed in order to give us a more rounded understanding of party support, performance, legitimacy and entrenchment at a local level. Other avenues for enquiry might include more nuanced appraisals of the performance of BNP councillors in the council chamber, examining how they seek to translate ideology into praxis through proposed council motions and minority budgets. What conclusions can we draw from attempts by BNP councillors to put their ideology into practice at a local level, in places such as Barking and Dagenham or Stoke-on-Trent, and what are the ramifications for community cohesion and indeed the white working-class communities that they purport to represent?

The BNP does not control any local authorities, which is at variance with the French experience, where the *Front National* has won control of a number of local councils with significant consequences. Researchers wishing to examine the impact of the BNP on local government and indeed upon local communities might consider viewing future BNP successes within such a comparative framework. BNP local councillors are typically isolated in small groups, or sit as individuals, and so do not have the numerical quorum required for proposing and seconding motions or proposing alternative budgets, and thus they have an extremely limited impact upon local politics. That said, how do their voting patterns distinguish them, if at all, not just from those of their numerically more fortunate colleagues in other localities, but also from other local councillors from other political parties with whom they sit? Through such detailed local studies, scholars can begin to draw wider conclusions about how the party seeks to implement its ideology at a local level and the potential ramifications of this.

The election of BNP councillors adds to the 'normalization' and legitimization of the party. What effect does this have on community cohesion in localities that have elected BNP representatives? Although this has not been the subject of scholarly study, *The Guardian* newspaper has reported that – according to police statistics – racially and religiously aggravated crime increased following the election of BNP councillors. The newspaper analysed police statistics from eleven forces covering twenty-nine wards in which BNP councillors had been elected, a sample of roughly a half. The picture was mixed. In eight wards, racial violence had increased following the election of a BNP councillor, against a wider reported decline across the remainder of the police forces' respective jurisdiction. Racial violence had declined in fourteen wards, in line with again a wider reduction, while no change was reported in four other wards, with not enough data prevailing in the remaining three for any inference to be drawn. The areas in which an increase was reported included the West Midlands, London and Essex and also included Eastbury ward in Barking, where incidences of racial violence, theft and criminal damage more than doubled following the election of a BNP councillor (*The Guardian*, 15 January 2010). Although one cannot posit a direct correlation between an increase in racial violence and the election of a BNP councillor (either before or after their election), because the picture is at present too statistically mixed and incomplete, those statistics that are available clearly highlight the need for further research into the impact of local BNP victories on community cohesion.

These ideas surrounding the construction of democratic legitimacy bring us to the final point concerning the BNP: the international perspectives that can be brought to bear upon the party and what these tell us about it. The comparison of the BNP with the German NPD at a local level, by Macklin and Virchow, highlights a number of common characteristics and indeed differences between the two parties. The chapter yielded a number of observations regarding the means through which far-right parties have sought to embed themselves in local communities, as a precursor to constructing the local 'legitimacy' necessary for an electoral breakthrough. Such observations could be furthered using other transnational comparisons drawn from a range of European parties and geographical locations, in order to refine our understanding of the factors required for constructing the 'legitimacy' necessary to achieve an electoral breakthrough, which might also help illuminate the extent to which far-right parties are the masters of their own destiny.

The comparative continental framework through which Roger Griffin surveys the ideological nature of BNP politics and, indeed, the assessment of the anti-immigrant politics of the BNP within a broader framework by Anthony Messina both take important methodological steps away from viewing the BNP as an insular phenomenon, even if their findings confirm just this observation.

The election of Nick Griffin and Andrew Brons to the European Parliament in June 2009 also highlights the enlargement of the parameters in which the BNP can now be said to operate. Mindful of the truism that you can tell a lot about a man by the company that he keeps, further study is needed, not just of the pan-European edifices that the far-right perennially attempts to erect. The most recent manifestation of this trend has been the Alliance of European Nationalist Movements (AENM) and, prior to this, the Identity, Tradition and Sovereignty (ITS) bloc that collapsed acrimoniously shortly after its foundation in 2007. What do such groupings tell us about the common ideological goals of the parties concerned? What do they tell us about the nature of far-right networking and how this impinges upon the 'moderate' image that the BNP wishes to project of itself to a domestic electorate? Indeed, the transnational networking and 'Europeanization' of the contemporary far-right provide fertile ground for further comparative research on this topic, which would require those academics not blessed with the gift of multilingualism to evolve their own transnational research partnerships in order to engage with this increasingly salient topic. There is also a need for further research into the nature of BNP activity within the European Parliament and the agenda the party's two MEPs are pursuing in Brussels and Strasbourg.

These preliminary observations, and doubtless there are others that have not occurred to either editor, will, it is hoped, serve as a stimulus for further research into the nature of the BNP and, indeed, other manifestations of extreme-right politics that may follow it.

Notes

1 See www.guardian.co.uk/politics/2009/oct/20/bnp-membership-list-analysis (accessed 30 January 2010).
2 See www.guardian.co.uk/politics/2009/oct/20/bnp-membership-list-analysis (accessed 30 January 2010).
3 See http://tv.bnp.org.uk/ (accessed 2 December 2009).
4 See http://bnp.org.uk/2009/10/english-defence-league-"honey-trap"-proscribed-by-bnp/ (accessed 30 January 2010).
5 See http://pitsnpots.co.uk/news/2010/02/bnp-and-edl (accessed 30 January 2010).

References

Bjørgo, T., Grunenberg, S. and van Donselaar, J. (2008) 'Exit from right-wing extremist groups: lessons from disengagement programmes in Norway, Sweden and Germany,' in Bjørgo, T. and Horgan, J. (eds) *Leaving terrorism: behind individual and collective disengagement*, London: Routledge.

Durham, M. (1998) *Women and fascism*, London: Routledge.

Eatwell, R. (2006) 'Community cohesion and cumulative extremism in contemporary Britain', *Political Quarterly*, 77: 204–16.

Eatwell, R. and Goodwin, M. (eds) (2010) *The new extremism in 21st century Britain*, London: Routledge.

Ford, R. and Goodwin, M. (2010) 'Angry white men: individual and contextual predictors of support for the British National Party', *Political Studies*, 58: 1–25.

Githens-Mazer, J. and Lambert, R. (2010) *Islamophobia and anti-Muslim hate crime: a London case study*, Exeter: European Muslim Research Centre.

Goodwin, M. (2010) 'Activism in contemporary extreme right parties: the case of the British National Party', *Journal of Elections, Public Opinion and Parties*, 22: 31–54.

Goodwin, M. (2011, forthcoming) *New British fascism: the rise of the British National Party*, London: Routledge.

Gottlieb, J. V. (2003) *Feminine fascism: women in Britain's fascist movement*, London: I B Tauris.

Klandermans, B. and Mayer, N. (2006) *Extreme right activists in Europe: through the magnifying glass*, London: Routledge.

Moore-Colyer, R. (2004) 'Towards "Mother Earth": Jorian Jenks, organicism, the right and the British Union of Fascists', *Journal of Contemporary History*, 39: 353–71.

Mudde, C. (2007), *Populist radical right parties in Europe*, Cambridge: Cambridge University Press.

Walker, M. (1977) *The National Front*, London: Fontana/Collins.

Wilks-Heeg, S. (2008) 'The canary in a coalmine? Explaining the emergence of the British National Party in English local politics', *Parliamentary Affairs*, 63: 377–98.

INDEX

Page numbers in *italics* denotes a table.